THE OTHER KASHMIR

Society, Culture and Politics in the Karakoram Himalayas

THE OTHER KASHMIR

Society, Culture and Politics in the Karakoram Himalayas

Editor

K. Warikoo

idsa

INSTITUTE FOR DEFENCE STUDIES & ANALYSES
NEW DELHI

PENTAGON PRESS

The Other Kashmir: Society, Culture and Politics in the Karakoram Himalayas
K. Warikoo (Ed)

First Published in 2014

ISBN 978-81-8274-797-5

Published by
PENTAGON PRESS
206, Peacock Lane, Shahpur Jat,
New Delhi-110049
Phones: 011-64706243, 26491568
Telefax: 011-26490600
email: rajan@pentagonpress.in
website: www.pentagonpress.in

Branch:
Prime Arcade
Office #11
1154 Saifee Street
Opp. M.G. Road, Camp
Pune-411001
Email: pentagonpresspune@gmail.com

In association with
Institute for Defence Studies and Analyses
No. 1, Development Enclave,
New Delhi-110010
Phone: +91-11-26717983
Website: www.idsa.in

Printed at Aegean Offset Printers, Greater Noida, U.P.

Contents

Preface

The Himalayas are an embodiment of divinity, of nature in its splendour, and of culture in the deepest sense of the word. The Himalayas are the highest and the most spectacular mountains in the world, separating the Indian sub-continent from the Tibetan plateau. The Hindu Kush, Karakoram and Pamir ranges are continuous, and are interlocked with the Himalayan mountain system, the region being most heavily glaciated, wild and rugged. By the Karakoram-Himalayan region geographers mean the whole complex mass of main and subsidiary ranges, outliers, spurs and foothills. When the lofty peak of K2 was discovered in Baltistan in early nineteenth century, it was locally known as Karakoram. William Moorcroft had heard this name in 1828, Cunningham in 1854, Hayward in 1870 and, finally, Montgomery applied the name K2 to the highest peak in the world. Major Montgomerie (of the Trignometrical Survey of India), General Walker (Superintendent of the Great Trignometrical Survey of India) and Clements Markham (then a geographer at India Office, London), adopted the name Karakoram 2 for the peak. Karakoram is home to more than 60 peaks (above 7,000 metres in height), including the K2, the second highest peak in the world (8,611 metres) after the Mount Everest (8,848 metres).

After much debate on the nomenclature of the mountain ranges, Major Kenneth Mason found it best to call the whole region bounded by the Hunza river, the Indus, the Shyok, and the Raskam-Yarkand river, the 'Karakoram Himalayas'. The boundaries of South and Central Asian countries converge along the Karakoram Himalayas, which lends unique geo-political and geo-strategic importance to the region. Abutting the borders of Afghanistan, China, Pakistan and India, and being situated in close proximity to Central Asia, the Karakoram-Himalayan region has been an important constituent of India's trans-Himalayan communication network in the continent and beyond.

The imposing geographical features and high daunting peaks did not prevent the region from being a complex of cultural interaction, overland trade and communication. This region is the cradle of ancient Indian culture, including Budhhism which spread in different directions in Central Asia, East Asia and South East Asia. Gilgit, Hunza, Chitral, Skardu, Leh-Zanskar and other frontier areas have been important mileposts on the famous Silk Route. It needs to be emphasized that the Karakoram-Himalayan region, or the 'Northern Areas' of the erstwhile State of Jammu and Kashmir, comprises Hunza, Nagar, Gilgit, Baltistan, Yasin, Astore, Chilas, Koh-Ghizar , Gupis , Punial and Ishkoman, and is the single largest territorial unit of the State. This area constitutes about two-thirds of the total area of 84,471 sq. miles of the entire Jammu and Kashmir State.

The region displays a wide diversity of cultural patterns, languages, ethnic identities, and religious practices. The entire region has been a melting pot of different cultures and faiths: Zoroastrianism, Buddhism, Hinduism and Islam. Moreover, a variety of languages such as Ladakhi, Balti, Shina, Burushaski, Gojali, Khowar, etc. exist in the region, and cross-border linkages between various ethnic-religious groups turn this frontier into a complex vortex of geopolitics. The induction and settlement of Punjabis, Pakhtoons, and the Taliban cadres by Pakistan as its calculated policy to colonise the Shia/Ismaili dominated region has not only changed its demographic balance but also led to the rise of sectarianism and religious extremism, often leading to violence and conflict. At the same time, the region has been witnessing a new surge in the revival of its indigenous languages, cultural heritage, and social practices. Due to its high and difficult mountainous terrain, isolated and remote location, and its distinct ethno-cultural characteristics, the region has specific requirements for its sustainable development. Similarly, the social and political aspirations of different indigenous ethnic-religious groups in Karakoram-Himalayas have remained suppressed due to geopolitical and religious factors.

The Karakoram-Himalayan region has been the subject of study by geologists, glaciologists, earth scientists, geographers, environmentalists, and anthropologists. Since 1985, a series of international annual meetings on the geology of the Himalaya-Karakoram-Tibet region have been organized periodically by various scientific bodies in Europe, USA, Japan, etc. by several scientific bodies. Professor I. Stellrecht and her colleagues have been conducting the Karakoram Culture Area Project at Teubingen University, Germany for the past 25 years. The late Professor Karl Jettmar of the Heidelberg Academy of Sciences, and the late Professor A.H. Dani of Pakistan launched a joint German-Pakistan project in the 1980s aimed at documenting and publishing the rock carvings and inscriptions found in the Karakoram-Himalayan region. This project is being continued under the leadership of Professor Jettmar's successor, Professor Harald Hauptmann of the Heidelberg Academy of Sciences and Humanities, Germany. Nepal has been carrying out the Hindu Kush-Karakoram Himalaya Mountain Partnership Project for some years. Academica Sinica, Beijing and Pakistan's Ministry of Science and Technology started the International Karakoram Project in 1980. Most of these works/projects have mainly dealt with the geosciences, glaciology, atmosphere, ecology, anthropology, etc. of this mountain region.

While the Indian State of Jammu and Kashmir has been the focus of national and international attention during the past six decades, the Gilgit-Baltistan region has eluded attention. This is mainly because this frontier area has been put under the iron curtain by successive Pakistani governments. Pakistan took over the administration of this area in 1948, enforcing Frontier Crimes Regulations (FCR). Pakistan's policy has been to segregate this strategic area from Pakistan-occupied Kashmir (POK) both in name and governance, and Pakistan's Federal Ministry of Kashmir Affairs has been directly administering this region. In early 1982, the late General Zia-ul-Haq, the then President of Pakistan, publicly announced that this area was never a part of the Jammu and Kashmir State before 1947, which evoked strong protests in Kashmir on both sides of the Line of Control (LOC).

It is against this background that this book presents diverse essays on the historical, cultural, geopolitical, strategic, socio-economic, and political perspectives on the entire Karakoram-Himalayan region. The essays have been contributed both by area/subject specialists and analysts from the region (Gilgit-Baltistan, Mirpur-Muzaffarabad, and the Indian State of Jammu and Kashmir) as also by well-known academics and strategic analysts.

The first chapter by Dr. Mohammad Arif presents the ancient and pre-Islamic history of Gilgit-Baltistan from an archaeologist's perspective; the second chapter by Professor K. Warikoo explores the links between this region and Central Asia in the pre-Islamic period. In Chapter 3, Dr. Ayaz Rasool Nazki recounts the experiences of his visit to Sharda Peeth located in the Neelum valley of Muzaffarabad, and re-lives its rich history, spiritual significance and importance for the composite culture of Kashmir. In the fourth chapter, Professor Mohammad Rafiq Bhatti of Mirpur records the diverse facets of the language, culture, and heritage of Mirpur. In the following chapter (Chapter 5), Senge Hasnan Sering, a Balti scholar and cultural activist, delves into the dynamics of cultural and identity politics in Baltistan in contemporary times. Chapter 6 by Professor K. Warikoo makes a historical-political study of the relationship between the Dogra State of Jammu and Kashmir and its frontier territories of Gilgit-Baltistan from 1846 till 1947.

The next few essays deal with strategic, political, and socio-economic perspectives on the region. Professor Warikoo and Major General (Retd.) Afsir Karim bring into focus the geo-strategic importance of the Karakoram Himalayan region in Chapter 7 and 8. In Chapter 9, Paul Beersmans brings out the state of political and democratic process in Gilgit-Baltistan during the past sixty years. Senge Sering examines the constitutional limbo in Gilgit-Baltistan in Chapter 10. Shaukat Kashmiri, Chairman of the United Kashmir People's National Party and a well-known politician of the region, provides insights into the role of political parties in Pakistan-occupied Kashmir and Gilgit-Baltistan (Chapter 11). Praveen Swami deals with the issues of modernity, migration, and identity in the Mirpur-Muzaffarabad region (Chapter 12). In Chapter 13, Dr. Shabir Chaudhary makes a detailed analysis of the problem of water resources in Pak-administered Kashmir and Gilgit-Baltistan, drawing attention to the construction of mega hydel projects by Pakistan in this region. Safdar Ali of Gilgit presents critical insights into the problems associated with the construction of Bhasha dam in Gilgit (Chapter 14). Dr. Priyanka Singh writes a critical essay on the political unrest in Pakistan-occupied Kashmir, based upon Pakistani press commentaries and news (Chapter 15). Baltistan's Manzoor Hussain Parwana, Chairman of the Gilgit-Baltistan United Movement, draws attention to the adverse impact of extremism in NWFP, Swat, and Chitral in the region (Chapter 16). Nasir Aziz Khan, Spokesperson of the United Kashmir People's National Party, evaluates the human rights situation in Pakistan-occupied Kashmir (Chapter 17). In Chapter 18, Alok Bansal explores the causes and the course of sectarian violence in Gilgit-Baltistan – the only territory under Pakistan's control that has a Shia Muslim majority. The book concludes with Wilson John's essay (Chapter 19) on the emergence of Pakistan-occupied Kashmir as an alternative sanctuary of extremist forces, and as the epicenter of global *jihad*.

New Delhi **K. Warikoo**

Contributors

Prof. K. Warikoo is Professor of Central Asian Studies, Jawaharlal Nehru University, New Delhi.

Mohammad Arif is former Deputy Director, Northern Circle of Archeology, Lahore, Pakistan.

Dr. Ayaz Rasool Nazki is Director, ICCR Cultural Centre, Srinagar, Kashmir.

Prof. Mohammad Rafiq Bhatti is Principal, Shah-e-Hamadan College of Business Administration & Commerce, Mirpur.

Senge Sering, a young academic and cultural activist from Baltistan, has worked with Aga Khan Development Programme in the region. He is currently President, Institute for Gilgit-Baltistan Studies,Washington.

Major General (Retd.) Afsir Karim is a well known defence analyst and Editor of *AAKROSH*, the quarterly journal on terrorism and international conflicts.

Paul Beersmans is President, Belgian Association for Solidarity with Jammu and Kashmir, Belgium.

Shaukat Kashmiri is Chairman, United Kashmir People's National Party.

Praveen Swami is *The Hindu's* Strategic Affairs editor, and Resident Editor of its New Delhi edition.

Dr. Shabir Choudhry is Director, Institute of Kashmir Affairs, London.

Safdar Ali of Gilgit is Spokesman, Balawaristan National Front.

Dr. Priyanka Singh is Associate Fellow at the Institute for Defence Studies and Analyses, New Delhi.

Manzoor Hussain Parwana is Chairman, Gilgit-Baltistan United Movement, Skardu, Baltistan.

Nasir Aziz Khan is Spokesperson, United Kashmir People's National Party.

Alok Bansal is Senior Fellow, the Centre for Land Warfare Studies (CLAWS), New Delhi.

Wilson John is Senior Fellow, Observer Research Foundation, New Delhi.

List of Maps and Photographs

1

Rock Art of Gilgit-Baltistan

Muhammad Arif

Gilgit-Baltistan, now famous for its rock art, enjoys an important position for being the home of indigenous cultures since pre-historic times. This land of winding valleys, and some of the highest peaks of the world where agriculture is possible on the river banks, is unique as three majestic mountain systems—the Himalayas, Karakoram and Hindukush—meet and interact here.

Rock carvings and inscriptions exist practically in every continent of the world; but it is only during the last twenty five years or so that these have been systematically documented and studied by international organisations, many of them sponsored by UNESCO. Experts have counted more than 800 sites of this primordial art, of which 144 are considered as the main site which have more than 10,000 figures in a restricted area. But no area is as attractive for scholars as has been discovered in Gilgit-Baltistan. Because of the presence of a diverse cultural and religious heritage, rock carvings of pre-historic, Buddhist, and post-Buddhist period are found co-existing in this region.

Realizing the importance of Rock Art as an authentic source of history, a Pakistan-German Study Group started systematic survey in Gilgit-Baltistan. The vast petroglyphs material found here has great importance in the study of life and culture of the pre-Islamic period. From the artistic viewpoint, the inscriptions provide valuable information for the study of the history of this area. Numerous rock engravings and inscriptions are found along the ancient routes. Fa-hien, the famous Chinese monk who passed through this area in 400 AD, describes in detail the route he took and the principal towns he crossed on his way. Except for a few references in the official annals of the Chinese Tang Dynasty, no written account of the history of this region is available. Even Chinese sources give only a little information about political events, and have nothing to say about social and cultural traditions of this area. On the basis of archaeological evidence, the history of Gilgit-Baltistan can be traced back to about 5,000 BC; but evidence regarding any pre-history is scanty. However, from the early centuries of the Christian era, archaeological information becomes more reliable, and deals with political and cultural aspects as well. It needs to be pointed out that no political event is mentioned as such in the archaeological source material available, though the existence of names of some important rulers already known from other places suggests the extension of their rule in this area as well.

A third source of information for the reconstruction of the history of this area is epigraphy which has, fortunately, recorded some dynastic names unknown to other sources. A few names of rulers are also to be found in Muslim historical and geographical literature. A. H. Francke, the author of *A History of Western Tibet* (London 1907), identifies the people of this region as Dards. But Dani calls them merely 'people of the rock art', and suggests that they may have been much older than the Dards and who may have copied their art and carried the tradition to Tibet. Different names have been given to the people and the region by the ancient Greek, Hindu, Chinese, Tibetan, and Muslim writers from the time of Herodotus (484 BC to 425 BC), right down to western travellers and historians of the nineteenth century.

Scythians or Sakas

The Scythian element in the population of Central Asia was dominant in the region called Turkistan. Scythian migrations had a great impact upon the regions to the south of Turkistan. They are known to have swept over the Persian plateau, and into Gilgit-Baltistan where they finally settled down. Several Scythian groups ruled over these areas one after another. Chinese evidence is clear about the movement of the Sai-wang (or Sakas) and the route followed by them, denying the claim of certain historians that the Sakas had penetrated through the Kabul valley. The route from Tashkurgan to the Little Pamir and onward into Wakhan along the Wakhjir river has been a traditional one. Here, the Boroghil Pass provided the main entrance southward towards the Darkot Pass that leads into the open green fields of Yasin. From Yasin one can go directly to Chilas, bypassing Gilgit.

Kharoshti inscription and rock carvings belonging to the Scythian period have been found at Chilas. Saka petroglyphs have been discovered at the principal river crossings at Shatial, Chilas, Gilgit, and Hunza. The petroglyphs at Chilas include drawings of Saka soldiers and herdsmen as well as representations of stupas and ibexes.[1] The sacred rock of Hunza Haldeikish also has numerous mounted horsemen and ibexes of the same period, with a series of Kharoshti inscriptions which include the names of Saka and Pahlava rulers. At Chilas-II, a carving depicts soldiers in Scythian dress standing in front of a person of high class, seated on a high backed chair. His name is given as Moga (Maues). There should be no difficulty in identifying this person with the Scythian ruler Maues, whose name occurs in the Taxila Copper Plate of Patika in the same form: as Moga.[2] Thus, one can assume that the Moga Mahata mentioned in the inscriptions at Chilas and at Taxila was the same person. The large number of horses and bullocks depicted in the rock carvings suggest a new transport system as well as cattle wealth which must have increased the economic prosperity of the region. Sakas have left proof of their art on the rocks of the Indus through carvings in Scythian-Siberian animal style.[3]

Pahlava or Parthians

The dynasty that reunited the fragmented empire of Azes II was that of the Pahlava or the Indo-Parthian king named Gondophares. The Scythians were succeeded by the Parthians belonging to the Gondophares group, and their inscriptions and coins in Gandhara are well known. One Kharoshti inscription of this ruler was found in the Gondophares Rock at Chilas at the point where the rivulet of Batugah joins the Indus.

At the Thalpan site, Parthian rock carvings are a witness to the movements of Parthians in this mountainous region. On one rock two human figures are depicted dressed in traditional long Parthian style coats.[4] Another rock exhibits two Parthian soldiers. On the whole, the Parthian period appears to have exerted a prolonged influence on the art of rock carvings in this region. Several carvings of this period showing animals, chariots, and other designs of an entirely new type seem certainly borrowed from the Iranian art of the time.

Kushans

Vima Kadphises, the successor of Kujala was the first emperor who extended the Kushana power into Gilgit-Baltistan. During this period, Kharoshti inscriptions appear to have been concentrated at Alam Bridge on the Skardu road, before the Gilgit River joins the Indus River. At Hunza Haldeikish also, Kushan inscriptions and carvings are found on the sacred rock on the riverside. At Chilas-II, there is an important inscription giving the full royal titles of Vasishka or Vajheshka. As the name has been real, Jhashkasa has the titles of Kaisarasa, Rajatirajasa, and Devadevasa.

It is through inscriptional evidence and rock carvings that we get to know that it was along the Gilgit branch of the Silk Road that Buddhism travelled from Gandhara to Khotan, Yarkand, Kashgar, and other places in Chinese Turkistan. We know that diplomatic relations were established between the Kushan and Chinese emperors from Chinese records. The Chinese source *San-Kuo-chih*, complied by Chien Shou (233-297 AD), refers to an envoy of the king of Yueh-Chih, who went to the court of the Wein, the day of Kuei-mao, i.e. 26 January 230 AD. The king Po'tiaw is usually identified with Vasudeva, a Kushan emperor.[5] A large number of Kharoshti inscriptions speak of the popularity of this script as a vehicle of communication. Several little states other than Chilas flourished in Gilgit-Baltistan, and it is very likely that they were connected by trade routes to Ladakh and Tibet on the one hand, and to China on the other.

With their capital at Peshawar, the Kushans established a strong empire in northern India and adjacent territories. Under Kanishka (78-144 AD), Kushan rule was at the peak of its glory. Kanishka's domain extended over the whole of northern India—from Peshawar to Mathura, Varanasi and even Sanchi, including Baltistan, Ladakh and some parts of eastern and western Turkistan. An inscription of the Kushan king Vima Kadphises, found at Khalatse in Ladakh, corroborates this view.

Culturally, present day northern Pakistan was brought in close contact with Central Asia under the Kushans. We find several carvings of the Buddha at Chilas at the sites of Thalpan, Shing Nala, Chilas-I, etc. which seem to be contemporary with Gandhara art. The early fifth century AD marks a new resurgence of Buddhism, with deep penetration of Gandhara art, and an incursion of many artistic forms that show extraneous influences. This intermixture of Indian influence, along with Gandhara trends, reminds of the relations between the imperial Guptas and the Kidar Kushans.

In the time of Shahpur, the Sassanian Empire was extended in the east, and we have reasons to believe that they must have brought Gilgit-Baltistan under their influence. This new contact appears to have introduced new cultural trends from Central Asia in this region. As a result, we have found two types of inscriptions: Sogdhian and Bactrian writing. Most of the Sogdhians were merchants who were going from one direction to another, which indicates the existence of a brisk trade between China and Central Asia through this region.[6] Karl Jettmar remarks that the Shatial Bridge was a junction in a trade system maintained by the Sogdhians. His explanation is based on the well known fact that many of the Trans-Asiatic routes in

Central Asia were traversed by merchants of Sogdhian origin. Their names suggest that many Sogdhians considered themselves as the 'Servants of Iranian deities'. In the upper Indus valley, there was one main emporium near Shatial, on the slope above the present bridge. Here, the merchants coming from the south presented their stocks, the exchange took place, and the partners returned to their respective homes. Sims-Williams has remarked on the 'heroic tinge' in the proper names occurring in many inscriptions. Sogdhian inscriptions were found at the sites of Thor North (Khalat Das or Tsotsol Ka Das), Oshibat (Thoril Das), Dadam Das, Thalpan Ziarat, etc.

It may be pointed out that only a corner in the sacred precinct near Shatial Bridge was reserved for Sogdhians. May be this sacred precinct is identical with the one that has been mentioned in a remarkable inscription translated by Sims-Willians:

> I Nanivandark, the (son of) Narisaf, have come on (the) ten (the day) and (have) begged a boom from the spirit of the sacred place, kirt that... I may arrive (home) more quickly, may see (my) brother in good (health) with joy.

Besides the inscription, *Tamgas* or emblems have also been found. *Tamgas* were, perhaps, originally conceived as owner's marks for branding cattle. This function has been preserved to the present day among Mongolian pastoralists. Originally they were used by the nomads of the 1st millennium AD as symbols for tribes, clans, families, and even individuals.

The Huns (5th-6th Centuries AD)

The ethnic identity of the Huns is very difficult to ascertain. It is generally believed that they were composed of several branches or groups of the same ethnic stock, which later came to be known as Turk, Mongol, Mughal, etc. They are known by different names: Huns in Sanskrit sources, Hon in Armenia, Ephthalite or Chionite in Persia, Xun in Sogdhian accounts, Hsiung-nu in Chinese history, Hun in European history, etc. The Chinese emperor Shih-Huangti (Chin dynasty) built the Great Wall of China in 246 BC to protect the country from the raids of these northern 'barbarians'. Their power grew stronger, and their empire extended from the Japanese Sea to the Volga region. The great Hun ruler Motum prided himself in being the 'Leader of all those who shoot arrows from horse back.' It is exactly this kind of horse and rider that we begin to see carved on the rocks throughout Gilgit-Baltistan from the latter half of the fifth century AD. They ride on horseback, stand or shoot from running horses, play on horseback, etc. They can be seen at Shatial, in Chilas, in Gilgit, in Hunza, and on many rocks and by roads along which their horses must have bruised their backs. They made a rapid advance throughout this region, and clashed not only with the earlier Kidarite Kushans but also extended their power right into the outskirts of Tibet and China.

Tibetan annals also mention the general persecution of Buddhists in Khotan, as a result of which the monks fled to Tibet and Bruza (Gilgit). But, as the Huns were against the Sassanian and the Roman powers, it appears that the old Silk Road Buddhist monasteries must have suffered adversely during their time. Yet, Buddhism continued to be followed by the local people. Another significant change in this period is the interlinking of all the regions of the empire into a closer cultural bond. As a result, we find the influence of Kashmir art on the rock carvings of the Chilas region as well as the influence of Chilas carvings on Buddhist art in China and the Far East.

Patola Shahis and Dards

The Patola Shahi dynasty has been identified from the well-known Hatun inscription (in the Ishkoman valley), the colophons of the Gilgit manuscripts, and from an inscription at Hodar. The word Patola is contained in the Arab name of the region, Bolor. Generally, it is known as the Dynasty of the Patola Shahis of Gilgit, as most of the documents which mention it come from this region. Its rule began in the fourth century AD. Inscriptions from the Alam Bridge site mention a group of persons appearing under the name of Palolo/Palara between the sixth and seventh century AD.

Hieun Tsang's famous work *Hsi-Yu-Chi* indicates that Bolor was a state which had only a restricted extension from north to south, but covered large strip of land from west to east. The persistence of the name for the respective area is proved by the use of the term 'prusava' for the Gilgit valley in a Saka itinerary describing the way from the north to Kashmir in the tenth century AD. According to the songs of the Bonona festival, the original place of this medieval settler,who finally reached Ladakh, was in Brushal and Gilgit.[7]

The author of the *Hudud al Alam* is more definite about the country. He writes that Bolor (Balur) is a vast country, and its king calls himself the son of the Sun. In his *Tarikh-i-Rashidi*, Mirza Haider Dughlat writes that Bolor is a country of infidels between Badakhshan and Kashmir. According to Hieun Tsang, it is situated in Pho-mi-lo or the Pamir. Stein informs that 'In the east, a road leads into Thou-fan or Tibet; in the north there is a road which reaches into Poliu'. The road to Thou-fan corresponds undoubtedly to the present route over the Zoji-la to Ladakh, and to Tibet. The road to

Poliu is represented by the present 'Gilgit Road'. According to Karl Jettmar, Bolor consisted of two parts: the eastern half, or Great Bolor or Baltistan; and the western half or Little Bolor, that is, Gilgit. However, Banat Gul Afridi, who served as Political Agent in Baltistan, says that Baltistan was never called Bolor by the natives of Baltistan. Shaw discovered that

> the name Bolor was still applied to Chitral by the Kirghiz. The vast territory to the west of Bolor is called She-mi, and is generally identified with Kafiristan, presently called Nuristan. Mirza Haider says that Bolor is bounded on the east by Kashghar and Yarkand, on the north by Badakhshan, on the west by Kabul-Naghman, and on its south lies the land of Kashmir.

According to this description, the place can be identified with both Gilgit and Chitral. According to the *Hudud-al-Alam*, Gilgit is called Bolor, and Ladakh is called Bolorian Tibet.

The famous 'Gilgit manuscript' mentions a certain Patola deva Shahi Vajradityanandi. One of the royal Gilgit inscriptions at Danyor gives the name of the donor as Sri Deva Shahi Surendira Vikarmaditya. Another manuscript of Mahamayuri gives the name Patola Shahi Shahanushai Sri Nava Surendraditya Nandi Deva. Since they patronised the Buddhist religion, it can safely be assumed that this religion might have prospered under their rule. Shahi was the title of the Dard rulers. Dani refers to the names of seven (Patola Shahi) rulers found in manuscripts and inscriptions.

As to the name *Dardadesa* (Dard Country) in Sanskrit literature, Aurel Stein writes:

> Dard settlements on the upper Kishanganga and its tributaries seem to have formed a separate little kingdom, called by a general name of *Dardadesa* in the Chronicle. This early and powerful Darda kingdom must be regarded as the background of the Kharoshti inscription near Alam Bridge. From the eleventh century onwards, the rulers of the Dardas were almost equal partners with the kings of Kashmir. Evidently, after many centuries of disorganisation, the Darda kingdom again formed a considerable military power. The king Vaisravanasena was the second oldest king of the Dards, preceded only by the Daradaraya referred to in the Kharoshti inscription at Alam Bridge.

The ancient name of the Gilgit Valley under its Hindu Rajas was Sargin, which was later known as Gilit, and which was later corrupted and called as Gilgit. However, the local people are still familiar with the ancient names of Gilit or Sargin. Chilas is known as Silathasa in the Saka itinerary, and Al Beruni's account calls it Shiltas.

The Tibetan intrusion in the region took place via Ladakh and Baltistan, where a number of their inscriptions and Buddhist carvings are found—at Manthal near the Satpara Lake, Skardu, and other places. Buddhist influence is in evidence in the Kargah rock-cut Buddha in Gilgit, and in Yasin from where it passed beyond the Darkot and Baroghil passes into Wakhan. Sri Deva Chandra Vikramaditya, apparently a Patola Shahi ruler, was the last in the line whose inscriptions are found at the sacred rock of Hunza.

On the basis of available folk traditions, the main ruling families may be placed in two geographic regions.

1. Those located in the Gilgit sub-region, and include the rulers of Gilgit, Nagar, Hunza, Punyal, Yasin, Ghizir, and even Chitral. This sub-zone also includes the tribal people of Goharabad, Chilas, Darel, Tangir, Harban, and down to Kohistan including Pattan, Jalkot and Kolai
2. Those who are located in Baltistan, including the rulers of Skardu, Khaplu, Shiger, Kharmang, Rondu, Astor, Tolti, and down to Kargil and Dras. The last two areas are part of Indian State of Jammu and Kashmir.

The rulers of Gilgit call themselves 'members of Trakhan dynasty'. While rulers of Skardu take the title *Maqpoon* (meaning head of the tribe), and those of Khaplu call themselves the *Yabgo*. The history of Baltistan has, in the remote past, been linked with Tibet on the one hand (and is mentioned as *Tibet-Khurd* in Mughal accounts), and with Kashmir (since Akbar's period) on the other hand. Modern history started here with the rise of British power in South Asia. In the first half of the nineteenth century, after the death of Maharaja Ranjit Singh on 27 June 1839, Gulab Singh helped the British to consolidate their grip in this area.

Shiva Cult

Shaivism and Buddhism certainly existed side by side in the mountainous territory of Gilgit-Baltistan. Shaivism revived in Swat valley during 6th and 7th century AD. During the 8th century AD, Lalitaditya Muktapida, a king of Kashmir, brought a large portion of Gilgit-Baltistan and tribes like the Tukhars, Bhutas, and Dardas, under his control. Lalitaditya built several Vishnu and Shiva temples, and also Buddhist viharas and stupas.

At the Daman Das site (east of the Hodur Village), the rock carvings depict the existence of the Shiva cult. According to A.H. Dani, a renowned scholar and archaeologist, the carvings in the region show veneration of Shiva in that period.[8] Shaivism in this region has been very complex, and has had very complex expression in the respective historical periods. At the Dadam Das site, there is a carved person wearing a loincloth round the hips, with long hair falling down the nape of his neck. In the right hand he holds a long *trishul*, which is crowned by a Swastika and crescent, and a conch shell is found on the right side of the *trishul*. A vertical strip on the forehead can be recognised as the third eye of Shiva, who is shown here with his typical emblem, the *trishul*. This representation of the Shiva figure at the Dadam Das site is not the only one. At the Thor North site, besides stupa carvings and animal figures, the picture of a six-armed deity is also found, dressed in kneeling trousers and a shirt. At its feet, a short trident is visible. It is clear from the six arms and the *trishul* that the displayed figure is that of Shiva. At the same site, another kind of Shiva can be observed. It is the representation of a man kneeling in front of *lingam* altar. A Brahmi inscription *Kakena*, left of the *lingam* fire altar, is also present. The carving represents Shiva veneration. Shiva worship is also documented in ophoric names, that is, *Shivadasa* or *Shiva-rakshita*, which are known from the inscriptions in Chilas and Taxila. The cult spread up to Afghanistan, where wall paintings from the Dilberzim temple ruins show Shiva sitting on the bull *nandi*.

Dani says that at the Hodar site, there are hardly any carvings that can be attributed to the Buddhist religion. It seems that Hodar was a stronghold of Brahmin followers, and that they had a large number of the local followers who joined them, along with their local traditions.[9] However, Karl Jettmar and his German colleagues suggest that the carvings and inscriptions found at the site are of the Buddhist period, and form a major part of the material from Hodar. There are numerous representations of *stupas* and Brahmi inscriptions.[10]

At Thalpan-I site (Thalpan Bridge), a drawing of a one-faced Shiva *linga* (*ekamukha linga*), is found, while on the three step *socle*, the bust of Shiva with the contour of a *linga* is present as well.[11] The *trishul* above Shiva's crown underlines this impression. The face is executed along simple lines, with special emphasis on the eyes; the expected 'third eye' on the forehead is very faint. His ears are decorated with big ear pendants. The presence of adherents of Shaivism is proved through many carvings depicting numerous representations of the *trishul*. The trident became a dominant feature in local artistic expression. If at all Shaivite religion spread here, its form was prominently seen in its *trishul* (trident) representation.

Two symbols are occasionally seen in the carvings: one is of *linga* (phallus) and the second is of *sankha* (conch shell). The first is associated with Shiva, and the second with Vishnu. Temple carvings are found at several sites. A decorated temple carved at Thalpan-IV site has a highly decorated conical *shikhara* (temple spire). *Lingam* (phallus altar) was also discovered in the Oshibat (Thoril Das) site. Shaivism was once the predominant religion in Kashmir. Kalhana mentions the existence of Shiva shrines of Vijayesa and Bhutesa even in pre-Ashokan days. On the basis of ethnographic evidence, Biddulph also mentions the Hindu period in the history of the Dardic people.

NOTES

1. A.H. Dani, *Chilas: the City of Nanga Parvat (Dyamar)*, Islamabad, 1983, pp. 91-128.
2. Ibid., pp. 63-64.
3. K. Jettmar, *Bolder and Dardistan* National Institute of Folk Heritage, Islamabad, 1980, p. 9.
4. A.H. Dani, no. 1, p. 122.
5. Ibid., p. 130.
6. Ibid., p. 131.
7. A.H. Francke, *A History of Western Tibet*, London, 1906, p. 95.
8. A.H. Dani, no. 1, p. 220.
9. Ibid., p. 34.
10. M. Bemmann and H. Hauptmann, *Rock Carvings and Inscriptions along the Karakoram Highway* (Preliminary Report), 1990, p. 3.
11. Ibid., p. 4.

Sogdhian Inscription from Ba Das, Chilas

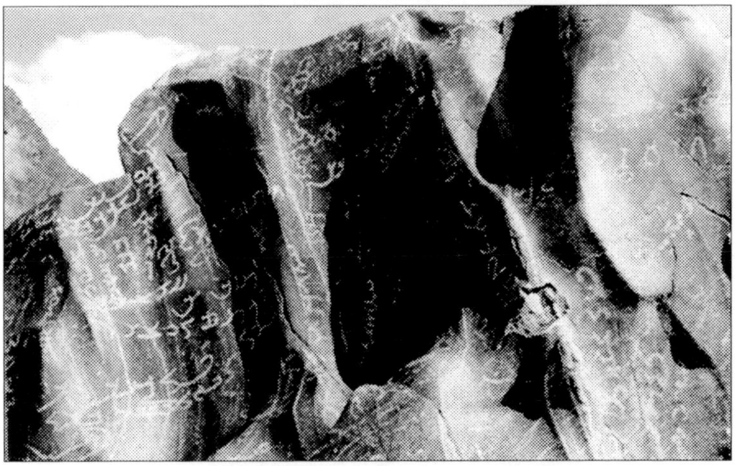

Boulders densely crowded with Soghdian inscriptions.

Brahmi Inscription from Ba-Das, (Chilas) Diamir

Shiva icon with six arms. A small trident is seen on his left side, Thor North

Ek Mukha Lingam from Thalpan bridge

A person kneeling before Lingam, Thor North

Lingam symbol from Oshibat (Thoril Das)

2

Karakoram Himalayas and Central Asia: The Buddhist Connection

K. Warikoo

Abutting the borders of Afghanistan, China, Pakistan and India, and being situated in close proximity to Central Asia, the Karakoram-Himalayan region has been an important constituent of India's trans-Himalayan communication network in the continent and beyond. The imposing geographical features and high daunting peaks have not prevented the region from being a complex of cultural interaction, overland trade, and communication. This region is the cradle from where ancient Indian culture, including Buddhism, spread to different directions in Central Asia, East Asia, and South East Asia. Gilgit, Chilas, Chitral, Baltistan, Ladakh, Zanskar and other frontier areas have been important mileposts on the famous Silk Route. The Karakoram-Himalayan region of India and Central Asia has shared a geo-cultural affinity and a long tradition of historical contacts that date back to antiquity. The movement of people, trade, and ideas, and the reciprocal cultural influences have enriched the horizons of human development, and left a deep imprint on the political, economic, and social life in the entire region.

Buddhist art, culture, and philosophy made a profound impact in pre-Islamic Central Asia. Buddhism spread to Central Asia in the 3rd century BC during Ashoka's time. Buddhist savants from India contributed to the spread of Buddhism in Central Asia and East Asia. One eminent scholar was Kumarajiva (344-413 AD) who broke political, geographical, cultural, and linguistic barriers for the propagation of Buddhism. The son of the

Kuchean princess Jiva and a Kashmiri Brahman father named Kumarayana, Kumarajiva went to Kashmir with his mother, and studied Buddhism for five years. On his return to Kucha, he stopped at Kashgar and studied Mahayana texts. On his return from Kashmir to Kucha, many Kashmiri missionaries accompanied Kumarajiva to propagate Buddhism.

Hieun Tsiang, the famous Chinese pilgrim and monk who travelled to India from 629-645 AD, mentions four important centres of Buddhism in Central Asia: Shan-shan (Kroraina), Khotan, Kucha, and Turfan. Kashmir played an important role in introducing Buddhism to Khotan which, in turn, played a key role in the transmission of Buddhism to China. Kucha was one of the most important centres of Buddhist learning. According to Hieun Tsiang, 'in Kucha there were more than 100 Buddhist monasteries, with above 5,000 priests, who were adherents of the *Sarvastivada* School, and studied in the language of India.'[1] From Kucha, Hieun Tsiang visited Aksu (Pohluka), where he found 'tens of monasteries with above 1,000 priests, all adherents of *Sarvastivada* School.'[2]

Hieun Tsiang came to India in 629/630 AD in search of Buddhist texts after an arduous journey across Central Asia. He spent fourteen years of his life (630-644 AD) visiting Buddhist monasteries on the Silk Route. Knowing both Chinese and Sanskrit, Huian Tsiang translated 77 texts into Chinese, and took back a great corpus of Buddhist texts to China. His itinerary included Balkh, Kafiristan, Swat, Gandhara, Bamiyan, Baltistan, Darel, Gilgit, Kashmir, Poonch, Badakhshan, Ishkashim, Wakhan, Shignan, Pamirs, Yarkand, Khotan, Kucha, Loulan, etc. Hieun Tsiang speaks of a 'carved wooded image of Maitreya Boddhisatva of a brilliant golden hue, 100 feet high,' in Talilo (modern Darel), describing it to be the work of Madhyantika'.[3]

In Polulo (modern Baltistan), he found 'some hundreds of Buddhist monasteries and some hundreds of priests'.[4] Travelling further to Kashmir (Kipin), Hieun Tsiang writes about the existence of hundreds of Buddhist monasteries, and about the people who were fond of learning and followed Buddhism and other religions.[5] Describing Kashmir as 'one of the most important and most famous lands in the history of the spread and development of Buddhism', the pilgrim relates the story of Madhyantika's visit to Kashmir, his propagation of Buddhism, and his building of 500 monasteries.[6] Hieun Tsiang throws sufficient light on the holding of a Buddhist Council in Kashmir by Kanishka, the ruler of Gandhara. He writes: 'The Council composed 100,000 stanzas of *Upadesa* sastras, 100,000 stanzas of *Vindya-vibhasa* sastras, and 100,000 stanzas of *Abhidharma vibhasa* sastras. King Kanishka had the treatises written on copper plates and enclosed these in stone boxes, which he deposited in a *stupa* made for the purpose.'[7]

On his return journey to Central Asia, Hieun Tsiang found 'hundreds of Buddhist monasteries with over 1,000 priests all following *Saravastivada* School' in Kashgar.[8] In Yarkand, there were 'some tens of Buddhist monasteries and about 100 priests, besides numerous *stupas* in memory of Indian *arhats* who had passed away'.[9] And, in Khotan, 'The system of writing was found to have been taken from that of India. The people were Buddhists, and there were above 100 monasteries, with over 5,000 priests, chiefly Mahayanists. *Arhat* Vairochana had come from Kashmir to propagate Buddhism here.'[10]

Charles Willeman, an eminent scholar of Buddhism from Belgium, refers to *Jibin*—a term in Chinese which, according to him, has been the territory of Udyana, that is, the Gilgit area of pre-Kushan times and which gradually developed to encompass the whole Gandhara cultural area and north western India including Kashmir.[11] It was during Kanishka's rule that Kashmir became the most important part of *Jibin*.[12] Willeman asserts that 'China's Buddhism mainly came from non-Kasmira *Jibin*, certainly the first centuries CE before Kumarajiva.'[13]

Patola Shahis, a local ruling dynasty of Gilgit which reigned from the sixth to eighth centuries AD, patronized the production of Buddhist Sanskrit manuscripts, bronze sculptures, and carvings of Buddhist images and inscriptions on rocks in the Karakoram Himalayan region. Oskar von Hinuber has reconstructed the chronology and genealogy of the Patola Sahis.[14] The names of Patola Shahi rulers, their family members and courtiers are mentioned among the donors in the colophons of Buddhist manuscripts discovered in the Karakoram-Himalayan region.[15] The dynasty and their court officials would 'participate in the Mahayan 'Cult of the Book' in which devotees made religious offerings by having many Buddhist *sutras* written down.'[16] One Patola ruler, Navasurendra, had his imperial titles inscribed in a Sanskrit stone inscription at Hatun in the Ishkoman valley in about 671 AD; it was written in the Proto-Sarada script.[17]

Discoveries of Buddhist Sanskrit manuscripts dating between the second and early eighth centuries AD in the Gilgit region provide evidence of the use of Sanskrit as the Buddhist literary language during that period.[18] That at least eight Buddhist monasteries survived in Gilgit long after the reign of Patola Shahis, is attested in a Khotanese Saka account, dating tenth century AD.[19] The images of Buddha located along the trade routes in the Karakoram-Himalayas and adjoining regions served as devotional landmarks for local patrons, devotees, visiting pilgrims, traders and travellers,[20] who would often make their religious offerings (*devadharma*) by carving Buddhist images, inscriptions, writing graffiti, etc.

About six miles from Gilgit town, there is a boulder with an engraving of Buddha carved out of the rock at the mouth of Kargah nullah. Hence it is called the Kargah Buddha.[21] Near Satpara lake, about eight kilometres south of Skardu, is a huge boulder on which a meditating Buddha surrounded by Bodhisattvas are carved.[22] The preponderance of rock carvings and inscriptions of pre-historic and Buddhist periods in the Gilgit-Baltistan area provide sufficient evidence of the prevalence of Buddhism in this region in pre-Islamic times. Several rock carvings of Buddha at the sites of Shaital, Thor, Thalpan, Shing Nala, Satpara, Kargah, Chilas, etc. still exist. Karl Jettmar and his team, of the Pakistan-German Study Group, have done pioneering work on the rock carvings and inscriptions in this region. Five volumes of *Antiquities of Northern Pakistan* (published between 1989 and 2004) provide studies of select inscriptions and petroglyphs in the region. The fifth volume, edited by Oskar von Hinuber (2004), is devoted to the sources for studying the Patola Shahis. Nine volumes of *Materialien zur Archaeologie der Nordgebiete Pakistans* (MANP) (published between 1994 and 2003), provide a detailed documentation of petroglyphs and graffiti at Oshibat, Shaital, Hodar, Shing Nala and Gichi Nala, Dadam Das and Chilas Bridge/Thalpan. The existence of drawings of *stupas*, Buddhas, Bodhisattvas and inscriptions testifies to the established presence of Buddhism in the Karakoram-Himalayan region.

The world famous Gilgit Manuscripts (*Lotus Sutra*), written on birch bark, were first discovered in 1931, just by chance, in a ruined *stupa* near Gilgit by cattle grazers. These manuscripts are Buddhist texts dating back to the 5th-6th centuries AD. The second lot of these manuscripts was discovered by Pandit Madhusudan Kaul in the course of his excavations in Gilgit in 1938. A major part of the Gilgit Manuscripts is in the possession of the National Archives of India which, in association with Soka Gakkai International, released the facsimile edition of 14th work in the *Lotus Sutra* series recently on 3 May 2012. Some portion of the Gilgit Manuscripts is stored in the Jammu and Kashmir Government's Libraries and Research Department in Srinagar, in an unsatisfactory state.

The drawings of *stupas*, Buddhas, Bodhisattvas and narrative scenes, and inscriptions on rocks are mainly located at river crossings or on the routes below mountain passes, which were traversed by traders, travellers or devotees. According to Jason Neelis, 'the largest concentrations of Buddhist petroglyphs are located south of Hunza-Haldeikish and Alam Bridge in the upper Indus valley between Chilas and Shaital.'[23] There are over one thousand inscriptions and seven hundred petroglyphs located at Shaital,[24] from where paths led through the Darel and Tangir valleys to Gilgit, Chitral, and onwards to Badakhshan. Drawings of 138 *stupas* have been found in Shaital, and over 130 such drawings at Hodar,[25] both being evidence of Buddhist presence in this region. Petroglyphs and inscriptions at Helor Das, Hodar and Dadam Das were made by local devotees as well as travellers and traders, as their religious offerings.'[26] Many Buddhist petroglyphs are reported to be 'concentrated near the modern bridge between Chilas and Thalpan.'[27] Buddhist petroglyphs, drawings of *stupas*, and Buddha narratives at sites around Chilas and Thalpan are ascribed to local patrons named Kuberavahana and Sinhote, who are reported to have donated these 'religious offerings'.[28]

A site at Shing Nala, located about 30 kilometres upstream from Thalpan, has a number of Buddhist petroglyphs including 156 *stupas*, and is believed to have 'functioned as a pilgrimage place' where devotees would make their own *stupa* drawings.[29] The existence of many Khoroshti and Brahmi graffiti written on rocks near Alam bridge[30] indicates that Buddhist travellers, monks, and devotees transited through this area, recording their personal names and titles, thereby pointing to the transmission of Buddhism through this region to Central Asia. Notwithstanding its difficult terrain—high and cold mountains, and very limited material resources—the Karakoram-Himalayan region acted as the transit zone for the transmission of Buddhism to Central Asia. Traders, monks, and local patrons, particularly the Patola Shahi dynasty of the 7th-8th Century AD, contributed to the establishment of Buddhist presence in the region.

Gilgit remains an important archaeological site, and reports of digging the ruins and illicit trading in manuscripts and antiquities have been coming in. When the Norwegian Broadcasting Corporation (NRK) team visited Gilgit in 2004 to investigate and document the activities of Martin Schoyen, the Norwegian multi-millionaire, for his film titled *Skriftsamleren* (The Manuscript Collector), Mozaffar Ali, the representative of the local administration in Gilgit, while standing in the Gilgit ruins, told the NRK,[31]

> Everyone knows that this is a historically important area. If the authorities had protected it, we could have had a museum here. But now there is nothing to stop the Pathans, the Europeans and others from enriching themselves. They have destroyed our cultural heritage.

The diversity and density of rock carvings (about 50,000 carvings and 5,000 inscriptions)[32] in Gilgit-Baltistan have turned the area into one of the most important petroglyph sites in the world. Unfortunately, over 30,000 carvings and inscriptions are doomed to be inundated due to the construction of Diamer-Bhasha dam. According to Harald Hauptmann of Heidelberg, a German archaeologist who has been working on the heritage of this area for quite some time, '37,051 carvings on 5,928 boulders will be inundated'.[33] The inscriptions are in Brahmi, Sogdian, Chinese and Tibetan languages, and some 80 per cent are in the Brahmi script. Hauptmann has also warned that some 3,000 *stupas* and a similar number of drawings will be submerged under the dam.[34] That the Water and Power Development Authority (WAPDA) of Pakistan (responsible for the construction of the dam), and its contractors Rogers Kolachi Khan and Associates (RKK) have realized the intensity of damage that will accrue to the region's heritage, there is hope of some arrangements being made to preserve these carvings. There are also reports about the Pakistan government's plans to construct two museums to preserve 33,000 rock carvings and Buddhist figures discovered from the site of the construction of the Bhasha dam.[35] Shakeel Durrani, former Chairman of WAPDA, is reported to have confirmed the plan to 'construct two museums, one each in Gilgit and Chilas, to preserve thousands of rock carvings'.[36] However, no such steps have been taken so far.

Obviously, it was through the Karakoram-Himalayan region—at the crossroads of ancient routes and cultures, which attracted travellers, traders and pilgrims, that Buddhism was transmitted to Central Asia and beyond. Several important places on the Silk Route system, such as Kucha, Balkh, Bamiyan, Khotan, Kashgar, etc., developed into important centres of Buddhism when parts of Central Asia and north-western India were integrated into a single kingdom under the Kushans. Findings of the Indian imprint in several other settlements in the Chu valley (Sokuluk, Shish Tube, Kara Djigach, Burana etc.) testify to a wide settlement of Buddhists along the Silk Route system. Archaeological excavations conducted in early twentieth century in Xinjiang—particularly at Yotkan, Dandan Uiliq, Niya, Loulan, Turfan, etc.—have unearthed some of the remnants of ancient Buddhist shrines and *stupas*, along with a rich treasure of Buddhist images, Brahmi and Kharoshti manuscripts, wooden tablets, and frescoes. The petroglyphs of *stupas* at Chilas and Thalpan have many similar features such as 'hemispherical or parabolic domes on three or four rectangular foundations like those of the *stupas* at Mauri Tim outside of Kashgar, Subashi near Kucha, Niya, Endere, and Loulan.'[37] Buddhist settlements extended upto Marghilan, Merv, Sogd, Eastern Turkestan (the Xinjiang region of China) in the 3rd and 4th centuries AD, and beyond in the valleys of Chu, Talas and Ili rivers in the Semirechie (Kyrgyzstan) in the 5th to 9th centuries AD).[38]

The Buddhist imprint is reflected in the architectural style of Buddhist temples and monasteries, paintings, clay and stone sculptures, bronze pieces, Sanskrit texts, etc.[39] Buddhists built huge cave monasteries in Bamiyan, the Kara Tepe complex in old Termez (southern Uzbekistan, called northern Bactrian Tokharistan in ancient times), Fayaz Tepe—Zar Tepe (about 80 kilometres from Termez in southern Tajikistan), Bezeklik in Turfan, Kyzyl, Kucha and Dunhuang. In the Semirechie region, archeologists excavated several Buddhist sites at Suryab in Ak Beshim, Naveket (Krasnaya Rechka), Sangarma Julya (the Kluchevskoye site of ancient settlements in Bishkek), all of which are reported to date back to 7th-9th centuries AD.[40] The Kyrgyz archaeologist Valentina Goryacheva describes the three temple sculptures of Buddha (7th-8th centuries AD) from Kuvinsky (Farghana, Uzbekistan), and Krasnorechensky (Semirichie, Kyrgyzstan) as 'the most monumental ones'.[41] However, small bronze images of Buddha Sakyamuni, Maitreya, Boddhisatva Avalokiteshvara were quite popular among the common people at that time.

Indian Buddhist texts/manuscripts written on birch bark were found in Merv (Gaur-Kalya, Turkmenistan 5th-6th century AD) by M.E. Masson and G.A. Koshelenko in 1962 and 1965; in Kafir Kala (southern Tajikistan) in 1968 by B.A. Litvinsky; in Zang Tepe (Uzbekistan) in 1961 by L.A. Albaum; and in Krasnaya Rechka (Kyrgyzstan) in 1983 by V.D. Goryacheva.[42] Such a rich heritage of Buddhist presence in Central Asia was destroyed by the Turks and Arabs.

Whereas the sculptures excavated at Khalchayan and Dalverzin-Tepe (both in Uzbekistan) depict the influence of Indo-Buddhist traditions, the discovery of a Buddhist cave monastery at Kara Tepe,[43] and the existence of lotus flowers and Brahmi inscriptions on the artefacts clearly demonstrate Indian cultural influences in this area. Frescoes found in Panjikent and Varakhsha also bear testimony to this effect. For instance, a painting depicting a blue dancer with a trident, and body draped in tiger skin, is linked to the legend of blue-necked Shiva (*Nilkantha*). Another painting shows a king hunting a tiger on the back of an elephant which is obviously based on the Indian experience. The discovery of a large number of manuscripts and archaeological remains depicting Indian traditions in the oasis settlements of Kucha, Khotan, Kashgar, Dunhuang, Panjikent, Varaksha, Khalchayan, Dalverian, Ajina Tepe, etc. testifies to the wide diffusion of knowledge and culture from the Western Himalayan region to Central Asia and onwards since ancient times. The existence of terracotta tiles in Harwan near Srinagar, depicting figures in the Central Asian ethnic type and dress style and also containing Kharoshti numerals of about 300 AD,[44] testifies to the Central Asian connection.

Being situated in the very centre of Central Asia, and deriving its name from the Sanskrit word *Vihara* (monastery), Bukhara retains its reputation as the holiest city, with hundreds of mosques and *madrassas*. The Chor Minar *madrassa* at Bukhara is a crude and miniature form of the Indian Char Minar at Hyderabad. Masjid Kalyan and Mir Arab *madrassa* in Bukhara continue to be the centres of important religious and social activity. Kalyan Minar is a prominent feature of Bukhara. One tall pole with a yak tail in the Kalyan minaret is reminiscent of old traditions.

Similarly Samarkand, situated on the bank of the Zarafshan river, was the very centre of the Silk Route system, and a major urban centre of erstwhile Sogdhian empire. It was the capital of Tamerlane (1372 to 1402 AD). At first sight, the Registan Square evokes feelings of awe and splendour. The grand and imposing scale of the three *madrassas* that form the three sides of the square, their exteriors decorated by intricate calligraphy and mosaic, make Registan a unique sight in Central Asia. The main gate, with two lions and the sun painted on its top, is still called *Sher Dor*, and is ample testimony to close historical ties with India. In the Bibi Khanam mosque in Samarkand, people are still seen to be tying cotton tags to the mulberry tree asking for a boon, reminding us of similar practices in India.

The local museum in Chimkent, a town in southern Kazakhstan, has a number of artifacts, particularly farming tools, household items, yurts, stone items, etc. which demonstrate close resemblance to the lifestyle in the Western Himalayas. Some Zoroastrian artifacts are also preserved here. Of relevance here are the artefacts preserved in Sairam, another ancient Kazakh town on the Silk Route. There is an ancient pillar, with Sanskrit inscriptions in Brahmi and Kharoshti script, in a local mosque at Sairam, which is also a mausoleum of the mother of the famed saint of Turkestan, Ahmad Shah Yasavi. In the small local museum, there is another such pillar, an old plough, a spinning wheel, an old manuscript in Arabic script, and other antiquities. One such pillar is reported to be in the Hermitage Museum, Leningrad. Recently, an ancient Buddhist site has been discovered in Sairam, where a lamp of the 12th century AD was found. The mausoleum of Aisha Bibi (12th century) in Dzhambol (Taraz) has a twelve-cornered dome, much like Indian temple roof tops. Symbols like the octagon and swastika are found engraved in some stone pillars. At another mausoleum of Karakhan (in Taraz), stone images and human figures are stored.

Talas is the birthplace of the Kyrgyz epic hero Manas, and the famous Kyrgyz writer, Changiz Aitmatov. Large stone pillars, and some stones with human figures locally known as Bal Bals which have been preserved in the Manas precincts, stand testimony to the pre-Islamic heritage of the Kyrgyzs. Manas has become the symbol of the renaissance of the Kyrgyz cultural and historical heritage in independent Kyrgyzstan. The hillock, locally named Karal Chaku, overlooking the Manas mausoleum, is considered sacred by the Kyrgyzs universally. The top of the Manas mausoleum is also like that of an Indian temple top rather than being dome-shaped. A large number of local people, both young and old, throng the place as pilgrims, and climb the hill top. No alcohol is served or taken within the Manas complex. The ancient tradition of worshipping hillocks, trees, rivers, sun, images and legendary heroes continues in Kyrgyzstan. Buddhism was prevalent in Kyrgyzstan, mainly in urban centres and towns along the Silk Route. That the symbol of sun occupies a central place in the national flag of Kyrgyzstan only reinforces the view that the Kyrgyzs continue to rever nature and its elements.

The ancient town of Tokmak is the site of the 21 metre high Buran tower. Here, one comes across the remnants of pre-Islamic and Buddhist heritage of Balasaghun, which used to be a flourishing trading and cultural centre on the Silk Route. This historic site, spread over an area of 36 square kilometres was declared as the Balasaghun National Park in 1977. The Buran tower was first restored in 1967-68, and again in 1978. The tower was constructed in the 11th century AD to commemorate the ascendancy of Islam in the region, and the totems (stone figures, locally called Bal Bals) lying throughout this area act as a reminder of its pre-Islamic past. These totems—sculptures carved in the likeness of the deceased persons—were erected in the memory of the dead. Interestingly, this tradition still continues, albeit in a modernized form of erecting concrete graves with stone pillars carrying portraits of the dead. This peculiar tradition would be an anathema in puritan Islamic countries. About 8 kilometres away from the Buran tower, there is the Ak Beshim archaeological site standing testimony to the ancient Buddhist settlements in the area.

Fragments of the Brahmi and Kharoshti script on birch bark were found in Krasnorechensk temple. These texts are believed to have originated from Kashmir—the main centre for the copying of Sanskrit manuscripts. Significantly birch bark manuscripts in Brahmi/Kharoshti found throughout Central Asia (Kafyr Kalan in southern Tajikistan, Merv, Bairam Ali in southern Turkmenistan, and Zang Tepe in southern Uzbekistan) are reported to have similar handwritings.[45] Similarly, Naveket temples are similar to sites discovered at Ajina Tepe, Fayaz Tepe, Kara Tepe, and Merv in Uzbekistan and Turkmenistan. Findings of bronze and stone artefacts, ceramic bowls modelled with Boddhisattvas, etc. in ancient sites, testifies to the location of monasteries along the Silk Route, and also to the constant flow of Indian traders, artists, craftsmen, monks and exponents from the Indian Himalayas.[46]

According to Kyrgyz archaeologists Voropoeva and Goryacheva, 'direct contacts between northern India and Tien Shan in VIII-IX cc, represented the golden age of Buddhist-Hindu culture in medieval Kyrgyzstan.'[47] Soviet archaeologist Bernshtam discovered (1933-54) at a number of ancient sites of Chui valley—Ak Beshim, Krasnaya Rechka, Karadjigach, Novopavlovka, Sokuluk etc.—works in the style of Gandhara art, which indicate the main contours of historical-cultural relationship among Tein shan, Eastern Turkestan, and India since the first century up to the 12th century.[48]

Bernshtam found the 'powerful influence of Buddhist culture of northern India on the culture of Semirechye.'[49] Two other Soviet archaeologists, Kyzlasov and Zyablin, excavated two Buddhist temples in Ak Beshim in the 1950s.[50] Both temples were found to be burnt and their sculptures destroyed around 8th century, after which they were not restored.[51] Kozhemyaho (1961-63) and Goryacheva and Peregudova (1980-88) carried out an investigation of two other temple sites dated 8th century in the Navekat (Krasnorechensk) settlement.[52] In 1961, a sculpture of the sleeping Buddha was excavated here, which is reportedly lying in a museum in Moscow. A Kashmiri bronze sculpture of Buddhisatva Avalokiteswara of the 8th century was also reportedly found here.[53] Many such Buddhist images (7th-8th centuries) and Brahmi/Kharoshti manuscripts found in Naveket are housed in the Archaeological Museum in the Kyrgyz Slovanic university, Bishkek, and the Museum of Institute of History, Kyrgyz Academy of Sciences, Bishkek.

Archaeological finds in Kazakhstan point to the introduction of Buddhism in southern Kazakhstan around 7th-8th century AD, and its spread in different parts of the country up to the 18th century AD. The petroglyph rock engravings of Buddha images and inscriptions at Tamgaly-Tas, about 50 kilometres north of Lake Kapchigai along the bank of the Ili River, fare the risk of damage due to the vagaries of nature. There are three main stone blocks which have large sized images of Buddhist deities and inscriptions in the Tibetan, Pali and Mongol scripts. Kazakh ethnographer and writer Chokan Valikhanov, who visited the site in 1856, was the first to study and document the Tamgaly-Tas petroglyphs by drawing some sketches of these rocks.[54] In 1981, the Alma Ata Regional Council of National Deputies decided to recognize and protect the Tamgaly-Tas petroglyphs. However, the site remains vulnerable to vandalism, as some parts of the figures are reported to have been damaged by throwing stones.[55]

There are several other archaeological sites pointing to the existence of Buddhist monasteries in various parts of Kazakhstan. Antonovka, which is located some 500 kilometres from Almaty towards the east, near the Jungarski Alatau Mountain, was excavated by K.M. Baipakov in 1998-1999. This Buddhist monastery is in ruins now. Other sites include the monasteries of Sumbe (in Kegen district), Ablaikit (in Semipalatinsk province), and Kyzilkent located 250 kilometres east of Karaganda.[56]

At the Hazrat Afak Khoja's shrine, situated about 5 kilometres away from Kashgar, which was built around 1639-40 AD and constructed in the Uyghur style, an extensive use of swastika and lotus symbols in the tile work on the exterior of this shrine is visible. It was declared as a Special Protective Site of Historical Relic of China on 13 January 1988. Robert Shaw, who visited Kashgar in 1868-69 AD, found the popular shrine of Hazrat Afaq decorated with yak tails, flags, and numerous huge horns of *ovis poli*.[57] During my visit to this shrine in June 2010, I found a Muslim priest with some of his devotees lighting a lamp and performing some traditional rituals. Khotan has been the most important commercial and Buddhist centre on the southern limb of the Silk Route, having had strong connections with India. Khotan has three main ancient sites: Ak Sepul, Yotkan, and Malik Awat. Relics and artefacts found by Stein in Yotkan are now lying in the British Museum. However, some antiquities from Yotkan and some other sites are placed in a shabbily arranged local museum at Khotan. Major Buddhist sites in Xinjiang have been stripped of their treasures, which were carried away by foreign archaeologists to museums outside China. Antiquities discovered in the desert between Maralbashi and Aksu are stored in a small local museum in Bachu (Maralbashi). These relics included Buddhist figures, statues of the monkey god, and wooden tablets with Brahmi inscriptions, etc. About 45 kilometres further from Bachu, there are remains of an ancient Buddhist site on the Tok Serai hills. Three to four stone images of Buddha, still exist here, though lying defaced. Kucha has been yet another important centre of Buddhism in Central Asia. On a visit to the famous Buddhist caves at Kumtura, Kyzyl and Kyzyl Gaha, one found paintings and frescoes of Buddha in different forms, monkey gods and a figure with a flute. Only 230 Buddhist caves out of original 330 are still intact in the Kucha complex. British and German archaeologists have taken away the paintings from these caves to their respective countries. Only 8 caves are now open to public view. Cave No. 17 has elaborate murals depicting Indian characteristics. A statue of Kumarajiva is erected in the Kucha cultural complex which is well maintained. These frescoes need to be reconstructed and preserved.

Korla, which is the new and modern oil city of Xinjiang, was an important trading centre having economic links with both China in the east and Central Asia in the west. On a visit to the local museum in the Korla town, one found several Buddhist artefacts, an image of Tara (which was excavated in Yenchi county of Korla), and also several folios in the Mongolian, Tibetan, and Kharoshti scripts. There was one round stone with *Om Mane Padma Om* inscribed on it, which is still preserved here. In Turfan, lie the ancient cities of Jiohe and Gaochang; here one can see traces of the ancient Buddhist monastic establishment. In the famed Bezeklik caves of Thousand Buddha near the Flaming Mountains in Turfan, there are a few remnants of the paintings of Buddha. Images of Buddha, monkey gods, etc. have now been recreated by Chinese authorities to attract tourists. The local museum at Turfan contains some painted pots, two small Buddha statues, and some mummies.

Thus, the task of identification, location, documentation, and dissemination of such a rich historical-cultural legacy assumes a priority. It is high time that concrete steps are taken towards the preservation of thousands of rock carvings, petroglyphs, inscriptions and images in the Karakoram-Himalayan region to save them from being obliterated.

NOTES

1. Thomas Watters, *On Yuan Chwang's Travels in India: 629-645 AD* (ed.) T.W. Rhys Davids and S.W. Bushell, 2nd edition, New Delhi, Munshiram Manoharlal, 1973, p. 60.
2. Ibid., pp. 64-65.
3. Ibid., p. 239.
4. Ibid., p. 240.
5. Ibid., p. 261.
6. Ibid., p. 265.
7. Ibid., p. 271.
8. Ibid., p. 290.
9. Ibid., p. 293
10. Ibid., p. 295.
11. Charles WIlleman, 'India's North-western Cultural Area and its Impact on China', in Lokesh Chandra and Radha Banerjee (ed.), *Xunzang and the Silk Route*, Munshiram Manoharlal, New Delhi, 2008, p. 139.
12. Ibid., p. 140.
13. Ibid.
14. For further details, see Oskar von Hinuber, *Die Palola Sahis: ihre Steininschriften, Inschriften auf Bronzen, Handschriftenkolophone und Schutzzauber: Matirialien zur Geschichte von Gilgit und Chilas*. Mainz, Phillip von Zabern, 2004.
15. Ibid., pp. 12-27, 77-83.
16. Jason Neelis, *Early Buddhist Transmission and Trade Networks*. Brill, Leiden, 2011, p. 172.
17. N.P. Chakravarti, 'Hatun Rock Inscription of Patola-deva', *Epigraphica Indica*, Vol. 38, 1953, pp. 226-231.

18. Jason Neelis, no. 16, p. 46.
19. See H.W. Bailey, 'An Itinerary in Khotanese Saka'. *Acta Orientalia*, Vol.14, 1936, pp. 261-262. See also, Oskar von Hinuber, no.14, pp. 74-76.
20. Jason Neelis, no. 16, p. 59.
21. *Mountains of Pakistan.* Islamabad, 2001, p. 66.
22. Ibid., p. 101.
23. Jason Neelis, no. 16, p. 278.
24. Ibid., p. 279.
25. Ibid., pp. 280-281.
26. Ibid.
27. Ibid., p. 283.
28. Ibid., p. 284.
29. Ibid., pp. 284-285.
30. Ibid., p. 285.
31. Staffan Lunden, TV Review: NRK (Norway), *Skriftsamleren* (The Manuscript Collector). *Culture without Context*, Issue 16, Spring 2005, pp. 1-8. http://www.mcdonald.cam.ac.uk/projects/iarc/culturewithoutcontext/issue16/lunden.htm accessed on 31 March 2013. This documentary was aired by the Norwegian Broadcasting Corporation (NRK) on September 7 and 14, 2004.
32 . See Harald Hauptmann, *Rock Carvings and Inscriptions along the Karakorum Highway*, Heidelberg Academy of Sciences and Humanities, 2006, p. 1.
33. 'Threatened Rock Carvings of Pakistan'. *Dawn*, May 18, 2011.
34. Ibid.
35. Mehtab Haider, 'Museums to House Buddha Carvings found from Bhasha Dam Site'. *Pamir Times*, May 3, 2013.
36. Ibid.
37. See Jason Neelis, no. 16, pp. 294-295.
38. Valentine Goryacheva, 'Buddhist Heritage of Central Asia', in K. Warikoo (ed.) *Bamiyan: Challenge to World Heritage*, Bhawana Books, New Delhi, 2002, pp. 41-42. See also, pp. 2, 3, 4.
39. Ibid.
40. Ibid., p. 46.
41. Ibid., p. 47.
42. Ibid., pp. 54, 55.
43. G.M. Bongard Levin, 'India and Central Asia: Historico-Cultural Contacts in Ancient Times', in Amalendu Guha (ed.), *Central Asia*, Vikas, New Delhi, 1970, p. 101.
44. R.S. Sharma, 'Central Asia and Early Indian Cavalry (c. 200 BC-1200 AD)', in Amalendu Guha (ed.), *Central Asia*, New Delhi, Vikas, 1970, p. 179.
45. V. Voropoeva and V. Goryacheva, 'Kyrgyzstan on the Great Silk Road and Cultural Relationship with India'. *Himalayan and Central Asian Studies*, Vol. 2, Nos. 3-4, July-December 1998, p. 79.
46. Ibid., p. 80.
47. Ibid., p. 73.
48. Ibid., pp. 74-75.
49. Ibid., p. 75.
50. Ibid.
51. Ibid., p. 76.
52. Ibid., p. 75.

53. Ibid., p. 77.
54. For further details, see Jean-Marc Deom, *Kazakhstan: The Petroglyph Site of Tamgaly-Tas. At* www.international.icomos.org/risk/2004/kazakhstan2004.pdf
55. Ibid.
56. P. Stobdan, 'The Traces of Buddhism in The Semireché.' *Himalayan and Central Asian Studies*, Vol. 7, No. 2, April-June 2003, p. 11.
57. R.B. Shaw, *The History of Khojas of Eastern Turkestan*, Calcutta, 1897.

Buddha: Rock Carving at Kargah Nulla, Gilgit

6th Century Gilgit: Buddha Shakyamuni (Metropolitan Museum of Art)

Meditating Buddha surrounded by Bodhisattvas, near Lake Satpara, Skardu

7th Century Gilgit: Palola Sahi Kingdom, Lion Throne Base

Gilgit 714 AD: Buddha Shakyamuni and Attendants (Asia Society Museum)

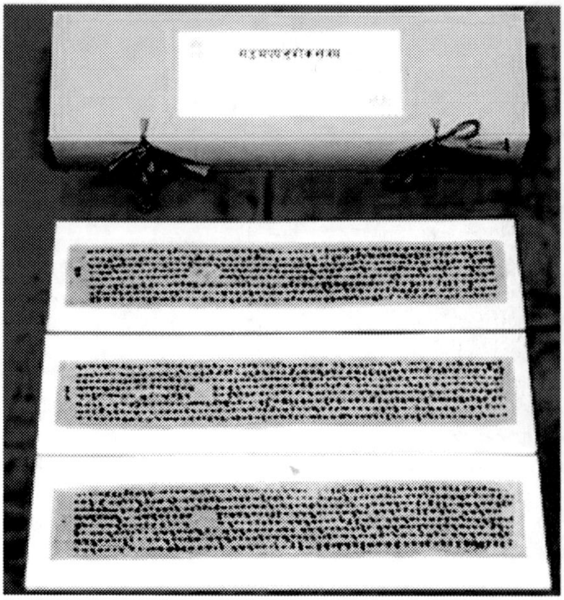

The Facsimile Edition of the Gilgit Lotus Sutra Manuscript

Petroglyph Depicting a Stupa with Attendant: 8th Century AD, Chilas

Petroglyph depicting Buddha Seated Beneath the Bodhi tree and a Stupa: 8th Century AD, Chilas

Avaloketishwara, Krasnarechka, Kyrgyzstan 8th-9th Century AD (Courtesy: K. Warikoo (ed.) *Bamiyan: Challenge to World Heritage.* New Delhi, Bhawana Books, 2002

Avaloketishwara, Novo Pakrovskoe, Kyrgyzstan (8th-9th Century AD)

(Courtesy: K. Warikoo (ed.) *Bamiyan: Challenge to World Heritage.* New Delhi, Bhawana Books, 2002

Crowned Buddha from Ak Beshim, Kyrgyzstan (7th Century AD) Courtesy: K. Warikoo (ed.) *Bamiyan: Challenge to World Heritage.* New Delhi, Bhawana Books, 2002

Eleven Headed Avaloketishwara, Chu Valley, Kyrgyzstan (8th-9th Century AD) Courtesy: K. Warikoo (ed.), *Bamiyan: Challenge to World Heritage.* New Delhi, Bhawana Books, 2002

Fragment of Buddha from Karasnarechka temple, Chu valley (7th-8th Century AD) Excavated in 1961 Courtesy: K. Warikoo (ed.), *Bamiyan: Challenge to World Heritage.* New Delhi, Bhawana Books, 2002

Buddha Images and Inscriptions, Tamgaly-Tas, Kazakhstan
Drawing by Chokan Valikanov, 1856

Buddha Head, Giaur-Kala (Southern Turkmenistan) excavated in 1962 Courtesy: K. Warikoo (ed.) *Bamiyan: Challenge to World Heritage*. New Delhi, Bhawana Books, 2002

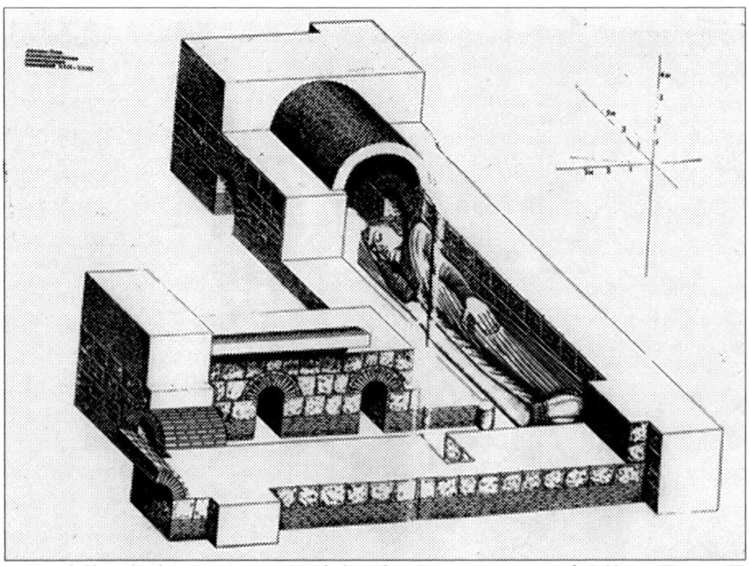

Sleeping Buddha (7th Century AD) in the Monastery of Ajina-Tepe, Tajikistan
Courtesy: K. Warikoo (ed.) *Bamiyan: Challenge to World Heritage*. New Delhi, Bhawana Books, 2002

Petroglyphs on Stone, Tamgaly-Tas, Kazakhstan
Photo: K. Warikoo

Horse Tail on the Pole at the Bahauddin Naqshband, Uzbekistan
Photo: K. Warikoo

Pole with Flag in a Buddhist Monastery in Ladakh
Photo: K. Warikoo

Reconstruction of Monastery Complex, Fayaztepa, Uzbekistan History Museum, Tashkent

Buddha Seated Beneath the Bodhi tree, Flanked by Two Attendant monks (in Limestone) Kushan period (1st-2nd Century AD) from Fayaz Tepe, Southern Uzbekistan, History Museum, Tashkent

Ruins of a Buddhist Monastery in Badakshan, Tajikistan.
Photo: K. Warikoo

Octagonal Tile excavated at Buddhist site, Karaganda, Kazakhstan
Photo: K. Warikoo

The Mauri-Tim Stupa, near Kashgar, Xinjiang

Kyzyl Caves, Kucha
Photo: K. Warikoo

Kumarajiva Statue, Kucha Cultural Complex, Kucha, Xinjiang
Photo: K. Warikoo

3

Sharda: History and Importance

A. R. Nazki

Kashmir is neither only a land nor only a people. It is, and has been in itself, a complete and perfect world in many respects. It is no coincidence that most of the ancient wisdom and philosophy that the Indian sub-continent is proud of, be it religion or about life itself, somewhere down the line has had either a Kashmiri origin or a Kashmir connection. When we speak of the ancient systems of thought that had a sway over vast tracts of land, and multitudes of men and women, the *Sharda* legend or philosophy readily comes to mind. The *Sharda* legend was undoubtedly born in the holy land of Kashmir, which was accordingly designated as *Shardapeeth* and *Shardamandala*. The only ancient temple dedicated to Goddess *Sharda* in the entire sub-continent was located in Kashmir. The script that is supposed to have evolved here is also named *Sharda*. Among the Western Himalayan scripts, the *Sharda* alphabet has pride of place. Evolved from the north western *Brahmi* a millennium ago in the 9th century AD, it remained in popular use for several centuries in an extensive area of the Western Himalayas, including the North West Frontier Province, Dardistan, Kashmir, Ladakh, and Himachal Pradesh.

Kashmiris of yesteryears perfected the doctrine of *Shakti* worship. The shrines dedicated to *Shakti puja* dot the entire valley. It is here in Kashmir that the goddess of power, *Durga*, is worshipped as '*Sharda* – the goddess of learning'. In a unique instance of mingling of the two different goddesses, *Sharda* in Kashmir has been described as the *Shakti* embodying three separate manifestations: *Sharda* (the goddess of learning); *Narda* or

Saraswati (the goddess of knowledge); and *Vagdevi* (the goddess of speech which articulates power). This is the beauty of Kashmir's philosophy and its thought system. In Kashmir, knowledge, learning and articulation occupy the highest positions, and all power, worldly and otherwise, flows from them. It is no wonder, then, that the shrine at Sharda is supposed to have been a place where, among other objects, books were also worshipped. This, in spite of the fact that *Nilmata Purana* refers to the shrine as a *Durga* temple, where *pasuhoma* (animal sacrifice) was obligatory even for the *Vaishnavites*. Thus, *Sharda* encompasses knowledge, learning, and articulation; and confers upon Kashmir and Kashmiris the distinct scholarship and wisdom associated with them. Not very long ago, Kashmiri Pandits greeted each other with the recitation:

Sharda werda Devi
Mokhshedata Saraswati
Namastase Namastase
Namo Nama

(*Sharda* who grants the boon of learning, scholarship and deliverance from woes of worldly life, I bow to thee.)

Outside Kashmir, Saraswat Brahmins who trace their ancestry to Kashmir, invoke *Sharda* as part of their popular rituals. The evening *sandhya* prayer of Chitrapur and some Vaishnav Saraswats of Karnataka contains the following verse:

Namastase Sharda Devi Kashmirapuravasini.

(We bow to *Sharda Devi* resident of Kashmir)

The evening *sandhya* of the Vaishnavis contains the following verse:

Saraswati mahamaya kashmirapuravasini
Stadresamantat tam saraswata mahamunium

(We bow to Saraswati; who is the great *maya* and resident of Kashmir and also to the great sage Saraswata residing in the neighborhood of *satadri*)

At their *yagnopavit* ceremony, some *Saraswats* in Karnataka move seven steps towards north (Kashmir), and then retrace them, thereby trying to keep their link with *Sharda* intact. *Maghatritya* or *gauri tritya*, celebrated on the 3rd of the month of *Magh* outside Kashmir as a feast for women and considered sacred to Parvati, is celebrated as the day of the initiation of learning among Kashmiri Pandits. Likewise, the 5th day of the dark fortnight of Baisakh (*Sripanchmi*) is observed as sacred to Goddess *Saraswati* by Kashmiri Pandits.

Thus, it is evident that the legend of *Sharda* pervades over everything in Kashmir, and has omnipresence in its social and cultural life. Through this thought system, Kashmiris have laid claim to knowledge and scholarship from ancient times. Through *Sharda*, they have kept alive the flame of enquiry, inquisitiveness, assimilation, and inference: all important milestones on the path to knowledge and wisdom. It is, perhaps, a unique instance of linking the pursuit of knowledge and the acquisition of scholarship with faith and religion in early times.

The *Sharda* Temple: Location

The ancient temple of *Sharda* is located in Neelam (Kishanganga) valley, just beyond the Line of Control in Pakistan Occupied Kashmir (PoK). The temple is located in a small village called Shardi or Sardi, near the confluence of Kishanganga and Madhumati rivers. Its location seems to be 74.2 E and 34.8 N. It is located northwest of the Wular Lake, about 40 miles as the crow flies. Another way of getting an idea about its location is that Kishanganga and Vitasta (Jhelum) rivers meet in Muzafarabad; Shardi and Sopore are about the same distance from Muzafarabad along two different rivers.

An old account records the following details about the temple as it existed prior to the Partition of India:

> The shrine of Sharda is situated in the Keran-Kishnganga valley at a hillock across the Kishnganga River on the bank of Madhmati, which joins it near the shrine. Surrounded by the snow-capped mountains and dense forests, it commands a panoramic view.

The gateway to the shrine is through an imposing staircase, with two flanking walls of massive construction. It has sixty four big steps, and three hundred, now faded, small steps. Each big step is twelve feet long, two feet wide, and one and a half feet thick. From the height of the staircase, an extensive view of the surroundings is available. The shrine occupies roughly four *kanals* of land, out of which two *kanals* is stone-filled. At the centre of this floored portion is the stone temple. Around it is a *dharamshala*. The roof of the temple is made of wood. In medieval times, the Rajas of Karnah used to store gunpowder at the shrine. Its explosion is reported to have blown off the original stone roof.

On my visit to the Neelam District of Pakistan occupied Kashmir in July 2007, the imposing staircase referred to was found intact, although the number sixty four may not have been correct. Only sixty three steps exist today, and a sign board erected in the vicinity of the complex also talks of sixty three steps and explains the religious significance of this number. The complex seems to be without any encroachments. The *dharamshala* doesn't exist, and the wooden roof has also vanished.

The sign board placed near the base of the staircase has a write up in Urdu.

> Noted Muslim historian Al-Beruni, in his book *Kitab-ul-Hind*, mentions Sharda in these words. 'Sharda is situated in the south-west of Srinagar. Indians consider the place as extremely holy and, on the eve of Baisakhi, people from all over India come to this place on pilgrimage, but due to snow and extremely difficult terrain, I could not visit the place myself.'
>
> During the reign of Kanishka I, *Sharda* was the largest academic institution in Central Asia. Side by side with imparting education in Buddhist religion, history, geography, structural science, logic and philosophy subjects were taught to perfection. This University had evolved its own script which resembles Devnagari and was known as *Sharda*. In conformity with this, the present village is also known as Sharda. This building was constructed by Kanishka I during 24 to 27 AD. The Sharda University building was constructed from north to south on a rectangular pedestal. Modern day engineers are overawed by the magnificent work of the structure. This building is different from all other ancient buildings in the subcontinent: in particular the centrally placed Sanctum presents a unique style of architecture which is very interesting. It [was] about hundred feet in height and [had] carvings on its walls on all sides. There is a doorway to its west. There is no trace left of a roof on top of the structure, however entry from the west is by means of sixty three steps. Even now, some tribals adorn an elephant with a crown made of sixty three ornaments before worshiping it. The number 63 has a religious significance in Asian history. Few figures suggesting Buddhist faith are even now visible on the walls. These have been engraved into the stones. There used to be a pond in the building which does not exist now. People afflicted with skin diseases would bathe in the pond and get cured, because water came to the pond from a sulphur spring situated two kilometers away. Historical references suggest that five thousand individuals resided at Sharda. The entire area between Sharda and Kishan Ghati was populated. Kishan Ghati is the name of a hill situated three kilometers away from the main building at

Sharda in the southeast direction, and is considered holy. There used to be a deep cave which had a huge statue inside and the dead were cremated under it, and the ashes immersed in the Kishan Ganga (presently the Neelam River). Sharda has been the abode of Naga tribes in the distant past, and their religious beliefs resembled those of Buddhism and Jainism. The majority of people are not aware of the real historical background of Sharda, therefore a lot of interesting stories are narrated to the visitors to the place. These are full of mythological lore. Anyhow, the building presents the picture of ruin and is a victim of neglect, its academic and instructional importance seems to be only a dream. (*Translation from Urdu by Ayaz Rasool Nazki*)

Who Constructed Sharda Peeth?

Nothing can be said for certain as to who constructed the *Sharda* shrine, or when it was constructed. Is the structure that now stands at the site the original construction? Or, was the present temple built on the ruins of an older site? These, and many such other questions, may never be answered conclusively. However, an effort could be made to establish the antiquity of the site through modern day scientific and technological investigations. Till such time when this becomes possible, we shall have to fall back only on the reported legends about the temple construction. Some say that the *Sharda* temple has a striking resemblance with the ruined cellas at *Kapatesvar kother* (Acchabal)—an indication that both these temples could have been built by the same person.

As per the popular legend, King Mutskund is credited with building the temple. It is an interesting story. The king was cursed with having the ears of a buffalo. He tried everything to get rid of these ears, but in vain. To hide this from his populace, he wore a turban which he would never remove. The barber who was called upon to the royal service would come to know of the king's ears, and to stop him from spreading this piece of royal information, he would be put to the sword. Barbers came at regular intervals and died at the majestic hands—till a particular barber was called in. He pleaded with the king for mercy, and promised to keep the secret at all costs. It so happened that after some time, the barber became very sick, and no treatment was of any value in curing his ailment. At last, the King sent his royal physician to treat him. The King's doctor examined the barber and said that his ailment was because of a secret that he was holding in his chest. The only remedy to this malady, as suggested by the doctor, was that the barber should divulge the secret. This the King would not allow.

Finally, it was decided that the barber should be taken to a forest, and there he should tell his secret to the trees, and thus get cured. Once in the forest, the barber shouted *Mutskund razas manshihind kan* (King Mutskund has buffalo's ears). The secret was out. The royal priests suggested to the King that if he took a bath in the *amarkund*, his ears would take the human shape. The King immediately set out on his journey towards the *amarkund*. However, as fate would have it, he ran into the Raja of Nagri in whose kingdom the *amarkund* was situated. There ensued a bloody confrontation in which King Mutskund was killed. A loyal cousin of the slain king succeeded in removing the corpse of the King, and carried it all the way to the *amarkund* where, as a result of a mishap, it fell into the *amarkund* and—lo and behold!—the King's dead body came to life, and the buffalo ears were also gone. The King stayed at the place for the night, and had a *darshan* of the Devi in a dream. The Devi ordered the King to build a magnificent temple at the site. The King returned to his kingdom, collected his forces and masons, and marched on the Nagri kingdom. The Nagri *raja* was defeated, and the magnificent temple was built at Sharda. The Raja is said to have got the stones used in the construction shifted from a place called Narda, which is located at least five kilometres away from Sharda, and can be reached only after a very steep and dangerous trek.

Shila Worship

It is reported that the object of veneration at the shrine was *shila*, a square stone slab with a rough surface. It was 8×8 feet, and 1.5 feet thick. The *shila* had a broken surface. As of now, there is no *shila* anywhere in the temple sanctum, although a few fragments of a different stone filled into an excavated gap in one of the walls suggest the possibility of these fragments being parts of the missing *shila*. The visible face of one of the pieces carries an embossed inscription which is difficult to decipher. The *shila* has a Sri Chakra and a few other figures marked on it. It is also recorded that the '*shila* covers what could have been a spring'. As it stands today, the temple does not have any spring; its floor is earth filled and no trace of water is visible in the entire compound.

The temple proper, or the sanctum sanctorum as it stands today, presents an imposing view. It is roughly 24×24 feet, with a height of about 30 feet still intact. Another feature mentioned by earlier chroniclers is the *Ganesh ghati* (Ganeshagiri) or the hill of *Ganesha*. This hill has cliffs shaped like an elephant nose. Ganesha hill is also the place where the famous castle of *Sirhasila* once stood. This natural feature can easily be discerned even now.

Pilgrimage to Sharda

Many ancient chroniclers have written about pilgrimages to Sharda. Alberuni, Abul Fazal, Bilhana and Kalhana have thrown light on the subject. Alberuni says: 'In inner Kashmir, about two or three days journey from the capital in the direction towards the mountains of Bolor, there is a wooden idol called *Sarda* which is much veneered and frequented by pilgrims.' For Bilhana, the goddess is said to

> resemble a swan, carrying as her diadem the glittering gold washed from the sands of the *Madhumati* stream which is bent on rivaling the Ganga. Spreading luster by her fame, brilliant like crystal, she even mounts Himalaya, the preceptor of Gauri, raise higher his head (his peaks) in pride of her residence here.

Kalhana refers to *Saradasthana* in connection with the memorable siege of *Sirhasila* castle, which took place in his own time. In connection with Sultan Zain-ul-Abidin's visit to Sharda, Jonraja wrote: 'The goddess Sharda broke her own image making the king an instrument'. Abul Fazal writes:

> at two days distance from Haehamun (Hayehome) is the river named Padmati (Madhumati) which flows from the Dardu country. Gold is also found in the river. On its banks is a stone temple called Sharda dedicated to Durga and regarded with great veneration. On every eighth *tithi* of the bright half of the month, it begins to shake and produces the most extra ordinary effect.

The pilgrimage to Sharda has seen ups and downs throughout history. It came under the influence of wars, turmoil and tribulations, as well as security concerns, and was sometimes suspended. It is said that, during Mughal and Afghan rule, the pilgrimage lost its importance. During the rule of Gulab Singh, the restless Bombas were suppressed, and the annual pilgrimage became a regular feature. The temple was repaired, and financial help was also made available to the hereditary guardians of the temple. All this came to a grinding halt in 1947-48—after the place came under Pakistan's control, and the pilgrimage was discontinued, and remains so. In the meantime, realizing the importance of *Sharda* to their faith as well as ethos, Kashmiri Pandits have erected a number of substitutes. Even before the Sharda temple became inaccessible, *Shardakunda* in the village of Tsatsa close to Harwan (Srinagar), remained a popular centre of the Sharda *yatra* for those who were unable to go to the actual Sharda shrine. Bandipur and Gushi were other places of Sharda pilgrimage.

Pilgrimage Routes

In the past, devotees could approach the shrine by two routes. Pilgrims could go from a place known as Gushi to another important station Hayehome via a spot known as Tiker. All three places fall in the district of Kupwara, on this side of the Line of Control. They would take a ritualistic bath in the Krsnag (Batnag) spring situated above the village of Drang, then passing through Rangvati forest, they would traverse the Rangvor meadow and reach Guthamman Marg. The next stop on this journey would take the devotees to Thejvann and then the fruit of their toil would be in sight. This was supposed to be the orthodox and blessed route to the shrine. This was the route taken by the legendry Rishi Sandilya.

The other route followed by the pilgrims from the Valley differed from the route outlined above. Pilgrims would go from Gushi to Dudiyal, avoiding Hayehome. This route would pass through the villages of Aura, Zirhoma, and Sitalvan pass. There was, again, a choice of following two routes from Dudiyal. The pilgrims coming from outside Kashmir would start their journey from Muzaffarabad, the present day capital of PoK. I also took this route when I visited the shrine in July 2007. The present day motorable, but extremely difficult mountain road, keeps to the left bank of the Neelam river for the most part of the one hundred sixty kilometres. It overlooks the Indian side of the Line of Control, and one can very clearly see the landscape on this side of the dividing line—so much so that one can easily count the number of chickens in the backyard of a farmer in Titwal or Keran from the other side.

Adi-Shankara's Visit: Fact and Fiction

One account of Adi Shankara's visit says: 'after he sat on the holy stone slab at Temple (Sharda), it gave him vision to compose *Saundriya Lahiri* in praise of Goddess Divine Mother (*Shakti*)', considered to be excellent piece of poetic devotion after *Panchastavi*. Further, he adopted *Sri Chakra* as reverence to Goddess Sharda and was conferred the honour of *Sharda Peeth*. Some accounts give us to understand that Shankaracharya ascended a temporal or a pontifical seat at the Sharda temple, and/or *Sharda Peeth* (referred by some as university), during his visit to Sharda Mai—a little known area near Karnah referred to as 'Sharda Mai', and stated as the location of the Sharda Peeth. An account of his visit has been composed by Madavacharya (1199-1276 AD), an erudite scholar who, after becoming ascetic, is referred to by the name of Vidhyaranya. His account was, subsequently, suitably versioned by followers of Shankaracharaya who had returned to Kashmir in the latter part of the 15th century, during Zain-ul-Abidin's reign.

While in the plains, they had become Shankaracharaya's devotees and generally followed *Shankaradivijya*—an extensive poetic work on the Adi-Shankara which was composed by Madavacharya in the 13th century, five centuries after Adi-Shankara. It is interesting that, during the 13th century, Islam had taken root in pockets in the south, and the Khilji armies were active in conversion to Islam. Many Hindu scholars of the south could not continue their religious inclinations, and found Kashmir an ideal place. This was one of the reasons for the extraordinary number of scholars of the Shaivite order visiting Kashmir during this period, and staying back for long durations or till they attained *Samadhi*. Madavacharya did not adhere to the religious activities as given in *Sankaravi Jaya-Kavya* (composed by Anantanandagiri in the 10th century AD) but adopted the tradition of writing flourishing accounts based on *Puranic* mythology, poetic imagination, and personal devotion which contained stories and events which, in most of cases, had no grounding in reality. His description of the Sharda temple is also believed to be similar, interspersed with ground landmarks, duly assisted by our own, little known scholars of that period.

These scholars, who gave this touch to Madavacharya's imaginative and expressive works were also devoted to Abhinavgupta (933-1015 AD), a Shaivite scholar of the highest degree. His ancestor Atrigupta, a scholarly Brahmin, was brought by Lalitaditya (697 AD to 733 AD) to Kashmir with him. One of the best authorities on Shaiva philosophy and various branches of Sanskrit literature (rhetoric and poetics), he wrote some forty works, including the *Tantraloka* (Light on Tantra), a comprehensive text on *Agamic Shaiva* philosophy and ritual. Abhinavgupta's literary period extended from 990-1015 AD. Some of his other works are: *Para-Trimshika Vivarna*, *Prataybhijna Vimarshini* (expurgated), *Pratyabhijna Vivriti*, *Vimarshini* (full), *Tantrasara*, *Parmarthasara*, and a commentary on the *Bhagvadgita* called *Gitartha-Sangraha*. It was Abhinavgupta whose brilliant and encyclopedic works established Kashmir Shaivism as an important philosophical school. After completing his last work on the *Pratyabhijna* system, he entered the Bhairava cave near Mangam with 1,200 disciples, never to be seen again. The legend of his entering the cave, never to return has been immortalized in the following folk verse in Kashmiri.

Bahshat Chaat Heth Su Bal Bramchari
Sari Heth Khot Shivlokas
Yete Khot Deh Heth
Kus DehDari
Abhinavgupta Acharaya Zan.

(With his 1,200 disciples, this *Brahmchari* went to *Shivlok* with all of them in mortal form, who dares such a miracle. Remember only *Acharaya* Abhinavgupta could do it.)

Sharda Peeth: Sharda University

Being associated with knowledge, scholarship and articulation, *Sharda* has always been seen as a seat of learning. The *Sharda* seminary or university trained thousands of scholars in the sciences and other branches of knowledge which were in vogue in those days. Some chroniclers believe that the university at Sharda housed as many as five thousand scholars at any given time. These seekers of knowledge came from far and wide, including furthest places in the sub-continent, Indo-China, Japan and China. The university seems to have further flourished during the Buddhist period. While presently, there is not much evidence on the spot which suggests the presence of such a huge facility, one can only be sure if a detailed and scientific archaeological study of the area is undertaken.

Earlier reports mention the presence of large square bricks (1.5 x 1.5 feet) at some distance from the shrine complex. The large size of these bricks is suggestive of the presence of huge tenements at the site. The majority of the chroniclers, however, do believe that a grand seat of learning did exist at the spot. The evidence is literary and tradition based. The general perception is that Adi Shankara visited the area, and interacted with scholars and pundits of high Vedic learning. The claim that the great Shankaracharya 'vanquished many learned disputants and seated himself triumphantly on the throne of omniscience' may lend credence to the fact that this, indeed, was an abode of great scholars.

There are many other references to *Sharda* being a great seat of learning. Alberuni narrates the story of a book—a grammar classic *Shishyahitavriti*—written by one Ugrabhuti, the tutor of prince Anandapala, son of king Jayapala. Following the established convention, the author submitted a copy of his book to *Sharda* university for approval which, unfortunately, was denied. The author approached the king for relief. At the insistence of the prince, a pupil of the author, the king ordered the dispatch of two hundred thousand dirhams, and gifts of a similar value to Kashmir, for distribution among those who had studied the book. This did the trick. The book was approved. There is also a report of king Jayasimha of Gujarat ordering the well-known Jain scholar to compile the great grammatical work, *Siddhahemacandra*. The scholar insisted that the work cannot be taken up without reference to the eight existing volumes of grammar available only at the *Sharda* library in Kashmir. The king is supposed to have sent his envoys to Kashmir for this purpose. Similarly, there is the report of one Ramanand Sanyasi from the south coming to the court of Zain-ul-Abidin, and the court historian Jonraja complementing his scholarship and articulation in the following words: 'that even Sharda Devi, the goddess of learning, was perplexed to cope with his unfathomable sea of knowledge'.

The Future of *Sharda*

Sharda symbolizes the origins of Kashmir's intellectual persona. It is most probably here that the confluence of the three water bodies, that organized the thought system associated with *Sharda*, was perfected. It is perhaps here that countless minds set the ball of introspection rolling, and followed every turn and twist of its course. Sharda was not an accidental happening. It was the culmination of a long drawn out belief in search and enquiry conducted by generations of men and women that came and went over the centuries. The seed was planted long ago, watered regularly over centuries, and finally the flower blossomed, and the fruit ripened. For many Kashmiris, *Sharda* symbolizes the faith and heritage of all Kashmiris. The preservation of *Sharda*, both in its physical form and its intellectual content, is extremely necessary. Political upheavals come and go; but heritage must stay, culture must prevail, and civilization must continue. *Sharda* has seen only one visitor from Kashmir during the last sixty years. It cries for attention and care. Political issues may not have any urgency. Kashmir may have waited for sixty years for peace and tranquility, and may have to wait for another sixty years; but *Sharda* has waited for too long, and got just one visitor after sixty years of waiting. *Sharda* is the abode of knowledge, the seat of scholarship and intellectual pursuit and its heritage must be restored.

Perhaps the best way of restoring *Sharda* to its original magnificence is to have all the universities in the state of Jammu and Kashmir (which includes the university at Muzaffarabad) come together to restore and preserve *Sharda* as it exists in the Neelam district across the Line of Control. Along with the restoration and preservation effort, let these universities develop a joint university campus at *Sharda* through a consortium of education. Let this campus be provided the services of academicians from every university in the State on a tenure basis. Let *Sharda* become a hub of not only scholarship but also of unity and brotherhood, as also promote the universal values of good against evil. Let *Sharda* continue with its mission of spreading the light of knowledge and truth. Let the sages and savants of yore be replaced by exponents of modern sciences, technology, and other intellectual pursuits.[1]

NOTE

1. The issue of the restoration of Sharda University was proposed during the course of my presentation in Jammu University on my return from Sharda in July 2007. I had made some suggestions then which are reiterated here.

The Signboard giving the Historical Background of the Sharda Fort (Qila)

Ruins of Sharda Peeth

Ruins of Sharda Peeth

Ruins of
Sharda Peeth

Ruins of
Sharda Peeth

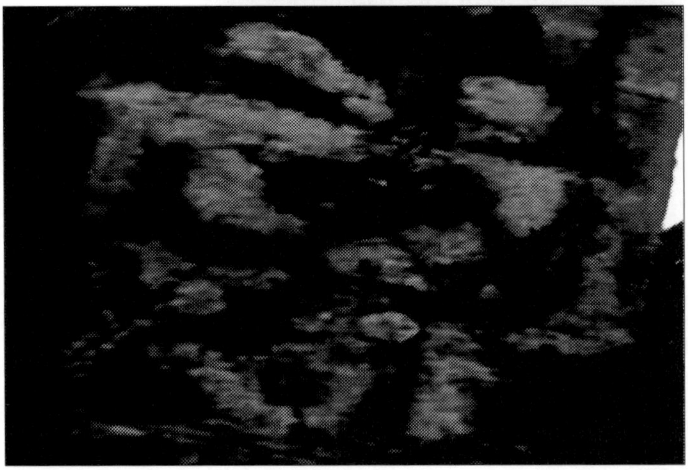

'Om' in Sharda
Script

4

Language, Culture and Heritage of Mirpur

Muhammad Rafiq Bhatti

Language, culture and heritage have been the cornerstones of civilizations—ancient, medieval and the present. It is very difficult to draw demarcation lines between the languages, cultures and heritage of different regions because these are often interwoven and overlapping. Language is the medium of expression of feelings, emotions, reason, prudence, passions and vision. Since time immemorial, mankind has evolved diverse modes of expression: different tongues, dialects or languages. A language is a living organism, which originates, develops and dies. There are so many languages that have died away, and are extinct.

Culture reflects the generally accepted macro and micro behavioural structure of a society. All practices that people undertake, adopt, or follow consciously for their economic, social, political, moral, religious or spiritual satisfaction come under the category of culture. These practices, rites, rituals, customs, traditions, arts, architecture, food and dress, etc. become part of every individual's and collective life, and pass on from generation to generation. This becomes the process of their history, and differentiates one community from other, one nation from other, and one time span from the other. It is like a tree that has its roots in the past, branches in the present, and shades in future.

The concept of heritage refers to the collected arts and science of a society preserved in different forms. It reflects the past, reforms the present, and regulates the future behaviour of individuals and societies. Different societies and nations have different stores of arts and science in their heritage. A major part of any heritage is attributed to past culture. In other words, heritage is past culture preserved in different forms.

Topography of Mirpur

Geographically, Mirpur is situated on the southern borders of the former State of Jammu and Kashmir. District Mirpur is situated 32.17 to 32.50 degree North, and 72.40 to 80.30 degree East on the world map. Before partition, its area was 1,627 square miles. Its southern and western borders touch the Gujrat, Jhelum, Gujar Khan and Rawalpindi districts of Pakistan. Before partition, Jammu province had five districts: Jammu, Kathua, Udhampur, Riasi and Mirpur. After partition, a major part of the former district of Mirpur fell into Pakistani administered Kashmir, and district Mirpur was further divided into two more districts: Kotli and Bhimber.

It is said that old Mirpur city was founded by the Ghakhar tribe in 1051 Hijri, or in the third decade of the 17th century AD. Some believe that the saint Hazrat Miran Shah Ghazi was the founder of this city. The shrine of Miran Shah Ghazi still survives, although the water of the Mangla dam keeps it submerged for nine months of the year. As the water level falls, and the shrine appears, people (pilgrims) visit the shrine, and hold *Urs* every year with zest and zeal. In 1967, old Mirpur city was evacuated due to construction of the Mangla dam. In its place, the new Mirpur city, just 5 kilometres towards the south, at Balla Gala, was populated.

The people of district Mirpur, including Kotli and Bhimber, speak a language called Mirpuri or Pahari, which is a blend of Punjabi, Dogri, Pothowari, Lahndi and Gojri. Recent research shows that Pahari Mirpuri language was earlier called Kharoshti. At present, Mirpuri in itself is not recognized as an independent language. It is known as Mirpuri Pahari, Mirpuri Punjabi, or Mirpuri Pothowari. But researchers believe that it is Mirpuri Pahari which is close to Prakrit or Pali. Rock carvings of Chitterpari near Mirpur town testify to this relationship. To quote Mohsin Shakeel, 'all the Pahari languages share many common grammatical features and lexical items'. The famous Pir Panjal range of mountains demarcates some of the Pahari languages spoken on its northeastern and southwestern slopes.

The leading literary work that identifies Mirpuri Pahari is *Saif-ul-Malook*, written by famous Sufi poet Mian Muhammad Bakhsh. *Saif-ul-Malook* is universally recognized as a book written in Mirpuri Pahari. The author himself belonged to District Mirpur. *Saif-ul-Malook* is a perfect and complete reflection of Mirpuri language, culture and heritage. Every year, the *Urs* of Mian Muhammad Bakhsh is celebrated at Khari Sharif with great religious, spiritual, and social festivities. The verses of *Saif-ul-Malook* are recited. People from far flung areas come and attend this *Urs*. It has great cultural significance. On this occasion, many groups come to recite *Saif-ul-Malook* with their musical instruments, and pay homage to the saint poet who is also known as the 'Roomi of Kashir' or 'Nightingale of Kashmir'. Old mosques, tombs, and shrines have recently been renovated by the department of Auqaf. The new expanded and modified buildings, along with the grand mosque, have made the place attractive for pilgrims, visitors, and for cultural congregations.

The Mirpuri language has three dimensions:

1. Mirpuri Pahari
2. Mirpuri Punjabi.
3. Mirpuri Pothowari.

George Grierson, a prominent scholar and the author of the *Linguistic Survey of India*, broadly divides the Himalayan range into three regions:

1. Eastern Pahari region.
2. Central Pahari region.
3. Western Pahari region.

District Mirpur falls in third region, that is, the Western Pahari region. However, geographically it is not true. District Mirpur lies in the south eastern part of the State of Jammu and Kashmir. Zabair Ahmed Qazi (Allama Iqbal Open University, Islamabad), who has conducted research on regional dialects and languages, observes that Grierson ignored the actual location of district Mirpur. Grierson acknowledges that 'Western Pahari consists of a great number of dialects varying from hill to hill.' No doubt, one does find a change in language after every 10 miles. But despite these varying accents, there is a general homogeneity in so far as the overall language of the region is concerned. For example the words 'mine' and 'thine/yours' are spoken as *mahra* and *twara* in Mirpur. In Kotli, they are spoken as *mera* and *tera*; and at other places, they are spoken as *asna* and *usna*. In Kotli, 'come' and 'go' are spoken *aana* and *jana*. In Mirpur, the same are spoken as *anran* and *janran*. Nasrullah Khan Nasar has classified Pahari alphabets in two categories, that is, Primary and Secondary.

The present inhabitants of this district are migrants from the adjacent areas of Punjab. However, over a period of time, they have evolved a form of language which is an amalgamation of different accents and dialects. Since the majority of the population has migrated either from Punjab or has been in socio-economic and cultural touch with Punjab, the Punjabi accent is dominant. But, one cannot call the spoken language Punjabi. The alphabets of Mirpuri Pahari as identified with reference to the phonetics recorded in *Chitka* are the same as those identified by Nasrullah Khan Nasar, with minor differences.

The people residing in areas of Mirpur adjacent to Rawalpindi speak with a Pothowari accent. Mirpuri and Pothowari are closely related. The languages/dialects used in the areas close to Jehlum, Dina, and Kharian also differ in accent. But with all these minor dialectical differences, the fact remains that District Mirpur has a distinct language. One may call it Mirpuri or Pahari. On the northern and eastern side of Mirpur—that is, in Poonch, Rajouri, Noshera, Riasi and Jammu—the language used displays an admixture of Poonchi, Gojri and Dogri accents. Due to the migration of Kashmiris from Indian administrated Kashmir, an important change in the Mirpuri language has taken place. Moreover, overseas migration from Mirpur to Europe, particularly to England, has also influenced the texture of Mirpuri Pahari. Urdu and English have adversely affected its nativity. Being the district headquarters and a developing modern city, Mirpur is losing its old linguistic identity. Due to changing patterns of life, food and dress, the Mirpuri language is also changing.

To conclude, Mirpuri is an offshoot of Pahari, and Pahari is itself is perverted form of Prakrit, a language which became popular during the Gandhara civilization. In ancient times, Mrpuri was written in the Gurmukhi script; at present it is being written in Shahmukhi. According to David Crystal, the author of *Encyclopedia on Languages*, Pahari is a group of languages belonging to the northwest group of Indo-Aryan spoken in the lower Himalayas. Nazir Tabassum, an expert on Pahari/Mirpuri languages, states that there are 60 sounds in the Mirpuri language, comprising of 38 consonants and 22 monothong vowels. *Chitka*, a journal of Almi Pahari Adbi Sangat (APAS), shows that good research is being done on Mirpuri. On the Pakistani side of Jammu and Kashmir, the Jammu and Kashmir Cultural Academy, Gojri Adbi Sangat, and the literary society Adbika, are working to perceive and promote Mirpuri language, literature and culture. *Tehzeeb*, a magazine of the AJK Cultural Academy, has also played a significant role in this respect.

Mirpuri Pahari Writers and Writings

So far as writings in Mirpuri Pahari are concerned, there is no record of any ancient or subsequent research work. But we find some rock and stone carvings which show that people here have been using a script close to *Sharda*. One sample was found from a water tank or *baoli*.

Since the use of the Shahmukhi script, one can classify the literary work of this district in three phases; classical, neo-classical, and modern. The work of the writers of these groups is mostly poetry.

In the classical group, there are a a number of writers and writings. Most of them were poets, and their poetry was over shadowed by Punjabi. Three representatives of first phase are listed below:

1. *Pir De Heer* by Syed Muhammad Shah of Khnayara Sharif Dadyal;
2. *Ishiq Prem Dian Sattan* by Syed Haider Shah Qalandar of Panag Sharif Kotli;
3. *Qissa Shah Behram* by Imam Bakhsh of Banah Khoiratta Kotli.

In neo-classical phase, the following names are popular.

1. *Se Harfi Hai Mubarka* by Pir Syed Naik Alam.
2. Hazrat Mian Muhammad Bakhsh of Khari Sharif Mirpur has authored more than a dozen books. His famous book *Saif-ul-Malook* has been recognized as the authentic record of Mirpuri Pahari language, culture and heritage. It is the master piece of Mirpuri Pahari literature.
3. Mian Muhammad Zaman of Baratla Kotli, popularly known as Zaman Channa (Channa was her beloved) was a romantic poet. His poetry is not fully published yet. But he is still popular among commoners, elders and youngsters.
4. Muhammad Ashraf Asghar of Bannah Khoiratta Kotli; his poetic collection is named *Phullan Bhari Changair*.
5. Al-Haj Nawab Din Bhatti of Saj Rajouri; his book published in Mirpur entitled *Ishiq Na Puchda Zatan* is a fine piece of literature in Mirpuri Pahari.
6. Khawaja Ali Bahadur of Machiary Mirpur. His book *Dukkan Dey Pandh* is also a representative of Mirpuri Pahari. The present author's book *Qarz-e-Hasna* is a critical analysis of Khawaja Ali Bahadur's poetic work.
7. Munshi Muhammad Ismail of Panjeri Mirpur is believed to have authored about one hundred books, the famous being *Saif-ul-Malook*.
8. Muhammad Khalil Saqib of Khari Mirpur is author of half a dozen books in poetry and prose, the famous one being *Khusbo-e-Faqar*.

Besides the above mentioned writers, other well-known names include: Qazi Muhammad Jan of Sehautha Mirpur; Ghulam Qadir, famous as Mian Kaka, of Samahni; Muhammad Alam Sozi of Dadyal; Haji Muhammad Hanif Soz of Boa Kalan Mirpur; Ch. Muhammad Siddique of Islamgarh Mirpur; Mian Zaman of Khari ;and Maqbool Ahmed Azad of Palak. These deserve special mention for their research work. It may be noted that the writings of classical and neo-classical writers are dominated by Punjabi. However, one cannot ignore their Mirpuri Pahari content as all these writers belong to this district, and they have their own linguistic identity.

Due to the increasing awareness about regional languages, culture and heritage, a number of young writers, both men and women, are inclined now towards their mother tongues, dialects, and languages. Along with poetry, modern writers of these districts also write prose. Thus, Ustad Saleem Rafiqi; Mrs. Shakh-i-Nibat; Haji Rana Fazal Hussain; Mazhar Javed Hassan; Rana Ghulam Sarwar Sehrai; Masoom Hussain Zinda; Muhammad Farooq Aseer; Muhammad Farooq Jarral; Jamil Ahmed Jamil; Qadeer Ahmed Qadeer; Dr. Mohsin Shakeel; Prof. Saeed Saqib; Mushtaq Shad; Zulfiqar Asad; Dr. Zahida Qasim; and myself are regular writers of poetry in Mirpuri Pahari. In prose, Ali Adalat; Dr. Sardar Haleem Khan; Professor Zubair Ahmed Qazi; Liaqat Ali Khan; Tariq Mahmood; Shamas-ur-Rehman; and myself have been making their contributions. *Chitka 2003*, a magazine of APAS, represents these contributions made by modern writers of Mirpuri Pahari, both in poetry and prose.

Organizations Promoting the Mirpuri Language

Though not properly registered, the following organizations are actively working for the promotion of the language, culture and heritage in Mirpur.

1. Almi Pahari Adbi Sangat.
2. National Institute of Kashmir Studies.
3. The Saif-ul-Malook Arts Academy.
4. The Jammu and Kashmir Writers Forum.
5. Adbika Azad Kashmir.
6. The Citizen Forum.
7. Mian Muhammad Bukhsh Society.
8. Tourism Department, AJK Government, Mirpur.
9. Radio Azad Kashmir, Mirpur.

Due to the efforts of these organizations, Mirpuri Pahari is being released of Punjabi dominance, and is becoming popular among new writers. Even those who favoured Urdu and Panjabi medium, are now writing in Mirpuri Pahari. The poetic taste of the public is also receptive to this trend. Needless to say, regional and local dialects and languages are the seed beds, as these are the springs, streams, rivulets, and rivers to join the seas and oceans of national languages. Thus, every effort should be made to promote them.

Since the inception of Radio Mirpur, popular Mirpuri Pahari programmes such as *Mahari Tehrt*, *Payara Desh* and *Karman Ni Chan* have been aired. Advertisements in Mirpuri Pahari are attractive for the trade, commerce and industries as different institutions of this district prefer their advertisements in Mirpuri. A private TV Channel, *Aap* also telecasts a programme named *Bazam-i-Sakhun* in Mirpuri. Outside Mirpur, particularly in the UK, migrants from Mirpur are taking keen interest in promoting the Mirpuri language there. A few years ago, they started a campaign in the UK to get Mirpuri recognized at Council level and now, in some areas of the UK, Mirpuri Pahari is accepted as a language. Ali Adalat, Shamas-ur-Rehman and their friends have been at the forefront for this successful struggle.

Mirpuri Culture

The cultural side of Mirpur is very rich. Living patterns, food and dress, in particular are different from the Punjab and Kashmir Valley. But a constant change is silently taking place in this context. About four decades ago, most men wore shirts and turbans, with a *chadar* on shoulders. Women attired themselves in *shalwar qameez* and a *chadar* over their heads. They also wore traditional ornaments. But now we see a deviation in the dress of both genders. Since 1970 onwards, there has been a shift in dress, foot wear, and ornaments. Due to local, regional and international migration, mobility and interaction, both men and women look different. Although, *shalwar qameez* is still popular among both the genders, yet shirts, trousers and even jeans are being worn openly. In towns, the *pyjama* has replaced the *shalwar*. However, people in the rural areas are even today tied to conventional dress. The turban that was a symbol of grace and dignity, is no longer in vogue. Due to the improved means of transport, camels, mules, horses and donkeys are used rarely.

Gypsies or Nomads

Many gypsies or nomads (the Bakarwals and the Pashtoons) also reside in the district Mirpur. They have a separate language, culture, and heritage in this area. They still keep herds, like goats, sheep, horses and mules. They still wear their traditional dress, that is, long shirts, loose *shalwars* and black turbans. The women also dress likewise, with embroidered headgear (*topi*) and *chadars*. But they are poverty stricken, and are slowly giving up their nomadic life. In the coming few years, these nomad Bakarwals will not be seen any more with their herds in Mirpur.

There is another group of nomads in Mirpur, which consists of the Pashtoons and the Afghans. This group is economically very sound, and some of them live in towns. But a large number of these nomads live in tents and straw huts close to neighbourhoods and still preserve their own traditions. They are very hard working and, instead of camels and donkeys, they now use tractors and other mechanical tools to earn their livelihood.

Migration from Mirpur

A large number of people from Mirpur have migrated to other countries, especially to the UK for employment. About one million Mirpuris are settled in the UK. It has helped them to improve their lifestyle and homes and buildings. Old designed houses made of mud, stones and wooden logs have become rare. In their place, beautiful concrete, spacious, decorated and furnished houses, with new styles of furniture, have been built. The use of electronic machines has also changed the domestic life style. Mirpur city is now called a mini-England. Even in rural areas of Mirpur, the old patterns of living have undergone a change. Agriculture is now a secondary profession. People do not keep animals. Rather, they buy their vegetables, milk and edibles from general stores. Agriculture has slowly given way to commercial and industrial enterprises. In place of oxen, yokes and ploughs, people now use tractors, thrashers, graders, and other mechanical tools in farming. In place of wells, there are tube wells, and bored pumps to extract water. Water supply schemes have made pitchers and the fetching of spring water a story of past. Now women do not go to deep wells to pull out water, and so have lost out on meetings with other women and the exchange of their joys and sorrows sitting close to each other on the walls of well.

Mangla Dam and Heritage

The construction of the Mangla Dam has adversely affected historical monuments such as temples, monasteries, forts, mosques, gurdwaras, tombs, tanks and graveyards. No steps have been taken to preserve or protect this architectural heritage. The fort of Burjun has no remains. The forts of Mangla, Ram Kot, Hari Pur, Bagh Sar, and Thuroochi are decaying. No effort by the public or private sector is being made to save these treasures of Mirpur. The monuments at Choumukh, the historical site of Mirpur, once a capital city, are nearing extinction. The *Sarai* of Saad Abad in Samahni is also withering.

Now a separate district, Bhimber has a rich cultural heritage which deserves our immediate attention. Historically, the cultural heritage of Bhimber dates back to times older than Mirpur. Besides the inn of Saad Abad and the fort of Bagh Sar, the lake of Bagh Sar, and the water reservoir or *baoli* at Mohalla Bawali, the Hathi Gate and the Shah Jahan mosque in

Bhimber city are breathing their last. The temple of Sangri and Banian, along with Gurdwara Ali Beg are calling for urgent steps to preserve them. Similarly, the decaying structure of a beautiful *baoli* at Sokasan needs attention. The fact is that, so far, we have consciously or unconsciously, damaged a major part of precious heritage of Mirpur. However, there much remains to be saved.

Games and Hobbies

At one time, the people of Mirpur were very fond of wrestling, kabadi, weight lifting, dog fighting, bull races, wrist holding, cock and button quail fighting. Camel and horse races were also held. Horse and cattle shows were held almost in all major places of this district. In these shows, people of all ages and groups participated with fervour. Now these games are on the decline. It is the responsibility of the ministry of tourism, sports and culture to revive, and promote them. These social activities on special festivals had great socio-economic value. These developed social relations, tolerance, and a spirit of competition. Harmony, cooperation, mutual co-existence, friendship, and tolerance were promoted by such sports and festivals. But now these social activities are on the wane in Mirpur.

Similarly, social gatherings at the tombs of mystics and saints were very popular, and were held regularly with faith and fervour. There are many such tombs and mystic centres in district Mirpur. The *Urs* of Pira Shah Ghazi Qalander, Mian Muhammad Bukhsh, Syed Naik Alam, Syed Lal Badshah, Mian Shah Badshah, Panj Pir, Dhular Shahab, Mai Toti, Mohra Sharif, Panag Sharif among others, have significant social and cultural value, as these provide opportunities to the people to mix together, and improve their social and cultural contacts. Before partition, social activities at these places were prominent. After partition, religious rites and rituals have come to the forefront, and relegated social activities to the background. This has depreciated cultural growth of a more balanced social nature.

Festivities

The rites and traditions of marriages in rural areas of Mirpur are still intact to some extent, even though new modern practices have crept in, especially in cities and towns. The construction of marriage halls, the use of cars in place of horses, and bridal cots for bridegroom and brides have become rare now, particularly in cities and towns. In place of folklore songs sung in marriage ceremonies, cassettes, videos and other musical instruments are played now. The social value and significance of marriage has also been decreasing. Due to inflation and the increasing cost of food stuffs, ornaments, and other accessories, the old graces in marriage ceremonies are in decline. Instead, a new social set up is under way. Folk dances, *bhangra*, wrist holding, weight lifting, and drum beating during the marriage procession are fading day by day. The holding of marriage processions for a night was very common a few decades ago. But now such festivities are not to be witnessed.

The people of Mirpur district have always been fond of music and dance. Single and double pipe flutes, tongs, *ik tara* and *shehnai* were the common musical instruments used in Mirpur since early days. *Bhangra*, *ludi*, and sword playing were also common until a few decades ago. Folk love stories, like *Namoo and Mitha* along with *Mahya* and *Tappa*, have been an important part of the folklore of Mirpur. The women of the district also danced and sang in marriage ceremonies. *Mehndi* particularly, is a very special festive occasion in marriages in which women wear colourful costly dresses and ornaments which make the ceremony very attractive. The fashion of wearing a *sari* is on the increase now.

Shair Khwani or the reciting verses from mystic poetry was a very popular social practice in Mirpur. Reciters from Pothowar and Pindi were invited to display their art. The harmonium, *tabla* and *chimta* were used by people in such performances. These classical musical instruments are very rare now. Radio and particularly television have sucked them out from the open air into tight studios.

Conclusion

The following steps need to be taken to promote the cultural heritage of the Karakoram Himalayan region.

1. The government of India and Pakistan must take confidence building measures and create an atmosphere of peace, tranquillity and cooperation. Mutual confidence, trust, and tolerance are the foundation stones for achieving these objectives.
2. Mistrust and hostility must be discouraged in both the public and private spheres.
3. People to people contacts must be encouraged at all levels. There should be free and easy exchanges of intellectuals, writers, artists and scholars between the two countries.
4. The educational, cultural and research institutions in both the countries should undertake joint research programmes.
5. The print and electronic media in the two countries should help in normalizing bilateral relations.
6. The universities in both countries should introduce the subjects of

archaeology, museology and heritage management at college and university levels so as to promote greater awareness and understanding of the ancient historical heritage of the Karakoram Himalayas.

7. During the construction of dams, roads and other mega projects in the region, care must be taken that archaeological monuments and sites are not destroyed. The ministries of tourism, culture and heritage, along with department of archaeology and other experts must be taken into confidence before undertaking such projects.

5

Political Dynamics of Culture and Identity in Baltistan

Senge H. Sering

As contemporary Baltistan evolves by developing socio-economic associations with its western neighbors, the political and cultural legacies associated with Ladakh and Tibet[1] continue to overshadow current developments. Ever since Pakistan occupied Baltistan in 1947 and separated it from Ladakh, the natives remain torn between their loyalties to their perceived country. Moreover, while they withstand religious persecution and cultural hegemony, they continue to struggle to preserve their social demography.

J.H. Bodley describes culture as the most important concept in anthropology which studies all aspects of human life: past and present. Human culture includes socially acquired knowledge, laws, morals, customs, habits, belief, the rules of behavior, myths, languages, rituals, art, technology, costumes, religion, economics, politics, and traditions of producing, cooking and presenting cuisine.[2] These cultural traits prevalent among a certain group of people define their social identity. When different societies interact, dominant social groups may induce abrupt and unnatural changes within subordinate groups to cause cultural shock, confusion and social disorientation. Such changes can also cause social polarization and deterioration. This may also endanger their identity by weakening their link with their ancestral past.[3] Subsequently, fear of cultural death compels them to counter such interferences. They re-evaluate their social evolution, and distance themselves from the community which remains instrumental in damaging their culture.

The people of Baltistan, who are proud of their Tibetan roots, have gone through similar unwarranted socio-political changes since Pakistan occupied this region over six decades ago. Many locals consider this to have been detrimental to their society, and as harming ethnic integrity and identity. As a result, they have been demanding the preservation of their native culture, the renouncement of religious extremism, separation from Pakistan, and reunification with Ladakh to revive their rich civilization.

From time immemorial, the regions of Baltistan, Gilgit[4] and Ladakh remained an area of contest between Mongol, Tibetan, British and Chinese powers, which engaged in infamous 'Great Game' to gain supremacy. Their armies clashed in these valleys, and over the mountain passes, on several occasions. On the other hand, these valleys and passes also provided passage to traders in the shape of Silk Routes, and facilitated the globalization of trade and commerce.[5] Not a lot has changed since then as Kashmir dispute continues to draw attention of modern global powers, while India and Pakistan struggle to gain and maintain hold on to these regions. Further, the ancient Silk Routes have transformed into the modern-day Karakoram Highway which links South Asia with Central Asia and China. Based on its geo-strategic location, the titles of 'Asia's crown's nest', 'fulcrum of Asia',[6] 'cockpit of Asia',[7] and 'crown of India'[8] are still true for this region.

Strong political and cultural links with Ladakh and Tibet gave Baltistan the famous name of 'Little Tibet'.[9] The region embraced many ethnic groups, like the Tibetans,[10] Mongols,[11] Scythians,[12] Mons[13] and Dards,[14] and its valleys became their social melting pot. According to Professor Lozang Jamspal of Ladakh, who teaches at Columbia University of New York and is an authority on Tibetan history, Language and Religion,[15] history is silent about the exact date when hordes of Tibetan nomads, farmers, and invaders started colonizing Baltistan. However, it happened in different periods of history, and they settled in Ladakh and Baltistan on permanent basis. Their numbers must have been very large, to the extent that they successfully Tibetanized Mons, Scythians and other Indian races, which shared the land with these immigrant Tibetans.[16] The fact that approximately 93 per cent of the population of Baltistan considers Balti, an off-shoot of Tibetan, as their mother tongue—although not all of them claim their ancestry as Tibetan—proves this fact.[17]

Balti Language and Culture

Balti, similar to Ladakhi, is a West Tibetan archaic dialect,[18] and is spoken in areas which previously constituted part of the Yarlung and Shang-shung Tibetan Kingdoms.[19] Balti shares 90 per cent of its nouns, pronouns, verbs and other literary and grammatical characters with Ladakhi and other archaic Tibetan dialects. The exceptions are the Balti loan words which are adopted from Persian, Hindi and English. Further, the pronunciation of Balti words significantly resembles the way classical Tibetan is written. Indigenous poetry, proverbs,[20] script,[21] folklore, sagas,[22] folk dances, songs,[23] wedding rituals, festivals, sports,[24] costumes, cuisine[25] and cottage industries clearly demonstrate that Baltis and Ladakhis share the same heritage. They construct traditional flat-roofed buildings which slope inwards[26]—in typical Tibetan style. Further, Baltis consider *Swastika*[27] auspicious, which is also revered by Hindus, Buddhists and Bons, and carve on wooden planks of historical mosques and *Khankah*.[28] Their centuries old traditions, passed on from one generation to another, make their native culture unique in the conservative environment of modern day Pakistan.[29]

Baltistan: The Citadel of Buddhism

While the Tibetans gave their language and culture to Baltistan, it was Baltistan which gave the great religion of Buddhism to Tibet. Ancient Baltistan served as the hub for the dissemination of Buddhism from India into Central Asia, Tibet and China. It was the Mons who brought Buddhism to Baltistan, and established religious links with Buddhist schools in Kashmir and Turfan (Xinjiang). In Tibetan texts, Baltistan is also known for its greatest Buddhist priest, Sbal-te Dgra-bchom, who erected the famous Skyor-lung monastery (may be modern day Skor-yi-Lungpa, which is less than 35 kilometers from Skardo town) in the vicinity of Skar-mdo, Si-Dkar (modern day Shigar) and Ba-sho valleys in 1168 AD. Records also show that the great Buddhist monastery of Skar-chung Rdo-dbying (may be modern-day Skardo, the capital of Baltistan) was laid in Rgya (may be modern-day Rgya-yul of Skardo valley) which was then the capital of Ladakh.[30]

During the reign of the Rmakpon Dynasty, Buddhism was still practiced; however, Islam had started to make inroads, and arriving Kashmiri preachers, who introduced the Sufi-Nurbakhshia and Shia faiths, successfully converted the heir of Rmakpon Gyalpo Bugha and the majority of his subjects. By the seventeenth century, Baltistan was completely Islamized.[31] Today, Shias and Nurbakhshis make up more than 93 per cent of the total population of Baltistan. The Sufi-Shia religion of Baltis makes the cultural identity of this region distinct, since the majority of the inhabitants of other Tibetan speaking areas follow Bonchos[32] and Buddhism. Despite this change, Balti Muslims never stopped revering supernatural beings, such as *Lha* and *Lhu*,[33] to seek good faith during rituals like *Mephang, Srub-la, Brok-kher, Sonbor, Ong-chus, Mindok Ltadmo* and *Losar*.[34] Even today, many ancient supernatural belief systems, especially traditions connected with agricultural and hunting practices,[35] are followed with subdued reverence.

Ladakh Wazarat

Although it is said that the change of religion of the Baltis distanced them from Ladakh, the political history of both areas remained inter-woven till the end of 1947. During that time, the Rmakpons of Skardo[36] and the Rnamgyals of Leh took turns in ruling both the regions.[37] In 1840, when the Dogras conquered both regions concurrently, they established Ladakh Wazarat.[38] Subsequently, the Dogras divided Ladakh into the Leh, Kargil and Skardo administrative units, and Skardo, the capital of Baltistan, was made the winter capital of Ladakh. Their union lasted for another 108 years, which enhanced the political and administrative bonding between people of similar ethnicity and culture. The separation of Ladakh and Baltistan occurred in 1947, due to the tragic partition of the Indian sub-continent. Subsequent wars between India and Pakistan over Jammu and Kashmir led to the closure of the Line of Control (LoC) and the locals, under the pressure of Pakistani authorities, shunned connection with their brethren in Ladakh.[39] In 1974, the 'Northern Areas'[40] was created to detach Baltistan and Gilgit from the rest of Jammu and Kashmir. This brought new complexities to the region's political identity.[41] Constitutionally, however, Gilgit-Baltistan is still a part of Jammu and Kashmir, and UN resolutions refer to Baltistan as Ladakh, or the Pakistani administered part of Ladakh.[42]

Baltistan suffered geographical, political, economic, religious and cultural loss due to the breakup of Ladakh, and these changes took place without the effort or the will of the significant majority of the local people.[43] When compared with Pakistani controlled Kashmir (AJK), the sense of alienation, deprivation, and marginalization is still very strong in Baltistan.[44] Nationalists assert that, due to its proximity to Central Asia and Tibet, Baltistan had been able to maintain special political and commercial leverage, which it lost after Pakistan closed the Kargil-Skardo, Nubra-Khapulo and Leh-Skardo roads.[45] Further, the forceful separation of the Ladakh Wazarat has deprived Baltis of political autonomy, and an administrative province, which was granted by Dogra rulers, and is now denied by Pakistani Muslim occupiers.

Cultural Oppression by Pakistan

Soon after its creation, the ruling elite converted Pakistan into an oppressive security state, and used tenuous communal ideology to marginalize ethnic and religious minorities. As the country was created in the name of Islam, other parameters used for the definion of national identity—like language, culture and race—gave way to the sole factor of religion, which served as a national rallying cry, and a tool in the hands of of the establishment to promote the *jihadi* expansionist agenda. Following social Darwinism, the rulers committed ethnocide, and the deliberate destruction of minority cultures while promoting social hegemony to colonize ethnic groups like Baltis. They exploited Gilgit-Baltistan for its natural resources and filled coffers in Islamabad. These inhumane policies have led them to be identified as theft in Baltistan, and to be seen as a permanent threat to its rich civilization. At the advent of 21st century, Baltistan continues to be a victim of Pakistan's cultural and political abuse. Called the 'last colony'[46] by many international political and cultural commentators, Pakistani authorities have retaliated by attempting to warp the history, demography, traditions, language, and indigenous script of Gilgit-Baltistan.

The ethnocentric ruling elite of Pakistan reject cultural diversity, and deny the right of the Balti language and script to be taught in government schools, causing irreparable damage to this native language. By maintaining that Balti script is profane and un-Islamic, the Pakistani government insists on using the Urdu script for Balti, which is claimed as the language of Islam, and therefore compatible with Pakistani identity.[47] However, the Urdu script restricts the accurate pronunciation of many Balti words. A famous Balti writer, Hassan Lobsang, found the contents of his book illegible when written in Urdu script.[48] Further, oral traditions and Balti folklore, including *Ling Gesar, Api Tso, Rgyalbucho Lobzang* and *Rgyalbu Srasbu* and many other cultural treasures, risk permanent loss in the absence of a proper script. If these are not documented in the original Balti script, they will be permanently erased from the minds of future generations.[49] Today, publications in Baltistan are undertaken in either Urdu or English, while religious services are performed in Persian. Developments such as these have opened the doors to a random adoption of foreign loan words to further adulterate Balti.[50] In the absence of an appropriate script, Balti will face distortion, deterioration, and ultimate extinction if not preserved immediately.

The disregard of the Balti national identity in Pakistan has meant that local cultural and religious beliefs are ignored when formulating school syllabi.[51] As a result, local youth are unaware about their political and cultural legacy, which creates social disorientation, confusion, as well as an inferiority complex. Today, many school children in Baltistan cannot even count numbers in their own language, and hardly know anything about their rich history. As a causal effect of anti-Balti policies, local youngsters have lost interest in traditional festivals like *Mephang, Losar* (New Year), *Mindok Ltadmo* and *Srup La*. As the Balti culture faces downfall, traditional dancers, singers, musicians, and story-tellers also see a decline in the demand for their services and, as a result, are losing their livelihoods. Today, many among them are forced to find alternative sources of income, like daily-wage labor. In the same way, the indigenous cottage industry of handlooms, cap-making, and shoemaking is collapsing. Likewise, due to the lack of state patronage, the national sport of Baltistan, archery, is almost extinct.[52] Traditional Balti doctors and surgeons called *Amchi* and *Aba* have lost their livelihoods as their services are not deemed important anymore.[53] In the name of national conformity, authorities discourage the promotion of Balti costumes, architecture, cuisine, and wedding rituals, thereby causing a decline in the means of social bonding and identity.

Abbas Kazmi, a famous Balti writer says,

> To wear our traditional clothes or even to speak Balti is considered a sign of backwardness. We dress and eat like the Punjabis even though many of their customs are just as foreign to us as those from the West.[54]

Irrelevant to local needs, the authorities nevertheless impose events such as Urdu poetic seminars, which further alienate Baltis from their indigenous poetry. The so-called modern architecture introduced by Pakistanis is alien to local surroundings and tradition. Many traditional buildings have been razed to the ground to give way to Punjabi architecture. Further, the names of villages are being changed to erase the historical connection of this region with Ladakh and Tibet. Given the strategic location of Gilgit-Baltistan, which is sandwiched between China, Central Asia, Afghanistan and India, Pakistan seeks to prolong its occupation of the region, and maximize benefits from local resources. This is being achieved by causing social paralysis, ethno-linguistic degradation, demographic change, and an ultimate disconnect with its natural roots in Ladakh and Tibet.

Demographic Change and Loss of Identity

The natives of Baltistan are very concerned about local demographic changes since their homeland is sparsely populated. They feel threatened that Pakistan intends to turn them into a minority in their own homeland, and appropriate all the natural resources found there. The occupiers understand that a permanent hold on this region can become a reality only after locals are converted into a minority, either by settling Pakistanis there or by creating circumstances in which a large number of Baltis abandon their homeland. Subsequently, mechanisms are employed to incur rapid demographic changes, and weaken the natives in their demands for basic rights. For instance, when Pakistan announced the construction of the Skardo-Katzura Dam: it is understood that this would convert Baltistan into a gigantic lake. For locals this meant population displacement and the loss of cultural base.[55] The dam will be the largest in South Asia, and would generate more than 15,000 megawatts of electricity. The primary beneficiaries of this dam will be North West Frontier (NWFP) and Punjab provinces. However, it will force more than two-thirds of Baltistan's population to re-locate, causing a demographic change and the death of Balti culture and identity. The project will submerge the habitable parts of Baltistan which also host the famous Buddhist and Bon archeological sites. Further, the construction of another dam in Diamer will cause similar damage to the social fabric of Diamer and Gilgit, and the surrounding areas.

Pakistan uses a two-pronged strategy to change local demography: on the one hand, Pakistani Sunnis are encouraged to settle in the region; on the other, both Shias and Nurbakhshis are systematically killed, and forced to become Sunni.[56] For centuries, the people of Gilgit-Baltistan, even though professing various religious sects, co-existed in a relatively peaceful manner; today state sponsored Shia persecution in last four decades has divided the region very sharply on sectarian lines. Regimes pursue the well-trodden path of divide and rule to maintain a political impasse so that Pakistani settlers get enough time to establish their predominance. They orchestrate in-fighting between local Shias, Sunnis and Sufis with the help of local accomplices who, in turn, receive benefits and other favors.[57] The massacre of Shias in 1988 and 2005[58] are examples of such government-led adventures, which have strengthened Sunni settlers in Gilgit-Baltistan.

Shia Genocide: The Issue of Identity

The genocide of Shias in May 1988 was a watershed in the history of Gilgit-Baltistan in that it was responsible for causing a permanent trust deficit. Sunni tribal *Lashkars* (hordes), after receiving a nod of approval from General Zia-ul-Haque, attacked Gilgit-Baltistan where thousands of people were massacred, and many women were raped and abducted. The intention was to undertake demographic change by force in this strategically located region. In his book titled *Shohda-e-Gilgit Baltistan* (Martyrs of Gilgit-Baltistan), M.A. Kaiser has detailed incidents of Shia massacre in Gilgit-Baltistan. He claims that the then Minister of Kashmir Affairs and Northern Areas (KANA), Qasim Shah, played an active role in organizing the *Lashkars*, providing them weapons, transportation, and other reinforcements as well as other logistical requirements to march into Gilgit and slaughter the Shias. He has provided details of more than 87 native Shias who were massacred in that month by the Pakistani invading tribals. This book, gives details of several martyrs of Gilgit-Baltistan massacred in 1988, 1992, 1999 and 2004-5.[59] A synopsis of the events detailed by Kaiser is translated below.[60]

> The attack, which commenced on 16 May 1988, lasted for 10 days. The *lashkar*, numbering anywhere between 80,000 and 100,000, were armed with modern light and heavy weapons, and came from NWFP and Punjab. They also included Afghan *Mujahideen* in large numbers. According to reliable sources, 12,963 *lashkars* were killed by the local Shias. At the same time, more than 100 locals were martyred. The writer met a Sunni cleric on 7 April 1987, one year before the genocide, who narrated to him[61] that, a few weeks earlier, they had all gathered in Besham, a town south in Gilgit on the Karakoram Highway, and met the Minister for KANA, Qasim Shah, who promised to talk to President Zia-ul-Haque to support their *jihad* against the infidels of Gilgit-Baltistan. The Minister also promised to arrange weapons and transportation. After fixing a deadline to commence the *jihad*, they dispersed. Subsequently, Mullahs went to their respective mosques in Swat, Besham and Kohistan, and issued a religious *Fatwah* (edict) persuading the Sunnis to join the *jihad* caravan to attack Gilgit. They announced from their mosques,
>
> 'If one Shia is killed, then you will be rewarded by Allah as a Ghazi (*jihad* veteran); but if you kill 7 Shias, then you will be raised with a companion of Prophet Mohammad (PBUH) on the Day of Judgment (reward for one who kills 7 Shias will be equal and same to what the companions of Prophet Mohammad will receive from God on the day of judgment). If you get killed while fighting the Shias, then you will go to paradise (as *shaheed* or martyr).'[62]
>
> On their way to Gilgit, the *jihad*-caravan members received weapons, medicines, explosives, grenades, and food supplies. Thousands of people from Kohistan, Darel-Tanger, and Chilas joined them. They rode to Gilgit in buses, vans and jeeps, and carried their heavy weapons on large Bedford trucks. In Bunji, 45 kilometers south of Gilgit, Colonel Aziz and Major Ilyas of the Pakistan army, welcomed the *lashkars* and promised complete support. As planned by Minister Qasim Shah, around 50,000 *lashkars* were going to attack Gilgit, and another 50,000 were to attack Skardo simultaneously. The attack was going to happen on the day of Eid-ul-Fitr (right after the end of the holy month of *Ramazan*) when the Shias would congregate for Eid prayers. Information about the attack was already provided to local

Sunni mosques and community centers in Gilgit. Military personnel in the check posts on the Karakoram Highway were ordered to provide full support, and call off the checking of vehicles.

On 16 May 1988, when the Sunnis of Gilgit town heard about arrival of the *lashkars*, they attacked the Shia Mohallah of Nagaral. Meanwhile, in Bunji, local Sunnis converted the Shias to 'Islam' (converted to Sunni faith), and hence their lives were spared. However, their houses were torched, upon which they fled to Gilgit-Baltistan. In Jaglot village, all the Shias (around 800) became 'Muslim', and their lives were spared too. However, they were also forced to migrate to Gilgit. When the *lashkars* arrived in Manawar, 25 kilometers south of Gilgit town, they burnt local (Shia) mosques and copies of the *Quran*. The next stop was Sakwar, which is a couple of miles away from the Army Headquarters. There, Colonel Aziz provided reinforcements to the *lashkars*. On the other hand, the Shias arriving in Sakwar from other parts of Gilgit to protect the local Shias were stopped, and their weapons were taken away. The Shias coming from Nagar-Hunza towards Sakwar were also stopped at the China Bridge by the army. There, Pakistani soldiers killed Havaldar Mohammad Shafih of Nagar who insisted on going to Sakwar. Meanwhile, the *lashkars* kept advancing towards Gilgit town without facing any hurdles. On the way, they slaughtered many Shias.

On the other hand, around 400 fighters from Haramosh, and many more from Baltistan, advanced to the border between Gilgit-Baltistan, and stopped the *lashkars* there. Eyewitness counted more than 90 Bedford trucks with ammunition and heavy guns which were moving towards Skardo. As the skirmish continued, women, children, and the injured from Haramosh were moved to Skardo. The Government did not provide any support, such as shelter, food and medicines, to these refugees and local Baltis took care of them. Realizing their failure to advance further into Baltistan, the *lashkars* burnt the villages of Haramosh and returned towards Jalalabad of Gilgit. Once they left, the Baltis confiscated what they had left behind, which included Pakistani military uniforms, belts and caps. This suggests that radicalized serving-soldiers also joined the slaughter campaign of Shias.

On 22 May, Jalalabad, the largest Shia settlement in Gilgit, was attacked. *Lashkars* carried hi-tech modern weapons which the locals had never seen before. Around 40,000 *lashkars* attacked the village, from both the north and the south of Jalalabad. They killed livestock, set houses, crops, mosques, Shia religious centers and copies of the *Quran* on fire. *Lashkars* took heavy loss, and hundreds of dead bodies were either thrown into the Gilgit river, or piled in Bedford trucks to

> be hauled back to Pakistan. Meanwhile, two groups of *lashkars*—belonging to Mullah Quddoos and Mullah Dawood—got involved in in-fighting; this also led to the death of many *lashkars*. On the fourth day of the attack, as victory was nowhere in sight, Minister Qasim Shah dispatched personnel from the Frontier Corps to Jalalabad to join the *lashkars*. The *lashkars* killed women, and looted jewelry and other valuables. Two girls were gang-raped by 20 men. (Many girls like these were either killed or taken away by the *lashkars*, since tens of local women are still missing.) Two dead bodies of local Shias were found later; they were covered in bullets (as if sprayed from close range) and then burnt to charcoal. Wall-chalkings on different sites read: 'Zia-ul-Haque Zindabad' and 'Our supreme leader Zia-ul-Haque and Qasim Shah'. Local eyewitnesses saw 22 Bedford trucks filled with dead bodies of *lashkars* which passed through Chhamugarh village, on the way to Pakistan. Around 100 mosques, 80 Shia religious centers (Imambargahs), and more than 1,000 copies of the *Quran* were burnt by the *lashkars* in those ten days. On 23rd May, Qasim Shah enacted a peace agreement, and the *lashkars* were given safe passage to return to Pakistan. No one was arrested or charged for arson, manslaughter, rape, or looting. In villages where Shias were a minority—like Gulapur, Bargo, Shakyot, Sharot and Singal—they were converted to 'Islam'. Those who refused were killed. Many women from these villages were raped, and taken to Pakistan via the Darel-Tanger valleys. Minister Qasim Shah arranged 13 trucks to evacuate those *lashkars* who were stranded in Gilgit.

As one looks back towards 1988, it is heart-breaking to learn that the Shia massacre has not only continued unabated since then but its frequency has increased manifold. For example, eighteen people—including the Director of Agriculture Department of Gilgit[63]—were killed as a result of Shia-Sunni clashes in 2008. However, the year 2009 saw more sectarian killings than the previous two years put together. It started in the middle of February when two Shias were killed in an attack on a van in Gilgit.[64] Then, on 17 June, ISI personnel arrested a Shia political activist, Sadiq Ali, and tortured him to death while in detention.[65] Two months later, when leader of the banned anti-Shia political party *Sipah-e-Sahaba of Pakistan* (SSP), Allama Ali Sher Hyderi, was killed in Sindh, the repercussions caused riots in Gilgit, leading to the closure of markets and heavy gun battles between Shias and Sunnis.[66] In September, two Sunni Pashtuns and three native Shias were killed in Gilgit. Further, a bus with Shia passengers coming from Baltistan was torched during the same month, causing casualties.[67] On 27 September 2009, a bomb rocked Gilgit town sparking off yet another bout of Shia-Sunni rioting.[68] Gun battles in the aftermath of the blast devoured more than twelve people, including Raja Ali Ahmed Jan, a prominent leader of the *Pakistan Muslim League*.[69] On 11 November, three employees of Pakistan State Oil, including the area Manager, Ali Mohammad, were killed and two others were seriously wounded near Gilgit. In short, the Government failed to take measures to contain sectarian killings.[70]

Supporting the Pakistani agenda of Shia elimination from Gilgit-Baltistan, pro-Taliban militant groups have established bases in the region, and carry out target killings of Shia religious leaders, lawyers, technocrats, and government officials. Prominent political and religious leaders, like Agha Ziauddin Rizvi of Gilgit,[71] Syed Asad Shah Zaidi,[72] and Allama Hassan Turabi, became targets of similar groups. Agha Ziauddin's death in January 2005 caused widespread clashes, leading to a six-month long curfew and emergency, and the loss of hundreds of lives. Allama Hassan Turabi, who was shot dead in Karachi on 14 July 2006, hailed from Baltistan, and his death is termed as a blow to the Shia rights' movement in Pakistan.[73] Zaidi was the Speaker of Northern Areas Assembly, when he was murdered in April 2009.[74] Ironically, no one has ever been arrested or punished for their heinous crimes of eliminating national leaders, which reflects both upon the Government's intentions as well as competence.

The Advent of the Taliban in Gilgit-Baltistan

Social polarization based on religion, and the Talibanization of Pakistan has meant more killings of Shias, and the continued arrival of pro-Taliban settlers in Baltistan and Gilgit in large hordes. Both elements will hasten demographic change, and bring harm to local ethnic solidarity. In Baltistan, Sunnis constitute around seven percent of the population, many of whom support the Talibanization of Pakistan.[75] Further, many Taliban that have escaped from Swat and the adjoining areas, have found shelter among the Sunni extremists of Gilgit.[76] The fact that more than 300 suspected terrorists were expelled from Gilgit in October 2008, mirrors one's fears that the presence of non-local Taliban is widespread in Gilgit-Baltistan.[77] In May 2009, when a bomb blast in Baltistan led to the arrest of two Sunnis and the recovery of explosive-making material and hand grenades from them,[78] very few thought it would stop here.

Although sniper shooting has remained the primary method of sectarian killings, owing to the Taliban influence,[79] bomb blasts have also become common. A few weeks later, law enforcement agencies arrested another person from Baltistan for possessing explosives and hand grenades. However, in July 2009 terrorists were successful in detonating a bomb in Bagrot Hostel, Gilgit, which killed two Shias and injured several other students.[80] Earlier, in June, a toy bomb severely injured two persons of Gultari-Baltistan. Reports have also surfaced of an Al Qaeda member, Abdullah Rehman, threatening to bomb a four-star hotel in Baltistan.[81] By October 2009, five more accused of supporting terrorism were arrested from Baltistan. One of them is the Principal of a private school, while another person (belonging to Kuru village) was arrested near Skardo airport for allegedly carrying sketches of the runway and trying to cut the metal fence around the runway. In October, three more people from Yugu village were arrested on suspicions of terrorism, and taken by agencies to an unknown place for interrogation.[82] The radicalization of local Sunnis is bound to evoke reaction as Shias would also radicalize in self-defense. This will only increase sectarian deaths, and spread fanaticism among the Shias, thus damaging the social fabric of the region.

Shias of Gilgit-Baltistan, who see local Sunnis establishing links with Taliban and giving them shelter to further their claim to the region, have lost hope of religious co-existence in Pakistan. Referring to the sectarian menace that has choked Gilgit-Baltistan both socially and economically, Allama Sheikh Mirza Yusuf Hussain, a religious head of Baltistan and close associate of Zulfikar Bhutto, condemned Taliban activities in Pakistan.[83] The late Kalon Mehdi of Skardo, the lone Balti Law graduate from Aligarh Muslim University, once pronounced that once the unification with Ladakh and Kashmir had brought culture and civilization to Baltistan; but now Baltis receive drugs, Kalashnikovs and *Wahhabism* as a gift for opting for Pakistan.[84] These remarks show a clear rejection of Pan-Islamic radical identity by the Baltis.

Political analysts believe that the Gilgit region, which borders on the NWFP, has become the de facto safe haven for the Taliban to consolidate and re-organize. They fear that if Pakistan army extends its scope of operation to Gilgit-Baltistan, then the locals will come under attack from both the Pakistani army and the Pakistani Taliban. This will leave no choice for the locals but to request international military forces to intervene, and save them from a state-cum-Taliban led genocide. The ongoing state-cum-Taliban led genocide of the Shias in the Parachinar district of FATA[85]—where, as per local accounts, more than 500 natives perished[86]—reinforces fears of possible combined attacks on Gilgit-Baltistan by both the military and the Taliban.[87]

If a military operation occurs, it will refresh memories of the infamous Kargil war which, according to the local nationalists, was a weapon of Pakistani military regime to weaken the Balti Shias on both sides of the LOC, and to destroy their resource base.[88] While more than four thousand local soldiers became cannon fodder as a result of the Kargil war,[89] it also displaced around 60,000 Baltis as refugees, many of whom have not been able to return to their homes yet. It is feared that the majority of children refugees relocated to Islamabad, Karachi and Punjab with their families, will forget their language and the sense of belonging to Baltistan. These strategies of demographic change have directly impacted social cohesion among the Baltis.

Pakistani Occupation and Poverty

The advance of the Taliban into Baltistan will threaten indigenous Sufi practices, traditions, and institutions. The Baltis are also well aware of how militancy has destroyed cultural and economic activities in the Kashmir valley during the past twenty two years. In case the Taliban gets control of the Karakoram Highway (KKH),[90] which is the lifeline of the region, it will cause the economic death of Gilgit-Baltistan. As a result, many will fall into a permanent state of poverty while others will abandon their homeland in search of livelihood, causing brain-drain and demographic changes. As discussed earlier, demographic changes and subsequent cultural annihilation is also caused due to poverty and joblessness. The occupying regime has successfully maintained a state of socio-economic neglect and, owing to that, the per capita income of Baltistan is below one-fourth of Pakistan's—that is, US$ 234 as against US$ 1,071 respectively, while the literacy rate is less than half of Pakistan's average.[91]

Illiteracy has a direct impact on the degradation of cultures and the extinction of languages. Illiteracy bars people from knowing about their political and cultural rights, and takes away the awareness to value the richness of one's civilization and its traditions. It eliminates the ability to protect one's culture and identity. It is both ignorance and poverty which let locals join Pakistani armed forces, and become cannon fodder during fruitless military *jihads* (like the Kargil war) even when they knew that it was going to destroy their own homeland. Today, Balti soldiers of the Northern Light Infantry Regiment (NLI) have been pushed into combating Taliban and Al-Qaida *lashkars* in Swat and FATA—the same *lashkars* who perpetuated the Shia genocide in Gilgit in 1988. Many local families have already lost their bread earners as a result of the Taliban targeting Shia soldiers of NLI.

As the vicious cycle of poverty continues, and the poorer Baltis remain subsistent on government based menial jobs, it gives regimes the leverage to expedite their assimilation into Pakistani culture. Other poor Balti parents are forced to 'sell' their children to Sunni *madrassahs* of Pakistan—many orphans naturally end up there—so as to benefit from free ration and lodging. In the garb of Islamic teaching, these children end up learning extremist ideology and alien customs.[92] Such teachings adulterate their emotional attachment to their native culture, and confuse them about their sense of identity. Many like them, who are susceptible to falling victim to the Taliban, become suicide bombers.

State Subject Rule (SSR): Local Demography and Identity

Baltistan is experiencing an artificial social osmosis. While poverty and Taliban threats are causing Shia exodus from their ancestral homes, an increasing number of Pakistanis are acquiring land in Baltistan, and claiming their stake as its citizens. The influx of Pakistanis started after 1974, when the regime of former Prime Minister Z.A. Bhutto abrogated State Subject Rule (SSR), a law introduced by the Dogra rulers of Jammu and Kashmir to bar outsiders from acquiring land in Baltistan and thereby preserving its demography, and encouraged a systematic settlement of Pashtuns and Punjabis there.[93] Such a government-sponsored strategy has damaged the social fabric of Baltistan, and provoked religious feuds which continue to simmer. The settlers get government jobs on a preferential quota basis. Further, non-local federal employees, army generals, and politicians have acquired huge tracts of land through government allotment schemes, which also act as a catalyst of social change.[94] Many of these wealthy newcomers exert power and influence in the socio-political arena by imposing their language and customs upon the locals, which further exacerbates the identity crisis. To counter such trends, leading religious leaders of Gilgit-Baltistan have been demanding the reinstatement of SSR. They are concerned that Pashtuns and Punjabis control local commerce.[95] Similar views are being expressed by religious students of *Imamia Students Organization* (ISO) and *Nurbakhshi Youth Federation* (NYF).

Located at the crossroads of Central Asia and China, Gilgit is acutely affected by Pakistan's expansionist policy, and bears the brunt of cultural damage where settlers have turned the locals into a minority in Gilgit town. Over the years, as the demographics have evolved in Gilgit town, and the population balance tilted in favour of the Sunnis, Pakistani authorities have re-organized political constituencies. In 1991, they sent larger number of Sunnis to the regional council, and enhanced the marginalization of Shias.[96] Since then, contests between Shia and Sunni candidates in at least two constituencies have remained neck to neck.[97] For the first time in 2004, both seats from Gilgit city were won by Sunnis in the assembly election. The tipping point in Gilgit-1 is the vote bank in the Amphari neighborhood with a mixed Shia-Sunni population where sectarian polarization helps the Sunni candidate gain the lead. Likewise, in Gilgit-2, the settlement of the Pathans and Punjabis has changed the demography, and this one-time *Pakistan*

Peoples Party (PPP) stronghold supported Hafiz Rehman of the *Pakistan Muslim League* (PML) in the 2004 elections.[98] The voters' list released shows more than an 85 per cent increase in the number of voters' in Gilgit-1 (from 28,146 to 47,835) and Gilgit-2 (from 34,517 to 62,048) in just five years,[99] of which the majority are non-locals. The Government is planning to increase the number of assembly seats after the November 2009 elections, and the above-mentioned additional voters in Gilgit city will lead to an out-of-proportion representation for Sunnis in the assembly.

The sectarian rift also complicates the political process in Gilgit-Baltistan. Pakistani regimes exploit strategic location, demography, and political connections of this region with Jammu and Kashmir for their own advantage, but provide fewer or no benefits to the poverty stricken and largely illiterate local masses. The political arrangements in Gilgit-Baltistan since Pakistan's occupation in 1947 have remained transitory. Even today, the region is neither a part of Pakistan, nor an autonomous region, nor an independent country. Suiting its needs and political convenience, regimes sometimes declare the region as a part of Pakistan, and on other occasions, a part of Jammu and Kashmir. Given the ambiguity, many among the local youth are not clear what they are struggling for, and what their political identity is. Pakistan created a political vacuum and a law and order crisis, when they abolished the once princely states and the time-tested administrative structures of Gilgit-Baltistan. While Islamabad refused to delegate power to local Shias through viable modern political structures, the despotic military rulers maintained ad hoc policies to govern the region with an iron fist. Basically, Pakistan has illegally ruled the region through presidential ordinances since 1947.

The regime does not trust the Shias for the delegation of absolute autonomy for which the locals have been struggling for several decades. The Sunni minority also sees the political empowerment of the Shias, and the recently announced self-governance and empowerment ordinance of 9 September 2009 (which the majority see as eyewash) as undermining their long term political and socio-economic interests in the region. The Sunni fear that the Shias will gain majority in the newly incepted Gilgit-Baltistan Legislative Assembly, which is expected to legislate on 66 articles pertaining to socio-economic and administrative issues, dissuades them from supporting political autonomy for Gilgit-Baltistan. Pakistani authorities will continue to exploit similar insecurities to consolidate control in Gilgit-Baltistan. Such policies will only alienate the Shias, and strengthen their demand for separation from Pakistan.

Pro-Pakistani Rhetoric

In the name of national integration and countering separatism, the Pakistani authorities spend substantial resources. This can only prolong the occupation of these regions, but cannot legalize it. In the process, many pro-Pakistani socio-cultural and political groups have surfaced which benefit from government grants and preferential treatment. Collaboration with the authorities helps them become wealthy and influential as individuals. But, this fails to promote the overall development of Baltistan. While the support of such groups to regimes prolongs Pakistani occupation, it also delays a timely solution to the Jammu and Kashmir dispute. In the end, those who benefit from an impasse on Jammu and Kashmir issue outnumber those who would like to see an expedited just solution.

A large number of Baltis who reside in Pakistan see Gilgit-Baltistan becoming its fifth province as a just and logical end to the political stalemate. Among them are the 'Simla Baltis' who migrated to Himachal Pradesh to find work, and later moved to Pakistani cities during the partition of India.[100] It is said that, before partition, more than 10,000 Baltis were settled in Simla alone, and that the Vice Chairperson of the city council was also a Balti. After partition, many Simla Baltis decided to move to Pakistan rather than returning to Baltistan.[101] After four generations spent in Punjab and Karachi, a majority of these Baltis have forgotten their language and traditions; however, they still have emotional attachment with Baltistan. Many Simla Baltis have joined a political group called *Gilgit Baltistan National Alliance* (GBNA), which favors the merger of Gilgit-Baltistan with Pakistan.[102]

Similar views are held by a large number of people of Hunza[103] who express their unhappiness over Pakistan's persistent claim of Gilgit-Baltistan being disputed, and a part of Jammu and Kashmir.[104] Among the Pashtun Sunni settlers, many would like to see these regions merged with the NWFP.[105] However, others among native Sunnis would like to see the region united with 'Azad' Jammu and Kashmir (AJK), which will grant them better bargaining power. The majority of such activists come from Astore and Diamer districts.

Proponents of the 'fifth province' argue that such a decision will also receive support from China which does not want the Talibanization of this region.[106] They state that the recent attacks of Taliban on Chinese workers in Pakistan, and the Taliban's support for the separatist movement in Xinjiang has forced the Chinese authorities to believe that a Shia majority province on its border, with no association with Taliban or the Xinjiang militants, will safeguard Chinese interests.[107] They also believe that China will not prefer the merger of these regions with NWFP or Kashmir (AJK) as this may make Gilgit a launching pad for Islamic *jihad* in Xinjiang. The recently proclaimed self-governance and empowerment presidential ordinance of Gilgit-Baltistan 2009 is claimed by many as a step in that direction.[108] Pakistan announced the so-called self-governance package as it does not want to see a Balochistan-like situation emerging on its border with China. The ordinance is viewed as a replica of the political order prevalent in AJK, by creating a province-like structure for Gilgit-Baltistan, with a separate upper house, legislative assembly, judiciary, public service and election commissions.[109] Interestingly, the ordinance also provides a separate definition for the people of Gilgit-Baltistan, who are mentioned as citizens of Gilgit-Baltistan rather than citizens of AJK or Pakistan.

Censorship, Divide and Rule Mechanisms and Pakistani Occupation

Analysts claim that the ordinance was proclaimed after succumbing to the pressures of international political and human rights institutions. However, these organizations, which include the International Crisis Group, Human Rights Watch, Freedom House, International Kashmir Alliance, United Kashmir Peoples National Party, and especially, the European Union which has emerged as the most vocal advocate of Gilgit-Baltistan, have termed it a hoax. It is heartening for locals that the Members of the European Parliament (MEPs) not only successfully put Gilgit-Baltistan on the international political map, but also challenged Pakistan's political role and oppression in the region. Members of the European Parliament (MEPs) expressed shock that these regions of Jammu and Kashmir, which otherwise attract so much international attention, were illegally separated from Jammu and Kashmir. It is difficult to imagine that this situation continued for so long without the world noticing that one of the four parts of Jammu and Kashmir was allowed to fall almost entirely off the map for more than six decades.[110]

For almost six decades, Pakistani authorities successfully kept these regions hidden from the rest of the world.[111] First, it was media censorship in Pakistan which prevented the international community from learning about the true political and social color of these backward and remote regions.[112] Then, Pakistan successfully created a void between the people of Gilgit-Baltistan and those living in Jammu and Kashmir by making the locals believe that the Kashmiris oppose the political rights and provincial status for Gilgit-Baltistan.[113] As regimes fanned the ethnic and religious divide between those living in Gilgit-Baltistan, it helped them pursue a divide-and-rule policy without much resistance. For instance, after the death of Deputy Speaker of the Northern Areas, Syed Asad Zaidi, Baltis accused the people of Gilgit for the murder despite the fact that the majority in Baltistan believed that a government-sponsored sectarian motive was behind it. Protestors in Baltistan exploited the murder issue, and demanded a separate administrative unit for Baltistan. At the same time, they blamed Gilgit for discrimination in jobs, services, educational quotas, and the denial of other basic rights.[114] Such an act did not go down well with the Shia minority of Baltistan (about 7 per cent of the total population of the region),[115] who, in some localities, then boycotted attending religious functions along with Baltis. In the end, authorities benefited with the timing of these speeches and rallies, since it encouraged both sectarian and ethnic conflict in Gilgit-Baltistan simultaneously.

Commenting on the situation, a member of the guidance council of the nationalist *Baltistan Students Federation* (BSF),[116] Ali Shigri said,

> The infighting between Gilgiti, Balti and Kashmiri groups makes us weak in our demand for political rights. Although we are part of Jammu and Kashmir, a majority of Baltis believe that the amalgamation of Gilgit-Baltistan with 'Azad' Kashmir (AJK) will adulterate the local Shia majority, and therefore lose political leverage. The Islamization of the Kashmir issue under the influence of *Wahhabism* is a concern for the Shias of Gilgit-Baltistan.

Due to these insecurities, nationalists have failed to reunify all regions of Jammu and Kashmir. Ali Shigri further said,

> Balti nationalism is important when it comes to reviving our culture and language; but for political struggle, it distances us from Gilgit and creates insecurities among the people of Gilgit for their own future. In reaction, many politicians in Gilgit become pawns in the hands of the Pakistani administration, further isolating and depriving the Baltis of their socio-economic and political rights. Baltis are made to believe that the dominant ethnic group, i.e., the Kashmiris, oppose the socio-economic and political rights for smaller groups. The reality is that Islamabad has absolute authority, and all policies are formulated by federal agencies. Due to similar insecurities, the reunification of AJK and Gilgit-Baltistan regions has not happened.[117]

Over the decades, the authorities have exploited the local Sunni minority to act as accomplices in order to maintain a political impasse. The Inspector General of Police (IGP) of Gilgit-Baltistan, Syed Tehseen Anwar, recently admitted that police personnel have worked for sectarian causes. He also acknowledged that the banned religious, political and *jihadi* outfits have sustained their networks in Gilgit-Baltistan.[118] A political leader of

Gilgit Baltistan United Movement (GBUM) from Skardo, Ghulam Shehzad Agha, says,

> Sectarianism is used as a tool by state to divide and rule, while confusing the masses about their true identity. Our actual history and identity has been distorted due to which today we are weak and deprived of our rights. As a result, frequent attempts have been made by the authorities to annex Gilgit to NWFP by falsifying political and cultural realities.[119]

Manzoor Parwana, Chairman of GBUM and the editor of the monthly magazine *Kargil International*, calls the activities of Pakistani agencies ideological terrorism, which brainwashes the youth. He says,

> The nationalists unite Baltis on the basis of ethnicity, common language and culture. However, religious organizations obstruct such efforts, and distort the concept of national identity among the youth. The conversion of Sufis in Wahhabi *madrassahs* and training as militants is continuation of such a policy. These orchestrated efforts by government agencies feed ignorance, create a confused sense of ever shifting identity, and hinder economic development and social stability, thereby weakening locals who otherwise will rise with a unified voice demanding self-determination. Baltis are made to believe that America, Israel, and India are the real enemies of Muslims. In reality, our common enemy is sectarianism, poverty, unemployment, favoritism, corruption and illiteracy. Instead of chanting slogans in favor or against a country, we should demand funds from Pakistani government to enhance literacy.[120]

Manzoor believes that Gilgit-Baltistan needs international support to gain political rights and to present its case forcefully and, if the *mullahs* promote anti-West feelings, then such a support may not come. *Mullahs* who deliver anti-West speeches and declare the West as an enemy of Islam, are actually lending a hand to the occupying regime. In the same manner, many religious scholars fan anti-Hindu and anti-Buddhist hatred with the objective of suppressing the cultural association of Baltistan with Ladakh, which is a predominantly Buddhist region.

The famous Balti writer Abbas Kazmi thinks that anti-West slogans will only prove Baltis as less tolerant towards other religions and societies. He laments that there are Shias who point fingers at the Taliban for their extremism, and yet engage in extremism and harbor hate towards non-Muslims and their cultures. Such a dichotomy is challenging for Shias, especially when they are struggling to evolve out of an over sixty five years old Pakistani political ideology. He also accuses the *mullahs* for distorting the political and cultural history of Baltistan, thereby creating confusion and lack of direction for the local youth. He believes that, similar to Taliban ideological influences, Iranian influences—especially trends associated with Islamic Revolution of Iran—have damaged true Balti culture and identity. He laments the loss of pre-Islamic cultural practices, which are not prevalent in the urban parts of the region.[121]

Self-Supported Cultural Development

Abbas Kazmi, Hassan Hasni, Hassan Lobsang, Hassan Hasrat and the late Wazir Mehdi are among those who refused to succumb to state interventions of censorship and extremism, and continued their efforts to preserve indigenous secular culture and promote genuine national identity. Risking the wrath of the authorities, they keep the youth interested in Baltistan's connection with Ladakh, Tibet, and Jammu and Kashmir. Famous writers like Yusuf Hussainabadi and Abbas Kazmi have called Wazir Mehdi an authority on Balti culture and history.[122] Further, Ghulam Hassan Hasni, who compiled Balti *Tamlo*[123] containing 900 Balti and Ladakhi proverbs, idioms and expressions, is revered by many nationalists. Audio and video recordings of Hasni's poetry sell like hot cake in Indian Ladakh.[124] Kazmi's book *Balti Folksongs* is a source of emotional bonding with the land.

Hassan Lobsang's *Balti Grammar* and *Bon Philosophy* are considered a great source of learning.[125] In *Bon Philosophy*, the writer has narrated the epic of *Soma-milik* which is about creation of universe. The epic-narrator has used the word *Ldan* (self-evolving), throwing light on the fact that the universe was not created but evolved as ocean water and blowing dust mixed and turned into three worlds or planets: upper world for *Lha* or Gods; the middle world for humans; and the lower world for *Bruk* or Dragons. In the first world, the mountains and sky (atmosphere) are blue and dragons live there. In the second world, the mountains and sky are white and the Gods live there. The third world has red mountains and sky and humans live there. The red color may have come from a mixture of water and dirt. After that, greenery evolved on the red earth, and gave birth to the auspicious tree of *Chandan* (sandalwood). Lobsang writes that the three worlds could mean earth, moon and sun, and their division into three separate bodies may resonate with the theory of the big bang. On the other hand, Kacho Sikander argues that the three worlds mean Baltistan, Ladakh and Tibet.

The museum set up by Hassan Hasrat opens up one's imagination regarding Baltistan since it encompasses thousands of years of Balti and Tibetan civilization. Professor Shesrab of Skardo College, who has named his sons Wangyur, Gergan and Tsering in Balti language,[126] commands respect among the local students, and teaches them the native script, *Yige Bakir Posingpa*. The *Baltistan Cultural Foundation* (BCF) was able to successfully convince the shopkeepers of Skardo market to install signboards in the Balti script. The BCF continues its efforts to protect Baltistan's pre-Islamic heritage, including the Buddha rock etchings.[127] BCF made efforts to produce the first Balti primary school book which, to this day, continues to benefit thousands of Baltis.[128] All these activities are taking place without any government financial support.

The Reconstruction of Identity

As Pakistan evolves socio-politically, the issue of Balti national identity goes under repeated reconstruction and redefinition. The lack of political stability in the country and the continued oppression of the Baltis has, once again, forced many to review the concept of nationalism, thereby, distancing themselves from the rest of Pakistan.[129] Political deterioration in Pakistan has created an internal crisis even for those Baltis who identify themselves as pro-Pakistani, as they feel as much threatened by the Taliban's advance to Baltistan and Gilgit. Many Baltis who previously ignored their secular cultural identity, are now returning to it. For example, leading religious scholars of Baltistan desire to see the Balti script and culture taught in government schools. The identity of the 'Northerners' imposed by Pakistan on the residents of Gilgit-Baltistan has also hurt these regions since the term 'Northern Areas of Pakistan' is also used by the international media for Swat and the adjoining areas of the NWFP. Due to the proximity of Gilgit-Baltistan with NWFP and Swat valley, local livelihoods, especially the tourist industry, has suffered gravely. Out of compulsion, even the pro-Pakistanis, who once favored the term 'Northern Areas', now use the historical name of 'Gilgit-Baltistan' for these regions.[130]

Transforming social perceptions in Gilgit-Baltistan are providing greater legitimacy to nationalists who believe that separation from Pakistan is the only answer to their socio-economic and political problems. Pakistan's failure to deliver basic rights in the last 65 years has garnered them support among youth, and their demands for self determination have become louder, even as the need to maintain their culture and identity is being felt acutely, It also shows how the people of Gilgit-Baltistan are increasingly accepting the fact that they are not part of Pakistan but of Jammu and Kashmir. The majority of educated youth believe that the authorities will continue to cause the cultural and economic downfall of Baltistan to sustain its occupation. They resent Pakistan for exploiting their natural resources without any benefit accruing to the locals. The Baltis believe that state persecution and the systemic erosion of Balti identity under Pakistani occupation is severe, and parallels alarmingly the Chinese persecution of the Tibetans. The deteriorating conditions of other ethnic minorities in Pakistan, like the Balochis and Sindhis, reinforce this view.

Nationalist and Separatist Movements: A Logical Conclusion

The lack of a centralized nationalist leadership has created space for several groups to formulate diverse ideas. However, they all agree on the agenda of separation from Pakistan through political struggle. Some of the groups are: the Gilgit-Baltistan United Movement (GBUM), the Gilgit-Baltistan Democratic Alliance (GBDA), the Balawaristan National Front (BNF), the Gilgit-Baltistan Thinkers Forum (GBTF), the Baltistan National Movement (BNM), the Karakoram National Movement (KNM), and the All Parties National Alliance (APNA).

For BNM, BSF and Ladakh-Baltistan People's Party, the cultural distinctiveness of Baltistan and its separation from the 'Northern Areas' is an important element on the road to self determination and merger with Ladakh. The involuntary incorporation of Baltistan into the 'Northern Areas' in 1974 has been a cause of concern for them, as it undermined their national identity and the right of reunification with Ladakh.[131] These groups demand the opening of the Skardo-Kargil road and the re-establishment of cultural and political links with Ladakh and Tibet. In 2008, thousands of Ladakhi refugees residing in Baltistan assembled in Skardo town and carried out a symbolic march towards LOC, which was then obstructed by the police. Backed by parties like the BNM, GBUM and BSF, they raised slogans of unification of Ladakh-Baltistan and the opening of Kargil-Skardo road.

Jawad, an ex-president of the BSF, believes that the BSF desired Gilgit-Baltistan to be the fifth province of Pakistan, and raised that slogan for over twenty years. The circumstances have changed since then, and now an increasing number of Baltis desire a separate and genuinely autonomous political set up. He says, "with LOC closed, Pakistan restricts us from learning about our political relationship with Jammu and Kashmir, which can empower local people, especially the students."[132] Similar views were expressed by Sher Mohammad of the BNM, who said,

> BNM brings religious harmony among different sects in Baltistan, and demands an autonomous state or merger with Ladakh based on our unique ethnic and linguistic character. We are part of the Jammu and Kashmir State and based on that, we desire reinstating Ladakh Wazarat.[133]

He believes that, as a start, Pakistan should extend the same political rights to Gilgit-Baltistan which currently prevail in AJK.[134]

Shakir Shamim, a famous Balti poet, reinforces these views and says,

> Pakistan has no direct and legal claim to Gilgit-Baltistan. We are part of Ladakh and Jammu and Kashmir, and our political rights will return to us only after we rejoin Jammu and Kashmir. Our cultural future is with Ladakh.

He has demanded that State Subject Rule (SSR) should be reinstated, and the settlers of the post-1947 era should leave the region. He further said, "In many ways, the reign of Dogra rulers was better as Shias had religious freedom and civic security."[135]

Others who support separatism pursue three options: firstly, that Gilgit-Baltistan should become an independent country; secondly, it should be merged with Jammu and Kashmir; and thirdly, it should become part of pan-Tibetan country.[136] Shehzad Agha of the GBUM believes that Pakistan will never allow Gilgit-Baltistan to become sovereign as it fears the emergence of a Shia State. He also believes that the reason behind Pakistan's refusal to open the Skardo-Kargil road is the religious and ethnic composition of Gilgit-Baltistan. Agha's remarks lead us to the views of those who desire to create a little Iran, or a Shia Republic in this mountainous hinterland. Along with Gilgit-Baltistan, they also desire the neighboring Shia districts of Kargil and Chitral to become its parts.[137] These ideas are prevalent among those who survive on Iranian 'Dollars', and lament Shia persecution in Pakistan. Their influences have led to the introduction of an Iranian dress code, the Persianization of the local language, and the promotion of Pan-Shia ideology. Many of them once favored the merger of Gilgit-Baltistan with Pakistan. However, government-led political and religious persecution of the Shias has forced them to change their opinion. Their inclination towards Kargil is mainly based on a common Shia religion rather than a common secular cultural heritage.

Grand Alliances: Baltistan on the International Political Map

The idea of separatism among Gilgiti youth is widespread, and many have formed alliances with Balti nationalists. A pan-regional political identity among Baltis and Gilgitis is emerging, along with existing linguistic and cultural realities. Supporters of such ideas belong to BNF, KNM, APNA and GBTF. GBTF is represented by Colonel Nadir and Wajahat Hussain, who are the sons of the late Gilgit war hero, Colonel Hassan Khan Jarral. They all believe in the creation of a free Balawaristan country, and consider the people of Gilgit-Baltistan as one nation called Balawar or the 'highlanders'. Since the past several years, 1 November—the Independence Day of Gilgit—is celebrated by these groups as the 'Day of Occupation by Pakistan', or simply 'the Black Day'. BNF considers the Balawar people as the fourth party to the dispute of Jammu and Kashmir. They resent the fact that Islamabad denies representation to Gilgit-Baltistan during talks with India on Kashmir.[138] Based on a common language and civilization, they would like to see Chitral, Kohistan and Ladakh becoming part of Balawaristan.

The dream of these parties to create an independent country comprising of Gilgit, Baltistan, Ladakh, Chitral and other neighboring districts seems a huge challenge, especially when there is no response from the Ladakhis, both Muslims and Buddhists, who are content as being Indians. The Indian intelligentsia as well as the government would also like to see the LOC converted into an international border. Under these conditions, BNF lacks diplomatic support from India to fulfill its goal. Moreover, the ethnic divide between the people of Gilgit-Baltistan prevents the BNF from becoming a popular separatist movement in Baltistan.

Baltistan's Shina population is approximately seven per cent.[139] New dimensions to their identity are also appearing. Shinas live in the valleys of Baltistan adjacent to the LOC. Wars between Pakistan and India have forced them to take refuge in Skardo town. There, they mingle with Shina immigrants of Hunza, Astore and Gilgit who have made Skardo town their home. Many of these immigrants are Shias, and they migrated from Gilgit due to the on-going sectarian problem. However, some also came here to establish businesses. Over the years, the Shinas of Baltistan and these new immigrants have formed social alliances based on cultural and linguistic affinity. In some villages, they attend religious congregations together. Many of them support the Free Balawaristan movement which threatens many Baltis, who feel detached from these local Shinas with whom they have shared Baltistan for hundreds of years. Simmering ethnic tensions between Baltis and Gilgitis may further distort the perception of nationality among Shinas of Baltistan.

A few years ago, the nationalists of Gilgit-Baltistan formed a political union called GBDA, reflecting the growth of separatist movement in the region. One constituent among GBDA is GBUM, which believes in the creation of a country composed of Gilgit-Baltistan only. GBUM has limited its movement to the disputed region of Gilgit-Baltistan, and believes that Ladakh, Jammu and Kashmir are part of India while Kohistan and Chitral are part of Pakistan. GBDA has formed another grand alliance with the separatists of AJK, and this alliance is called APNA. They believe in reunification with Jammu and Kashmir and separation from Pakistan. They demand the lifting of restrictions on trade and people-to-people contact across the LOC.[140] Kashmiri political groups, like International Kashmir Alliance (IKA) and the JKPNP, have expressed their desire to unite with GBDA and APNA to strengthen their rights' movement in all parts of Pakistan-occupied Kashmir.

Although divided in their opinions and efforts, the separatists are gaining ground. In the coming years, they may be able to lend a hand in bringing the Kashmir dispute to its logical end. The Northern Areas Chief Executive, Mir Ghazanfar Ali, once stated that the nationalists have become popular enough to win a majority during assembly election.[141] He accused the local nationalist leader, Abdul Hamid Khan, of being the 'Altaf Hussain'[142] of Gilgit-Baltistan who has strong support among the local educated youth.[143] If support of various international rights' groups and political forums continues for the GBDA and APNA, then very soon they might become a real driving force to achieve political autonomy for Gilgit-Baltistan.

In October 2009, several members of the European Parliament (EUP) incepted a political lobbying group called Friends of Gilgit-Baltistan (FoGB).[144] GBDA and APNA is terming the inception of FoGB as a great success. Earlier, in May 2008, EUP passed a resolution with an overwhelming support of 522 members demanding political and cultural rights for the people of Gilgit-Baltistan. The resolution reiterates respect for ethnic identities and confirms that the society of Jammu and Kashmir is multi-ethnic and multi-religious. Such tireless efforts of members of the EUP have helped put Gilgit-Baltistan on the international political map.[145] The fact that an institution like the EUP recognizes the disputed status of the Gilgit-Baltistan region and its separation from Pakistan, is very encouraging for those who ultimately desire 'Azadi' (independence) from Pakistan.

NOTES

1. According to the famous 10th century Muslim geographic work *Hudud-ul-Alam*, and the 16th century historical narration *Tarikh-i-Rashidi*, Baltistan was a Tibetan province, located between Ladakh and Gilgit. When the Tibetan Yarlung dynasty disintegrated at the end of 1000 AD, Baltistan became part of the Tibetan Zhang-zhung (pronounced Shang-shung) dynasty. After 1100 AD, many decentralized fiefdoms emerged in Baltistan. See http://www.scribd.com/doc/21208422/Bot-Sinha-C-Nirmal-Gilgit-and-Swat pp 51; http://www.ssi-austria.at/ssi-engl/kyunglung-light_of_kailash-text.htm; http://www.scribd.com/doc/13988117/Chogyal-Namkhai-NorbuThe-Ancient-Kindgom-of-Shang-Shung
2. J.H. Bodley, *Culture, Online Encyclopedia* 2002, at http://www.encarta.msn.com.

3. Aziz Ali Dad argues that Gilgit-Baltistan presents a case of disharmonious interaction between state, religion, and culture, which is characterized by the hegemony of one group over the others. He writes that, in 1947, Baltistan and Chitral were separated from Ladakh and Gilgit respectively, which resulted in cultural disintegration. Today, the society of Gilgit-Baltistan suffers due to the disharmony created by the state and religious groups, which has greatly marginalized the local culture. See http://www.pamirtimes.files.wordpress.com/2009/06/state-religion-and-culture-in-gilgit-baltistan1.pdf pp 1-9.
4. In the past, the Tibetan empire extended to northern Afghanistan and Central Asia, and made Gilgit its province. In medieval times, Gilgit was the cultural and commercial transit post between Bhota (Tibet) and Suvastu (Swat). In 727–737 AD, the Tibetan king, Khri-Lde-gTsug-bRtan, once again extended his domain to Gilgit. Bon priests of Tibet sought refuge in Gilgit, and gave the region its Bon religion. For some historians, the word Gilgit or Gilit is Tibetan, composed of two syllables, Rgyal (victory/superior) and Skyid (happiness/wealth). Tibetans pronounce it gyal-kit, which is very similar to Gilgit or Gilit. Even today, many tribes in Chilas (District Diamer) call themselves Botto, which is a changed form of Pod, the ancient name of Tibet. Gilgit remained a province of the Tibetan Yarlung Empire until the death of King Glang Darma around the 10th century AD. See also, A. H. Francke, *History of Western Tibet*. Patridge, London, 1907; K.S.K. Sikandar, *Qadeem Ladakh: Tarikh-o-Tamaddun*, Leh, Kacho Publishers, 1987, p. 62; http://www.koshur.org/Linguistic/7.html; http://www.scribd.com/doc/21208422/Bot-Sinha-C-Nirmal-Gilgit-and-Swat pp. 47-55; http://www.ssi-austria.at/ssi-engl/kyunglung-light_of_kailash-text.htm; http://www.scribd.com/doc/13988117/Chogyal-Namkhai-NorbuThe-Ancient-Kindgom-of-Shang-Shung.
5. Peter Hopkirk, *The Great Game*, Oxford University Press, Oxford, 1990, pp. 449-450.
6. http://www.gastellier.be/Amaury/gilgit.htm.
7. http://www.kashmiraffairs.org/Manzoor_Parwana_revival_gilgit_baltistan_sovereignty.html.
8. http://www.indianexpress.com/news/gilgitbaltistan-india-must-speak-up/509001/0.
9. Historians and travelers have used the term Little Tibet for Baltistan. The Dogra rulers and the Mughals called this region *Tibet-e-Khurd*, which also means Little Tibet in Persian. Kashmiri chronicler Srivara called it Suri-Bhutan or Apricot Tibet due to the abundance of apricots in the region. Locals call their land Baltiyul, Rangyul, Phayul, Dreyul, Lhayul and Tibet. See B.G. Afridi, *Baltistan in History*, Emja Book International, Peshawar, 1988, p. 8. Ancient names used for Baltistan are Nang-gong by Central Tibetans, Palolo by the Chinese, Polu by western neighbors, Posal by the Mons, Byltae by Ptolemy, and Balor by the Arabs. See K.S.K. Sikander, no. 4, p. 258.
10. According to authoritative Tang Annals, Tibetans were a nomadic and pastoral people who lived on the steppes in the west and north of China. See Senge Hasnain Sering, 'Balti Language and Script', Skardo: Society of Asian Civilization, Pakistan, 20 August 2000; Friedrich Ratzel writes that they were one of the cultured races of Inner Asia. According to him, the word Tungustic is also used for Tibetans. See Friedrich Ratzel and A.J. Butler, *The History of Mankind*, Macmillan, Princeton, 1898, Vol. 3, pp. 313, 349, 354 and ff. Their language is prevalent in the modern-day Chinese provinces of Xizang (U and Thsang in Tibetan), Chinghai (Amdo in Tibetan), Sichuan (Khams in Tibetan), Gansu and Yunnan. See also J. Leyden, 'On the Language and Literature of Indo-Chinese Nations', *Asiatic Researches*, Vol. 10, 1808, p. 209 and ff. It is also the pre-

dominant language in Bhutan, and is spoken in parts of India, Pakistan and Nepal. The areas of India and Pakistan in which this language is spoken include Baltistan, Purig, Zanskar, Chang-thang, Ladakh, Lhahul, Spiti, Kumaon, Kunawar, Garwal, Sikkim, and Arunachal Pradesh in the Karakoram-Himalayan belt. As Tibetan is spoken over a vast mountainous area, some differences in pronunciation have appeared, and for this reason, very few people can understand or speak each other's dialects. After listening to a Balti tape, Namgyal Tsering, President of the Sydney branch of the Australian Tibetan Society, who comes from the Thsang province of Tibet, claimed to comprehend approximately only 40 per cent of the Balti dialect. For the majority of Tibetans worldwide, the Lhasa (the capital of Tibet) dialect is the standard. However, this is not true for the West Tibetans (Baltistan, Ladakh, Lhahul, etc.).

11. G.T. Vigne is of the view that the Baltis and Ladakhis are a mixture of Tatar (Mongol), as well as Indian and Aryan blood. He may be using the term Aryan for the Scythians since it is mentioned separately from Indians. The Tatars arrived from east and north, while the Aryans and other Indian races came from the west and the south, and the bank of Indus became their melting pot. See G.T. Vigne, *Travels in Kashmir, Ladak and Iskardo.* 1844, p. 248, (reprint by Sagar Publications, New Delhi, 1981. See also, A.H. Francke, *Ladakh: The Mysterious Land,* 1905, p. 12, (reprint by Ess Ess Publications, New Delhi, 1980). Sikander claims that the inhabitants of Baltistan belong to the Tungustic nation, who lived in the north east of present-day Mongolia, and arrived in Baltistan via Dzungaria (Xinjiang). See K.S.K. Sikander, no. 4, p. 46.
12. The Scythians, Parthians (pre-Mongol Central Asians) and the Kushans were pushed south of the Pamirs and the Karakoram by other dominant races. Rock-etchings and carvings in Gilgit-Baltistan and Ladakh substantiate this fact. Among some Baltis, light skin and brownish hair could suggest the racial mixing of Scythians and Tibetans. Many authors are of the view that it was the Scythians rather the Greeks who settled in present-day Chitral, Gilgit, Baltistan and Ladakh. See also, *Man & Life*, Calcutta, Vol. 26, 2000, p. 227; Rahul Sankrtyayana, *History of Central Asia*, Calcutta, 1964, pp. 11, 12, 105; http://www.visitnorthernareas.gov.pk/history.htm
13. The Mons was a superior race of north India who brought Buddhism to Baltistan and Ladakh. They engaged with the arriving Tibeto-Mongols, and were later suppressed to accept a lower class in society. It is believed that they ruled Baltistan and the surrounding areas for around 500 years. Today, the Mons of Ladakh and Baltistan speak Tibetan dialects as their mother tongue. The people of Zanskar call all those from Kashmir, Jammu and Himachal, Mon. The aboriginal people of Bhutan and Sikkim were called Mon by Tibetans since they lived south of the Himalayas. See also K.S.K. Sikander, no. 4, pp. 41, 44; A.H. Francke, *Antiquities of Indian Tibet*, Calcutta, 1926, pp. 19-24.
14. The Dards are an Indian race. The Shins of Gilgit and Chitralis are collectively called Dardic people. Their language is closely related to Sanskrit. On their way to Gilgit, Baltistan and Ladakh, they followed the Indus; however, some of them also travelled along the Pir Panjal Range and the Kishanganga valley towards Skardo and Kargil. Most of them came as nomads; but others were brought by the Baltis who exploited their martial skills. Following the Indus in the eastward direction, they moved to Spangong Tso, which borders modern-day Tibet and Ladakh. Many Dards of Ladakh and Baltistan have been Tibetanized; but the majority were able to preserve their language and customs. See also K.S.K. Sikander, no. 4, p.79 and ff; G.T. Vigne, no. 4,

p. 300; A.H. Dani, *History of Northern Areas of Pakistan*, Sang-e-Meel, Lahore, 2001, pp. 25, 156, 400; Karl Jettmar, *Ethnological Research in Dardistan*, 1958, pp. 79-97, at http://www.jstor.org/stable/985355.

15. In 2005, I took a six-month long Tibetan language course at Columbia University with Professor Jamspal.
16. Y. Hussainabadi, *Tarikh-i-Baltistan*, (in Urdu), Skardo, 2003, p. 18.
17. In the 9th century, Baltistan went through an intensive Tibetanization process in terms of its language and religion after it became part of Tibetan Shang-shung Dynasty. http://india_resource.tripod.com/balti-human-rights.html
18. Tibetan dialects void of tone are grouped under 'West Tibetan archaic dialects', which include Balti, Purigi, Zanskari, Ladakhi, Lahuli and their respective sub-dialects, spoken by around 650,000 people in India and Pakistan http://www.koshur.org/Linguistic/7.html. These dialects are also called Stod Skad (the broader nomenclature meaning superior language, which includes gNari-skad and Chang-skad). West Tibetan finds its closest linguistic cousins in the very far north east, in Amdo around the blue lake in Chinghai of China, and in Khams in east Tibet. Balti, along with Amdo and Khams dialects, is of utmost importance for the understanding and re-construction of the language history of Tibet and Burma. See J. Averi, 'The Tibeto-Burman Group of Languages', *Transactions of American Philological Association*, Vol.16, 1885, Appendix, xvii and ff. These dialects are a monosyllabic form of speech, with a highly complicated phonetic system. See Lobsang G. Hussain, *Balti Grammar*, Berne, 1995, pp. I-III. The notion archaic means that Balti has preserved ancient forms of vocabulary, phonetics and grammar, which is similar to classical Tibetan texts from the 8th century AD onwards. On the level of phonology, many of the complicated initial consonant clusters of written Tibetan are found in Balti. See G.A. Grierson, *Linguistic Survey of India-Tibeto-Burman Family*, Delhi, 1909, pp. 1-37. Balti retains a good deal of old compound consonants of classical archaic Tibetan. See A.F.C. Read, *Balti Grammar*, Royal Asiatic Society, London, 1934, p. 10. The old consonants, which would seem to have been generally sounded and spoken twelve centuries ago, when the Tibetan written character came into existence, and which, at any rate, are marked by the primitive system of writing, have prevailed in Balti. Every one of them can still be disinterred, somewhere or other, from some local particularity of language, and thus even the very diversity of modern practice can be made to bear testimony to the standards imposed by the classical period. See, H.A. Jaschke, *A Tibetan-English Dictionary*, Motilal Banarasidas, Delhi, 1887, pp. I and ff; IX and ff.
19. Lobsang G. Hussain, Ibid., pp. I-III.
20. For details, see H. Hasrat, *Baltistan Tehzib-o-Saqafat*, Baltistan Publications, Skardo, 2007, p. 103 and ff.
21. Although the art of Tibetan writing was developed centuries ago, present Tibetan alphabets were adopted from India only in the year 632 AD. When Srungthsan Gampo (ca 617-650), the great Yarlungpa King, was the patron of Buddhism in Tibet, he sent his minister Thonmi Sambhota to India to prescribe a suitable script for their language so that Buddhist teachings could be translated from Sanskrit into native language. The minister spent fourteen years in India learning Buddhism as well the Sanskrit (*Devanagri*) script, and transformed *Devanagri* to devise alphabets for Tibetan. Other linguists say that the Tibetan script is very close to Pali. The major translation works from Sanskrit to Tibetan, include *bKa-gyur* (the Book of Commandments) and the great book of exegesis, *Stan-gyur*. Two distinct characters, *dBu-chen* (head possessing) and

dBu-med (headless) were developed. The *dBu-chen* script has mostly been used for writing manuscripts, textbooks, etchings and religious texts. The *dBu-med* style is commonly used by the Tibetans in general. The Tibetan writing pattern is from left to right—similar to English and Hindi. The alphabet is comprised of thirty consonants and five vowels. The vowel 'a' is inherent in all consonants. See G.A. Grierson, no. 18, pp. 1-37. Today, Tibetan religious etchings are found on rocks, historical monuments and buildings in different parts of Baltistan.

22. For further details on folk tales, see H. Hasrat, no. 20, pp. 250-342. Story-teller Ghulam Hussain can be heard narrating these sagas during the winter. Hussain Blaghari, famous Balti radio producer and drama writer, also possesses a collection of many sagas and folksongs of Baltistan.
23. For details on Balti folksongs, and classical dance and music, see M. A. Kazmi, *Balti Lok Geet*, Islamabad, 1985, pp. 41-47, 109-120, 133, 135, 181, and 183.
24. For details about polo, the national sport of Baltistan, see H. Hasrat, no. 20, pp. 459-520.
25. For details on Balti cuisine, see M.A. Kazmi, *op. cit.*, pp. 31, 32.
26. See K.S.K. Sikander, no. 4, p. 640.
27. Called *Yung-drung* in local language, and considered the sign of prosperity.
28. Sufi religious centres.
29. As part of an ancient civilization going 5,000-6,000 years, Baltis profess the concept of the creation of the earth and living beings. The theory of the creation of human beings is called *Pho-gsum Mo-gsum* (three males and three females). The creation of the universe is presented through the epic of *Soma-milik*, which narrates that the universe was created upon ocean water and blowing dust, and mixture of both created the earth and the mountains. The concept is quite different from the biblical narratives of the West. See Lobsang G. Hussain, *History of Bon Philosophy: History of Baltistan, Ladakh and Tibetan Belief System*. Hunza Printing Press, Gilgit, 1997, pp. 92-112.
30. A.H. Francke, no. 13, p. 183 and ff.
31. The Islamization of Baltistan was completed in the 17th century. In Gilgit, the process took even longer than Baltistan. See http://www.jstor.org/stable/1571229?seq=4
32. Before professing Buddhism, Baltis practiced Bonchhos or Bonism which is a form of Shamanism. See http://www.tibetreisen.com/zjwh/ ShowArticle.asp?ArticleID=2119
33. Qurban is the designate person of the village Thwar in Baltistan to make offerings to *Lha* to honor them. If *Lha* are not happy, they can impact weather, as also the quantity of glacial water and rain that the farmers need for irrigation. They make offerings to *Lha* and sing classical songs to prevent rain during harvest time. When hunters go to hunt, they come to Qurban to seek his advice, and request him to make offerings to *Lha*.
34. *Losar* is the local New Year festival which comes around December 21. *Mephang*, which means fire throwing, is one of the rituals practiced during *Losar*. *Lha-Lhu* is venerated during different rituals of *Losar* so that the farmers will have ample water for irrigation, and hunters will hunt enough antelopes, deer and sheep to meet their food needs. Also, during the glacier regeneration process, offerings are made to *Lha* to seek their support. *Srub-La* is the festival to mark the harvest. *Brok-kher* marks the occasion of taking yaks to higher pastures. *Sonbor* is a festival to start sowing. *Ong-chus* marks the collection of grain after the harvest. *Mindok-Ltadmo* is the spring festival of flowers, and marks the beginning of the warm season and the end of cold winter. The details of many festivals are available in H. Hasrat, no. 20, pp. 400-422.

35. Supernatural beings like *Lha* and *Lhu* are believed to own wild animals as pets, and hunters seek their permission by making offerings before embarking on a hunting trip. Hasrat writes that the Baltis have formulated hunting rules to conserve animal species, and that the violation of these rules makes *Lha* unhappy. See H. Hasrat, no. 20, p. 242.
36. When the Tibetan Shang-shung Dynasty disintegrated around 1,100 AD, Baltistan came under the rule of local Rajas. The first to rule were the Lonchhe, followed by the Brak-Mayur rulers. Other famous groups to hold sway over Skardo and the surrounding areas include Rgyalbu Srasbu, Rgyalbucho Lobzang, Kuru Asancho and Si-dkar Gyalpo. See, Hashmatullah Khan, *Tarikh-i-Jammu*, Lahore, 1968, p. 449; H. Hasrat, no. 20, p. 85. During 1200-1300 AD, Palolo established their dynasty at Skardo. Then, the Rmakpon Dynasty took over the reins, and their twenty-four succeeding generations ruled Baltistan. In 1840, Rmakpons were defeated, and the Dogras conquered the region. Some of the great Rmakpon rulers united the western Tibetan regions under their sway (1590-1680 AD). Their empires spread from Chitral in the west on the Afghanistan border, to western Tibet in the east, including Gilgit, Ladakh, Ngari, Chang-thang, Purang and Stod-Ling. See also, G.T. Vigne, no. 4, p. 251 and ff; B.G. Afridi, *Baltistan in History*, Emjay Book International, Peshawar, 1988, pp. 36-37.
37. Hashmatullah Khan, *Tarikh-i-Jammu*, Lahore, 1968, pp. 276 and ff; 285; 452 and ff.
38. Ladakh (including Baltistan) and Gilgit formed the western regions of Jammu and Kashmir, and remained under Dogra rule. Before 1947, the borders of Jammu and Kashmir touched Afghanistan and the former Soviet Union. A. Lamb writes that Jammu and Kashmir has five regions: first, there is Kashmir proper, the so-called Vale along the upper reaches of the Jhelum River; second, there is the State of Jammu; third, there is the Poonch district; fourth, the very extensive tract of Ladakh and Baltistan; and finally, there is Gilgit region in the northwest, comprising Gilgit, Gilgit Wazarat, Gilgit Agency, Yasin, Ishkuman, Hunza and Nagir. See A. Lamb, *Kashmir: A Disputed Legacy 1846-1990*, Oxford University Press, Karachi, 1992, pp. 17-18. Josef Korbel, Member of the United Nations Commission for India and Pakistan (UNCIP), believed that the term Kashmir applies only to the Kashmir valley whereas the official name of the state is the State of Jammu and Kashmir. The state consists of several regions. Its heart is the famous Vale of Kashmir; south of it is the Jammu province; to the east is Ladakh; and to the north of it is Baltistan; further north are the regions of Hunza and Nagir; and on the west of them, is the Gilgit agency, composed of several districts. West of the Vale are the districts of Muzaffarabad, Riasi, Poonch and Mirpur. See J. Korbel, *Danger in Kashmir*, Oxford University Press, London, 1954, pp. 5, 6, 92 and 202. During the reign of Ranbir Singh, the Jammu and Kashmir state was administratively arranged as: Jammu, Kashmir, Ladakh (including Baltistan); and Gilgit; and the Frontier districts (which included Chitral).
39. In 1963, a political party called *Ladakh-Baltistan United Front* (LBUF) was launched. It remained active until 1975. It was led by Ibrahim Baltistani, Malika Baltistani and Nasim Changezi. The party created awareness about the political connections of Ladakh and Baltistan, and their shared civilization. In 1972, the party changed its name to *Ladakh-Baltistan United Organization* (LBUO). See Y. Hussainabadi, no. 16, p. 297. Before the Bhutto era (1971-1979), Gilgit-Baltistan was considered by both locals as well as the Pakistani government as part of Jammu and Kashmir, and therefore, part of 'Azad' Jammu and Kashmir (AJK). For instance, Babu Ishaq Shigri of Baltistan became the political representative of the refugees of Baltistan in the 'Azad Kashmir'

State Council. He was representing the 'Simla Baltis' who were residing in different parts of Pakistan. See, H. Hasrat, no. 20, p. 66. Later, Bhutto abolished the set up and disjoined Gilgit-Baltistan from AJK in the 1970s.

40. Technically, the Northern Areas of Jammu and Kashmir comprised of Gilgit Agency, Chilas, Hunza, Nagar, Koh Ghizar and the Tribal areas west and south of Gilgit Agency. Further, the British leased parts of Jammu and Kashmir didn't include Gilgit Wazarat, the Gilgit sub-division, and Baltistan. See, Mirza Hassan Khan, *Shamsher se Zanjeer tak* (From Sword to Chains), K2 Publishers, Rawalpindi, 2002, pp. 120-121.
41. S. S. Hamza, *Gilgit-Baltistan Lawa ke Dhana par* (Gilgit-Baltistan at the Threshold of Volcanic Lava) (in Urdu), Orient Printers, Islamabad, 1995, pp. 5, 49, 60 and 62. The author is an ex-member of the Northern Areas Council.
42. UNCIP resolutions refer to Baltistan as Ladakh or the Pakistani-administered part of Ladakh. The agreement between the government of Pakistan and Azad Kashmir is reproduced below:

    ...the second part, postulated in part III, was relevant as by virtue of that part of the agreement, the sphere of administrative jurisdiction was divided among the component parties to the agreement. The matters assigned to the government of Pakistan were listed under caption "A". These subjects were eight in number. It contained the responsibilities of the government of Pakistan in respect of all affairs of Gilgit and Ladakh, the area, at the relevant time [Baltistan under present circumstances, as the rest of Ladakh is under control of the Union of India], under the control of Political Agent, at Gilgit.

    See page 140 (No 151) of the High Court of Judicature, Azad Jammu & Kashmir: Verdict on Gilgit-Baltistan.
43. The separation of Gilgit from Jammu and Kashmir happened as a result of a military coup led by Muslim soldiers of 6th Regiment of Jammu and Kashmir against the Dogras. At that time, Gilgit Scouts decided to support the Dogras on the condition that the Maharaja raise their pay, and declare Gilgit Scouts a regiment. It was only after the 6th Regiment marched to Gilgit town that the soldiers of the Gilgit Scouts joined the coup. Local civilians were supportive of the decisions taken by their respective Rajas. Except for the Raja of Rondu, the remaining thirteen Rajas of Gilgit-Baltistan declared their loyalty to the Dogra ruler of Jammu and Kashmir. See Mirza Hassan Khan, *op. cit.*, 2002, pp. 113, 114, 123, 125, 134, 135 and 145–150.
44. http://www.tibet.ca/en/newsroom/wtn/archive/old?y=2006&m=4&p=23-2_1
45. Senge Hasnain Sering, 'Baltistan: Fifty Two Years of Agony', *ACHA Peace Bulletin*, June 5, 2002 at http://www. asiapeace.org
46. M.H. Parwana, *Sach Likhna Jurm Hai* (Telling the Truth is a Crime), GBUM Publishers, Skardo, 2005, p. 112.
47. The fact that Pakistan was carved out of the mainly Muslim-majority areas of India resulted in the division of ethnic groups. The break-up of Pakistan in 1971 and the creation of a new independent Bangladesh were based in part on the language variable, which proved to be a more powerful ethnic factor than a common Muslim identity, which was the ideological basis for creation of Pakistan.

    Similar movements periodically challenge the integrity of Pakistan. Such movements prevail in all provinces of the country, including Sindudesh, Pakhtoonistan and Greater Balochistan. Government circles are hesitant to allow ethnic and linguistic development except for Urdu, which they see as binding the country together. See K. Warikoo, 'Language and Politics in Jammu and Kashmir', in P.N. Pushp and K. Warikoo (eds.),

Jammu, Kashmir and Ladakh: Linguistic Predicament, Har Anand, New Delhi, 1996, p. 185.

A central Indian language, Urdu is spoken by only 8 per cent of the population of Pakistan, whereas the remaining 92 per cent has to learn it as any other foreign language. During the era of Mehmud Ghaznawi, Urdu evolved out of the grafting of Persian and Arabic vocabulary on the grammatical stem and basic stock of the West Hindi dialect of *Khari Boli* (Standing Language). The language found the support of Central Asian soldiers and Indian traders. Initially, it evolved in Lahore, which was to become the political and cultural center of Muslim rulers. In order to ensure the success of Urdu as a national language, Pakistani authorities took every possible step to empower Urdu at the risk of destroying indigenous languages. P.N. Pushp and K. Warikoo, Ibid., p. 201; http://www.koausa.org/Languages/Warikoo.html.

The National Language Authority (*Muqtadira Qaumi Zaban* or the MQZ) of Pakistan is an institution that promotes the interests of Urdu in Pakistan. Because the responsibility of the MQZ is to broaden the usage of Urdu in the country, the script is being used for other languages, irrespective of whether it suits their phonetics or not. In his speech delivered at Skardo in August 2001, F. M. Malik, the Chairman of MQZ, termed the indigenous language and script as profane. He opposed the efforts of local NGOs to set up signboards in the local script, and also prohibited the publication of a Balti primer in the local script.

48. Historically, one can prove that Sanskrit-based scripts (including Tibetan) are best suited to the needs of Balti phonetics. When Islam was introduced in Baltistan, the Tibetan script was discarded and Persian was adopted; however, it failed to accommodate linguistic requirements. Scholars then had to invent another script which was taken from Sanskrit, and the Moravian missionaries of Baltistan found it phonetically suitable to Balti. See B.G. Afridi, no. 9, pp. 29-30.

During the time of Dogras, a group of scholars considered only Hindi to be best suited for writing the Balti language, while others preferred the Roman script. Experiments with the Balti language continue even today, and a Balti textbook in Urdu script was published in 2002. However, this fails to address linguistic technicalities and suppresses its richness. Subsequently, the majority of Baltis have rejected this government-led initiative. Prominent Balti scholars, like Lobsang, Kazmi, Hasni, Blaghari, have stated that the Persian script, with or without modifications, can not adequately represent Balti. However, the Pakistan government refuses to allow the Balti script to be taught in schools. Government-backed groups propagate that religious scholars in Baltistan oppose the restoration of indigenous script, which is not true. During interviews, the Head Imam (Leader) of Baltis, Sheikh Hassan Jafri (1999) and Shiekh Jawad (2005) appreciated the setting up of Balti signboards, and the publication of a Balti primer in the indigenous script.

49. King Gesar, also known as *Ling Kesar*, *Lha Kesar* or *Gyalpo Kesar* in Ladakh and Baltistan, is a famous Tibetan Epic, which is also narrated in Mongolia, Tibet, Nepal, Bhutan, China, and Hunza. The epic hero Ling Gesar and his wife Lhamo Brugum are considered Lha. A person from the Nar village of Baltistan has admitted to receiving financial support from Lhamo Brugumo, which made him extremely wealthy. See H. Hasrat, no. 20, p. 234.

Other famous epics are *Apithso Phara*, *Shing-mkhan Gsosbu*, *Shing-mkhan Chandan*, *Salima Chocho*, *Rgyalbu Srasbu*, *Rgyalbu-cho Lobzang*, *Sring-chik nang Ming-chik*, *Sbrul gostan*, *Song Shiring Chocho*, *Dre-yuli Behram*, *Phara Thsongpa*, *Gseri Lhaskang*, *Xlung rta*, *Mutigi*

Chocho, among others. The absence of a written language and an adequate script has threatened the existence of Balti epics which, as a result, will disappear very soon. See Y. Hussainabadi, no. 16, pp. 347, 352; http://www.koshur.org/Linguistic/7.html.

50. H. Jaschke is of the view that the spread of Islam led to the deterioration of language and script in Baltistan. He states,

    the vowels and the super scribed consonants, for the most part are still sounded at each extremity of the whole territory, within which the language is spoken, both on the western and the eastern frontiers of Tibet, alike in Khams, which borders central China and in Balti, which merges into Kashmir...Now about twenty degrees of longitude separate Balti from Khams, and the former, embracing Islam, long since cut itself adrift from spiritual and religious cohesion with Tibet, and there, too, the dialect in other respects has greatly deteriorated, has admitted many foreign elements and has fallen altogether from the position of a literary language.

    See H.A. Jaschke, *A Tibetan-English Dictionary*, Motilal Banarasidas, Delhi, 1987.

    After conversion to Islam, the adoption of loan words from Persian became much more common, since it was the language of Muslim preachers. Then, the Dogra rulers of Jammu and Kashmir also adopted Persian as the court language, which impacted Balti language significantly. Even after the creation of Pakistan, Persian was considered the honorific language. For instance, in 1949, when the Pakistani Prime Minister, Liaqat Ali Khan, came to Skardo, his welcome speech was delivered in Persian instead of Urdu. See H. Hasrat, no. 20, p.290.

    However, Vigne argues that although foreign rulers and languages impacted Balti deleteriously, the core essence of the language being Tibetan was not altered. Vigne states, 'The Tibetan dialect of Baltiyul differs from that of Ladakh, as Arabic letters are often used.' However, this innovation is remarkable for certain parts of the cultural vocabulary only, as for example, in the vocabulary of religion and administration. It has not affected the basic core vocabulary much, where we find a few words common to the Brushaski and Indo-Aryan Shina neighbours. See G.T. Vigne, no. 4, p.267.

51. On 14 August 2003 (the Independence Day of Pakistan), curfew was imposed in Gilgit as local Shias burnt government buildings and protested against their socio-political repression. The protesters demanded that religious school syllabi in government schools in Gilgit-Baltistan should accommodate the Shia belief system since Shia Muslims are the predominant group in the region. This is the second such incident since 1999, when more than 30 political activists from the Gilgit region observed the Independence Day of Pakistan as 'Black Day', leading to arrests.

52 For further details of local professions and livelihoods, see H. Hasrat, no. 20, pp. 210-226.

53. *Amchi* and *Aba* hold on their traditional status in Ladakh and Tibet. In Khapulo and Gangche of Baltistan, practices are partially prevalent. My uncle Mohammad was treated for hepatitis by an *Amchi* in 2002. For details about *Amchi* and *Aba* practices in Baltistan, see H. Hasrat, no. 20, pp. 521-530; see also, G.T. Vigne, no. 4, p. 317.

54. For details of local costumes and dress code, see M.A. Kazmi, *op. cit.*; H. Hasrat, no. 20, pp. 156-169; http://www.tibet-foundation.org/nl/nl29.pdf pp 4-5; Tarik A. Khan, 'Little Tibet: Renaissance and Resistance in Baltistan.' *Himal*, May 1998.

55. http://www.dawn.com/weekly/dmag/archive/050710/dmag5.htm

56. Some of the forced conversions happen due to physical and mental torture. I happened to meet one Balti Shia who became Sunni after militants abducted and tortured him. Further, Nurbakhshi children are regularly taken to Sunni *madrassahs* lured by free

ration and lodging, and financial help to parents. Poverty forces parents to 'sell' their children to religious seminaries, as the government fails to support the educational needs of such children.

57. Clerics from both sides have been used by the government to create social disorder and political impasse. In one such incident, intelligence agencies released a Punjabi cleric, Ghulam Reza Naqvi, from prison 'to be sent to Gilgit to keep the pot of sectarian violence boiling'. His release was granted after negotiations with a banned Sunni outfit, *Sepah-i-Sahaba Pakistan*, which also got their leader Maulana Mohammad Ludhianivi freed from jail; http://www.dailytimes.com.pk/default.asp?page=2006%5C05%5C21%5Cstory_21-5-2006_pg3_1
58. M.A. Kaiser, *Shohda-e-Gilgit-Baltistan* (Martyrs of Gilgit Baltistan). Islamabad, R.S. Publications, 2005, pp. 25 and 296.
59. The book has 356 pages and many illustrations.
60. M.A. Kaiser, no. 58, pp. 25-50.
61. During this conversation, Kaiser had pretended to be a Sunni from Gilgit
62. See M.A. Kaiser, no. 58, p. 28.
63. http://hunzatimes.wordpress.com/2008/12/27/five-of-a-family-killed-in-gilgit-attack-updated-news-news/
64. http://www.facebook.com/group.php?gid=40756234671
65. http://www.ahrchk.net/ua/mainfile.php/2009/3193/
66. http://pamirtimes.net/2009/08/17/violent-protests-in-gilgit-over-murder-of-ali-sher-hyderi/
67. http://www.blogcatalog.com/blog/pamir-times/854fb8cae3214331a32604745d595c27
68. http://www.thenews.com.pk/updates.asp?id=87717
69. http://pamirtimes.net/2009/09/28/pml-leader-raja-ali-ahmad-jan-shot-dead-in-konodas-gilgit/
70. http://mygilgit.wordpress.com/2009/11/page/2/
71. http://pakistantimes.net/2005/01/14/top1.htm
72. http://pamirtimes.net/2009/04/21/asad-zaidi-deputy-speaker-nala-shot-dead-in-gilgit/
73. http://en.wikipedia.org/wiki/Allama_Hassan_Turabi#Early_life
74. http://www.thefreelibrary.com/PM+grieved+over+assassination+of+Syed+Asad+Zaidi.-a0198311457
75. All the ten persons of Baltistan who have been arrested on charges or suspicions of promoting or supporting terrorism are Sunnis.
76. http://dardistannews.wordpress.com/2009/06/02/taliban-hiding-in-gilgit-baltistan-operations-in-gb-asian-human-rights-commission-press-release/
77. http://www.dawn.com/wps/wcm/connect/dawn-content-library/dawn/news/pakistan/nwfp/300-suspected-people-expelled-from-n-areas-gilgit
78. http://dardistannews.wordpress.com/2009/05/
79. http://dardistannews.wordpress.com/2009/06/02/taliban-hiding-in-gilgit-baltistan-operations-in-gb-asian-human-rights-commission-press-release/
80. http://pamirtimes.net/2009/05/23/bomb-blast-at-hostel-in-gilgit-city/
81. http://weeklybaang.blogspot.com/2009/04/weekly-baang-karachi-voloum-02-issue-08_3275.html
82. Information received in October 2009 during my visit to Baltistan.
83. Shiekh Yusuf states that sectarianism received a boost during the tenure of Mehtab

Abbassi as Minister of KANA. The Pakistani para-military is accused of meddling in local politics and taking sides with the local Sunnis. Shiekh believes that peace cannot return to Gilgit-Baltistan if the Pakistani para-military—like the Frontier Corps—continues their presence in the region. He further said that the jihadi elements arriving in Gilgit-Baltistan have maligned Islam, and impacted the society negatively. See, *Weekly Qayadat*, Gilgit-Baltistan, Vol. 32, Issue No. 1, November 2009, pp. 4-10.

84. Information received from his nephew Ali in October 1999, a few years after the death of Mehdi.
85. In this district of Pakistan where Shias were a majority, the percentage of Shias has reduced from 85 to 55, owing to Sunni settlements as well Shia genocide that has continued unabated since 1980; http://infidelsarecool.com/2008/06/29/taliban-killing-up-to-30-shia-muslims-a-day/
86. http://www.countercurrents.org/jawad150409.htm; http://ammar360.com/2009/03/07/holocaust-of-shias-in-parachinar/
87. http://www.bbc.co.uk/urdu/pakistan/story/2008/04/080430_kurram_jirga_sen.shtml
88. The *Kargil International Magazine*, banned on September 8, 2004, published regular articles on this topic.
89. Nawaz Sharif, the then Prime Minister of Pakistan admitted 4000 deaths of NLI soldiers of Gilgit Baltistan; http://infao5501.ag5.mpi-sb.mpg.de:8080/topx/archive?link=Wikipedia-Lip6-2/803754.xml&style.
90. The Karakoram Highway (KKH) passes through the Shangla district which remained in the control of the Taliban for few weeks in 2008-2009. KKH connects Pakistan with China, and passes through Gilgit-Baltistan. It is a source of income for local traders and shopkeepers. It also brings essential commodities and food items from both Pakistan and China.
91. AKRSP Socio-economic Survey of Northern Areas and Chitral (SESNAC) 2005, current estimates are US$264; http://www.finance.gov.pk/finance_blog/?p=238; http://finance.kalpoint.com/pdf/highlights/todays-pick/per-capita-income-falls-to-1071.pdf.
92. Until the late 1990s, when Nurbakhshis did not have their own Sufi *madrassahs*; they sent their children to Wahhabi *madrassahs*.
93. During the reign of Prime Minister Z. A. Bhutto (1971-1979), SSR was abolished, paving way for Pakistanis to settle in Gilgit-Baltistan.
94. For example, the government razed a historical market in Gilgit under the pretext of modernizing the structure, and later awarded ownership of the newly constructed shops to Pashtun settlers.
95. Agha Ziauddin, supreme leader of Gilgit, continuously opposed Pakistani settlements in Gilgit-Baltistan and, as a result, was killed.
96. See Y. Hussainabadi, no. 16, p. 305.
97. http://www.ciaonet.org/wps/icg449/icg449.pdf (pp:16)
98. http://pakistantimes.net/2004/10/14/top2.htm
99. http://www.app.com.pk/en_/index.php?option=com_content&task=view&id=87988& Itemid=2
100. Hasrat writes that the neighborhood where Baltis lived in Simla was called 'Tibeti Mohallah', and the name was later changed to 'Baltistani Mohallah' by the Baltis. During those days, Baltis were known as Tibetan, Bhotia or Ladakhi, which was seen as synonymous with being Buddhist. The Muslims of Ladakh, therefore, preferred

the word Balti for themselves, which later became the common term. According to another narration by Sheikh Ghulam Hussain of Gulabpur, he experienced the same situation in Iran, as well as in the city of Quetta in Pakistani Baluchistan. He states that the Baltis studying or settled in those regions resented the word 'Tibeti', the appellation that the Iranians and Afghanis ascribed to Baltis.

101. See B.G. Afridi, no. 9, p. 18.
102. In a statement, GBNA Chairperson Malika Baltistani, who was leading the *Ladakh Baltistan United Front* in 1963, demanded complete independence from Pakistan, and rejected the self-rule package. She writes, 'We demand that this Constitutional package may immediately be abolished and Gilgit-Baltistan may be granted self rule and independent status under the fourth-option proposed by Gilgit Baltistan National Alliance to the United Nations in 1996.' http://balawaristantimes.blogspot.com/;http://www.balawaristan.net/index.php?option=com_content&view=article&id=1748%3Agilgit-baltistan-conference-in-new-york&Itemid=64
103. There is a fear that if the region fails to become part of Pakistan, the Baltis will merge with China or Tajikistan. This view of the Tajiks and Wakhis of Gilgit, and the students and NGO workers was expressed to me. By comparison, they think China is a developed country, and the people of Hunza will benefit from China. The people of Gojal (Hunza) and some parts of northern Ghizer have ethnic and linguistic connections with the people of Badakhshan, Wakhan, and southern Xinjiang.
104. http://gbtimes.wordpress.com/2009/09/27/130/
105. Many Pashtun settlers supported *Awami National Party* (ANP), a political party of NWFP, during the Gilgit-Baltistan Legislative Assembly election of November 2009. Some of them would like to see Gilgit merged with NWFP.
106. http://www.scribd.com/doc/20987918/Empowering-Gilgit-Baltistan.
107. Such groups also believe that China wants to gain the sympathies of the people of this region to counter any advances by USA or India.
108. http://www.thesouthasian.org/archives/2009/empowering_gilgitbaltistan_or.html
109. http://www.sananews.com.pk/english/2009/09/15/gilgit-baltistan-empowerment-and-self-governance-order-2009/
110. A conference on 'The Constitutional, Political, and Socio-economic Conditions of Gilgit-Baltistan', organized by the International Kashmir Alliance, and held in the European Parliament in Brussels on 8-9 April 2009, was attended by many MEPs, including Baroness Emma Nicholson.
111. http://www.scribd.com/doc/21208422/Bot-Sinha-C-Nirmal-Gilgit-and-Swat.
112. Several local magazines, which aspired to promote freedom of expression, were banned by Pakistan, which include *Balawaristan Times, Kargil International Magazine*, and *Weekly K2 Newspaper*.
113. *Kargil International Magazine* (Monthly) Volume 11, Issue 14, February-March 2003, p. 23.
114. For more than two decades, the Baltis have struggled for the creation of a separate administrative division for Baltistan. In the year 2000, the then Prime Minister of Pakistan, Nawaz Sharif, visited Baltistan. Local communities from all walks of life, including school children, held rallies and demanded the creation of a separate administrative division for Baltistan. This was granted later that year. However, Pervez Musharraf stalled the implementation of this decision after staging the coup against Sharif. However, the government of the *Pakistan People's Party* (PPP) has declared

Baltistan a separate administrative division, and appointed a commissioner.

115. See H. Hasrat, no. 20., p. 45.
116. BSF proudly boasts its Ladakhi roots by displaying *Swastika* on its party flag.
117. Ali Shigri was interviewed in July 2009 in Islamabad. Please see, the monthly *Kargil International Magazine*, Volume 11, Issue 14, February-March 2003, p. 15.
118. *Weekly Qayadat*, Gilgit-Baltistan, Volume 32, Issue No. 1, November 2009, pp. 4-10.
119. Agha was interviewed in Skardo in July 2009; the NWFP claim over Gilgit is based on their definition of a 'common culture', and the fact that, like other agencies of NWFP, the Chitral and Gilgit regions of Jammu and Kashmir became British Tribal Agencies.
120. http://skardu.blogspot.com/2009_03 _01_archive.html
121. Scholars like Kazmi and Lobsang have written several articles on this issue.
122. Both called him their teacher. Banat Gul Afridi, author of *Baltistan in History*, 1988, received the bulk of the information for his book from Wazir Mehdi.
123. http://depts.washington.edu/icstll39/abstracts/icstll39_hasnain.pdf
124. Since the last few years, Ladakhi songs have also become popular in Baltistan, and most of the music shops carry Ladakhi audio and video tapes.
125. In August 1992, Lobsang produced the book *Od* (Light) with 500 sayings of prominent international personalities of various schools of thoughts, of both old and modern eras.
126. Balti youth are, once again, adopting Balti secular names like Tsering, Senge, Lobsang, Mayur, Mutik, Sang-sang, and Shesrab which shows their love for 'everything' Tibetan. See Khan, 'Little Tibet: Renaissance and Resistance in Baltistan', *Himal Magazine*, Nepal, May 1998; see also, H. Hasrat, no. 20, p. 155.
127. H. Hasrat, no. 20, pp. 200-210.
128. In 1999, I initiated the project of setting up sign boards on shops in indigenous Tibetan script, and the BCF joined in the efforts later. Initially, the local shopkeepers contributed financially to set up their signboards. The first major contribution came from G. Amin Beg of the Gojal Northern Areas, who was working as the Manager, Enterprise Development for Aga Khan Rural Support Program in Skardo during that time. Baqir Haideri and I utilized this money, and set up more than ten signboards in the Skardo market. Both religious and secular communities of the region appreciated the effort. This encouraged us to send a proposal to the Australian Tibetan Society (ATS), which later provided funding for the same project. Professor Estelle Dryland of Australia played a vital role in getting this funding. Today, signboards are evident on shops, offices and schools.
129. The demand by the majority in Baltistan to have a political set up, which currently prevails in AJK, shows their desire for genuine autonomy and separation from Pakistan.
130. http://www.bbc.co.uk/urdu/pakistan/story/2008/06/080627_gilgit_tourism_fz.shtml
131. http://pamirtimes.files.wordpress.com/2009/06/state-religion-and-culture-in-gilgit-baltistan1.pdf: pp. 2 and ff.
132. Jawad was interviewed by this author in Skardo in July 2009.
133. On 4 January 2001, the Baltistan Union of Journalists and the Press Club, Skardo, co-hosted All Parties Conference (APC) on the topic 'Kashmir Issue and Future of Gilgit-Baltistan'. More than 26 participants, representing mainstream as well as nationalist and regional political parties, attended the conference. In a decision taken by 15 out

of 26 members, the resolution stated that Pakistan and India should open the Kargil-Skardo road for trade and people-to-people contact, and Ladakh Wazarat should be re-instated prior to the 1947 position.

134. Sher Mohammad was interviewed in August 2005.
135. Shamim was interviewed in July 2009 in Skardo.
136. The famous writer of Baltistan, Ghulam H. Lobsang promoted the cause of Pan-Tibetan identity among Baltis for many years, and published magazines to propagate the cause. From 1987 and onwards, Lobsang published five journals collectively called *Mimang Rgyasrid* (People and their Territory), with sub-headings of *Lobsang* (April 1987) *Kesar* (August 1987), *Losar* (November 1987), *Yuli* An (April 1988), and *Sang* (November 1990).
137. The Shias of Baltistan assert that historically Chitral was part of Baltistan for more than 100 years during the era of Rmakpons, and the game of Polo was introduced by the Baltis in Chitral. See Hashmatullah, *op. cit.*, p. 17.
138. http://www.swarthmore.edu/Admin/cooper_grants/dpi/speakers/tshering.php
139. Shin is the predominant ethnic group of Gilgit, and they speak a language called Shina which is closely related to Chitrali and Kashmiri. Today, they form a small minority in Ladakh and Baltistan.
140. Before 1947, the trade items which were exported from Baltistan to Ladakh, Kashmir, Simla, Tibet and Yarkand included woollen garments, pashmina shawls, pottery made of jade stone and koro-stone, earthen and wooden utensils, carpets and blankets made of yak and sheep hair, bronze-ware, silverware, turquoise jewelry, dried fruits, yak butter, sheep, marble-ware, and herbs. See Y. Hussainabadi, no. 16, p. 359.
    Now, exports from Baltistan have completely stopped, except for potatoes and some dried fruits. Imports from Islamabad and China are rising, and even local clothing and food items come from outside.
141. http://pamirtimes.net/2009/07/04/nationalists-of-gilgit-baltistan-likely-to-defeat-pro-pakistan-parties-ghazanfar-ali-khan/
142. Altaf Hussain is the Chairperson of *Muttahidda Qaumi Movement* (MQM) and resides in the UK. He has been accused by Pakistani agencies of working against state interests, and provoking the people of Sindh to seek separation from Pakistan. The MQM is the fourth largest political party of Pakistan, and enjoys overwhelming support among the Hindustani migrants who settled in Pakistan after Partition in 1947.
143. http://www.dailytimes.com.pk/?page=2009\06\30\story_30-6-2009_pg7_33
144. http://www.unpo.org/content/view/10307/83/
145. Baroness Nicholson of European Parliament (EUP) was spearheading the resolution passed in favor of Gilgit-Baltistan by the EUP in 2008. She condemned Pakistan for refusing political rights to Gilgit-Baltistan.

6

The Making of a Frontier

The Relationship between Kashmir and its Frontier Territories

K. Warikoo

Historical Background

Though the ancient history of the Karakoram-Himalayan region is shrouded in obscurity, the region has been referred to as *Daraddesa* (corresponding to present day Gilgit and adjoining areas) and *Polulo* (corresponding to present day Baltistan) in several ancient sources. The entire region is also referred to as Bolor, Baloristan or Balawaristan. Whereas Gilgit was under the reign of *Palola* or *Patola* Shahis who practised Buddhism during the 6th to 8th centuries, Baltistan remained Buddhist upto the 15th century. That this frontier area has been part of the Indian political and cultural system is corroborated by historical evidence. Thousands of rock carvings, inscriptions, petroglyphs etc. spanning the Karakoram-Himalayas provide clinching evidence of the prevalence of Hindu and Buddhist faiths and rule since ancient times. Fourteen rock edicts of the Mauryan emperor Ashoka dating to mid-3rd century BC in the Kharoshthi script and detailing both the king's moral teachings and administrative orders inscribed on huge boulders, have been found along the Karakoram Highway.[1] Ashoka is referred to here by his titles of *Devana Priya Priyadasi Raja* (The King, Beloved of the Gods, of noble appearance).[2] A number of inscriptions in Brahmi, Kharoshthi, and Hindu temples with engravings of *Swastika*, *Trishula* (trident) and Buddhist figures found at Shatial, Thor, Hodur and Chilas also point to the existence of Hindu faith and rule in the region in ancient times.[3] A Kharoshthi inscription near Chilas mentions *Uvimadasakesa* (a name referring to the second emperor Vima Kadphises).[4] Kharoshthi inscriptions belonging to Kushana period are concentrated at Alam Bridge, 25 miles west of Gilgit.[5] The Sacred Rock at Hunza also has Kushana inscriptions and carvings.[6]

It is thus quite clear that Dardistan was a constituent unit of Kanishka's empire. Kalhana's *Rajatarangini* refers to the military exploits of King Lalitaditya of Kashmir (6th-7th century AD) in the Gilgit region. Similarly, Gilgit-Baltistan formed a part of the medieval Kashmir Sultanate of Shahbuddin and Zain-ul-Abidin. Even when the local chiefs asserted their independence, they continued to be influenced by Indian culture and way of life. Even in modern times, they have been known by their titles such as *Raja* and *Mehtar*, the latter being the corrupt form of the Sanskrit title *Mehattar*. Life size images of Buddha carved out of rock; an abundance of Buddhist inscriptions throughout this region; the discovery of the famous Gilgit MSS (in the early 1930s) etc. are living testimony of the Indian cultural influence in this frontier area. Even as late as in the nineteenth century, the Muslims of Gilgit were found to be lax in their practice of Islam. Major J. Biddulph, who joined as Political Officer in Gilgit in 1877, is emphatic that 'Buddhism was no doubt the religion of the country at the time of Shin invasion. There seem good grounds for supposing that the religion of the Shins was of the Brahminical type.'[7] According to him,

> till a very recent period burning the dead was practiced. The ashes were carefully collected and buried in rude wooden boxes, sometime carved out of a solid block, or in round earthen jars. The bones are neatly packed in the boxes, which have previously been lined with birch bark.[8]

However, Biddhulph found that 'the burning of the dead ceased to be practiced more than sixty years ago'[9] (that is, around 1810 AD). Biddulph ascribes the 'names of many of the rulers and of a number of places, not only in the Indus and Gilgit valleys, but also in the Chitral Valley,' to Brahminical origins.[10] It was actually the Sikh Commander, Nathu Shah who was Muslim by religion and Syed by caste and was functioning as Kashmir's governor at Gilgit for several years, who made his subjects follow Islam more strictly. According to Frederic Drew, who for several years was the British Joint Commissioner in Ladakh, the people of Astor used to cremate their dead—which practice was changed to that of burial after the arrival of Nathu Shah in 1842 AD.[11] Yet, they continued to light some fire near the grave.[12]

Baltistan

In ancient times, Baltistan was under the sway of Kushans who introduced Buddhism here. However, in the 7th century AD, the Tibetans expanded their authority to this region, only to be expelled in early 8th century by Lalitaditya Muktapida of Kashmir. The presence of Buddhist inscriptions and rock carvings in Baltistan, and the survival of Tibetan/Buddhist names, dialect and script to this day points to the prevalence of Buddhism, and the existence of active socio-economic contacts between Baltistan and Ladakh. In the 13th century, the Muslim adventurer Ibrahim Shah is reported to have come to Baltistan, married a local princess, assumed power, and founded the Makpon dynasty.[13] The Muslim missionary, Mir Shamsuddin Iraqi—who came to Baltistan in the 15th century—spread Islam, and established the Nurbakhshiya order here. Quite a large number of people in Baltistan continue to follow the Nurbakhshiya sect of Islam. Ali Sher Khan, who ruled Baltistan from 1595 to 1633, established matrimonial and friendly relations with the Mughal rulers.[14] However, following Ali Sher's death, internecine feuds amongst his sons and successors led the Mughal rulers Shah Jahan and Aurangzeb to extend their authority over Baltistan.[15] However, during the decline of the Mughals, the Balti chiefs regained their authority, which lapsed again when the Afghan Governor of Kashmir, Haji Karim Dad Khan sent a large force to Skardu in 1779 AD and brought Baltistan under Kashmir's control.[16] Whereas the Afghans were defeated in Kashmir by the Shikhs in 1819 AD, Baltistan witnessed internecine feuds amongst its chiefs. Ahmad Shah, the powerful chief of Skardu, sought the assistance of the Sikh rulers of Kashmir (1832-1834 AD) in his fight against the chief of Khaplu.[17] The internal feuds among the local chiefs facilitated the Dogra general Zorawar Singh's military campaign in the region. This brought Baltistan under the control of the Sikh/Dogra rulers of Kashmir. Zorawar Singh established a military post at Skardu in a newly built fort, and appointed a *Thanadar* (Commander) to supervise the garrison.

Before Gulab Singh became the Maharaja of Jammu and Kashmir under the treaty of Amritsar (1846), he as the Raja of Jammu under the Sikhs had conquered the whole of Ladakh, including Skardu (Baltistan).This was all thanks to his trusted and dynamic military commanders Zorawar Singh and Diwan Hari Chand. Maharaja Ranjit Singh—the Sikh potentate who had long coveted Ladakh due to its being transit route for shawl wool and a big revenue earner—recognized Gulab Singh's conquest of this frontier region. The area was thus brought under the full administrative control of the Jammu and Kashmir State. When the treaty of Amritsar was signed in 1846, the British not only recognized Gulab Singh as the Ruler of Jammu and Kashmir but also of Ladakh and Baltistan. In 1899, Baltistan, Ladakh and Gilgit were merged into one 'frontier district', and placed under *Wazir-i-Wazarat*.[18] Two years later, in 1901, a separate district of Ladakh was established which incorporated the Skardu, Kargil and Layya tehsils.[19] The areas of Gultari, and from Pari to Kharol were included in the Kargil tehsil.[20] Now onwards Skardu became the winter headquarters of the Ladakh district. Amar Nath Pragal of Jammu was the last Wazir of Skardu, before he was brutally killed by Pak raiders when they occupied Skardu in August 1948.

Skardu was part of the state revenue and judicial systems. Its revenue was assessed from time to time, and the settlement reports describe the quantum and method of revenue collection. In his report published in 1904 by Maharaja Pratap Singh's government at Jammu, J.L. Kaye, the Settlement Commissioner, mentions the *ilaqas* of Haramosh, Rondu, Shigar, Kiris, Parkutta, Tolti, Khaplu and Chorbat, as parts of Skardu.[21] Local Rajas were granted *jagirs* which were inherited by their family, in recognition of their services to the Kashmir Durbar. As per the records of 1939, such Rajas from Baltistan included Raja Nasir Ali Khan, Ilaqadar of Khapalu (holding a jagir of Rupees 12,000/- per year), Raja Mohammad Ali Shah, Ilaqadar of Skardu (holding a jagir of Rupees 7,500/- per year), Raja Ali Sher Khan of Kharmang (holding a jagir of Rupees 9,632/- per year), and Raja Abdulla Khan of Ladakh who belonged to the old Raja family of Rondu (with a jagir of Rupees 5,000/- per year).[22]

Under the direct control of Kashmir, Kashmiri shopkeepers and traders started settling in Skardu. They engaged in the *pashm* bushiness, and also set up shawl weaving units. Since Skardu was linked to Ladakh, it facilitated shawl-wool trading. In this manner, Baltistan got integrated with the Jammu and Kashmir State economically too. In fact, colonies of Baltis settled in Kashmir where they worked as agricultural labour, and did other jobs as well. Baltis even went to Jammu and the Punjab plains where they remained engaged in road-making, barrack-building and small trade. Moreover, the Maharaja of Kashmir formed a separate Regiment of Baltis in his State army, which had a distinct Highland kilt and a head dress.[23]

Gilgit

Dardistan or Gilgit is the land of Dards or Dardic speaking people. During the 6th-8th centuries, Gilgit remained under the *Palola* or *Patola Shahis*, who patronized Buddhism. According to local traditions, Sri Badat was the last Buddhist ruler of Gilgit.[24] However, in the medieval period with the advent of Islam, the local chiefs embraced Islam, even though Buddhist traditions were retained. Zoroastrian rituals too appear to have been followed by the local people right up to the 19th century, even though they had accepted Islam.[25] The local chiefs of Gilgit belonged to the Trakhan dynasty, the word Trakh originating from the name of the Gilgit ruler Torra Khan.[26] The Gilgit region included Gilgit, Nagar, Hunza, Punial, Yasin, Ghizar, Gor, Chilas, Darel, Tangir, Harban and even Chitral—all of which had close links with the Trakhan dynasty.[27] This is distinct from the Baltistan region which included Skardu, Khaplu, Shigar, Rondu, Astor, Karatshe, Tolti and even Kargil and Dras.[28] This historical and geopolitical divide is evident even today in the form of the Gilgit (Dardistan) and the Baltistan regions.

During the first quarter of the 19th century, Gilgit witnessed a series of internecine feuds, killings, and conflicts. It was in 1842 that the Sikh rulers of Kashmir sent a force led by Colonel Nathu Shah to Gilgit at the request of Karim Khan, the brother of Raja Shah Skander of Gilgit who had been killed, and his kingdom usurped by Gour Rahman of Yasin. The Sikh forces defeated Gour Rahman and established themselves in Gilgit. However, Gour Rahman returned, and attacked the Sikhs who got reinforcements from Kashmir. Finally, after negotiations, it was decided that the Sikhs would hold Gilgit, and Gour Rahman gave his daughter in marriage to Nathu Shah, the commander of the Sikhs.[29] The Chiefs of Hunza and Nagar, who were the allies of Gour Rahman, also gave their daughters to Nathu Shah.[30]

Karim Khan was installed as the Raja of Gilgit Tehsil, with the Sikhs wielding the real authority. To quote Frederic Drew, Nathu Shah established a Sikh force at Gilgit under a *Thanadar* (Commander).[31] In this manner, by 1842, the Sikh rulers of Kashmir brought Gilgit and its areas in Chilas, Astor, etc. under their control. And, when Gulab Singh acquired Jammu and Kashmir State by the Treaty of Amritsar in 1846, the Gilgit region came into his possession. Nathu Shah and the Sikh forces now took service under the Dogra ruler, Gulab Singh. On his part, Gulab Singh asked Nathu Shah to continue to administer this frontier.

Soon afterwards, Gour Rahman, together with the chiefs of Yasin, Punial and Hunza, attacked the Kashmir forces in Gilgit, and killed Nathu Shah along with Raja Karim Khan of Gilgit. They attacked and occupied the Dogra fort of Gilgit, leading to the ouster of the Dogras from the area for some time.[32] However, Maharaja Gulab Singh sent two columns of Dogra troops—one from Astor and the other from Skardu—who defeated Gour Rahman, and installed Karim Khan's son Muhammad Khan as the chief of Gilgit.[33] Two officers, Bhup Singh and Sant Singh, were appointed as administrators.[34] But again, in 1852, Gour Rahman launched a surprise attack on the two Dogra forts at Gilgit and Naurpura, and Killed Dogra soldiers.[35] Thus, Gilgit again slipped out of Kashmir's control, till it was reconquered by Maharaja Ranbir Singh in 1860.[36]

In 1860, Maharaja Ranbir Singh sent a strong contingent of 3,000 Dogra troops under the command of Colonel (later General) Devi Singh Narainia to attack Gour Rahman's forces in Gilgit.[37] Gilgit fort was taken over by the Dogra forces after Gour Rahman and his *Wazir* Wahab were killed.[38] Now, Ali Dad Khan, a descendant of the old Raja of Gilgit, was made the nominal chief of Gilgit, under the subordination of the Kashmir ruler.[39] Soon after, on 16 September 1860, Devi Singh took over the adjoining territory of Yasin and installed Azmat Shah, a son of the old ruler, as the Governor of Yasin.[40] In Punial, the local chief, Raja Isa Bahadur, who had fled Yasin to escape the wrath of Gour Rahman and had sought refuge in the Maharaja's court at Srinagar, was reinstated by Devi Singh.[41] Isa Bahadur now took over the territory of Ishkoman, which was previously part of Yasin.[42] But soon after, Mulk Aman son of the late Gour Rahman, attacked Yasin and forced Azmat Shah to flee. It was only in 1864 that Yasin was finally subjugated by a Dogra force led by Genral Hoshiara. Now, Yasin was placed under Mir Wali, brother of Mulk Aman, who signed an agreement on 4 September 1864 declaring his subservience to the Maharaja of Kashmir.[43] The decade of recurring conflict between the Dogra forces and unruly tribes in this frontier ended in 1870 when the chiefs of Hunza and Nagar also signed agreements with Maharaja Ranbir Singh, accepting the suzerainty of Kashmir.

Though the British tried to restrain Maharaja Ranbir Singh in his determined efforts to tame the unruly tribes in and around the Gilgit frontier, the Kashmir ruler stuck to his stand that the frontier territories of Baltistan, Gilgit, Yasin, Punial, Hunza and Nagar formed a part of Kashmir territory.[44] And, in 1870, the British Indian government stated 'categorically that Gilgit was included in the territories formally ceded to the Maharaja by treaty' (of 1846).[45] However, the circumstances of Hayward's murder at the hands of the Mir of Yasin, and the unhindered advance of Russians in Central Asia upto the Pamirs, convinced the British about the necessity of strengthening Kashmir's control over this turbulent frontier. While encouraging Ranbir Singh to secure an effective control over the territory 'lying between the Kashmir frontier and the passes south of Hindu Kush, namely Chitral, Mastuj, Yasin and their dependencies,' the British secured the right to station an Agent at Gilgit to monitor the events on, and beyond this frontier.[46] Captain J. Biddulph was appointed on 22 September 1877 as Officer on Special Duty at Gilgit, with

> the duty of collecting and furnishing reliable intelligence of the progress of events beyond the Kashmir frontier and to cultivate friendly relations with the tribes beyond the border in view to bring them gradually under the control and influence of Kashmir.[47]

Biddulph was also instructed not to 'interfere with the internal administration of the Maharaja's territories'.[48] But, Biddulph found himself surrounded by a network of local intrigues. The matter came to a head when Hunza and Yasin launched a successful assault on Gakuch and Sher Kila on 28 October 1880. The precarious situation on the Gilgit frontier was compounded by the inaccessibility of Gilgit which was connected with Srinagar by a rough track running over high mountains for 230 miles, and was open to traffic for six months only. Finally, in July 1881, it was decided to withdraw the Gilgit Agent. However, the Agency was only kept in abeyance till 1888, as the British reserved their right to re-appoint the Officer at Gilgit when necessary.

Afghan pressures on Chitral, which had submitted its allegiance to Kashmir in 1878, assumed seriousness in 1882 when Kabul claimed its territory as 'one of the protected states.'[49] The reported Russian intrigues in and around Chitral and the Panjdeh crisis of 1885, only crystallized the British military resolve to make elaborate arrangements for the defense of the north-western frontier. It coincided with the death of Maharaja Ranbir Singh in September 1885 and the installation of his son Pratap Singh as the new Maharaja of Kashmir. The British lost no time in re-designating the Officer on Special Duty in Kashmir as the full-fledged British Resident in Kashmir. On the new Maharaja's protesting against this unilateral British decision, he was divested of the effective powers of a ruler in 1889, and his powers were vested in a Council which was to work under the overall control of the British Resident. The Gilgit Agency was re-established in 1989 under Captain A. Durand as the British Agent. The need to strengthen Kashmir's hold over its frontier territories had assumed urgency due to a joint attack by Hunza and Nagar on the Kashmir forts at Chaprot and Chalt in early 1888. Now, the construction of the Jhelum Valley cart road, the Jammu-Sialkot railway, and the military road connecting Gilgit with Srinagar was expedited under the direct instructions of the British Resident in Kashmir. The Jammu and Kashmir State forces were reorganized into a newly created Kashmir Imperial Service Corps and local levies in Gilgit and placed under the command of British officers. New schemes for the defense of the British Indian northern frontier in and around Gilgit were initiated. Steps such as the building of air landing facilities, establishing wireless communication, and the strengthening of forces in Gilgit, Hunza, Chilas, Chitral, etc. under the direct command of British officers were taken.

However, with the increasing influence and power of the British Resident in Kashmir, the authority of the Maharaja of Kashmir and his representatives declined in the frontier. Nevertheless the greater part of the expenditure on account of the Gilgit Agency, and the administration of these districts was borne by the Jammu and Kashmir State. The expenditure covered not merely the cost of the maintenance of the Agency at Gilgit and the State troops at Gilgit but also the cost of making roads, establishing dispensaries and schools, as well as other normal functions of the administration within the territories themselves. The total expenditure of the State on the Gilgit Agency, excluding the settled portion of the Gilgit Wazarat, from 1889 (when the Agency was established for the second time in order to strengthen the defences on this border) upto 1935 (when the lease of Gilgit was executed) was about three crore rupees. As against this immense expenditure, the State received only a nominal revenue from the Political Districts.

In 1926-27 for instance, the State paid about 10 lakhs of rupees for the upkeep of the Agency and all its activities, both in the political area and outside it. About half this expenditure was spent on military affairs, and 1.5 lakh was spent on public works, and about 1 lakh was spent on 'political' matters, such as the upkeep of the Agency staff, the Gilgit Scouts and levies, entertainment, travelling and other allowances, and many miscellaneous expenses. This also included the subsidies to the local chiefs and Governors, and their relatives. The remaining expenditure amounting to 2 or 2.5 lakhs was incurred in respect of schools, hospitals, medical matters, veterinary department, stationary and printing, the upkeep of the Agency gardens, and other minor matters. As against this huge expenditure of 10 lakhs, the revenue received by the State in 1926-27 amounted to about 0.5 lakh rupees only.

Soon after the restoration of full powers to Maharaja Pratap Singh in 1922, and with the accession to the throne of Maharaja Hari Singh in 1925, the new Maharaja began to assert his authority in this frontier. He objected to the flying of the Union Jack, and insisted that only the State flag would fly in his frontier territories. A long correspondence with the British Indian authorities ensued to resolve this anomalous position of dual authority in the frontier. The British Resident in Kashmir sent a Memo to the Durbar, admitting therein the fact that 'the interests of the British Government and the Kashmir State on the Gilgit frontier are common interests'. He then put forth a new proposal to the Government of India by which

> the appointment of Political Agent, Gilgit, should be abolished and in his place a Political Officer should be lent to the Kashmir State to hold the appointment of Governor of Gilgit and to conduct political relations on behalf of the Government of India and the Kashmir Government with the Political Districts.[50]

The main features of the proposal were:

(a) The abolition of the Political Agency.

(b) The bringing of the unsettled districts under the full administrative control of the State.
(c) Cementing relations between the Maharaja and the frontier Chiefs and nobles.
(d) Maintaining the prestige of the Government of India on the frontier without detriment to the prestige and the rightful authority of the State.
(e) Transfer of the Indus Kohistan and Kandia to the North West Frontier Province.
(f) The flying of the Union Jack side by side with the State flag on the Chilas and Gupis forts.

However, before these proposals could be given a practical shape, internal disorders in the State broke out. The matter was discussed by the Political Committee, India Office, in London in its meeting of 18 November 1931. Soon after, on 26 November 1931, the Secretary of State for India sent a telegram to the Government of India giving explicit instructions for asking the Resident in Kashmir

> to suspend any further action in pursuance of his proposals ,as the recent events in Kashmir give us an opportunity and make it desirable to reconsider proposals for future of Gilgit Agency which were put forward informally as basis for discussion.[51]

Eventually the proposal was withdrawn by the Resident at the instance of the Government of India. This was mainly because British fears had increased after the success of the Bolsheviks in Central Asia, and particularly when the Soviet authorities became too close to Chinese warlord regimes in Xinjiang. Thus, the British used the circumstances of domestic political pressure caused by the Muslim upheaval and riots in Kashmir to coax Maharaja Hari Singh to accept the new proposal of leasing the Gilgit Agency to the British for 60 years. The lease agreement, which was signed by the Maharaja of Kashmir and Colonel L.E. Lang, the British Resident in Kashmir, on 26 March 1935, authorized the Viceroy and Governor General of India to assume the civil and military administration of the Gilgit Agency, subject to the condition that the territory would continue to be included within the dominion of His Highness the Maharaja of Jammu and Kashmir, and that the rights pertaining to mining would also be reserved for the Kashmir Government.

Before the Jammu and Kashmir Government handed over the administrative control of the Gilgit Agency to the British Indian Government under the terms of a 60 year lease in March 1935, the area of the Gilgit frontier was divided into three categories of administration: the

Gilgit Wazarat; Political Districts; and the Unadministered Area[52] as detailed below:

1. Gilgit Wazarat, comprising the Tehsil of Gilgit (including Bunji) and the Niabat of Astor. This area remained under the direct control of the Kashmir Durbar, and was administered by a *Wazir-i-Wazarat*.
2. The Political Districts comprising Hunza, Nagar, Punial, Yasin, Ishkoman, Kuh-Ghizar and Chilas.
3. The Unadministered Area comprising Darel, Tangir, Kandia, Jalkot, Sazin, Shatial and Harban

When asked about what the political status of the Unadministered Area was, the Chief Commissioner, North West Frontier Province clarified to the Survey of India that 'Tangir, Darel and Jalkot are not part of the NWFP'.[53]

The lease terminated with the partition of India in 1947. Being highly conscious of the strategic importance of this area, the Dogra ruler Maharaja Gulab Singh and his successors, not only incorporated this northern frontier as part of the newly founded state of Jammu and Kashmir, but also maintained administrative control over this region till 1947.

Hunza and Nagar

Hunza and Nagar were two small principalities bordering on Gilgit. Though their inhabitants spoke the same language—Burushaski—and came from the same stock, both Hunza and Nagar were persistent rivals. Soon after Maharaja Ranbir Singh's accession to the throne in 1857, when the Kashmir ruler was in a stronger position, the Raja of Nagar started paying tribute to the State, and received as a feudatory a subsidy from it. In 1870, after these had been quelled by Kashmir forces, treaties were entered into with the Chiefs of Hunza and Nagar. They remained under the suzerainty of the Kashmir Durbar, though they retained full autonomy in managing their internal affairs. They regularly paid an annual tribute to the State, in lieu of which they were granted *jagirs* in Kashmir.

The chief of Nagar gave a guarantee of safety for trade and commerce between Gilgit and Nagar, and undertook to pay compensation in case of any loss. He also provided for the keeping of hostages at Gilgit as a guarantee for good conduct, the supply of military assistance when required, and the payment of tribute. Lastly, there was an undertaking to bring the Raja of Hunza—who was still recalcitrant—and his son (as well as the son of his Wazir) to remain in attendance on the Maharaja. as also to arrange the handing over of the forts of Chaprot, Nomal, etc., to State troops. In the same year (1870), the Raja of Hunza, Ghazan Khan, gave a similar undertaking, and was granted an annual subsidy.

The undertaking signed by the Chief of Nagar in 1870 is reproduced below.[54]

(i) We undertake to confer with Ghazan Khan, the Raja of Hunza, that his son, as also the son of his *Wazir* should remain in attendance on the Maharaja of Kashmir, and in case he does not agree, we shall send our forces against him.

(ii) If any *Motabar* of Hunza comes for secret work into our State, we shall kill him.

(iii) We shall ask Raja Ghazan Khan to hand over the forts of Chaprot and Nomal; if he agrees well and good; if not, we shall march against him and take their possession by fighting it out.

(iv) Intercourse between the Gilgit and the Nagar subjects of the Maharaja and others will continue. If any loss occurs, we shall be held responsible.

(v) One real son of the Raja of Nagar and one son of the *Wazir* will remain always in the services of Maharaja.

(vi) Friends of the Maharaja will be considered friends; and his enemies, taken as enemies.

(vii) In case the Maharaja of Kashmir will demand any force, the same will be supplied without any hesitation, well equipped.

(viii) That in return for the *Khilat* granted to Raja Jaffar Khan, annually the following *Nazrana* will be presented: Horses = two; Gold = 21 Tolas, Apricots = 5 loads.

The Raja of Hunza also gave an undertaking of peace after his continued hostilities were quelled by Kashmir forces. His undertaking even acknowledged not only his dependence on Maharaja Ranbir Singh but also that such dependence had existed during the reign of Gulab Singh. The undertaking given by Raja of Hunza is reproduced below.[55]

> By the Holy *Quran*...
>
> I am Raja Ghazan Khan, son of Raja Ghazanfar Khan and Grandson of late Saleem Khan of Hunza. Whereas my father, the late Ghazanfar Khan, remained under the control of Kashmir for a long time, especially the deceased Raja was obedient to the Maharaja, I also agree to remain obedient and present the tribute in the same manner. Hence, on my own accord, without force or pressure, I depute my *motabir*, *Wazir* Fazal Khan and accept the following terms:
>
> 1. The following *Nazarana* will be paid by me to the Maharaja annually:
>   (i) Gold = 12 *tolas*
>   (ii) Horses = 2

In return, a *Khilat-Fakhira* and 2000 Srinagari coins will be granted to me, and also a *Khilat* to my *Wazir*.

2. The revenue of Chaprot that has been fixed from older times, will be paid annually at Gilgit.
3. One *Motabir* of mine will always remain present in Gilgit, and he will be paid thirty rupees per month by the State, and one *Motamid* will yearly present to the Maharaja the annual *Nazarana*.
4. The friends of the Maharaja will be my friends, and his enemies will be my enemies.
5. If a force be required in Gilgit, I shall place my troops at the disposal at the Maharaja for service, and I shall not spare my effort in doing the service.

As this agreement has been written after swearing on the Holy *Quran*, no change whatsoever will take place on my part.

Signed, Fazal Khan

Whereas Nagar remained docile and subservient, Hunza used any available opportunity to rebel against the authority of the Kashmir Government. By 1891, both Hunza and Nagar were brought under the effective control of the Maharaja by the use of military force. This was done to remove any apprehension over Russian attempts to explore the strategic overland routes to India via Gilgit, Hunza and Chitral. A study of the accounts of various operations conducted to quell this rebellion shows that the Jammu and Kashmir State government bore the brunt of the fighting as well as the expenditure involved in this campaign. British officers commanding the Imperial Service Troops were acting on behalf of the Maharaja.

The Acting British Agent at Gilgit conveyed the news of the victory to the Maharaja on 26 December 1891 in the following words: 'The Nagar Raja and his people have made their submission. Major General Suran Chand as usual took a prominent part in the day's proceedings'. On the successful conclusion of the Hunza-Nagar operations, the Queen and the Secretary of State for India sent their congratulations to the Kashmir Durbar.[56]

The *Sanads* granted by the Maharaja of Kashmir to the Rajas of Hunza and Nagar on the suppression of the rebellion of 1891 stated the following:

> Whereas the State[57] has recently been in armed rebellion against my authority and whereas in consequence thereof, you have justly forfeited any rights which you may have possessed as ruler of the said State[58] and whereas by reason by your submission and in consideration of your promise to abide by the following conditions it is though desirable to appoint you as ruler of the said State'.

> 'Further, you are informed that the permanence of the grant conveyed by this Sanad will depend upon the ready fulfillment by you and your successors of all orders given by the Jammu and Kashmir State, with regard to the conduct of relations between the State and the States and tribes adjoining it, the administration of your territory, construction of roads through your country, the composition of such troops as you may be permitted to retain, and any other matters in which the Maharaja of Jammu and Kashmir for the time being may be pleased to intervene. Be assured that, so long as your house is loyal to the State of Jammu and Kashmir and to the British Government and faithful to the conditions of this Sanad, you and your successors will enjoy favour and protection.

Though these *Sanads* gave Kashmir unlimited rights of intervention not only in the external but also in the internal affairs of the Chiefs, in actual practice Hunza and Nagar enjoyed full autonomy. In 1927, the subsidies of the Mirs of Hunza and Nagar were increased, being borne equally by the Government of India and the Kashmir Government. The chiefs of Hunza, Nagar, and Mehtar of Chitral visited Srinagar in 1926 to take part in the *Raj Tilak* (Coronation) ceremony of Maharaja Hari Singh. In fact, the Rajas of Hunza and Nagar were also reported to have visited Srinagar in 1947,[59] and reaffirmed their allegiance and solidarity with the Maharaja.

Yasin, Kuh, Ghizar and Ishkoman

Yasin had established treaty relations with the Kashmir Durbar during the reign of Maharaja Gulab Singh. A representative of Yasin used to go to Kashmir via Gilgit, with presents of hawks and dogs as tribute to the Kashmir ruler who would reward the nobles of Yasin. As per the old Kashmir records, the *Wazir-i-Wazarat* of Gilgit, Ram Kishan wrote a letter to Pahalwan Bahadur of Yasin, informing him about the grant of the annual *Mukarrari* (subsidy) of Rs. 2,700/- to him.[60] Later, upon the establishment of the Gilgit Agency, Yasin was included in its Political Districts.

Yasin, Kuh, Ghizar and Ishkoman were placed under Governors. Up to 1905, Yasin and Kuh were separately governed. On the defection of the Ghizar Governor in that year, Ghizar was incorporated with Kuh and Yasin. In 1911, Yasin was separated, and these territories became the three Governorships of Yasin, Kuh-Ghizar and Ishkoman. These Governors held the position of paid officials and had no hereditary rights. They were paid by the Kashmir Durbar, and they paid tribute to Kashmir—or rather, Kashmir took a share of the revenue. There was an advanced military post in Kuh-Ghizar which was the corridor leading up to Chitral, and onwards to Afghanistan and Central Asia. In 1911, Kuh-Ghizar was placed under

Raja Murad Khan, the head of an old Skardu family long settled in Gilgit. The Kashmir government paid his full salary of Rs.1,600 per year,[61] besides revenue, etc. valued at about Rs.5,000 per year.

Punial

Punial was conquered by Kashmir in 1860, and a *Jagir* was conferred on Raja Isa Bahadur. It paid no tribute because it was under the sovereignty of Kashmir, being actually administered by the *Wazir* as part of the Gilgit *Wazarat*. When the Gilgit Agency was re-established in 1889, Punial was included in it as a part of the Political Districts. It continued to be under the *Wazarat*, and the *Wazir* investigated serious offences such as murder. However, the British Agent now intervened in the internal affairs of Punial. In the due course of the time, the Agency assumed complete control of the *jagir,* although it remained under the suzerainty of Kashmir.

Chitral

As per Jammu and Kashmir government records, since 1864, the Mehtar of Chitral, Aman-ul-Mulk, used to send his *Nazrana* (tribute) through his representatives—sometimes his brother Makhmul Shah—to the Maharaja of Kashmir.[62] When, in 1885, Nizam-ul-Mulk, the eldest son of Mehtar Aman-ul-Mulk visited Jammu, he was treated as the State guest till he went to Calcutta to meet the Viceroy. On his return, he continued to be a State guest and, at the time of departure, was granted a *Rukhstana* of Rupees 3,125/- for himself, in addition to the *Khillats* granted to him and his family and dependents.[63] The Maharaja's growing influence and power in the frontier areas coincided with the Russian advance into Central Asia up to the Pamirs.

The events on the frontier were moving very fast, the Afghan war was in the offing. The British were anxious to isolate Afghanistan, and eliminate a possible threat from Chitral. The Mehtar of Chitral was also feeling threatened by the Afghan Government. Being unable to render him any direct assistance to meet the Afghan threat, the British encouraged Maharaja Ranbir Singh of Kashmir to accept the position of suzerain over Chitral, and to hold out the assurance of assistance to the Mehtar. In his letter of 15 May 1877 to the Maharaja of Kashmir, Lord Lytton wrote on the subject of extending his suzerainty over the Mehtar of Chitral.[64]

> It was suggested that the Ruler of Chitral should promptly be informed that, having accepted the suzerainty of the Maharaja of Kashmir, he was not at liberty to change for the suzerainty of Kabul, that Your Highness would doubtless take such measures as you deem suitable for the protection of your feudatory, but that the British

> Government if need be, would afford you countenance and material aid. I have since been informed by Major Henderson of your Highness proposal to dispatch a messenger with a present to the Ruler of Chitral and of availing yourself of the services of an Afghan refugee to ascertain the precise state of matters in Bajour and Dir, and I have already communicated my entire approval of the action proposed to be taken by Your Highness.
>
> I shall be glad to receive from time to time similar friendly communications from Your Highness regarding the State of affairs upon the frontier of Kashmir, and I shall esteem it a favour if you will cause Major Henderson who has my entire confidence to be promptly and fully informed of the progress of events.

In a second letter, dated 2 August 1877 on the same subject, the Viceroy wrote to the Maharaja:

> With regard to the conditions of allegiance, I share your Highness' opinion that they would be as brief and as little onerous as possible consistently with the main objects to be secured; with this view it will suffice, in my opinion, if the document embodying these conditions contains:-
>
> > 'First, an express recognition by the Chitral Chief of Your Highness suzerainty,
> > secondly, an arrangement for the exchange of representatives, and
> > thirdly, an agreement by Your Highness to grant Chitral Chief such annual subsidy as may be determined so long as he faithfully carries out the terms of his allegiance.
>
> ...it would appear, however, both from the remarks made to Major Henderson and from the information which has reached the British Government that Rahmatullah Khan, the Chief of Dir, who lately tendered his allegiance to the Kabul Ruler, now repents of the course adopted by him and is anxious to withdraw. I can give him no hope of being recognized as a protected foundatory of the British Government, but should Your Highness be willing to accept his vassalage and deem such course desirable for the object we have in view, I will gladly recommend that Chief to make a tender of allegiance to the Kashmir State.
>
> In conclusion, I have to suggest to Your Highness that although for the present it appears unnecessary to send troops into Chitral, yet in as much as events may happen which may render Your Highness to cause a careful examination to be made of the passes loading to Chitral, and full information should be collected as to the character of the roads, the supplies available, and other matters likely to be of use in the event of military operations in those parts becoming unavoidable.

Eventually, as a result of the negotiations, Aman-ul-Mulk, the ruler of Chitral signed the following treaty of allegiance with the Maharaja of Kashmir in 1878.[65]

> With the sincerity of purpose and the cordiality of will, I (the Aman-ul-Mulk) do hereby execute this deed on my own part and on the part of my children, consisting of the following articles:
>
> **Article 1**
>
> I engage that I will always sincerely endeavour to obey and execute the orders of His Highness the Maharaja, the Wali of Jammu & Kashmir, that I will overtly and covertly consider his Highness's well-wishers and friends as my friends and enemies of his Government as my enemies, that I will present the following 'Nuzerana' to his Highness annually as an acknowledgement of his paramount power:
>
> Three horses
> Five Hawks
> Five tezi dogs (hounds)
>
> **Article 2**
>
> One confidential agent of His Highness shall always reside in Kashka (Chitral) and another at Yasin. Due attention and consideration shall be paid to them.
>
> In the like manner a confidential agent of mine shall reside at the Maharaja's Durbar, and another on the part of the ruler of Yasin shall remain at Gilgit for the purpose of carrying out His Highness orders.
>
> **Article 3**
>
> I shall receive a yearly mawajib (subsidy) of Rs. 12,000/-, Srinagar Coinage, from His Highness Government, on condition of my acting upon the above articles and giving satisfaction to His Highness in every way.
>
> If one of my sons be appointed in the place of one of the agents (above mentioned), His Highness will assign him an extra allowance:
>
> To self — Rs. 10,000/-
> To Sardar Nizam-ul-Mulk — Rs. 7,000/-

For a very long time, the *vakil* of the Maharaja resided in Chitral, and used to send regular diaries and newsletters to the Maharaja of Kashmir. But things did not to remain quite in this region of perpetual intrigue and political turmoil. Soon, the Mehtar of Chitral engaged in a military conflict with the forces of the Maharaja as well as of some of the smaller principalities. This resulted in some of his territories being detached from his rule and handed over to more loyal chiefs. Aitchison gives an account of these developments in the following words:

> Mehtar Pahalwan Bahadur, a member of the Khushwaqt family, acknowledged the suzerainty of the Kashmir State, from which he received a subsidy; but he failed to act up to his engagements, and in 1880 he invaded Punial. Yasin was occupied in his absence by Aman-ul-Mulk of Chitral, and Pahalwan having failed in his attack on Punial, fled from the country. Aman-ul-Mulk was permitted by the Kashmir Durbar to incorporate the whole tract in his own territory; and with their consent, he gave Ghizar to Mohammad Wali, Yasin proper to Mir Aman, and retained Mastuj himself. After the fresh disturbances created by Pahalwan Mahadur in 1882, Aman-ul-Mulk turned Mir Aman out of Yasin and put his son Afzal-ul-Mulk in his place, the Kashmir Durbar agreed to this action.

According to the Annual Administration Report of Jammu and Kashmir State for the year 1880-81 'the Mehtar of Chitral undertook to guarantee the remittance to the Maharaja of the annual *Nuzzrana* by the person entrusted with the administration of these three sub-districts. The Maharaja's influence and power at the court of Chitral at this time was so high that when, in 1886, a part of the Afghan Boundary Commission was returning to India via Gilgit, the Government of India requested the Maharaja to issue orders to the Mehtar of Chitral to arrange transport and make other arrangements for the Commission while in Chitral. The map prepared and published by the Tignometrical Survey in 1874 not only showed Hunza, Nagar and Chilas but also Chitral within the territory of the Jammu and Kashmir State.

When the British virtually took over the administrative control of the Jammu and Kashmir State after Maharaja Ranbir Singh's death, Chitral affairs also underwent a drastic change. In 1889, the Political Agency was established at Gilgit; and in 1891, a subordinate Political Agency was established in Chitral as well to more effectively watch and control the situation there. After the death of Aman-ul-Mulk in August 1892, the British installed Nizam-ul-Mulk as the new Mehtar of Chitral and stationed troops in Ghazi. Captain Younghusband was appointed as Political Officer at Mastuj.

In 1894, Nizam-ul-Mulk, the Mehtar of Chitral was murdered by his own half-brother, and trouble after trouble followed, till the British Agent was besieged in Chitral fort, and a relief expedition became necessary. That the Kashmir troops played a major part in the Chitral campaign led by Robertson in 1895 is well known. On the restoration of peace in Chitral, the Khushwaqt districts on the west of the Shahdur range, (the boundary between the Chitral and Gilgit Agencies) were severed from Chitral. Yasin, Koh-Ghizar and Ishkoman were now administered by Governors whose position was that of paid officials, with no hereditary rights. But the

Governorship of Yasin was held by a member of the Khushwaqt family. To quote Atchison, 'The revenue of the districts is taken by the Governor, but a certain proportion is credited to the Kashmir Durbar as tribute. The Governors and certain headmen under them receive fixed stipends from the Kashmir Durbar'.

After this, the Shuja-ul-Mulk, the 15 year old son of late Aman-ul-Mulk, was enthroned as the Mehtar of Chitral on 2 September 1895 'in the name of Kashmir as suzerain and with the authority of the Government of India.'[66] At the same time, the British established the Malakand Agency in 1895, and transferred the administration of Chitral from Gilgit to Malakand.

In his letter No. 1851, 7 April 1913, to the Chief Minister to the Maharaja of Jammu and Kashmir, the Resident in Kashmir S.M. Fraser informed about the new arrangements made by the Government of India at the end of Chitral war of 1895.

> They comprised inter-alia the partition of Chitral into two tracts—the Katur country which was to consist of Chitral proper with the neighbouring country, and Khushwaqt country namely Mastuj, Lasspur, Ghizar, Kuh and Yasin. The control of the Mehtar, it was proposed, should extend over the former only, while the latter should be administered by the British Agent, Gilgit, on behalf of the Kashmir Durbar. At the same time, it was suggested that the subsidy paid jointly by the Government of India and the Kashmir Durbar to the Mehtar of Chitral should be continued.
>
> In carrying these proposals into effect, the Government of India directed that Shuja-ul-Mulk should be given a subsidy of Rs. 1000/- p.m., and in consideration of the loss to him of the revenue from the separation of the Khushwakt country, he should be given an additional sum of Rs. 8000/- a year.
>
> It was further decided that the British Agent Gilgit should, on behalf of the Kashmir State, appoint and pay the Governors and headmen of the Khushwaqt country who, except in the case of Mastuj and Laspur, should have direct relations with him. As a matter of convenience, it was decided that the Governor of Mastuj and the Hakim of Laspur should correspond with the political Officer in Chitral. This arrangement was followed till 1896, in which year the Chitral Agency was transferred from Gilgit to the Political Agent, Dir, Swat and Chitral. As a consequence, the Governorships of Mastuj and the district of Laspur were transferred to Chitral whereas Yasin remained with the Gilgit Agency.

Due to the war clouds looming large on the political horizon in 1914, and the extension of the German influence to the Middle East, the British were inclined to keep the frontier outpost of their Indian Empire on a more secure basis. Thus, the Resident conveyed to the Kashmir Government certain proposals with regard to this on 7 April, 1913.

> For some time past, the Mehtar of Chitral has claimed that the districts of Mastuj and Laspur should be placed under his control. The Government of India, after giving the question their full consideration, are disposed to accede to the wishes of the Mehtar of Chitral on the resignation or death of Mehtajoo Bahadur Khan, the present Governor of Mastuj, provided the Kashmir Durbar are willing to continue the present subsidy by them to the Mehtar of Chitral.
>
> As the Mehtar of Chitral acknowledges the suzerainty of Kashmir, I am to request that you will place the above proposal before His Highness the Maharaja, and ascertain for the information of the Government of India whether he has any objection to the same. I am to say that if the contemplated proposals are put into effect, the Government of India hope the Durbar will agree to continue the payment of Rs. 8000/- as subsidy to the Mehtar, and Rs. 10,000/- as salaries and allowances to officials and headmen of Chitral as heretofore subject in the latter case to the condition already mentioned.

The Kashmir Durbar agreed to these proposals of the Government of India and, as a result, an agreement was executed by the Mehtar on 2 April 1914 according to which Mastuj and Laspur were transferred to his direct administration. Article 1 of this agreement reads as follows:

> I acknowledge the suzerainty of His Highness the Maharaja of Kashmir and Jammu and in token thereof will resume the annual payment of the following Nazrana;
>
> (a) 3 horses
> (b) 5 hawks
> (c) 5 tazi dogs (hounds).

That the Mehtar of Chitral or his son followed the custom of payment of *Nazrana*, is evident from the following facts:

(a) While visiting Jammu in December 1921, the Mehtar of Chitral presented *Nazar* to the Maharaja as his suzerain.
(b) His son attended the Raj Tilak celebrations of Maharaja Hari Singh in 1926, and paid a *Nazarana* to him.
(c) The State, on its part, continued to pay the annual subsidy to the Mehtar.

The Mehtar personally visited Jammu in April 1939, and had long discussions with the then Prime Minister, Sir Gopalaswami Aiyangar, discussing the draft of the new agreement. Since the Gilgit *Wazarat* had already been leased out to the Government of India in 1935, the idea of a fresh agreement was given up. Subsequently, after the creation of Pakistan, Chitral has continued to be part of Malakand of North West Frontier Province.

Chilas

The relationship with Chilas district began early in the rule of Maharaja Gulab Singh who had sent a punitive expedition to Chilas in 1851-52 to curb the Chilasi marauders who used to raid the Astor valley. From that time, the Chilasis not only undertook to pay tribute to the Maharaja but also sent hostages, who remained in Kashmir until relieved by another batch so that some were always there to ensure the good conduct of the Chilasi tribesmen. After the conquest of Chilas by the Kashmir Government in 1851, the Maharaja imposed a tribute of gold dust upon the country and arranged for its administration as part of the Gilgit districts. The people of Chilas approached the government of the Maharaja for the redressal of wrongs in the manner of ordinary subjects of the State.

However, the autonomy of the Chilasis was guaranteed, while the right of the Kashmir State to construct roads, and place a limited number of troops in that territory was secured. After the re-establishment of the British Agency in Gilgit in 1889, Chilas and the neighbouring tribes were included in the political districts. Chilas was made a sub-division of the Agency, and was placed under the control of the Assistant Political Agent, and this control extended to the neighbouring territories of Darel and Tangir.

Shinaki Republics

The territory of the Shinaki republics of the Indus valley extended from Ramghat, where the Astor River joined the Indus on the right bank, and Jalkot on the left bank of the Indus. Within this area, the people were grouped in communities, each community comprising a republic in itself. These were Darel (with Khanbari), Tangir, Kandia or Khilli, Seo, Harban, Sazin, Jalkot and Chilas.

Thor

Like Chilas, Thor had been a tributary of Kashmir, and in the events which led up to the occupation of Chilas, the Thor people appear to have acted conjointly with the Chilasis. In 1893, at the request of the inhabitants, Thor was incorporated in Chilas; a *Sanad* was granted to the people, and they were given service money, provided by the Durbar, in return for a yearly *Nazrana* of 12 male goats paid to the Maharaja of Kashmir.

Darel

Darel had been paying an annual tribute of gold dust to the Durbar ever since 1866, when Maharaja Ranbir Singh's troops raided the territory. This tribute was paid through the Governor of Punial, a Raja whose family had influence in Darel owing to the relative geographical positions of Darel and Punial.

Tangir

Raja Pukhtun Wali was a Khushwaqt who had settled in Tangir after the Chitral disturbances of 1895. In 1898, he opened correspondence with the Political Agent in Gilgit and sought recognition as the ruler of Tangir. At the same time, he continued to build up his position, both in Tangir and Darel, and was recognized as their Chief in 1911.

Jalkot

Jalkot was, like others, a principality under the suzerainty of Kashmir and was included in the territories of the Gilgit area.

Conclusion

The historical evidence and contemporary records discussed above show that Skardu, Gilgit, Hunza, Nagar, Chilas, Astor, Gupis, Kuh-Ghizar, Punial, Ishkoman, Yasin, Darel, and Tangir, etc. were part of the territories of Jammu and Kashmir State till 1947. Whereas the Kashmir government exercised direct authority over Gilgit, Bunji and Astor which were part of Gilgit Wazarat till 1947; Skardu, Rondu, Shigar, Tolti, Khaplu, etc. were part of a tehsil in the Ladakh district. However, the chiefships of Hunza, Nagar and Governorships of Punial, Yasin, Chilas, Kuh-Ghizar, Ishkoman and the tribal territories of Darel, Tangir, Thor, Kandia, Jalkot, Shatian, Harban, etc. were feudatories of the Kashmir Durbar, which received tribute from them but were allowed internal autonomy in their local administration.

When the British left the sub-continent in August 1947, the area of the Gilgit Agency reverted back to Maharaja's control. Maharaja Hari Singh appointed Brigadier Ghansara Singh as new *Wazir-i-Wazarat* (Governor) of Gilgit, who assumed charge on 31 July 1947. On 1 August 1947, illuminations in the entire Jammu and Kashmir State celebrated the resumption of the civil and military administration of Gilgit. However, Major Brown, the British Commander of Gilgit Scouts, organised and led a revolt of the Gilgit Scouts and arrested Brigadier Ghansara Singh, the Kashmir Durbar's *Wazir-i-Wazarat* at Gilgit. On 4 November 1947, Brown hoisted the Pakistani flag at Gilgit and handed over the area to Pakistan, which appointed its own Political Agent. Though Indian forces, supported by the people of Kashmir led by Sheikh Abdullah, the popular leader of National Conference, pushed back Pakistani armed forces from the Valley of Kashmir, Pakistan succeeded in occupying Gilgit, Baltistan and the adjoining frontier territories. When the ceasefire was declared in January 1949, Kashmir Valley, Jammu, Ladakh and Kargil were left within India, and Pakistan occupied a vast territory of Mirpur, Muzaffarabad and Gilgit-Baltistan.

Subsequently, by a mere stroke of pen, Pakistan divided the occupied territory of Kashmir into two: (i) 'Azad Jammu and Kashmir' or Pakistan Occupied Kashmir (POK), comprising Muzaffarabad, Mirpur, Bagh, Neelam, Sudthi, Rawlakot, Bhimbar, Kotli; and (ii) Gilgit-Baltistan. Due to its strategic importance, Pakistan enforced federal control over Gilgit-Baltistan and renamed it the 'Northern Areas'. Later, 2700 square miles of the Gilgit-Baltistan area was ceded to China in March 1963, in exchange for China's support.

Covering an area of about 28,000 square miles, which is 5 to 6 times more than that of POK, the Gilgit-Baltistan region comprises 7 districts under the new administrative arrangement.

(i) Skardu and (ii) Ganche have been part of Skardu/Baltistan—the erstwhile Tehsil of the Ladakh District of Jammu and Kashmir.
(iii) Gilgit includes former Gilgit Tehsil
(iv) Hunza-Nagar
(v) Diamir includes Chilas, Tangir and Darel.
(vi) Astor
(v) Ghizar includes Gupis, Punial, Ishkoman and Yasin.

In early 1982, General Zia-ul-Haque publicly announced that these areas were never part of Jammu and Kashmir State before 1947. It evoked a lot of protests in Jammu and Kashmir on both sides of the LoC. At a huge May day rally in May 1982, Sheikh Abdullah, the then Chief Minister of Jammu and Kashmir State, declared that 'the whole of PoK, including Gilgit, constitutes the territory of the State'. In fact, General Zia had brought this area at par with the other provinces of Pakistan by declaring it as Martial Law Zone 'E' with its own Martial Law Administrator in 1977, which was not done in the case of POK. Ever since then, there has been simmering discontent in POK about this de facto merger of Gilgit-Baltistan with Pakistan. Demands have been made to hand over its administration back to the POK government.

In 1990, a petition was filed before the High Court of 'Azad Kashmir' pleading that the 'Northern Areas' be considered a part of 'Azad' Jammu and Kashmir, and that their separation is illegal. Advocate Raja

Muhammad Haneef[67]—who argued the case of constitutional status of Northern Areas on behalf of the petitioners Haji Amir Jan and Abdul Aziz in the 'Azad' Kashmir High Court—made the following points:

(i) That 'Northern Areas' were historically a part of State of Jammu and Kashmir.

(ii) In the July 1947 elections to the Jammu and Kashmir State Assembly, Raja Jagmat Dadool Nano, Chewing Rinchen, Raja Fateh Ali Khan, Ahmed Ali Khan, Raja Raza Khan and Muhammad Jawad Ansari were elected the members from the 'Northern Areas'.

(iii) In 1949, the 'Azad' Kashmir government was not in a position to look after the 'Northern Areas' due to the lack of communications. Therefore, the administration of 'Northern Areas' was transferred to the government of Pakistan by the 'Azad' Kashmir government in April 1949.

(iv) Clause 6 of the Sino-Pak Agreement signed in March 1963 provides that 'Northern Areas' are a part of the State of Jammu and Kashmir.

(v) On 15 July 1991, the 'Azad' Jammu and Kashmir Assembly demanded that the local administration of the 'Northern Areas' should be handed over to the 'Azad' Kashmir government in terms of the AJK Interim Constitution, 1974.

(vi) None of the Constitutions of Pakistan, 1956, 1962, 1972 and 1973 recognise that the 'Northern Areas' are part of Pakistan.

In its written statement lodged before the AJK High Court, the Pakistan government admitted that 'Northern Areas' were not a part of Pakistan territory, and that the Constitution of Pakistan and other laws were not applicable to the 'Northern Areas'. It also admitted that the 'Northern Areas' were a part of the State of Jammu and Kashmir. In its written statement, the 'Azad Kashmir' government pleaded that the 'Northern Areas' were part of Jammu and Kashmir . The *AJK Muslim Conference* President, Sardar Muhammad Abdul Qayyum Khan, lodged his written statement in the AJK High Court pleading that 'Northern Areas' were part of the State of Jammu and Kashmir. Abdur Rashid Torabi of the *Jamat-e-Islami*, Abdul Khaliq Ansari of the *Plebiscite Front*, and G.M. Mir of the *National Liberation Front* also supported this petition. The 'Azad' Jammu and Kashmir High Court gave its judgement in March 1993 declaring that the 'Northern Areas', (Gilgit-Baltistan) are legally part of Kashmir, and ordered the 'Azad' Jammu and Kashmir government to assume administrative control of 'Northern Areas'.

Pakistan challenged this verdict in the Supreme Court of 'Azad Kashmir', which gave its verdict in September 1994, ruling that 'Northern

Areas' are part of the State of Jammu and Kashmir but are not part of 'Azad Jammu and Kashmir'. This only reflects the anomalous position of Pakistan on the Kashmir issue, both in theory and practice.

NOTES

1. Ahmad Hasan Dani, *Human Record on Karakorum Highway*, Islamabad, n.d., p.18.
2. For full text of these rock edits, please see Ibid., pp. 20-22.
3. Ibid., pp. 30, 34.
4. Ibid., p. 35.
5. Ahmad Hasan Dani, *History of Northern Areas of Pakistan*, Islamabad, 1989.
6. Ibid., p. 122.
7. J. Biddulph, *Tribes of the Hindoo Koosh*, (Reprint), Bhavana Books, New Delhi, 2001, pp. 112-113.
8. Ibid., p.113.
9. Ibid., p.114.
10. Ibid., p.115.
11. Frederic Drew, *The Jummoo and Kashmir Territories: A Geographical Account*. London, 1875. (Reprint) Oriental Publishers, New Delhi, 1971, p. 429.
12. Ibid.
13. Ahmad Hasan Dani, no. 5, p. 215.
14. Ibid., p. 222.
15. Ibid., p. 223.
16. Ibid., p. 224.
17. Ibid., p. 225.
18. Ibid., p. 320.
19. Ibid.
20. Ibid.
21. Cited in *Statement of Facts on Gilgit, Hunza, Nagar, Yasin, Punial, Chitral and Skardu*. Srinagar, n.d., p. 15.
22. See, *Revised List of Ruling Princes, Chiefs and Leading personages of the Jammu and Kashmir State and the Gilgit Agency*, Government of India, New Delhi, 1939, pp. 12, 16.
23. Frederic Drew, no. 11, p. 358.
24. A.H. Dani, no. 5, p 163.
25. Ibid., p. 160.
26. Ibid.
27. Ibid., pp. 161-62.
28. Ibid., p. 161.
29. Frederic Drew, no. 11, pp. 437-38.
30. Ibid., p. 438.
31. Ibid.
32. Sukhdev Singh Charak, *Life and Times of Maharaja Ranbir Singh (1830-1885)*, Jay Kay Book House, Jammu, 1985, pp. 167-168.
33. Ibid.
34. Ibid.
35. Ibid., pp. 168-69.
36. Ibid., p. 169.

37. Ibid.
38. Ibid., p. 170.
39. Ibid.
40. Ibid.
41. Ibid., pp.170-171.
42. Ibid., p. 171.
43. Ibid., p. 173.
44. K. Warikoo, *Central Asia and Kashmir: Study in the context of Anglo-Russian Rivalry*, Gyan Books, New Delhi, 1989, p 157.
45. See 'India to Punjab' dated 16 May 1970, cited in G.J. Alder, *British India's Northern Frontier, 1865-95*, Longmans, London, 1963, p. 101.
46. Ibid., p. 158.
47. *Foreign & Political Department 67-X (Secret) of 1930*, 1-28, National Archives of India, New Delhi.
48. Ibid.
49. *Foreign Secret April 1882*, 353-360, National Archives of India, New Delhi.
50. *D.O. letter from Lt. Col. G.D. Ogilvie, Resident in Kashmir dated 18 December 1930, Foreign & Political Department, 67-X (Secret) of 1930*, 1-28, National Archives of India, New Delhi.
51. See L/P&S/12/3287 No. 24/3, India Office Records, London.
52. E.B. Howell, Resident in Kashmir to the Director, Frontier Circle, *Survey of India*, 12 January 1928, *Foreign Political 71-X (Secret) 1928*, National Archives of India, New Delhi.
53. See Letter from Secretary to Chief Commissioner NWFP to Director, Frontier Circle, Survey of India, July 18, 1927.
54. Sukhdev Singh Charak, no. 32, p. 190.
55. Ibid., p. 191.
56. See Resident's D.O. letter dated 31-12-1891 to the Maharaja of Kashmir.
57. The Kashmir Durbar objected to the use of the term State (as was done by C.U. Aitchison) and requested the Resident in Kashmir to replace it with the term Chiefship, which in its opinion would correspond to the term *Riyasat* used in the original Persian text of the *Sanad*. The British Resident, however, preferred to use the term Principality.
58. Ibid.
59. A.H. Dani, no. 5, p. 345.
60. Sukhdev Singh Charak, no. 32, p. 195.
61. See Political Agent in Gilgit to First Assistant to Resident in Kashmir, 17 February 1930, *Foreign Political 242-X (Secret) 1930*, National Archives of India, New Delhi.
62. *Statement of Facts on Gilgit, Hunza, Nagar, Yasin, Punial, Chitral and Skardu*, no. 21, p.13.
63. Ibid., p.14.
64. *Sec. Procs.* 30-60 B, July 1877, National Archives of India, New Delhi.
65. C.U. Aitchison, *A Collection of Treaties, Engagements and Sanads relating to India and Neighbouring Countries Vol. IX, Part II, The treaties relating to the State of Jammu and Kashmir*, Calcutta, 1892, p. 372.
66. Robert A. Huttenback, *Kashmir and the British Raj, 1847-1947*, Oxford University Press, 2004, p. 122.
67. Raja Muhammad Haneef, AJK Court Verdict on Northern Areas, *Muslim*, March 18, 1993.

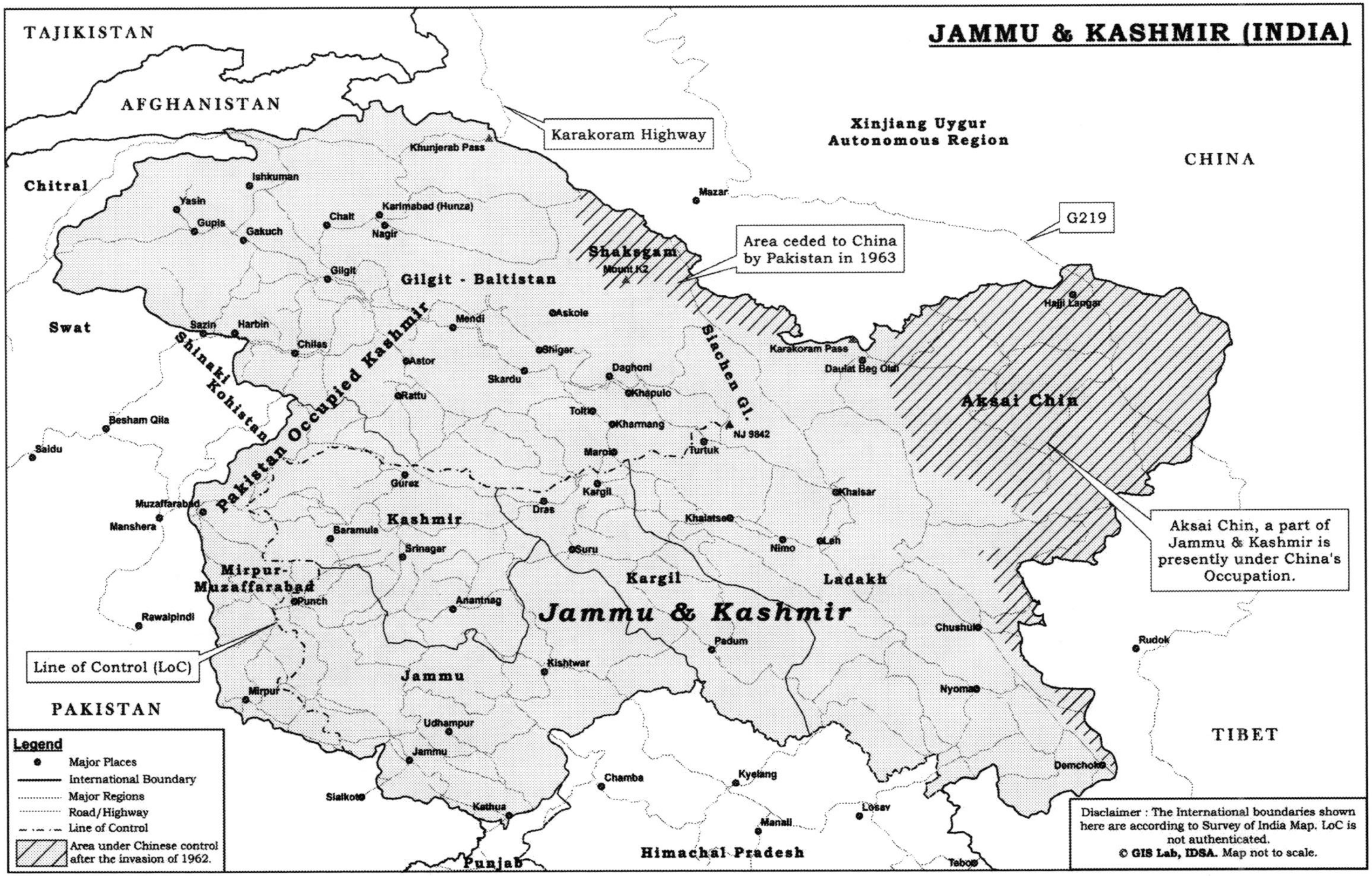
JAMMU & KASHMIR (INDIA)
TAJIKISTAN
AFGHANISTAN
Karakoram Highway
Xinjiang Uygur Autonomous Region
CHINA
G219
Area ceded to China by Pakistan in 1963
Chitral
Swat
Khunjerab Pass
Ishkuman
Yasin
Gupis
Gakuch
Chalt
Karimabad (Hunza)
Nagir
Gilgit
Gilgit - Baltistan
Shaksgam
Mount K2
Mazar
Sazin
Harbin
Chilas
Mendi
Askole
Shigar
Skardu
Astor
Rattu
Daghoni
Khapulo
Tolti
Kharmang
Marol
Siachen Gl.
NJ 9842
Turtuk
Karakoram Pass
Daulat Beg Oldi
Hajji Langar
Aksai Chin
Shinaki Kohistan
Pakistan Occupied Kashmir
Besham Qila
Saidu
Muzaffarabad
Manshera
Gurez
Kargil
Dras
Kashmir
Baramula
Srinagar
Khalatse
Khalsar
Nimo
Leh
Suru
Kargil
Ladakh
Aksai Chin, a part of Jammu & Kashmir is presently under China's Occupation.
Mirpur-Muzaffarabad
Punch
Anantnag
Jammu & Kashmir
Rawalpindi
Padum
Chushul
Rudok
Line of Control (LoC)
Kishtwar
Jammu
Mirpur
PAKISTAN
Nyoma
Udhampur
Jammu
TIBET
Demchok
Sialkot
Chamba
Kyelang
Kathua
Losav
Manali
Punjab
Himachal Pradesh
Tabo
Legend
Major Places
International Boundary
Major Regions
Road/Highway
Line of Control
Area under Chinese control after the invasion of 1962.
Disclaimer : The International boundaries shown here are according to Survey of India Map. LoC is not authenticated.
© GIS Lab, IDSA. Map not to scale.

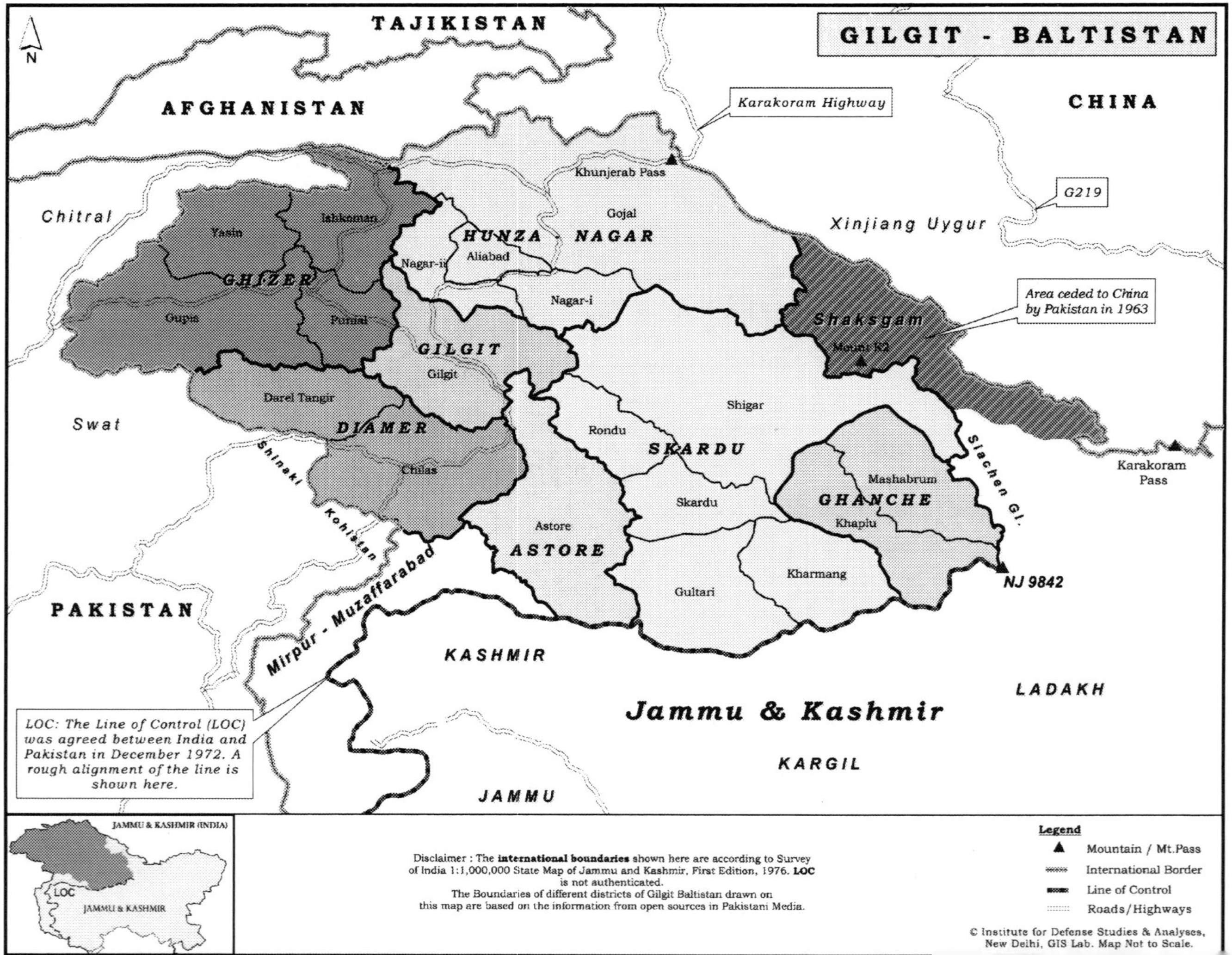
GILGIT - BALTISTAN
TAJIKISTAN
AFGHANISTAN
CHINA
PAKISTAN
Karakoram Highway
G219
Xinjiang Uygur
Area ceded to China by Pakistan in 1963
Shaksgam
Mount K2
Karakoram Pass
Khunjerab Pass
Gojal
HUNZA - NAGAR
Aliabad
Nagar-ii
Nagar-i
Chitral
Yasin
Ishkoman
GHIZER
Gupis
Punial
GILGIT
Gilgit
Darel Tangir
DIAMER
Chilas
Swat
Shinaki
Kohistan
Mirpur - Muzaffarabad
Shigar
Rondu
SKARDU
Skardu
Astore
ASTORE
Gultari
Kharmang
Mashabrum
GHANCHE
Khaplu
Siachen Gl.
NJ 9842
KASHMIR
Jammu & Kashmir
LADAKH
KARGIL
JAMMU
LOC: The Line of Control (LOC) was agreed between India and Pakistan in December 1972. A rough alignment of the line is shown here.
JAMMU & KASHMIR (INDIA)
LOC
JAMMU & KASHMIR
Disclaimer : The international boundaries shown here are according to Survey of India 1:1,000,000 State Map of Jammu and Kashmir, First Edition, 1976. LOC is not authenticated.
The Boundaries of different districts of Gilgit Baltistan drawn on this map are based on the information from open sources in Pakistani Media.
Legend
Mountain / Mt.Pass
International Border
Line of Control
Roads/Highways
© Institute for Defense Studies & Analyses, New Delhi, GIS Lab. Map Not to Scale.

7

Geo-Strategic Importance of Gilgit-Baltistan

K. Warikoo

Pakistan occupied territory of Jammu and Kashmir (PoK) includes highly strategic areas of Gilgit, Hunza, Nagar, Chilas, Astor, Darel/Tangir, Gupis, Ghizar, Punial, Ishkoman, Yasin and Baltistan (Skardu, Shigar, Kharmang and Ghanche), all situated at the tri-junction of the Hindu Kush, Karakoram and Pamir mountains, where the frontiers of India, China, Pakistan, Afghanistan and Central Asia meet. Since this frontier area is interlocked with the Himalayas, it is highly important for the security and defence of north and northwestern frontiers of India. The importance of the Himalaya as the natural frontier of India in the north is immersed in Indian ethos and psyche.[1]

अस्त्यूत्तरस्याँ दिशि देवात्मा हिमालयो नाम नगाधिराजः ।
पूर्वापरौ तोयनिधी वगाह्म स्थितः प्रथिव्या इव मानदण्डः ॥

[In the north (of our country) stands the Lord of Mountains and the very embodiment of divinity—the Himalaya, like a measuring rod of the earth spanning the eastern and western oceans.]

This is how Kalidasa in his *Kumara Sambhava* described the Himalaya as *devatma*—a divine personality, and as the measuring rod spanning the eastern and western oceans, thereby pinpointing the northern frontiers of India.

The very fact that the boundaries of China, Pakistan, India, Afghanistan and Tajikistan converge at Gilgit-Baltistan, lends a unique geostrategic importance to this region. It is through this area that the Karakoram Highway passes providing Pakistan direct land access to Central Asia. The PoK has been an important constituent of India's trans-Himalayan communication network in the continent and beyond. The imposing geographical features and high daunting peaks[2] did not prevent the region from becoming a complex of cultural interaction, overland trade, and communication. Important land routes—Leh (Ladakh)–Yarkand–Kashgar crossing Khardung La pass over the Karakoram range, and Gilgit-Hunza-Kashgar across the Khunjerab and Mintaka passes, pass through this region. Whereas the Leh-Yarkand route, which used to be the main artery of trade and communication between India and Central Asia remains closed since 1949, the Gilgit-Kashgar route has been developed into the Karakoram Highway providing China direct land access through Pakistan.

This region is the cradle from where ancient Indian culture including Budhhism spread to different directions in Central Asia, East Asia and South East Asia. Gilgit, Hunza, Chitral, Skardu, Kargil, Leh and other frontier areas have been important mileposts on the famous Silk Route. The region displays a diversity of cultural patterns, languages, ethnic identities and religious practices. The entire region has been a melting pot of different cultures and faiths—Zoroastrianism, Buddhism and Islam. Whereas a variety of languages—Ladakhi, Balti, Shina, Burushaski, Gojali, Khowar, etc. exist in the region, the cross-border linkages between various ethnic-religious groups turn this frontier into a complex vortex of geopolitics. Its potential for instability and conflict is furthered by the ethnic-religious jigsaw prevailing in this trans-Himalayan region, as people of the Buddhist and Islamic (Shia, Sunni, Ismaili, Nurbakshi) faiths are concentrated in various areas and are vulnerable to extraneous influences. The induction and settlement of Punjabis, Pakhtoons and the Taliban cadres by Pakistan as its calculated policy to colonise this Shia/Ismaili dominated region has not only changed its demographic balance but also led to the rise of sectarianism and religious extremism often leading to violence and conflict.[3] At the same time, the region has been witnessing a new urge for the revival of its indigenous languages, cultural heritage and social practices. Similarly, the social and political aspirations of different indigenous ethnic-religious groups in Gilgit-Baltistan have remained suppressed due to the geopolitical and religious factors.

Covering an area of about 28,000 sq. miles (about 73,000 sq. kms) Gilgit-Baltistan has seven districts—Gilgit, Skardu, Diamer, Ghizer, Hunza Nagar, Ghanche and Astor, with a total population of about two million. Whereas the entire population of Hunza, Punial, Yasin, Ishkoman and Gupis are Ismailis (followers of Agha Khan), the people of Nagar and Baltistan

(Skardu, Ghanche) are Shia Muslims. Gilgit has 60 per cent Shias and 40 per cent Sunnis (mainly Punjabi and Pakhtoon settlers from Pakistan). Chilas, Astore and Darel/Tangir have a Sunni Muslim majority. Pakistan secured direct administrative control of Gilgit-Baltistan by virtue of the Karachi agreement with the Presidents of 'Azad Kashmir' and the Muslim Conference on 28 April 1949 by detaching this area from PoK and terming it as 'Northern Areas'. Ever since, this region has been directly governed by the Ministry of Kashmir and Northern Affairs (KANA) from Islamabad. Obviously, this arrangement has come in handy for Pakistan in its military colonisation of the area and in its dealings with China including the ceding of about 2,100 sq. miles[4] territory in Skaksgam and Muztagh valleys of Gilgit-Baltistan. On the other hand the 'Azad Jammu and Kashmir' (AJK) has had a modicum of democratically elected governments and assembly. AJK has an area of 5,134 sq. miles (13,297 sq. kms) and a population of over 3.2 million. For administrative purposes it has been divided into eight districts – Muzaffarabad, Neelam, Mirpur, Bhimber, Kotli, Poonch, Bagh and Sudhnoti. The people of AJK who are Sunni Muslims speaking Punjabi, Pothowari, Mirpuri, Pahari/Gojri languages, have very little in common with those of the Gigit-Baltistan region. Pakistan, besides maintaining regular army detachments and Northern Light Infantry (NLI) formation, has been operating scores of training camps for terrorist groups like *Lashkar-e-Toiba, Harkat-ul-Mujahideen, Jaish-e-Mohammad, Hizbul Mujahideen, Al Badar, Harkat-ul-Ansar,* etc. at Marol, Baghicha, Dou, Dhappa, Skardu, Daral, Astor, Bunji, Damiyor, Gilgit (in Gilgit-Baltistan) and at Muzaffarabad, Bagh, Kotli, New Mirpur, Tain, Kahuta, Rawlakot, Manshera, Palandri, Bhimber (in AJK) for carrying out proxy war against India.[5]

Major international land frontier disputes pertain to this area. Whereas India and Pakistan have been locked in a conflict over Kashmir since 1947, the Sino-Indian border dispute remains to be settled. Any cross-border fraternisation of people living in the region on ethnic and religious lines is a potential source of conflict in the region and a security threat. With the disintegration of erstwhile USSR and the emergence of newly independent Central Asian states—all having predominantly Muslim population, a new geopolitical situation has arisen across the northwestern Himalayas. In the past, this region served as a gateway to India for numerous invasions and influences from Central Asia and West Asia. Even in contemporary times, India has had to experience successive military aggressions from Pakistan in 1947, 1965, 1971, 1999 (in Kargil) and in the form of a proxy war in Kashmir that has been going on for more than twenty two years now, besides the Chinese military offensive in 1962 from across the Himalayas. The situation has become adverse for India from the security point of view, as China has been consistently providing diplomatic, military, logistics, physical and financial support to Pakistan to enable it to consolidate its grip over the strategic frontier area of PoK and Gilgit-Baltistan.

Shadow of 'Great Game'

In the last quarter of the 19th Century, the British activated their policy in this frontier area, with a view to monitor the Russian movements in the Pamirs and Central Asia. During the period of the 'Great Game', the importance of the Hindu Kush-Karakoram-Pamir region had become clear to the British as it was the meeting point of the Kashmir frontiers in Gilgit, Hunza and Chitral, of the Afghan provinces of Badakhshan and Wakhan, of the Russian territory of Kokand and of the Sarikol area of Chinese Turkestan.[6] It was seen as a gateway for any foreign invasion of India. The British strategy geared itself to the task of creating a barrier between Russian and British empires right on the Pamirs, simultaneously extending their effective control over the frontier areas in Gilgit, Hunza, Chitral and Yasin through the Maharaja of Kashmir. The British used Ladakh and adjoining areas in Gilgit, Skardo, Hunza and Chitral as 'frontier listening posts' to monitor the developments in Central Asia and Xinjiang throughout the Dogra period. With these strategic considerations, the British encouraged the Maharaja of Kashmir to bring the warlike and unruly Dardic tribal chiefs inhabiting the obscure mountainous valleys of the Hindu Kush and Karakoram under his effective control.[7] The Maharaja was given the freedom to choose any means from conciliation to military expeditions or both and was provided with the necessary arms and ammunition too. The idea behind several military expeditions carried out jointly by the Kashmir forces and the British officers against Hunza, Nagar, Chitral and Yasin was to put the defence of north and northwestern frontiers on a firm footing.[8] Once these unruly tribes were coerced into subjugation to Kashmir, a strong military garrison was established at Gilgit, thus making it the nucleus of the whole defence arrangement.[9] The importance of Gilgit as a convenient base for extending the British influence up to the territories lying south of the Hindu Kush had now been fully realised. To quote Alder, it was a 'natural choice' being situated at the 'hub of routes leading off to all parts of Dardistan'.[10] According to E.E. Knight, the celebrated author of *Where Three Empires Meet*, '...the value of Gilgit to the Kashmir State, commanding as it does the Indus Valley and the mouth of the Hunza river, and so holding in check the unruly tribes in either side. Gilgit, the northernmost outpost of the Indian Empire covers all the passes over the Hindoo Koosh, from the easternmost one—the Shimshal, to those at the head of the Yasin river. Possession of the Gilgit valley affords a direct communication through Kashmir territory to the protected state of Chitral'.[11]

In 1874–75, the British Indian government sent several experienced officers like Col. Gordon, Biddulph and Trotter to survey the Wakhan, Pamir and Sarikol region. Gordon's disclosures about the existence of a practicable road from the Russian military post of Osh across the Alai to Sarikol brought into sharp focus the strategic importance of this area. When Gordon pointed to the vulnerability of India from the direction of Wakhan via Ishkoman and Baroghil passes, the need to strengthen the British position in the tribal territories of Gilgit, Yasin and Chitral assumed importance. The discoveries made by Biddulph during his exploration in the Wakhan area during 1874 and at the passes lying south of the Hindu Kush during 1876, only reinforced Gordon's viewpoint. By 1876, the British Indian government was convinced about the necessity of extending Kashmir's control over Chitral and Yasin, right up to the south of Ishkoman and Baroghil passes. The incorporation of Kokand by Russia, which pushed the Russian frontier beyond Osh, only catalysed the British forward policy in this region.

It is against this background that Lord Lytton enunciated the future course of action to be taken in this frontier belt, which he finally conveyed to Maharaja Ranbir Singh personally at Madhopore on 17 and 18 November 1876.[12] Lytton impressed upon the Kashmir ruler the need to strengthen the Indian frontiers by assuming control over the territory that lay between the HinduKush and Kashmir frontier, in order to secure command of such passes as were thought to be practicable for the passage of Russian forces.[13] To the British, it was now of vital importance that the states like Chitral and Yasin 'should come under the control of a friend and ally' like the Maharaja of Kashmir 'rather than be absorbed by powers inimical to Kashmir'.[14] However, while encouraging Ranbir Singh to obtain 'an effective but peaceful control over the countries lying between those passes and Kashmir frontier namely Chitral, Mastuj, Yasin and their dependencies',[15] the British secured the right to station an agent at Gilgit 'to collect information regarding the frontier and the progress of events beyond it'.[16] The Kashmir ruler, however, relented to this measure only after obtaining written assurance from Lytton that the Gilgit agent would in no case interfere in his internal administration. The Maharaja also volunteered to connect Gilgit, Srinagar and Jammu with the British Indian telegraph system. After having obtained Kashmir's concurrence, the formal announcement of the appointment of Captain J. Biddulph as Officer on Special Duty in Gilgit was made on 22 September 1877. He was assigned the task of collecting information about the topography and resources of the territory beyond the Kashmir frontier and to extend the British influence among the tribal people by cultivating friendship with them.[17] Though Biddulph succeeded in keeping track of the Russian movements in Badakhshan, Afghan Turkestan and Kokand, he could not win the support of the Kashmir Durbar officials posted in Gilgit. Obviously, the Kashmir Durbar disparaged the foisting of a British agent on its territorial jurisdiction. The assault by Hunza and Yasin on Gakuch and Sher Kila on 28 October 1880 proved to be the proverbial last straw for the Gilgit agent. Finally, it was decided in July 1881 to withdraw the Gilgit agent, who was, however, reinstalled in 1888.

The year 1885 was marked by the despatch of two exploratory missions, one under Colonel William Lockhart,[18] the Deputy Quarter Master General of India, to survey the lands south of the Hindu Kush via Gilgit and Chitral, and the other under Ney Elias to Chinese Turkestan and the Pamirs. Meanwhile, the Defence Committee's recommendation for extending the Srinagar-Rawalpindi cart-road to Gilgit and Chitral,[19] had been approved by Dufferin. The new Commander-in-Chief, F. Roberts, even suggested, "We should have political control over the country around Chitral and Gilgit in order to secure the approaches to the former by the Dora pass and to the latter through Wakhan'.[20] The purpose of Lockhart's mission was to establish friendly relations with Chitral and Kafiristan and to obtain accurate information about the routes, passes and resources of the country lying below the Hindu Kush.[21] During 1885–86, he not only surveyed about 12,000 square miles of the territory of Gilgit, Chitral, Hunza, Taghdumbash Pamirs and all the important passes across the Hindu Kush,[22] but also secured the Chitral ruler Aman-ul-Mulk's promise to allow the passage of British troops through his territory in the event of a Russian attack from that side.[23] Lockhart wanted the British Indian government to develop Gilgit as the defensive nucleus of Dardistan and establish there a garrison of locally raised troops under a British commandant carrying out both the political and civil functions.[24] By May 1887, the Secretary in the Foreign Department (GOI) H.M. Durand, too had reached similar conclusions. By recommending the re-establishment of the Gilgit Agency with a garrison of Kashmir troops and local levies, Durand wanted the British Indian government to adopt a more active policy towards this northern frontier so that in the event of any difficulties with Russia, Kashmir would not be 'more or less shaky and inclined to hedge'.[25] It was in October 1887 that more clear directives reached the Resident in Kashmir regarding the revised policy of the Indian government about the frontier defence. He was informed:

> Time has come for establishing on the north-west frontier of Kashmir an effective political control, which will enable us to watch the passes of the Hindu Kush and the country beyond, and a military organization sufficient both to control the Chiefships over the border and also to check, in the event of war with Russia, any demonstration towards the passes not backed by a respectable force.[26]

The need to strengthen Kashmir's hold over its frontier tributaries assumed urgency in view of a joint attack by Hunza and Nagar on Kashmir posts at Chaprot and Chalt in early 1888, and due to the Chinese links with Hunza. It was against this backdrop that Dufferin decided to depute Capt. A.G.A. Durand (younger brother of the Foreign Department Secretary, H.M. Durand) on a mission to Gilgit. He was required to 'report on the military position at Gilgit with reference to the recent tribal disturbances and to future possible complications with Russia, and to work out a scheme for rendering Gilgit secure without the aid of British troops and for dominating from Gilgit, through the Kashmir forces, the country upto the Hindu Kush; thus rendering Kashmir territory thoroughly secure against attack...'[27] On his return in late 1888, Capt. Durand proposed the re-establishment of a political agency at Gilgit and stationing of about 2,000 Kashmir troops there to function under four British officers.[28] He also recommended the improvement of the Kashmir-Gilgit-Chitral road and the early completion of the telegraph line to Gilgit.[29] It was proposed that the local chiefs of Chitral, Punyal, Hunza and Nagar be encouraged by grant of increased subsidies to them.[30] Lord Lansdowne, who succeeded to the Viceroyalty in December 1888, accepted Captain Durand's recommendations. He was optimistic of success this time, 'We shall have the upper Hindu Kush well watched, and the countries to the south of it closed against interference from China and Russia and Afghanistan, and we shall get some useful information from the districts beyond. We shall be protected against any *coup de main* from the northward and we may eventually succeed in establishing our influence in Kafiristan also. We shall thereby have provided for a really important part of our scheme of frontier defence, and at small cost to ourselves'.[31] Accordingly, Captain Algernon Durand alongwith two British officers Dr. Robertson and Lt. Manners Smith arrived in Kashmir in April 1889 to make preparations for their journey to Gilgit.[32] Durand who left Srinagar for Gilgit in mid-June 1889, was formally appointed as the British Agent at Gilgit in July 1889. Durand's position was quite different from that of his predecessor Biddulph, as a British Resident had already been appointed in Kashmir in 1885. Now the virtual administration of Dardistan (Gilgit, Hunza, Nagar, Astor, Yasin, Chitral, Gor, Chilas, Darel, Tangir and Kohistan) passed into the British hands through their agent, though the Kashmir Governor at Gilgit continued to exercise civil authority over this territory.[33]

Lord Curzon, who before assuming the Viceroyalty of India (1899–1905) travelled extensively in this frontier even up to the Pamirs, was convinced that protection of the British colonial state in India required dominance of the strategic Himalayan neighbourhood to stem any incursions by other interested regional state actors like Russia and China. The idea of developing 'buffer states' formed an integral part of this strategic philosophy and formed the crux of efforts to develop an integrated external policy paradigm during his term in India. Curzon sought to 'extend the idea of "buffer zones"—whether notionally independent like Afghanistan or under British control like the North West Frontier Province—to India's strategic Himalayan neighbourhood in a proactive but composite manner'.[34]

India's Gateway to Central Asia

Enjoying a central position in the network of overland caravan routes that were linked to the Silk Route, the Karakoram Himalayan region acted as an important gateway to Central Asia. However, during the nineteenth and early twentieth centuries, the extent and pattern of Indo-Central Asian exchanges were influenced on the one hand by the state of diplomatic relations between the three empires—Britain, Russia and China, and on the other hand by the level of influence exercised by the Dogra rulers of Jammu and Kashmir. The Dogra rulers followed a consistent and proactive policy in this strategic frontier, which facilitated their direct and friendly communication with the neighbouring Central Asian chiefs and also to keep abreast with the rapidly changing course of events in the neighbourhood.

The extent and pattern of overland Indo-Central Asian trade carried through Ladakh fluctuated from time to time due to the changing political situation in Central Asia. During the years 1919 to 1931, goods worth about Rs 285 lakhs were exported through Ladakh to Xinjiang, whereas merchandise valued at about Rs 330 lakhs was imported from Xinjiang into Ladakh and India during the same period.[35] However, the Indo-Central Asian trade through Ladakh, which scaled an unprecedented height of over Rs 68 lakhs during the financial year 1920–21,[36] finally ceased to flow since 1949 following the communist take over of Xinjiang and its subsequent closure to outside traffic. The Government of India and the then Prime Minister Jawaharlal Nehru were acutely conscious of the importance of the frontier areas of Gilgit and Baltistan as India's only overland corridor to Central Asia. That explains why Nehru as the first prime minister of India wrote a letter on 20 August 1948 to UNCIP Mission, which was finalising the ceasefire agreement, asserting the authority of Jammu and Kashmir over the 'northern areas'. He wrote:

> The authority of Govt. of J&K over the sparsely populated and mountainous region of the J&K State has not been challenged or disturbed, except by roving bands of hostiles or in some places like Skardu. The Commission resolution, as you agreed in the course of our interview on the 18th, does not deal with the problem of administration or defence in this large area. We desire that, after Pakistan troops and irregulars have withdrawn from the territory, the responsibility for the administration of the evacuated areas should revert to the Government of Jammu and Kashmir and that for defence to us. We must be free to maintain garrisons at selected points in this area for the dual purpose of preventing the incursion of tribesmen, who obey no authority and to guard the main trade routes from the state into Central Asia.[37]

Responding to Prime Minister's letter, the Chairman of the UN Commission for India and Pakistan (UNCIP), Joseph Korbel in his letter of 25 August 1948 to Jawaharlal Nehru assured that the matter of defence administration of Northern Areas 'could be considered in the implementation of 13 August 1948 resolution'.[38] However, the Commission later resorted to subterfuge declaring that it would study the situation in those areas. Bringing this fact to the notice of the Security Council, one of the Commission members, Dr. Chyle submitted a minority report on 1 December 1948, giving some interesting insights on the inner workings of the UNCIP, which in his view was 'heavily influenced in its decisions and judgements by Western strategic considerations and designs'.[39]

When the UNCIP asked the UN Secretary General to send to Kashmir 40 military observers and a military adviser, the then Security Council Chairman, M. Jacob Malik (of USSR) called a meeting of the Council and proposed to draw these military observers from all the five countries represented on the Commission—Argentina, Belgium, Colombia, USA and Czechoslovakia. Malik's suggestion was brushed aside and foreign military observers drawn from the armies of USA, Canada, Australia, Belgium and Norway were despatched to Kashmir.[40] The US member on UNCIP mission had brought with himself military and political experts and a large staff of field workers to make on the spot survey of this strategically important area in order to assess its value for military and air bases. It may be recalled that at the height of the cold war era, the USA and Britain were obsessed with the rise of Communist China and Soviet Union near the borders of Pakistan and India, and were desperately looking for a foothold in this strategic frontier of Gilgit to monitor the developments in Xinjiang, Tibet, Afghanistan and Central Asia.

Dr. Oldrich Chyle, the Czechoslovak member of the UNCIP in his minority report[41] blamed the Commission for the failure of its efforts for reaching a 'positive solution of the whole problem'.[42] He pointed out, '...cancellation of the joint Indo-Pakistan political conference; the unauthorised proposal for arbitration; the disclosure of the secret memorandum on arbitration to the Governments of the United States of America and Britain before being presented to the governments of India and Pakistan, and its use by President Truman and Prime Minister Attlee, in a synchronised action for a public interventionary pressure',[43] were the principal factors responsible for undermining the mediatory role of the Commission. Dr. Chyle while referring to the problem of 'Northern Areas' stated that in the resolutions of both, 13 August 1948 and 5 January 1949, '...the Commission entirely omitted to concern itself with the situation in strategically very important territory to the north of Kashmir'.[44] By the time the Commission decided to study the situation, the Pakistan army contrary to the provisions of the 13 August 1948 resolution, had occupied these strategic regions and presented the Commission with a *fait accompli*. Dr. Chyle in his report to the Security Council explained:

> The Government of India submitted a reservation in respect of the resolution, dated 13 August 1948, concerning its right to administer the northern territory, of which, on the basis of the military situation then existing, it maintained, that it could not be put on par with the 'Azad territory' to the west of Kashmir. Instead of rectifying the aforesaid shortcoming by a formal rider to the resolution—which in fact the Government of Pakistan sanctioned only five months later the Commission replied by a letter dated 25 August 1948 in which it acknowledged to the Prime Minister of the Indian Government the receipt of his reservation and stated that 'the question might be examined when the resolution of 13 August 1948 was implemented....
>
> While the Government of India made on 20 August 1948 a clear reservation regarding the position in the Northern Area—two weeks after that, Government of Pakistan, in its aforesaid notification made a claim of great consequences mortgaging practically the political future of vast territories in the State of Jammu and Kashmir where the Pakistan army or forces under its High Command could have gained upper hand.
>
> The Commission claims that at that time had no practical means to its disposal to verify the factual situation in the different parts of the State of Jammu and Kashmir. This is, however, exactly the reason why the Commission should have been firm at least on the legal ground

> and not to have taken course to empty promises.
>
> The Commission facing later on the materially changed situation in the Northern Areas is bound to admit that while the reservation of the government of India of 20 August 1948 may be legally valid, it is physically impossible to implement it.[45]

The Government of India did not pursue the matter to its logical conclusion.

Strategic Advantages of Pakistan

Whereas after 1947, Ladakh including Kargil has been a province of Indian state of Jammu and Kashmir, a sizeable portion of the Ladakh territory (Baltistan, Raskam, Shimshal and Muztagh valley and Aksai Chin) besides the Gilgit region have been under the occupation of Pakistan and China after 1947–48. Out of a total area of 2,22,236 sq. km, only about 45.6 per cent, i.e. 1,01,387 sq. km remains in the Indian State of Jammu and Kashmir. The Kashmir valley covers only 7.2 per cent, i.e. 15,948 sq. kms. Ladakh covers 59,146 sq kms constituting 26.6% and Jammu region spans about 26,293 sq km, i.e. about 11.8 per cent. The Pakistan occupied territory of Jammu and Kashmir covers 35.1 per cent, i.e. 86,000 sq km of the total territory (13,297 sq km in AJK and 73,000 sq km in Gilgit-Baltistan). China occupies about 37,555 sq km (16.9 per cent) in Aksai Chin and 5,180 sq kms (2.3 per cent), which was ceded by Pakistan in Shimshal, Muztagh and Raskam area to China in 1963. Issues like Pakistan's aggression in Ladakh and Baltistan in 1947–48, the heroic resistance by Ladakhis, the repulsion of Pak invasion, and the circumstances leading to non-recovery of Baltistan/Skardo from Pak control, became even more relevant during the Pakistani intrusion in Kargil in 1999, which further underscores the need for effective security management of the Indian Himalayan frontiers. The Kargil crisis unleashed latent nationalism and fierce patriotism throughout India cutting across regional, religious and caste barriers. The people of India demonstrated exemplary courage, deep-rooted sense of national unity and commitment to the territorial integrity of India and resolve and willingness to sacrifice their lives for defending the Himalayan borders of India. It also brought into focus the vulnerability of Indian positions in Kashmir along the Srinagar-Dras-Kargil-Leh strategic highway, due to Pakistan controlling the heights overlooking this highway. It only shows, how unprepared the Indian military and foreign office authorities were, at the time of delineating, first the Ceasefire Line (CFL) in 1949 and later the Line of Control (LoC) in 1971–72. Successive political leaders have allowed the battle to be lost at the negotiating table even if it was won at the battlefront at high human costs. The ground reality is that India continues to suffer huge material and human losses in defending the Siachen glacier, which is easily accessible to Pak forces from their base in Khapalu, Skardo. Similarly, the Dras-Kargil road is vulnerable to even sniper fire by enemy forces, which are occupying the heights.

Even though Kashmir has been the focus of national and international attention during the past 65 years, PoK and Gilgit-Baltistan have eluded attention. This is mainly because this frontier area has been put behind an iron curtain by successive Pakistani governments. Pakistan took over the administration of this area enforcing Frontier Crimes Regulations (FCR). The Muslim Conference, which assumed power in POK in 1947 with Muzaffarabad as the capital of 'Azad Jammu and Kashmir', was not even allowed to open its branch in Gilgit-Baltistan region. Pak policy was to segregate this strategic area from POK both in name and in governance. In addition, by the Karachi Agreement of April 28, 1949, signed between Pakistan government, 'Azad Kashmir Government' and the Muslim Conference, Pakistan assumed full control over Gilgit and Baltistan region. There has been no representative from this region. Ever since, Pakistan's Federal Ministry of Kashmir Affairs has been directly administering the 'Northern Areas'. Even though the 1949 agreement became defunct after the promulgation of the 1974 Interim Constitution of POK by Z.A. Bhutto, Pakistan did not let 'Northern Areas' to be part of 'Azad Kashmir'. Moreover, when in July 1977, General Zia-ul-Haque promulgated martial law in Pakistan, he declared 'Northern Areas' as Martial Law Zone E. In early 1982, late General Zia-ul-Haque, the then President of Pakistan publicly announced that this area was never a part of Jammu and Kashmir State before 1947, evoking protests in Jammu and Kashmir on both sides of the LoC. In fact, late Sheikh Mohammad Abdullah, the then Chief Minister of Indian State of Jammu and Kashmir while addressing a huge May Day rally at Iqbal Park in Srinagar in May 1982 reiterated, '...the whole of PoK including Gilgit constitutes the territory of the State'. Subsequently, the state government issued a White Paper detailing the historical evidence of Gilgit-Baltistan area being part of Jammu and Kashmir.[46]

The draconian Frontier Crimes Regulation was replaced by the Northern Areas Governance Order of 1994 by late Prime Minister, Benazir Bhutto, which with some amendments was later renamed as The Legal Framework Order by President Musharraf in 2007.[47] In 2009, the Zardari government taking cognizance of the local demands for restoration of its original name, issued the Gilgit-Baltistan Empowerment and Self-Governance Order, in a bid to deflect criticism over human rights violations in the region.

The Gilgit-Baltistan region is a clear case of colonisation by Pakistan, having no representation in Pakistan's parliament. No local has ever been appointed to the post of Chief Secretary or the Police Chief, who are either Punjabis or Pathans. There has been deep resentment in the Gilgit-Baltistan region over the mal-treatment of Northern Light Infantry (NLI) soldiers by Pakistan, who were killed or injured during the Kargil war. Over 900 NLI troops are reported to have been killed and about 1,000 injured. The people of Gilgit and Baltistan retain bitter memories of Pakistan having refused to accept the dead bodies of NLI soldiers from the war front in Kargil. Composition of the NLI, which was earlier dominated by the Shias from 'Northern Areas', has now been drastically changed with the introduction of quotas for other Pak forces, particularly Punjabis and Pathans. Ambivalence in Pakistan's Kashmir policy is best reflected in its political and constitutional relationship with the region. While insisting that Jammu and Kashmir is disputed territory, Gilgit-Baltistan are neither included in the definition of territories of Pakistan as per its constitution of 1973 (Article 1), nor does the AJK Interim Constitution of 1974 define this area as under its administrative control.[48]

On 16 October 1990, two persons from 'Northern Areas' and one from Pak-occupied Kashmir filed a joint petition in the High Court of Azad Kashmir pleading, '...the Northern Areas are part of "Azad Jammu and Kashmir"', and their separation is illegal, which has resulted in depriving the residents of these areas from legitimate rights of representation in the 'Azad' Kashmir government, the assembly, the council and other institutions. The Pakistan government in its reply did not deny that these areas were part of the State of Jammu and Kashmir before 1947. After hearing arguments, a full bench of the AJK High Court in its judgement on 8 March 1993, declared that Gilgit-Baltistan are legally part of Kashmir and asked the 'Azad J&K Government' (AJK) to assume the administrative control of Northern Areas, and to set up the judicial set up there.[49] However, Islamabad ruled out the merger of 'Northern Areas' with 'AJK'. Ahmad Sadik, Secretary of the Ministry of Kashmir and Northern Affairs (KANA) reacted by stating, 'AJK government was responsible only for the administration of Azad Jammu and Kashmir. It had no jurisdiction in the Northern Areas'.[50] Pakistan, which challenged this verdict in the Supreme Court of 'Azad' Kashmir, did not deny that Northern Areas were part of the State of Jammu and Kashmir as on 14 August 1947. The Supreme Court gave its verdict in September 1994, ruling that 'Northern Areas' are part of the State of Jammu and Kashmir but are not part of 'Azad Jammu and Kashmir'.

Sino-Pak Axis: Implications for India

The Chinese occupation of Aksai Chin area of Ladakh, provides it with the vital link between Xinjiang and Tibet. Soon after the defeat of India by China in the 1962 war, China and Pakistan signed a border agreement in March 1963 following which Xinjiang's border with PoK was delineated and demarcated with Pakistan ceding about 5,180 sq. kms area in Shaksgam and Muztagh valleys of PoK to China. Though the Sino-Pak agreement of 1963 accepted and recognised that 'it did not affect the status of the territory of Jammu and Kashmir', both China and Pakistan went ahead with building the 1,330 km long Karakoram Highway. Now this highway is being expanded and rebuilt to make it an all-weather highway and an expressway. Railways, and oil/gas pipeline[51] are planned through it thereby giving immense strategic advantage to China in terms of speedy transport of its armaments and military forces, securing easy access to the sea, the resources of Central Asian Republics, the energy supplies from West Asia, etc. China is also working on the construction of 19 tunnels in Gilgit-Baltistan,[52] besides helping Pakistan in the expansion of its network of feeder roads and bridges in this area. China has already built feeder roads through Shaksgam, Raskam and Shimshal valley (ceded by Pakistan to China in 1963), linking Gilgit to Khotan, which is connected to Qinghai province of China through the Qinghai-Golmud Highway.[53] Currently, over 60 Chinese public and private sector companies and over 10,000 Chinese personnel are reported to be working on about 250 projects in PoK and Gilgit-Baltistan.[54] China is also reportedly laying a fibre optic cable line linking Rawalpindi, the military headquarters of Pakistan, Gilgit-Baltistan and PoK with Xinjiang.[55] There have also been reports of China establishing its Consulate in Gilgit.

Here it would be instructive to reflect upon the Chinese experience in Xinjiang. While this remote northwestern region has been brought closer to China's mainland both by air, rail and road network, notwithstanding the enormous distance and inhospitable deserts between the two regions, China has also connected Xinjiang with PoK by building the strategic Karakoram Highway. Besides, China has extended Xinjiang's overland transportation links through Kashgar and Yarkand to Central Asia-Kyrgyzstan via the Osh, Turgart and Karamik passes; Tajikistan via Osh, Sary Tash and Murgab; Kazakhstan by building Alashanko, Khorgos and several other border ports. This road network is being linked to the Karakoram Highway running through PoK, so that these Central Asian countries secure access to the sea via Pakistan. Besides, cis-Pamir mountain territories of Karategin, Garm, Tajikabad, Jirghital, Darvaz and Tavildara in Tajikistan are being linked to Kyrgyzstan and the Kashgar region of

Xinjiang by the formation of a transport and economic corridor through Suhov and Kyzyl Su (in Kyrgyzstan), through Sary Tash in the Pamirs, and via Irkeshtam to Kashgar in China. This 750 km route is reported to have no high passes or inaccessible sections and can be operational throughout the year. There already exist roads on some sections of this route and the whole section from Dushanbe to Kashgar (750 to 800 kms.) has asphalt or pebble stone cover. Only a few sections of this road are reported to be unmetalled. This transport network known as the Euro-Asian highway will embrace the Pamirs and connect the Central Asian countries of Tajikistan, Kazakhstan and Kyrgyzstan with Xinjiang and Pakistan though the Karakoram Highway. This author during his field visit to the Gorno-Badakhshan region of Tajikistan in October 2011 travelled upto Langar, the last village in Wakhan and found that a road is being planned towards Gilgit and Pakistan via Langar (in Tajik Wakhan). The Tajikistan government, thus, seeks to secure access to South Asia through this corridor. China is already well entrenched in Tajikistan, in terms of its monopoly over trade, cargo transportation, political influence and road connectivity. Both these developments pose a serious security challenge to India besides cutting off its overland access to Afghanistan and Central Asia.

The latest Chinese plans to build a Special Economic Zone (SEZ) in Kashgar and connect it by a major rail network with Pakistan through PoK, along the Karakoram Highway, poses a serious security challenge to India in Kashmir and Ladakh. Pakistan's President Asif Ali Zardari during his visit to China in early July 2010 urged the China Northern Railways Corporation (CNR) to form a consortium with the Pakistan Railways to concretise the planned rail link between Kashgar and Pakistan.[56] Pakistan's Ambassador to China, Masood Khan in an interview given last year disclosed that the 'pre-feasibility work on the proposed railway line has been completed'.[57] This railway line, which runs from Kashgar in Xinjiang through PoK and onwards will join Pakistan's railway network at Havelian. Work on the Chinese side is almost completed and train is already running upto Kashgar and Khotan. China is also providing 500 million dollars for repaving and widening the Karakoram Highway.[58] Recent reports suggest that China has taken over the management of Gwadar port in Pakistan.[59] As such, China is implementing its plans to have direct access to the Arabian Sea through the Karakoram Highway and Pakistan. China is thus, not only securing an alternative route for its trade with West Asia, but is also augmenting its airborne and naval capabilities, thereby posing serious threat to the security of India.

China has a close and strategic, defence and intelligence sharing mechanism with Pakistan. China's defence minister visited Pakistan on 20 May 2010. This visit was followed by the visit of Pakistan's Army Chief, General Ashfaq Kayani to Beijing in June 2010, during which, both countries reaffirmed their strategic and security ties. Both China and Pakistan conducted joint anti-terror military exercise in the Ningxia Hui Autonomous Region to coincide with the sensitive first anniversary of Urumqi riots. The drill named 'Friendship 2010', which was conducted between 1–11 July 2010, was the third of its kind and it took place against the backdrop of heightened security measures in Xinjiang.

That China opened a new high attitude airport at Ngari in Tibet (4,300 metres) claimed to be the highest airport in the world facing Ladakh, demonstrates China's determination to integrate and consolidate its physical presence in outlying provinces of Xinjiang and Tibet, by building quick and efficient means of air communication. This will not only facilitate direct flights between Ngari, Lhasa, Southern Xinjiang and mainland China, but also pose a direct threat to Indian positions in Ladakh. For the past few years, China has been making incursions in the Ladakh sector, particularly in Demchok, Chushul, Spanggur, Hot Springs, Depsang and the Pangong Lake areas. Time, the prevailing geopolitical situation and the rapidly expanding physical reach of China even within Central Asia, Pakistan, PoK and Gilgit-Baltistan, are all going to work to the advantage of China. This situation calls for bold and out of the box solution to the vexed problem.

Conclusion

Due to its geo-strategic location abutting the borders of China, Pakistan and Afghanistan, and being in close proximity to Central Asia, Jammu and Kashmir is the strategic frontier of India in its north. Jammu and Kashmir offers India the only overland access to Central Asia. However, independent India lost the opportunity of having direct overland access to Xinjiang and Central Asia after it allowed Pakistan to illegally occupy the vital strategic territory of Gilgit-Baltistan and PoK in 1947–48. India needs to safeguard its interests in this strategic frontier by securing direct overland access to Afghanistan, Tajikistan and other Central Asian countries, and to ensure that it has a peaceful, tranquil and benign neighbourhood. Taking into account the concept of strategic frontiers, India needs to determine the area within which no hostile or potentially hostile focus is to be allowed to exist or develop, so that its national security is not threatened.

Both houses of the Indian parliament unanimously passed a resolution on 22 February 1994 expressing deep concern over 'Pakistan's role in imparting training to the terrorists in camps located in Pakistan and occupied Kashmir, the supply of weapons and funds, assistance in infiltration of trained militants including foreign mercenaries into Jammu and Kashmir with the avowed purpose of creating disharmony and subversion'. The resolution firmly declared:

(a) The State of Jammu and Kashmir has been, is and shall be an integral part of India and any attempts to separate it from the rest of the country will be resisted by all necessary means;
(b) India has the will and capacity to firmly counter all designs against its unity, sovereignty and terrorial integrity;
(c) Pakistan must vacate the areas of the Indian State of Jammu and Kashmir, which they have occupied through aggression.

The parliament of India has thus, laid the policy framework in terms of retrieving its lost territory in Jammu and Kashmir. Time has come for India to take all necessary steps to reverse its adversarial situation and free itself of the strategic bottleneck it has been facing due to the continued illegal occupation of PoK and Gilgit-Baltistan by Pakistan. This will enhance the prestige and stature of India among the neighbouring countries of Central Asia and Afghanistan, which are eagerly looking forward to see India playing a balancing role vis-à-vis China in the region. It will finally resolve the vexed Kashmir problem, which has been sapping the energy, resources, morale and profile of the Indian nation state, both within and outside the country. By doing so, India will secure its appropriate international position proportionate to its size, population, geopolitical position, economy and status of a rising power.

NOTES

1. K. Warikoo, *Himalayan Frontiers of India*, Routledge, London and New York, 2009, p. viii.
2. The region boasts some of the highest peaks in the world–700 peaks above 6,000 metres, 160 peaks above 7,000 metres and 5 above 8,000 metres (K-2=8,611 metres, Nangaparbat=8,126 metres and Gasherbrum=8,035 metres).
3. In February 2012, 18 Shias from Gilgit-Baltistan were target-killed by gunmen, after they were identified while travelling in a bus. In August 2012 at least 22 Shia passengers, who were going to their homes in Gilgit from Rawalpindi were gunned down at Mansehra area of Khyber-Pakhtoonkhwa after they were identified as Shias and brought down from their buses. See Anita Joshua, '22 Shias shot dead in Mansehra.' *The Hindu*, August 17, 2012, p. 13.
At least 16 people were killed and over 50 other injured in sectarian violence in Gilgit-Baltistan in early April 2012. See, 'Day after 16 people killed in Sectarian violence, curfew imposed in Gilgit.' *Indian Express*, April 5, 2012, p. 12.
4. P. Stobdan, 'Gilgit and Baltistan: The Historical Dimension,' in Virendra Gupta and

Alok Bansal (eds.), *Pakistan Occupied Kashmir: The Untold Story*, Manas, New Delhi, 2007, p. 48.

5. See Maloy Krishna Dhar, 'An Itinerant's Journey through Pakistan occupied Kashmir,' in Virendra Gupta and Alok Bansal, Ibid., pp. 134-136.
6. For further details see, K. Warikoo, no. 1, pp. 14-35.
7. Ibid., p. 16.
8. Ibid., p. 17.
9. Ibid.
10. G.J. Alder, *British India's Northern Frontier, 1865-95*, Longmans, London, 1963, p. 11.
11. E.E. Knight, *Where Three Empires Meet*, Longmans, London, 1905, pp. 288, 290-91.
12. K. Warikoo, no. 1, p. 19.
13. See Memo of conversation held at Madhopore on November 17 and 18, 1876 between the Viceroy and Maharaja of Kashmir, *Foreign Secret*, July 1877, National Archives of India, pp. 34-60B.
14. Ibid.
15. Lytton to Salisbury (Secretary of State), June 11, 1877, cited in Ibid.
16. Ibid.
17. T.H. Thomson, Secretary, Foreign Department, Government of India to J. Bidduph, September 22, 1877, *Foreign. Pol. A.*, February 1878, National Archives of India, pp. 117–137.
18. He was later elevated to be the Commander-in-Chief of India.
19. See D.K. Ghosh, *Kashmir in Transition, 1885-93*, World Press, Calcutta, 1975, p. 159.
20. Cited in Ibid., p.160.
21. Government of India to the Secretary of State, August 28, 1885, *Foreign Sec. F.*, December 1885, National Archives of India, pp. 118–24.
22. G.J. Alder, no. 10, p. 155.
23. *Foreign Sec. F.*, January 1888, National Archives of India, p. 115–18.
24. Ibid.
25. Cited in D.K. Ghosh, no. 19, p. 166.
26. H.M. Durand to the Resident in Kashmir, October 18, 1887, *Foreign Sec. F.*, January 1888, National Archives of India, no. 23.
27. H.M. Durand to Capt A.G.A. Durand, June 22, 1888.
28. A.G.A. Durand, *Report on the Present Military Situation in Gilgit*. Simla, 5 December 1888, p. 14.
29. Ibid., p. 45.
30. Ibid., p. 14.
31. Cited in G.J. Alder, no. 10, pp. 163–164.
32. A.G.A. Durand, *Making of a Frontier*, London, 1899, p. 120.
33. Ibid., p. 198.
34. Vijay Kapur, 'India's Himalayan Frontiers', in K. Warikoo, no. 1, p. 49.
35. K. Warikoo, no. 1, p. 8.
36. Ibid.
37. *Reports of United Nations Commission for India and Pakistan (June 1948 to December 1948)*, Ministry of External Affairs, New Delhi, pp. 17–18.
38. Ibid.
39. P.N. Jalali, 'The Gilgit Dimension of the Kashmir Frontier,' in K. Warikoo, no. 1, p. 45.
40. Vijay Kumar, *Anglo-American Plot Against Kashmir*, People's Publishing House, Bombay, 1954, p. 95.

41. UN Security Council, S/1430/Add. 3, December 16, 1949.
42. Ibid., p. 2.
43. Ibid.
44. Ibid., p. 3.
45. Ibid., p. 3.
46. See *Statement of Facts on Gilgit, Hunza, Nagar, Yasin Punial, Chitral and Skardu*. J & K Government, Srinagar, p. 16.
47. Senge H. Sering, 'Constitutional Impasse in Gilgit-Baltistan (Jammu and Kashmir): The Fallout', *Strategic Analysis*, Vol. 34, No. 3, May 2010, p. 354.
48. M.A. Niazi, 'Northern Areas' Status: Forty five years of ambiguity', *Nation*, March 12 and 13, 1993, pp. 1, 4.
49. 'AJK High Court declares Northern Areas part of Kashmir.' *Pakistan Observer*, March 9, 1993.
50. 'Govt. Rules Out Merger of N. Areas with AJK.' *Frontier Post*, March 11, 1993.
51. For further details see, Senge H. Sering, *Expansion of the Karakoram Corridor*: Implications and Prospects, IDSA Occasional Paper No. 27, 2012, p. 64.
52. Ibid., p. 24.
53. Ibid., p. 10.
54. Ibid., p. 27.
55. See Saibal Dasgupta, 'Optic Fibre line to link China and Pak Military', *Times of India*, October 21, 2013, p. 20.
56. 'SEZ signals China-Pak Rail Link.' *Times of India*, July 8, 2010.
57. Anant Krishnan, 'China's POK rail link plan gain Traction.' *The Hindu*, September 2012, p. 4.
58. Ibid.
59. Rahul Datta, 'With Gwadar in kitty, China expands logistic', *The Pioneer*, February 3, 2013, pp. 1, 6.

Convoy of Chinese Cargo Trucks coming via Kyzylart Pass (Kyrgyzstan)-Karasu (Xinjiang)-Khorog-Darvoz-Dushanbe
Photo: K. Warikoo

Author standing at Kharog-Julandi-Murghab-Kulma-Osh Highway
Photo: K. Warikoo

Joint Tajikistan-China Cargo Terminal, Kharog
Photo: K. Warikoo

View from Langar, Wakhan (Tajik Badakhshan)
Photo: K. Warikoo

From the left: Prof. Voldosh of Khorogh, Headwoman of Langar with her husband, and Prof. K. Warikoo at Langar
Photo: K. Warikoo

8

The Karakoram-Himalayan Region

Geopolitical Perspective

Afsir Karim

The Hindu Kush, the Karakoram and the Western Himalayas were the arena of the 'Great Game' of the nineteenth century played between the British and Czarist Russia. This area is once again the arena of a new 'Great Game' initiated by American-Russian rivalry but carried forward and played in a different context by Pakistan—by introducing the Islamic card. Pakistan provided safe haven to the Taliban and the Al Qaeda after the American invasion of Afghanistan according to a well-calculated move to reestablish them in Afghanistan once the American forces had left the area. The geo-political and strategic arena of the new 'Great Game' of Pakistan extends from the Hindu Kush to the Karakoram-Western Himalayan region. In this game, the Gilgit-Baltistan area is an important focal point of China-Pakistan strategic agenda against India.

The US administration coined the term AfPak in the context of war in Afghanistan, reflecting that Afghanistan and Pakistan are inextricably linked by geography and ethnic affiliations. The linkage, however, extends beyond AfPak to other neighbouring tracts in South and Central Asia as well. A link in this chain that cannot be ignored is where the Karakoram and the Western Himalayas meet, a remote region, which is emerging as the new playground of fundamentalist forces. Pakistan is relocating a number of its indigenous terrorist groups to this area to create another epicentre of fundamentalism that would provide a safe haven for the Al

Qaeda and other transnational players of terrorism, far removed from prying eyes.

This region also provides an excellent springboard for the extremists to plan attacks, and send fighters to support insurgency in India and Afghanistan. They can, in fact, use the difficult mountainous terrain of this area to hide, train, and send fighters to support insurgency in any part of South and Central Asia. If the fundamentalist forces are allowed to assemble and regroup in the remote areas of the high Karakoram-Himalayan ranges, they will pose a catastrophic international security challenge very soon.

The heights of Gilgit-Baltistan region also serve as a springboard for Pakistani aggression directed towards Dras, Kargil and Ladakh.The road running from Gilgit to Skardu across the Indus river leads to Kargil and Ladakh, and in the north along the LoC, to Siachen via Khapalu. Routes from Gilgit via Babusar and Burzil pass provide easy avenues for infiltration and sneak attacks in Gurez valley and adjacent Karen area. Occupation of this region by Pakistan has put India at great disadvantage both strategically and tactically, since India has been denied access to Afghanistan and Central Asia. It has also increased its vulnerability to hostile forces that may attack targets in Kashmir, Kargil and Ladakh from their bases in this region.

Close cooperation between China and Pakistan through this area has great geo-strategic significance as it provides a short direct land route between these two countries. The Pakistan-China tie up here on the one hand and the rising tide of fundamentalist forces on the other, with its centre in Gilgit-Baltistan pose a serious threat to India and other neighbouring countries. Annexation of this area by Pakistan in 1947 provided great strategic advantages to Pakistan. It created a direct link with the Chinese provinces of Tibet and Xinjiang, and the Central Asian Republics. Pakistan also blocked all land routes between India and these regions, which has proved to be a long-term major strategic set back. India has yet to find a way to get around this strategic bottleneck.

This region shares common borders with the Wakhan valley of Afghanistan in the northwest, China's Xinjiang region in the northeast, Jammu and Kashmir in the south and southeast, the Pakistani occupied area of Kashmir in its south and Pakistan's North-West Frontier Province to the west. The area is thinly populated. As per the last census (1998), the population of Gilgit-Baltistan was about 870,347 spread thinly over an area of about 72,971 square km^2.

The Gilgit-Baltistan region is located in the shadow of high mountain ranges of the Karakoram and the Himalayas, with the Pamirs to its north, and the Hindu Kush to its west. Mount Godwin-Austen or K2 the second highest mountain in the world and three of the world's longest glaciers outside the Polar regions are found in this region. Despite the ruggedness and desolation of the terrain, this area has been a bone of contention between the Russian and British empires in the19th century because it was a concealed gateway to South Asia. China was a minor player at that stage, but in the present era, China is a major player in this region. Gilgit-Baltistan is a disputed area which is a bone of contention between India, Pakistan and China.

Construction of the Karakoram Highway (KKH) in 1986 brought about a major change in strategic landscape of the region in favour of China and Pakistan. It not only provided a direct land link between these two countries, but also gave China access to the Indian Ocean region via a short land route. China has since been involved in development of Gwadar port in Baluchistan and enjoys all civil and military port facilities there.

The Karakoram Highway, aptly known as the Friendship Highway in China, was built jointly by Pakistan and China and it took 20 years to complete. It connected China and Pakistan across the Karakoram mountains through the Khunjerab Pass, at an altitude of 4,693m (15,397ft). The KKH is also called National Highway 35 (NH35) and due to its high elevation and the difficult terrain in which it was constructed, it is also referred to as the 'Ninth Wonder of the World'.

The KKH generally follows the alignment of the ancient Silk Road and runs approximately 1,300 km from Kashgar in Xinjiang to Islamabad. The Pakistani part of the highway is 806 km long; it starts from Havelian, near Abbottabad. An extension of the highway was also constructed to meet the Grand Trunk Road at Hassan Abdal, near Islamabad. The KKH crosses the Indus river at Thakot, and continues along the river until Bunji, where the Gilgit river joins the Indus. The highway passes via Gilgit, and goes to Nagar and Hunza, along the Hunza river. In this region, it passes through areas, which are within 250 km of China, Tajikistan, Afghanistan and Pakistan; and where three great mountain ranges, the Hindu Kush, the Karakoram and the Himalayas come very close to one another.

Political Status of Gilgit-Baltistan, 1947–2008

Gilgit-Baltistan was a part of erstwhile state of Jammu and Kashmir until Pakistan occupied this region in 1947. In 1935, the British Indian government coerced the Maharaja of Jammu and Kashmir to lease Gilgit

Wazarat the north of Indus and its dependencies to the British for a period of sixty years. It was, however, made clear in the lease agreement that the leased area would remain an integral part of Kashmir State. In 1947, the British government terminated the lease agreement of Gilgit Wazarat and the political agent of Gilgit handed over his charge to Brig. Ghansara Singh, the Governor appointed by Maharaja Hari Singh of Kashmir. However, Major William Brown, a British officer, who was the Commandant of the Gilgit Scouts, sabotaged the transition with the aim of facilitating the occupation of this region by Pakistan. Brown and his second in command, Captain A.S. Mathieson, staged a revolt by the Gilgit Scouts to take complete control of the Gilgit Agency and offered it to Pakistan.

Political unrest has, however, continued since the occupation of Gilgit-Baltistan by Pakistan in 1947, mainly because Pakistan not only neglected development of the area but also oppressed the people. In 1970, Pakistan created a new administrative unit, the 'Northern Areas' in the Gilgit agency, comprising the Baltistan district of the erstwhile Ladakh Wazarat, and the states of Hunza and Nagar. However, political protests started against Islamabad in 1971 when a political group called the Tanzeem-e-Millat (TM) started a political movement in Gilgit despite the ban on political activities. In 1974, Johar Ali Khan, the founder of the party, called a strike for repealing the Frontier Crime Regulations (FCRs) and for the grant of basic rights to the people. The agitation turned violent, the Deputy Commissioner ordered the Gilgit Scouts to open fire on the agitators and disperse them. The Scouts refused to open fire on fellow Shias and it was reported that the Deputy Commissioner opened fire himself, killing one agitator. The crowd dispersed but Johar Ali Khan and 15 others were arrested and sent to jail. Later a large crowd raided the jail and freed them.

Following these violent incidents, a notification disbanding the Gilgit Scouts for refusing to fire on the agitators was issued. The disbanding of Gilgit Scouts left a large number of Shias out of job; this alienated the community further and triggered the demands of an independent state. Law and order in 'Northern Areas' generally deteriorated further as the nationalist movement seeking independence, gradually gained momentum. The rise of violence was directly related to Pakistan taking recourse to brutal suppression of Shias; this triggered sectarian violence in a region where Sunnis, Shias and Ismailis so far coexisted without any confrontation.

The main demand of the Gilgit-Baltistan United Movement (GBUM) has been an autonomous status of the area comprising Gilgit and Baltistan. According to the GBUM, the region became independent in November 1947. When the suzerainty of the Dogra rulers of the Kashmir ceased, people never opted for Pakistan and it was occupied by force. The GBUM demanded that the Gilgit-Baltistan region be declared an independent state called 'Republic of Gilgit-Baltistan' and that the Legislative Council should be given the status of an 'Independent Constituent Assembly' and be given rights granted to the existing 'Azad Kashmir Legislative Assembly'.

The Balawaristan National Front (BNF), another political party has been demanding independence of an even larger entity called Balawaristan that would include the regions of Baltistan and Ladakh (including Kargil) as part of Balawaristan. Sometimes Chitral was also included in the new entity. The BNF was formed on 30 July 1992 under the leadership of Nawaz Khan Naji. Abdul Hamid Khan, Mohammad Rafiq, Shujaat Ali and Engineer Akbar Jan were active members of this organisation.

The party demanded a sovereign and independent Republic of Balawaristan comprising of three provinces and made people aware that they have been deprived of all rights by Pakistan, which had illegally occupied the area in violation of recognised international laws or principles. It condemned and deplored the method of Pakistani aggressors and chalked out a programme to demand their rights and freedom. In April 1993, the BNF gathered support of all political groups of this region and formed a platform against the Pakistan government. During this period, the situation became tense as people from both Shia and Sunni sects were attacking each other at the instigation of Pakistani agents. The BNP brought various political factions together and the formation of an alliance called Muttahida Mahaz was announced. On 23 March 1994, an ultimatum was given and a protest meeting was held on 24 March 1994, which was dispersed by the Pakistani forces. In April 1994, a large public gathering in Shahi polo ground in Gilgit sent a strong message to the Pakistan government, which now announced another package 'Northern Areas' Legal Framework Order 1994'. However, this package was rejected by the Mahaz.

Until October 1994, political parties were banned here. However, the Benazir Bhutto government allowed political parties of Pakistan to extend their activities to the 'Northern Areas' (NA) and set up branches there in 1994. The Pakistan Peoples Party (PPP), the Pakistan Muslim League (PML), the Muttahida Qaumi Party of Altaf Hussain, the Jamaat-e-Islami and the Tehrik-e-Jaffria Pakistan (TJP), a Shia party, opened branches in the 'Northern Areas'. The Inter-Services Intelligence (ISI) on the other hand encouraged the Sipah-e-Sahaba Pakistan (SSP), a Sunni extremist party, which has been campaigning for the declaration of the Shias as anti-Muslim, to expand its activities in the NA to counter the activities of the TJP.

The NA was ruled directly from Islamabad by the Minister of State for Kashmir and Northern Areas Affairs with the help of six officers, the Chief Executive Officer (CEO), the Commissioner, the Deputy Commissioner, and the Inspector-General of Police (IGP), the Judicial Commissioner and the Chief Engineer, Public Works – all deputed from outside. While the posts of the CEO and Chief Engineer were generally filled by serving or retired army officers, the other posts were filled by officers taken on deputation from Punjab or the NWFP. There was no right of appeal against the judgements of the Judicial Commissioner; even the Pakistan Supreme Court had no jurisdiction over him.

Pakistan's military remained the arbiter of the Kashmir policy; it did not allow delineation of the region's constitutional status. As a result, the NA were not included in any development schemes and the region made little progress. Unlike the other part called 'Azad' Kashmir, the NA remained under the Legal Framework Order (LFO) issued in 1994, an administrative instrument of suppression and denial of basic rights. Many observers believed that the main reason behind denial of basic rights was that the NA was a Shia-majority area under the Sunni dominated Pakistan.

Despite a clear verdict by the Supreme court of Pakistan directing Islamabad to extend fundamental rights to the NA, Pakistan made no move to do so and the region continued to be ruled from Islamabad through the Federal Ministry for Kashmir Affairs and Northern Areas (KANA). The Northern Areas Legislative Council (NALC), the region's elected legislature, remained without power, and civil and military bureaucrats administered the region.

Islamabad encouraged Sunni groups to exploit the local Shias and harass them. The Sunni cliques were first inducted for promoting sectarian strife during General Zia-ul-Haq's regime resulting in anti-Shia violence and Shia-Sunni clashes in the region. Under General Pervez Musharraf, the military-Sunni groups continued suppressing the Shias besides promoting Sunni extremism.

All movements demanding autonomy or independence were brutally suppressed by the army and the NA were governed under the Frontier Crime Regulations (FCR) framed by the British for the people for criminal tribes of the areas bordering Afghanistan. The people were not given passports and were not allowed to travel or migrate abroad. Every resident had to report to the local police station once a month and all movements from one village to another had to be reported to the police. Collective fines were imposed on entire villages for crimes or any law violated by any individual of the village. It is obvious that Pakistan held this area by brute force and gave no rights to the people because of the fear that they will secede from Pakistan.

No Pakistan government took any concrete steps to address the wider issues of development and the lack of empowerment of the people of the NA. This situation created great discontent and gave a fillip to extremist groups who focused on their jihadi goals. Moreover, Musharraf's cynical use of the Shias as gun fodder during Kargil war created bitterness against Pakistan's military regime. He actually left them to die on the heights of Kargil and even their dead bodies were not collected after the war so they could not even be given a decent burial at home.

Change in Status, 2009

A major change was announced in 2009 in the status of NA, it was given a new name and identity called 'Gilgit-Baltistan Autonomous Region'. The Pakistan Cabinet approved a self-governance reforms package for the NA aimed at giving it internal autonomy besides changing its nomenclature. The people were now given the right to elect members for the National Assembly and were permitted to take active part in the national affairs of Pakistan.

Prime Minister Syed Yusuf Raza Gilani while addressing a press conference announced that the 'Gilgit Baltistan Empowerment and Self Governance Order 2009' would replace the earlier 'Northern Areas' Legal Framework Order 1994'. The prime minister revealed that a high-powered committee under the chairmanship of the minister for KANA, prepared the reforms package with a view to providing autonomy to the area. Giving its salient features, Gilani said 'the Gilgit-Baltistan Assembly will formulate its own Rules of Procedures, while legislation on various subjects pertinent to governance will be done by the Council and Assembly in their respective jurisdiction'. He said the area would be given full rights as 'Azad Jammu and Kashmir' (known to us as PoK); however, it could not be given provincial status as per the Constitution. Regarding any impact of this change on the UN, Gilani said both Foreign Office and the 'Azad' Kashmir President had been taken on board before the decision'. In reply to a question, he said, '...the Council did not need parliament's shelter as it had its own Rules of Business, while Boundary Commission had already been constituted'.

The New Order has fifteen major parts. The new name of NA of Pakistan shall be Gilgit Baltistan as proposed under Article 2(f) and there shall be a Governor of Gilgit Baltistan as proposed under Article 20, who shall be appointed by the President of Pakistan. Until the election of the new Legislative Assembly, the federal minister for KANA would act as governor. Gilani clarified that the chief minister would be elected by the Gilgit Baltistan Legislative Assembly, who would be assisted by six ministers. There shall be a provision of two advisors to the chief minister; the Legislative assembly would have directly elected 24 members, besides six women and three technocrats.

Gilani said the decision shall empower the Gilgit Baltistan Council and Assembly to make laws. The subjects under which the Assembly shall now have power to make laws have been increased from 49 to 61 while the Council shall have 55 subjects. In order to empower the Council and the Assembly on financial matters, there shall be a Council Consolidated Fund under article 54, and Gilgit Baltistan Consolidated Fund under article 55. A detailed item wise budget shall be presented before the Gilgit Baltistan Assembly as being practised in Pakistan and shall be accordingly voted upon as suggested in article 56.

The Chief Judge of Supreme Appellate Court shall be appointed by the chairman of the Council on the advice of the governor and other judges shall be appointed by the chairman on the advice of the governor after seeking views of the Chief Judge, he added. The Chief Judge and Judges of the Chief Court shall be appointed by the Chairman of the Council on the advice of the governor on the same pattern as is being practised in AJK. The number of judges has been increased from three to five and the tenure of the present judges of the Supreme Judiciary has been protected in the draft.

Gilani said, another step to empower the people of the areas, is the establishment of Gilgit Baltistan Public Service Commission and Gilgit Baltistan Services under Articles 80 and 81. He stated that Auditor General Gilgit Baltistan would be appointed by the governor on the advice of the council as is the case in AJK (PoK). A Chief Election Commissioner under Article 82 as well as Auditor General besides emergency provisions under article 83 and 87 respectively would be appointed.

What benefits the new arrangements will give to people of area will be known after the actual functional arrangements come into being. Besides being a move to placate the people of the region, it is deft political decision that this area will no longer be part of the disputed territory of Kashmir, but a part of Pakistan, and this is a part of the new 'Great Game' Pakistan is playing in this area.

The New 'Great Game'

The relocation of several religious Sunni organisations in various parts of occupied Kashmir and the motivation behind giving a new political status to NA is a move to establish complete control over the area besides separating this area from J&K. It is also á signal that this region will not figure in talks or agreements between India and Pakistan on J&K. This area plays a crucial role in the new 'Great Game' that Pakistan is playing in the region; however, the arena of Pakistan's new 'Great Game' extends to the entire J&K state and far beyond.

Pakistan is fast turning into the most dangerous place with a civil war brewing, the Al Qaeda, and the Tehrik-e-Taliban controlling almost two thirds of the country where the writ of the Pakistan government does not run. Moreover, the army and the ISI are independent power centres that do not always obey the government. The problems of Pakistan are multiplying as homegrown terrorists are launching operations everywhere from their local hideouts. The country is divided between a strong military and weak civilian government, ethnic factions and Sunni-Shiites adding to the growing threat to stability and security of the country.

Pakistan is walking a tight rope by pursuing a policy of fighting the local Taliban in some sectors while allowing certain groups to regroup and continue attacking the American led Coalition forces across the border in Afghanistan. Pakistan, which has about 100 nuclear warheads, wants to convey a plain message to the US administration that they cannot hope to stabilise Afghanistan without Pakistan's help. However, since Pakistan is under attack now by indigenous Taliban factions and there are sharp ethnic, religious and regional differences, the situation has become rather precarious for the country and it may lead to violent fragmentation of the society.

The US has, however, still failed to accept the fact that ties between Pakistan and the Afghan Taliban are of a permanent nature and their mutual dependence will continue regardless of the American pressures and agenda. Pakistan is supporting the cause of Islamic groups and its leaders, like Gulbeddin Hekmatyar as it has a long-term strategic aim of establishing a client regime in Afghanistan.

Pakistan's policy is based largely on the pattern of the 'Great Game' of proxy wars and sabotage played in this region between Great Britain and Russia who competed for bigger strategic space in Afghanistan and Central Asia in the 19th century. Pakistan proclaims that it needs to create strategic depth to defend itself better against India and believes that this can only be achieved if a pro-Pakistan Islamic regime is established in Afghanistan.

However, there has been a long-standing border dispute between Pakistan and Afghanistan on the status of the Durand Line drawn by the British in 1893. The differences may continue to vitiate the relations between the two countries regardless of the dispensation there. Afghanistan's frontier with British India was drawn by Sir Mortimer Durand in 1893 and agreed upon by representatives of both governments. The border, which was given the name Durand Line divided Pashtun tribes living in the area with the aim of reducing their potential of creating trouble in British India.

Autonomous tribal agencies were controlled by British political officers; these agencies were carved out with the help of tribal chieftains whose loyalty was generally bought through liberal doles. The British only used force to put down serious uprisings in the tribal areas; otherwise, they generally left the tribes alone. After independence, Pakistani leaders assumed that they would inherit the British frontier and Afghan policy. Once the British left the subcontinent, Afghanistan demanded a Pashtun state, which would include the Pashtun tribes living on both sides of Afghanistan and Pakistan border creating a serious rift between the two countries.

There was a demand of an independent Baluch state linking Baluch areas in Pakistan with Iran and a small strip of Baluch territory in Afghanistan but these demands subsided once Pakistan initiated the jihadi movement against the Soviet army with support from America and Saudi Arabia. When the Soviet army eventually withdrew from Afghanistan, the US left Afghanistan in a state of flux and quit the scene; Pakistan and the Mujahedeen took full advantage of this situation and created the Taliban regime. However, this dispensation failed to establish peace mainly due to faction fighting and assumed an aggressive and dangerous fundamentalist shape that threatened the entire region.

Pakistan's quest for strategic depth can translate into reality only if there is a client state in Afghanistan. However, the Taliban regime failed to give a concrete shape to Pakistan's aim of achieving strategic depth against India because the Al Qaeda sponsored attack on America, and the American invasion after 9/11 in 2001 changed the entire scenario and power equations in the region. Pakistan became a close ally of America and the Taliban regime was dismantled. How the Taliban staged a second come back can be best described by the double game Pakistan has been playing as part of its larger great game that is still unfolding in this region. Pakistan knows that the most reliable ally in this game would be a Taliban regime and not an American supported democracy.

Once Afghanistan is tamed, the fundamentalist irregular forces trained by the Pakistan army would be able to operate against Indian troops from the Gilgit-Baltistan region with impunity to unsettle India in Kashmir. To achieve this, Pakistan fosters the Taliban as an asset; in this game plan they must not be abandoned and clandestine support for them must continue regardless of American interests. Notwithstanding the Pakistani offensive in the tribal areas and show of support for the Americans, Pakistan was loath to attack its strategic assets like Siraj Haqqani and even Hakimullah Mohssud, with an eye on them in the event of the US/NATO withdrawal from Afghanistan. The hazards of double-dealing and the problems it can create are evident even if this game is played with great deftness.

Conclusion

Although Pakistan is engaged in a peace process with India, it continues to play the old game of cross-border terrorism. India's geographic depth, growing economic clout and military might rules out any military adventure but that does not stop Pakistan from carrying on proxy war and asymmetrical warfare to keep India's military off balance.

The decision to continue to back or tolerate the Taliban is part of Pakistan's grand design for positioning itself as a major player in a contemporary version of the 'Great Game' in the region, Pakistan may fight the local Taliban, but will never give up the option of supporting Islamist insurgents in Kashmir or stop covert support to the Afghan fundamentalist forces. Pakistan is unlikely to relent unless it finds the cost of this policy unbearable. Moreover, the unfolding events show that US and the West have succumbed to Pak stratagems of co-opting the Taliban in the future set up in Afghanistan.

Any accord between Pakistan and India or between Pakistan and Afghanistan seems remote. Pakistan's meddling in Kashmir and Afghanistan is unlikely to stop although an end to this interference is an essential requirement for durable peace in the region. The conflict in Afghanistan and the fundamentalist geostrategic thrust in South Asia are the key elements of the new 'Great Game' being played by Pakistan. Much like the old 'Great Game', of the 19th century, the world's powerful nations are once again involved in South and Central Asia. Today the United States is playing a leading role, but Russia and the new regional powers such as China, Iran, India and Pakistan have entered the arena in a big way. In the meanwhile the transnational oil corporations are also pursuing their own agendas on the sidelines. Despite the high profile offensive against the local Taliban, Pakistan has been making all diplomatic, military and clandestine efforts to push forward its basic agenda of establishing a pliant regime in Afghanistan.

Pakistan is trying to get the maximum benefit as an ally of the USA to further its strategic interests in South Asia and Afghanistan, even though it has been entangled in terrorism and civil strife. Pakistan is still pursuing a policy that would allow the local Taliban to mount insurgent attacks across the border on coalition forces, to show Americans as well as Afghan leaders that they cannot stabilise the country without Pakistan's help.

Pakistan's role as the staging ground for operations against the Soviet forces in Afghanistan between 1979 and 1988 is well known, but it must be realised that Pakistan's aim of extending its influence into Afghanistan was the main motivation of Pakistan for joining this war. Pakistan's policies toward Afghanistan were largely influenced by its perceptions of creating strategic depth against India and a need to open a secure route to oil rich Central Asia. Concerns about security against India and ambitions to push its strategic frontier westward have got Pakistan involved in a new 'Great Game' of intrigues and espionage much like the original 'Great Game'.

The Pakistan army is reluctant to take any action against the Afghan Taliban, whom they see as assets against growing Indian influence in Afghanistan. Its operations in South Waziristan are directed against the 'foreigners', mainly Uzbeks, Chechens and Arabs who the local tribes have refused to hand over to the army according to the regional code of honor of defending guests.

Disparate militant groups that evolved into Pakistani Tehrik-e-Taliban though distinct from their Afghan counterpart, are led by individuals such as Nek Muhammad, a well known veteran of the Afghan war and a sworn enemy of the US presence in Afghanistan. The abolition of administrative institutions, such as the office of the Political Agents that served as the federal government's link with the tribal *maliks* (chiefs), has worsened the situation. Pakistan is in the midst of a political storm that is challenging its ability to maintain cohesion within the country or stopping an Islamic revolution from looming large on the horizon. Pakistan has an endemic problem of ethnic and sectarian violence but the threat from a well-armed and organised Islamist terrorist groups now pushing for *Sharia* laws adds a new and more dangerous dimension to the country's security.

The Pakistan army understands the threat posed by jihadis to the country, but also sees them as allies and a force that can provide a favourable dispensation in Afghanistan and help in continuing the so-called *jihad* in Jammu and Kashmir. The Pakistan army's efforts to roll back *Tehrik-e-Taliban* have shown mixed results and many western observers believe that the effort is half-hearted as the ISI and the Pakistan army are still helping the Afghan Taliban.

Pakistan refuses to break the fundamentalist strangle hold of the Deobandi and Wahhabi terrorist groups; they have full freedom to continue operations in Afghanistan and Kashmir. New outfits created by the ISI and Deobandi-Wahhabi *Maulanas* were responsible for the rise of various radical groups in Pakistan who in league with *Tehrik-e-Taliban,* are now threatening the very existence of Pakistan by a destructive internal war.

9

Political and Democratic Process in Gilgit-Baltistan

Paul Beersmans

Gilgit and Baltistan are situated in the northwest of Jammu and Kashmir, with a surface area of over 70,000 sq km, which is almost one third of the total surface area of Jammu and Kashmir. It has a population of about two million, which is totally Muslim. These areas are under the control of Pakistan.

Gilgit, the western part of the 'Northern Areas', was 'liberated' by the rebellious Gilgit Scouts, which were composed of locally recruited soldiers and were under the command of a British officer, Major W. A. Brown. On 1 November 1947 they put the Governor of Gilgit, Ghansara Singh, the highest representative of Maharaja Hari Singh of Jammu and Kashmir, in jail and declared Gilgit independent with a War Council assuming power. The British officers supported the rebels but it is not clear if their attitude was due to personal security considerations, due to their sympathy with the rebels or due to secret orders that they had received from the British government to keep under control at any price this observation post overlooking the former Soviet Union. A few days later, the War Council decided to use the services of an administrative officer from the newly established Muslim country, Pakistan. On 16 November 1947, the Pakistani government sent a third class magistrate, a Naib Tehsildar as Political Agent to Gilgit Agency who, from then on, would have all decisive powers. From the first day, this Pakistani Political Agent managed to divide the local simpleton people into sects because the majority of the rebellious forces were Shias and Ismailis. After his death, Major W. A. Brown received a high Pakistani award for his 'heroic' deed.

The 'liberation' of Baltistan, the eastern part of the 'Northern Areas', would not be as easy as that of Gilgit. There the fighting continued until a cease-fire between India and Pakistan came into effect on 1 January 1949. On 27 July 1949, India and Pakistan accepted and signed the Truce Terms. The positions held at that moment by both sides would determine the course of the Ceasefire Line (CFL) and the extreme eastern border would become the Siachen glacier.

On 28 April 1949, the links between Gilgit-Baltistan and Pakistan were formalised through the signing of the 'Karachi Agreement' by the representatives of the government of Pakistan, of the Government of 'Azad' Kashmir and of the *Muslim Conference*. In this agreement, it was stipulated that 'all affairs of the Gilgit and Ladakh areas were under the control of Pakistan through their Political Agent in Gilgit'. One may note that Baltistan has been named in this agreement as Ladakh, because Baltistan, and the part of this area under Pakistani control, was then a district of Ladakh. Afterwards, the denomination of 'Northern Areas' was introduced to indicate the complete northern territory under Pakistani control. The Political Agent in Gilgit was the representative of the Pakistani government and had full powers. All the key positions in administration and in the power structure were in the hands of the Pakistan government and the 'Northern Areas' were separated from 'Azad' Kashmir. Here, Pakistan was in a difficult position. On the one hand, Pakistan had taken the stand that the 'Northern Areas' were under direct federal control, but on the other it had to maintain that the 'Northern Areas' still belonged to Jammu and Kashmir.

Until 1974, the administration of the 'Northern Areas' would be run under the Frontier Crimes Regulation Act. Through this act, fundamental rights were denied to the population of the 'Northern Areas'. Political activities and parties were not allowed and no democratic or judicial rights were granted. In 1971, Zulfiqar Ali Bhutto installed a 'Northern Areas Advisory Council'. As the name indicates, this Council had only advisory powers.

The 'Northern Areas' were meted out step-motherly treatment. There was very little investment in development, limited possibilities for education, poor medical infrastructure and no possibility to appeal against the verdicts pronounced by the sitting judge appointed by Pakistan. Important decisions were taken by Islamabad, over the head of the local population. On 2 March 1963, a bilateral agreement was signed through which a part of the 'Northern Areas' with a surface area of 5,180 sq. km was handed over by Pakistan to China and in the 1970s the Karakoram Highway was constructed straight across Gilgit.

Slowly but surely, this situation led to resistance among the population and in addition to this, religious differences came to surface. This needs some explanation. It is true that the population was almost completely Muslim but it belonged to different sects within Islam. Most of the population is Shia, but there are also Sunnis and Ismailis. The latter are concentrated in Hunza, Punyal, Ishkoman, Gupis and Yasin, the former states of this region. Their spiritual leader, Prince Agha Khan, lives in France. After the fall of the Shah in 1978, Iran became a Shia Islamic republic and naturally supported the fellow believers in the 'Northern Areas'. On the other hand, Pakistan is mainly a Sunni state and as a consequence, it has better relations with the Sunni population in the 'Northern Areas', ignoring the basic demands of the Shia and Ismaili Muslims.

The Shias strive for a fairer treatment, autonomy and demand for the fifth province while the Sunnis on the other hand favour a complete integration of the 'Northern Areas' into Pakistan. Agha Khan tried to calm down feelings and to form bridges between the two sects with his Ismaili followers, which has so far worked as a stabilising force. Nevertheless, trouble started in May 1988 when thousands of armed Sunnis came down to Gilgit city from neighbouring tribal areas and attacked the Shias living there with the full support of the then military dictator General Zia-ul-Haq. During these riots, it is estimated that over a hundred people, mostly Shias, were killed. Several Shia villages were totally destroyed, women were kidnapped and religious places and Shia mosques were burnt down. The Shias are convinced that General Zia-ul-Haq, had set the stage for sectarian tensions with the aim of strengthening his position in the 'Northern Areas', which was still considered to be of vital importance for the security of Pakistan. Since then Gilgit city has been ghettoised into Sunni and Shia areas. Followers of *Sipah-e-Sahaba Pakistan*, the Sunni militant wing in Pakistan, were supposted to have taken position in Qila-e-Jhangri, a fort in Gilgit city. The peace and tranquillity of Gilgit hung in balance as extremist Sunni and Shia organisations prepared to fight it out.

In 1990, some political activists of the 'Northern Areas' filed a petition at the High Court of 'Azad' Kashmir seeking the confirmation that the 'Northern Areas' were an integral part of Jammu and Kashmir and consequently that the authority over these areas had to be handed over to the Government of 'Azad' Kashmir. In March 1993, the High Court of Judicature of 'Azad' Jammu and Kashmir passed an extended and detailed verdict on Gilgit and Baltistan ('Northern Areas') stating that the 'Northern Areas' were without any doubt an integral part of Jammu and Kashmir and consequently the Government of Pakistan should revert the control of the administration of the 'Northern Areas' to the Government of 'Azad' Kashmir. The Government of Pakistan and the Government of 'Azad' Kashmir went into appeal against this verdict in the Supreme Court of 'Azad' Kashmir. This court confirmed that the 'Northern Areas' were an integral part of Jammu and Kashmir but declared that it did not have jurisdiction over the decision to revert the control of the administration to the Government of 'Azad' Kashmir, as these areas were under the direct control of Pakistan. As the next step, the case was transferred to the Supreme Court of Pakistan. This court of justice passed a very striking judgement. The court was of the opinion that it had no power to hear a petition that was related to a territory, which did not belong to Pakistan. After this round of juridical sparring, the situation of the 'Northern Areas' stood as follows:

1. they were a part of Jammu and Kashmir but they were neither a province of Pakistan nor a part of 'Azad' Kashmir;
2. they were ruled directly from Islamabad through a Northern Areas Council headed by Pakistan's Minister of Kashmir and Northern Areas Affairs (KANA);
3. an Islamabad-appointed Chief Executive, normally a retired Pakistani military officer, was to be the local administrative head;
4. the Northern Areas Council was to meet only when Pakistan's Minister of KANA convened it.

In order to meet up to a certain extent, the aspirations of the population of the 'Northern Areas', the Northern Areas Council Legal Framework Order was introduced in 1994. This legal framework stipulated among others:

1. there shall be a Chief Executive of the 'Northern Areas' who shall be the Federal Minister of KANA (Art. 3);
2. the Chief Executive shall appoint a Deputy Chief Executive from among the members of the Northern Areas Council (Art. 4);
3. the Chief Executive shall, in consultation with the Deputy Chief Executive, appoint, from amongst the members of the Northern Areas Council, not less than three and not more than five advisers at Gilgit (Art. 5);
4. the Northern Areas Council shall consist of 24 members—including the Deputy Chief Executive and the advisers, elected from the various districts in the 'Northern Areas'. Two women members shall

be nominated by the Chief Executive in consultation with the Council. The Chief Executive shall be the Chairman (Art. 6).

The powers and functions of the Northern Areas Council were included in making the laws with respect to the municipal functions as may be specified by the Government of Pakistan, to suggest improvements in matters concerning administration of the 'Northern Areas', to advise the Provincial Government on local bodies, and to assign priorities for development schemes. (Article 17)

The Council and its members were required to declare (under oath of office) their true faith and allegiance to Pakistan and uphold the sovereignty and integrity of Pakistan, strive to preserve the Islamic Ideology, which is the basis for the creation of Pakistan, strive to preserve and to maintain religious/sectarian harmony in the 'Northern Areas', and not indulge in any activity prejudicial to this cause.

The Government of Pakistan governs Gilgit-Baltistan through the Federal Ministry of KANA. The executive head was the Chief Commissioner who was appointed by this Ministry and was only answerable to it. Gilgit-Baltistan, thus, remained totally under the bureaucratic rule of Islamabad. The people of Gilgit-Baltistan did not have any fundamental rights. The Judicial Commissioner had no jurisdiction to enforce these rights. He also had no say in the appointments and the transfers of subordinate court judges. The people of Gilgit-Baltistan had no say in deciding what laws should govern them. The KANA ministry exercises the powers of the provincial government for Gilgit-Baltistan and by notification, extends the laws of Pakistan and such amendments as it thinks fit to Gilgit-Baltistan. By a notification, the Civil Procedure Code was amended, taking away the powers of the civil courts to grant temporary injunctions against the government.

The Northern Areas Council was headed by the minister of KANA and met as and when called by the minister. The members could not convene a meeting. The relevant orders required that a meeting of the Council should be called every two and a half months. However, in practice, the minister did not convene meetings for months. The Council, in any case, had no real power. It could not form a government, could not legislate and had no say in the administration. It could not suggest development schemes.

The main function of the councillors seemed to be receiving dignitaries from Pakistan. The police in Gilgit-Baltistan have no separate prosecution mechanisms or crime branch nor is there a forensic laboratory. No newspaper is published in Gilgit-Baltistan. There are a few local language weeklies and monthlies, but these are printed elsewhere. Amir Hamza, a local high-ranking police officer and influential politician, was clearly not satisfied with these arrangements and he stated, 'Our Northern Areas Council is actually a municipal committee. It is a facade created by the Government of Pakistan where the Council members are given cars and rooms but no authority'.

In the meanwhile, a number of political parties came into being. Six political parties formed an umbrella organisation, the Gilgit Baltistan Democratic Alliance, demanding complete freedom from the occupation of Pakistan and an independent democratic government for the local indigenous people. These parties were: the Balawaristan National Front (Chairman - Abdul Hamid Khan); the Karakoram National Movement (Chairman - Mohammad Iqbal); the Gilgit-Baltistan United Movement (headed by Manzoor Hussain); the Bolor Research Forum (chaired by Amanullah Khan); the Bolor Labour Party (with Ehsan Ali as organiser) and the Progressive Youth Front (headed by Baba Jan). This alliance is of the opinion that there can be no solution until and unless the two million people of Gilgit-Baltistan are taken into confidence.

Other political parties in Gilgit-Baltistan are: the Pakistan Peoples Party (PPP) for the 'Northern Areas' (This party also exists in Pakistan and in 'Azad' Kashmir.); the Muthidda Qaumi Party strives for its own administration in the 'Northern Areas' without interference by the Pakistani bureaucracy; the United Kashmir People's National Party strives for a federal structure for the whole of Jammu and Kashmir. (This party also exists in 'Azad' Kashmir.); the Jammu and Kashmir Liberation Front, Gilgit-Baltistan. (This party also exists in 'Azad' Kashmir and strives for a united independent Jammu and Kashmir.); the Jammu and Kashmir National Liberation Front. (This party also exists in 'Azad' Kashmir); the Gilgit-Baltistan National Conference; the Jamaat-e-Islami, Northern Areas. (This party also exists in Pakistan and in 'Azad' Kashmir.)

Notwithstanding the efforts to calm down tensions by making some concessions, the situation in the 'Northern Areas' remains strained. When it was announced in 1996 that the Chitral Scouts and the Frontier Constabulary would be replaced by a new regiment named the 'Northern Areas' Scouts, there arose expectations of getting jobs. During the recruitment process for this regiment, it became clear that all plum jobs were allocated to Punjabis and Pakhtoons. The situation grew tense and the students of the government degree college called a strike. In the ensuing violence, which resulted in several deaths, many government offices, the government rest house, the houses of the non-local Judicial Commissioner and Deputy Commissioner, central post office and a police post were looted and burnt down. The Pakistani armed forces took over the administration and imposed curfew. In 1997, while the 50th birthday of Pakistan was celebrated in Pakistan as golden jubilee, the Balawaristan National Front and the Karakorum National Movement appealed to the people of the 'Northern Areas' not to participate in these festivities. They marked this day as a 'Black Jubilee'. As a result, hundreds of political leaders and workers were arrested under framed sedition charges and tortured. In 1998, an American tourist was killed and his wife injured seriously and although nobody claimed responsibility for this attack, it was assumed that the intention was to discourage tourists visiting the 'Northern Areas'. This could also be an attempt to internationalise the growing problems in Gilgit.

A Pakistani journalist described the general situation in the 'Northern Areas' as follows:

> Local sentiments are slowly turning against the way Islamabad governs the Northern Areas. Democracy has not arrived here. The whole region is governed by a Northern Areas Council which has no power at all and which is elected through a system similar to the 'Basic Democracies' method of Ayub Khan. Like many other areas of the country there is a feeling of alienation. The Punjabis and the Pathans have all the good government jobs.

The People of Gilgit-Baltistan are deprived of their basic human rights and are treated in a step-motherly fashion by Pakistan. The situation can best be explained by the below mentioned facts:

1. There is no university in Gilgit-Baltistan.
2. There are no professional colleges. Only 12 high schools and two regional colleges with no post graduate facilities exist.
3. There is very low literacy rate. Adult literacy is 14 per cent for males and 3.5 per cent for women.
4. Even when local people are qualified, they find it extremely difficult to get government jobs. If after rigorous tests and favours they are employed, they are paid 25 per cent less than non-native entrants from Pakistan are paid.
5. There are no local daily papers, no local radio and television stations.
6. According to the most recently available data, there is just one doctor for 6,000 inhabitants.
7. Piped water supply is virtually non-existent and two third of the population has no electricity in an area where winters are extremely harsh.

In the political sphere, the population of the Gilgit-Baltistan puts forth the following demands.

1. The 'Northern Areas' should become an autonomous area or even an independent state with the possibility of electing its own legislative assembly and having a democratic structure, which could take decisions and run the administration.
2. Some pro-Pakistani parties demand self-rule in the 'Northern Areas'.
3. All Pakistani officials should be recalled.
4. All Pakistani forces should be withdrawn in accordance with the resolutions of the United Nations Commission for India and Pakistan.
5. The allotment of land to foreigners, including Pakistani nationals, should be revoked as this is in violation of the State Subject Rules.
6. All Pakistani laws, orders etc. should be cancelled.
7. No tax/duty should be collected from Gilgit-Baltistan until they get the right to take decisions through their democratically elected representatives.
8. Necessary steps be taken to solve the problem of unemployment and the local population should have priority to get the available jobs.
9. The material and social infrastructure: roads, power and water supply, medical facilities, education, etc. should be improved.
10. The 'Northern Areas' should have its own juridical system including an independent High Court and Supreme Court like any other independent and democratic country of the world.
11. Steps must be taken to exploit the mineral and natural resources of the 'Northern Areas' and to promote tourism-trekking and mountaineering. The benefit of these activities should go to the local population.
12. Talented students should get the chance to continue their studies in 'Azad' Kashmir or in Pakistan.

The Kargil war in 1999 further fuelled discontent in the 'Northern Areas'. The Northern Light Infantry, 70 per cent of which comprises of local people, was used for the Kargil incursions. The Northern Light Infantry suffered heavy casualties as the Shia and Ismaili soldiers were pushed into suicidal missions by Sunni officers from the 'mainland'. After the war, Pakistan refused to receive the bodies of the Northern Light Infantry soldiers and the Pakistani army initially refused to give any compensation.

Later, a meagre compensation was given to the families of those killed in the Kargil heights.

Unrest erupted in Gilgit in June 2001 and again two years later, following protests from Shia organisations over the Islamic textbooks that were introduced by the Ministry of Education of Pakistan as part of the curriculum for the schools in the region, ignoring Shia beliefs and practices. The Shias claimed that they were being forced to study the same books as those prescribed for Sunni students by the Sunni clergy, and not those approved by the Shia clergy. According to the Shia leaders, the textbooks promoted Sunni thought and values and were an attempt to fuel sectarian hatred between the two sects. Hundreds of schoolchildren boycotted classes and staged protest rallies in Gilgit but to little effect.

Following the recommendations of the Pakistan Supreme Court to extend legislative, financial and administrative powers alongside an independent judiciary with writ jurisdiction to the 'Northern Areas', the first Northern Areas Legislative Council was elected in 2000. It was granted powers to legislate on local matters and impose local taxes, but the overall structure was left unchanged with the result that Pakistan's Federal Minister of KANA continued to be the Chief Executive. When the rest of Pakistan voted for a new civilian government in the October 2002 elections, the population of the 'Northern Areas' remained outside the political process.

After the October 2004 elections for the Northern Areas Legislative Council, the Ministry of KANA failed even after five months to announce the Northern Areas Legislative Council cabinet required to be set up under the Northern Areas Legal Frame Work Order of 1994. The 24 directly elected members of the Legislative Council were administered the oath of their offices on 21 November 2004 for a five-year term and they elected the Deputy Chief Executive, Speaker and Deputy Speaker on 23 November 2004. However, the posts of six designated technocrats and six women from each district were not filled up.

Violence erupted again in January 2005, after some gunmen assassinated the popular Shia leader Syed Agha Zia-ud-Din. At least 14 people were killed and shoot-at-sight curfew was imposed to curb the unrest. According to Dr. Shabir Choudhary, these riots had many dimensions, some of which are as follows.

1. People are not happy about Pakistan's attempt to change the demography of the area. In complete violation of the State Subject Rules, Pakistan has settled thousands of Pakistanis, Afghans and other nationals in the area, and made the local people of Gilgit,

Chilas, Skardu and Gahkoch, a minority in their own area.

2. Non-local people control local administration, local business and transport, etc.
3. There are lack of opportunities, poor health and educational facilities and widespread unemployment and poverty.
4. Islamabad has its direct control over the region, which has no identity of its own and there is lack of liberal and democratic practices.
5. Introduction of Pakistani political parties and religious rivalries has torn apart the fabric of the local social and cultural traditions.
6. Attempts to introduce new textbooks ignoring the declared opposition of the people resulted in burning of schools and clashes, and the issue is still very much alive in the minds of the people.
7. Nationalist parties have increased their activities, and have challenged the legal and constitutional basis of the rule by Islamabad.

After a clash between Pakistan Rangers and students in October 2005 in Gilgit, in which at least 15 people were killed, the law and order situation has been deteriorating. In November 2005, the Human Rights Commission of Pakistan blamed the Government of Pakistan and the security forces for the volatile situation in Gilgit-Baltistan. The Commission demanded an immediate cease-fire by the Rangers who were clashing with the local population to curb continuing unrest, and an investigation by an independent judicial commission into the violence persisting in the city since January 2005. According to the International Crisis Group, between June 2004 and October 2005 as many as 100 people died in sectarian violence. Apparently, it was difficult to stop sectarian violence in the 'Northern Areas' and this was affecting the rest of Pakistan. The non-local administration in Gilgit showed a fundamental lack of understanding of the Shia majority of the population. As long as this does not change, violence can flare up again at any time.

In October 2007, Pakistani President Pervez Musharraf announced a package of reforms that would change the Northern Areas Legislative Council into the Northern Areas Legislative Assembly, devolving fiscal and legislative powers to locally elected politicians. The package would also allow for the election of a Chief Executive accountable to the assembly, but it would maintain federal control over the judiciary and the top executive post of Chairman. The region would continue to be administered under the Legal Framework Order rather than a constitutional framework like in 'Azad' Kashmir. Most groups, including the Jammu and Kashmir Liberation Front and the Gilgit-Baltistan United Movement rejected these moves as insufficient because they lacked a solid constitutional foundation and guarantees of judicial independence. The imposition of a state of emergency in Pakistan on 3 November 2007, led to widespread restrictions on political rights and Musharraf's planned reforms for the 'Northern Areas' were put off indefinitely.

On 29 August 2009, Syed Yousuf Reza Gilani, Prime Minister of Pakistan announced a package for Gilgit-Baltistan by terming it as self-governance and internal autonomy. The package was finalised by a high powered Committee under the Chairmanship of Qamar Zaman Kaira, from the Punjab province in Pakistan and a minister of KANA, Islamabad. Giving details of the Order's salient features, Gilani said that the Gilgit-Baltistan Assembly would formulate its own Rules of Procedures, while legislation on various subjects pertinent to governance would be done by the Council and Assembly in their respective jurisdiction. The Prime Minister of Pakistan stated that the area would be given full rights as 'Azad' Jammu and Kashmir (AJK), however, it could not be given provincial status as per the constitution. Regarding any impact on the UN document on Northern Areas, Gilani said that both Pakistan's Foreign Office and the AJK president had been taken onboard before the decision. Gilani stated,

1. There shall be a Governor of Gilgit-Baltistan as proposed under Article 20 and shall be appointed by the President of Pakistan.
2. The chief minister will be elected by the Gilgit-Baltistan Legislative Assembly, who will be assisted by six ministers.
3. Legislative Assembly will have directly elected 24 members, besides six women and three technocrats.
4. The decision will empower the Gilgit-Baltistan Council and Assembly to make laws. The subjects under which the Assembly shall now have the power to make law has been increased from 49 to 61, while the Council will have 55 subjects.
5. The Chief Judge of Supreme Appellate Court shall be appointed by the chairman of the Council on the advice of the government and other judges shall be appointed by the chairman on the advice of the governor after seeking views of the chief judge.
6. The Chief Judge and judges of the Chief Court shall be appointed by the chairman of the Council on the advice of the governor on the same pattern as it is being practised in AJK.
7. The number of judges has been increased from three to five.
8. An auditor general for Gilgit-Baltistan will be appointed by the governor on the advice of the Council as is the case in AJK.
9. There shall be an election commissioner under Article 82 as well as

an auditor general besides Emergency Provisions under Article 83 and 87 respectively.

10. A Boundary Commission shall be constituted.

Despite claims of granting self-governance or internal autonomy, it is the governor who has been vested with powers by the government of Pakistan. All the powers rest with the President of Pakistan as approving authority, the Prime Minister of Pakistan as Chairman of the council, both of whom are not elected by the people of Gilgit-Baltistan, and the Pakistani minister of KANA, who will be the governor and vice chairman of the Council. The governor and chairman of the Council are the supreme authority. The Gilgit-Baltistan Council would be chaired by the prime minister, who will not be elected by the people of Gilgit-Baltistan, while an un-elected governor, to be appointed by the president, would act as vice chairman of the Council. This arrangement is being seen as a major ploy to control the elected representatives of Gilgit-Baltistan, to use the new political set up as a rubber stamp to facilitate the construction of six mega dams including Diamer/Bhasha dam and to merge Gilgit-Baltistan into Pakistan by ignoring the will of its two million people.

It is for the very first time in the history of Pakistan that a serving federal minister has been appointed as governor of a political entity. Though the position of chief minister has been created, he would not be authorised to form his cabinet. The governor would form a cabinet, albeit with 'advice (which is not legally bound)' of the chief minister. The elected Legislative Assembly would not be able to elect the chief minister. He would not be elected by the Gilgit-Baltistan Legislative Assembly, but selected by the (governor and chairman) Council.

The Gilgit-Baltistan Legislative Assembly is not authorised to discuss a large number of vital issues related to governance of the region. The real power vests with the Gilgit-Baltistan Council, whose head will be the Pakistani Prime Minister as chairman, which will not be elected but selected like in the case of Pakistan occupied Kashmir.

Nobody from Gilgit-Baltistan was taken into confidence before issuing this order. Even the so-called Northern Areas Legislative Assembly (NALA) was not taken into confidence. Even the local chief executive of NALA, Meer Ghazanfar was not aware of this package before the announcement.

Although Gilgit-Baltistan will have its own Legislative Assembly, in practice, it would not have much work to do as the Council chaired by the Prime Minister of Pakistan and outnumbered by Pakistani members will take most decisions; and the Assembly will have no power to challenge any of the decisions. The Gilgit-Baltistan Assembly would not be allowed to discuss or legislate on issues relating to defence, security, interior and foreign affairs and finance. It will have no power to legislate against the principles of *Sharia*, and in case of any confusion, it can approach the Islamic Ideology Council of Pakistan. Furthermore, just like in Pakistan occupied Kashmir, no one will be allowed to legislate or work against the ideology of Pakistan.

However, one good thing about the package is that Pakistan has acknowledged that these areas are not 'Northern Areas' and that they should be called Gilgit-Baltistan. People have appreciated the change of name; otherwise, all those who matter have rejected the package and called it an eye-wash. Historically, Gilgit-Baltistan was not merged into Pakistan proper due to the concern that this might undermine the country's claim on Kashmir. It was not merged into 'Azad' Jammu and Kashmir , the southern most political entity within the Pakistan-controlled part of the former princely state of Jammu and Kashmir, because it could complicate the settlement of the Kashmir issue.

It is interesting to note that on the Indian side of the LoC, politicians and separatist leaders have the right to travel to all parts of Jammu and Kashmir state. Despite a large concentration of security forces, separatist leaders have used this right to travel to Ladakh and Jammu to conduct political activities. On the Pakistani side of the LoC, however, where apparently 'azad' people live, politicians and political activists have no right to travel to Gilgit-Baltistan areas. A few years back, the Prime Minister of 'Azad' Kashmir expressed his desire to visit Gilgit-Baltistan. He was told categorically by the Federal Ministry of KANA that he cannot go there, that he was Prime Minister of 'Azad' Kashmir and that Gilgit-Baltistan does not fall under his jurisdiction. In addition, the separatist leaders from the Indian side, while visiting the Pakistani side, were not allowed to visit the 'Northern Areas'.

Pakistan has constantly propagated the thesis of self-determination in Jammu and Kashmir State. Curiously, in Gilgit-Baltistan, Pakistan has suppressed, and continues to seek the total circumvention of this very principle. Although successive governments have pledged to review the situation in this area, being of vital strategic and economic importance to Pakistan given its location on the trading route between China and the Central Asian Republics, to date no affirmative action has been taken. This attitude confirms the popular perception in Gilgit-Baltistan that Pakistan is only interested in their territory and not at all in granting them their basic right of self-determination.

10

Gilgit-Baltistan of Jammu and Kashmir in Constitutional Limbo

Senge H. Sering

Gilgit-Baltistan is part of the Pakistani occupied Jammu & Kashmir (PoK), which has been under the absolute control of the federal government since 1949.[1] The strategically located region borders the Xinjiang region of China to the north; Afghanistan and Tajikistan to the north-west; Chitral to the west; Dir, Swat, Kohistan and Kaghan districts of NWFP of Pakistan to the south; Muzaffarabad (PoK) and the Kashmir Valley to its south-east, and Ladakh and Tibet to the east. Before the disintegration of J&K in 1947, Baltistan was part of Ladakh, and along with Gilgit, these regions were administered from Srinagar.[2]

In April 1949, Pakistan forced the leaders of 'Azad' Kashmir (AJK)[3] to temporarily hand over Gilgit-Baltistan and established direct federal rule there. The so-called Karachi Agreement, was signed by Sardar Ibrahim and Chaudhary G. Abbas of the All J&K Muslim Conference without the will and consultation of the local people.[4] The agreement transferred all affairs of Gilgit-Ladakh[5] to Islamabad and thereafter deprived the Kashmiri leadership of any future political, judicial and economic role in the region. It also led to the end of political autonomy. Even after making Gilgit-Baltistan a de facto part of Pakistan, the constitutional limbo continues as a policy to reap benefits from both the Kashmir dispute and for resource exploitation through illegal occupation. Local nationalists consider this agreement as a major hurdle to attaining constitutional and judicial rights for their region. Terming April 28 as a Black Day, the leaders of

Balawaristan National Front, All Parties National Alliance (APNA), and Jammu Kashmir National Awami Party (JKNAP) appealed to the government of Pakistan to annul the "unilateral and unconstitutional" agreement. They believe that history will not regard the Kashmiri leadership with any respect because of the Karachi Agreement by which Gilgit-Baltistan was ceded to Pakistan. Future generations in the state of Jammu and Kashmir in general and in Gilgit-Baltistan in particular would be hard pressed, to find the legal, moral and political authority on the basis of which Muhammad Ibrahim, the President of 'Azad' Jammu and Kashmir (AJK), Ch. Ghulam Abbas, President of *All Jammu and Kashmir Muslim Conference*, and M. A. Gurmani, Minister without Portfolio on behalf of Government of Pakistan structured this agreement and surrendered the land and people of Gilgit-Baltistan to an occupying force. The government of AJK and the Muslim Conference have had no representation in Gilgit-Baltistan till date and the surrender was without any reference to the people or leadership of Gilgit-Baltistan.

Until the end of the era of Field Marshal Ayub Khan, Gilgit-Baltistan was deemed as part of J&K under the temporary control of Pakistan owing to the fact that there were no channels of communication and transportation between the two parts of J&K. Islamabad, fearing the weakening of its diplomatic stance on Kashmir, refused to merge the region into Pakistan. So, Pakistan did not completely disconnect Gilgit-Baltistan from J&K, which could have allowed it to benefit from Muslim votes in case a plebiscite on the future status of J&K took place. Therefore, it continued to allow local leaders to represent the region in the Kashmir Council. For instance, Babu M. Ishaque of Shigar-Baltistan was a member of Kashmir Council in 1962. During the same time, political parties like the Ladakh-Baltistan United Front of Malika Baltistani and M. A. Changezi worked for the reunification of Baltistan with Ladakh. However, the legal status of Gilgit-Baltistan was left undefined in successive constitutions leading to transitory political arrangements. Today, the region is neither a part of Pakistan, nor an autonomous region or an independent country. Pakistan created a political vacuum and a law and order crisis, after the princely states and the time-tested administrative structures of Gilgit-Baltistan were abolished. While Islamabad failed to create modern political structures to delegate powers to the locals, the despotic military rulers continued to govern them with an iron fist. Yet again, it detached Gilgit-Baltistan from the rest of PoK (Muzaffarabad–Mirpur) and brought it under Islamabad's de facto control to enhance strategic depth and establish a contiguous border with China. Once the Karakoram Highway (KKH) was built, Gilgit-Baltistan provided Pakistan the geo-strategic bridge to cement its relations with China.

Until 1975, Pakistan administered Gilgit-Baltistan like a colony[6] under the draconian and inhumane Frontier Crimes Regulation (FCR),[7] which was finally abolished by Z.A. Bhutto during his visit to Gilgit. Originally it was a British law devised to control the tribal agencies, which was then extended to Gilgit-Baltistan. It has 64 articles which deny basic human rights. For instance, according to Article 40 of FCR, if a person is accused of a crime and remains at large, then his whole tribe will be held responsible for his supposedly wrong act and the government is allowed to punish any person of his tribe or the whole tribe on his account. This does not exempt even children and FIRs show two-year old children receiving jail sentences for crimes committed by their uncles and father. Again, if a crime is committed in a house, then the owner and residents of that house are punished without any further investigation. The FCR denies the right to appeal, and the decision of the Political Agent is final.

The aftermath of 1971 war forced India and Pakistan to sign the Simla Agreement formalising the Line of Control (LOC) which divides J&K. In effect the agreement allowed Pakistan to further integrate the parts of Kashmir under its control. It gave Islamabad the leverage to abolish the princely states and integrate them into the federal structure. The chiefships of Hunza and Nagar were thus integrated and amalgamated with Gilgit during that period. Islamabad annexed Chitral and merged it with NWFP during the same period. India protested against the annexation of Chitral but in vain. The agreement also allowed Pakistan to be accepted as a party to the J&K dispute, which was until then considered to be a dispute between the people of J&K and its Dogra ruler, who acceded to India. So the Kashmir dispute became even more complex with the involvement of three parties; the representatives of J&K, India and Pakistan, dealing either bilaterally or trilaterally on the matter and creating communication gap between disputing parties. When Bhutto came to power, he abolished the FCR and christened Gilgit-Baltistan as the 'Northern Areas' of Pakistan. From then onwards, Pakistan ruled Gilgit-Baltistan with ad hoc ordinances without constitutional cover. The term 'Northern Areas' was applied firstly to provide a pseudo-legal cover to Pakistan's occupation of the region and deny its historical association with J&K; secondly, to erase the pre-1947 political realities and indigenous identities, that are closer to Ladakh, Kashmir and Tibet, rather than other parts of contemporary Pakistan. Ethnic identities are seen as threat by the proponents of Pakistani nationalism, who are obsessed with the religion-based two-nation theory, and regard the ethnic and racial links of Gilgit-Baltistan with India as a threat to the social fabric of their country, because it seeks to evolve as a Muslim state. Further, the historical name also draws attention to the

UNCIP resolutions, which demand that Pakistan withdraw from these regions and reunite them with J&K. The fact that, UNCIP resolutions use the name Ladakh for modern-day Baltistan is also concealed by Pakistan. Gilgit-Baltistan comprises five different regions of Jammu and Kashmir, which are:

- Baltistan—a part of Ladakh Governorate;
- Gilgit Subdivision constitutes major part of Gilgit region including Gilgit town, which was retained by the Dogras and ruled directly from Srinagar;
- Gilgit Agency comprising of some parts of modern Gilgit, Ghizar and Diamer districts. It was leased to the British by the Maharaja of Kashmir in 1935 for sixty years and was returned to the Dogras before the partition of India;
- Gilgit Wazarat or the modern Astore district. When the British created the Gilgit agency, its part on the left bank of the Indus River, i.e., Astore valley became a Wazarat and remained part of the Kashmir province until 1947;
- Darel-Tangir, the tribal territories of Jammu and Kashmir, are part of the present day Diamer district.

When General Zia-ul-Haque imposed martial law, he extended it to Gilgit-Baltistan and went one step ahead of his predecessors in claiming the region as integral part of Pakistan. As a symbolic gesture, he allowed two members, one each from Gilgit and Baltistan, to represent the region in the national parliament. He also appointed one advisor from the region to the federal cabinet. It was during Zia's era that Pakistan made itself the principal party to the dispute, despite the fact that the UN requires Pakistan to vacate PoK to pave the way for a just solution to the Kashmir dispute. In 1948, Pakistan was given 90 days to vacate PoK, so that a decision and plebiscite could take place. Since Pakistan refused to withdraw from its occupied parts, the option of plebiscite became irrelevant and the political future of Gilgit-Baltistan, has since been in the doldrums.

When Benazir Bhutto came into power, she brought the people of J&K back into the limelight and claimed to promote the cause of Gilgit-Baltistan by passing the Northern Areas Governance Order of 1994,[8] which for the first time allowed the setting up of a local regional council. She posted Pakistani bureaucrats at Gilgit and ruled the region with some semblance of political representation. However, absolute authority remained in the hands of the Chief Executive of Gilgit-Baltistan, who was a Punjabi appointed from Islamabad. Further, Ministry of Kashmir Affairs and Northern Areas (KANA) had the absolute authority to advise, formulate and approve budget for the region. The same ordinance was renamed, as the Legal Framework Order of 2007 with some amendments by President Pervez Musharraf.[9] As international pressure grew for granting genuine political rights to the people of Gilgit-Baltistan, President Asif Zardari signed another ordinance—the Gilgit-Baltistan Empowerment and Self-Governance Order of 2009.[10] The term self governance in the current ordinance is a strategic move to defuse the pressure of international organisations, which are demanding genuine political and judicial rights for the people of Gilgit-Baltistan and also for appeasing the locals.[11]

Self-Governance Ordinance: Tool of Annexation

Liberal commentators say that the presidential ordinance is nothing but a continuation of ad-hoc ordinances without a constitutional cover.[12] It is basically a repacking of Legal Framework Order of 1994 with few amendments.[13] Political leaders from the Indian Kashmir and Muzaffarabad —the capital of Pakistan-controlled Kashmir—have termed the ordinance yet another violation by Pakistan of the UNCIP resolutions. For those among the natives of Gilgit-Baltistan who call themselves pro-Pakistani, the package is somehow disappointing. Their demand to see Gilgit-Baltistan as the fifth province of Pakistan and having representation in the Pakistani parliament remains unfulfilled. The officials justified the decision by stating that:

> ...the Northern Areas will have self-rule on the pattern of 'Azad' Kashmir. They will have province-like autonomy but will not constitutionally be a province. Had the Northern Areas been given the status of a constitutional province, there might have been a reaction from outside the border.[14]

Pakistan's Prime Minister Gillani echoed a similar opinion and said that, "since Gilgit-Baltistan is not a constitutional part of the country and is linked with the Kashmir issue, we can not give them representation in the parliament." Although 'elements from outside the border' and 'Kashmir issue' are presented as excuses by Pakistan for denying genuine autonomy to the people of Gilgit-Baltistan. In reality, it is Pakistan's own colonial design to maintain a firm grip on these regions which provide the only safe and stable link to China as well as Central Asian markets and natural resources.

The spokesperson of the Balawaristan National Front (BNF) reacted by saying that if Pakistan is claiming to follow the AJK model, then the people of Balawaristan (Pakistan occupied Gilgit-Baltistan) should also be allowed the reinstatement of State Subject Rule (SSR), as well as a penal code, a prime minister, president and a Supreme Court of their own. He pointed out that the constitution of Pakistan and UNCIP resolutions bar Pakistanis from interfering in the administrative affairs of Balawaristan. This package is a prelude to governor's rule and will only strengthen Pakistani colonialism since the Pakistani PM and governor will have a veto on any laws passed by the Legislative Assembly.[15] Manzoor Parwana, Chairman of GBUM was of the opinion that just like the Chairman of the Northern Areas Legislative Assembly, the governor will be an outsider, either from Punjab or NWFP, who will act like the Viceroy of Pakistan.[16] Similar concerns were expressed by Allama Shiekh Mirza Yusuf Hussain of Baltistan who believes that the self-governance ordinance, reflects Pakistan's dishonesty and lack of sincerity. He further says that federal political parties make false promises and have no genuine and sincere interest in benefitting the locals. "The people of Gilgit-Baltistan should have their own regional political party," he demanded.[17]

Liaqat Baloch of the Jamaat-i-Islami reacted by saying that instead of an elected chief minister (of the legislative assembly) who will be a local politician, the non-elected and non-local governor will have the authority to choose and appoint the ministers. The authority of the governor to hire and fire the ministers will only lead to horse-trading and political manipulation. It will make the members of the legislative assembly more loyal to the governor rather than to the chief minister who is supposedly the chief executive. The two-tier system, in which a minister is appointed by the governor, but is answerable to the chief minister, will only make the system more ambiguous and inefficient. Further, the annual budget would be presented before the Gilgit-Baltistan Assembly but will be approved by the bureaucrats of the KANA Division in Islamabad. The members of the Assembly will be visiting the KANA bureaucrats more often than attending the assembly sessions so as to ensure funds for their constituency and secure future terms in elections. Likewise, the federally dominated Gilgit-Baltistan Council will overshadow the locally elected Assembly. Out of 15 nominated members of the Gilgit-Baltistan Council, eight will be Pakistani citizens and an in-built majority status for Pakistani federal ministers will give Pakistan veto over local members of the council. Further, the governor is also the vice chairman and voting member of the council. This gives him extra powers and leverage over the chief minister and veto right in both cases, whether, the bill is passed by Assembly or the Council. These matters will restrict the legislative authority of the assembly.

In violation of the UNCIP resolutions, the Pakistani prime minister has been given certain rights in the ordinance, such as the right to appoint three advisors to the chief minister who will hold status of provincial ministers. In other provinces or AJK, the prime minister of Pakistan does not any have such rights. The prime minister of Pakistan as well as the governor will also have the veto power to overrule any bill passed by the legislative assembly. Pakistani officials also claim that the 'Northern Areas' fall under the direct jurisdiction of the president of Pakistan.

It is feared that the ordinance will extend the right of 'citizenship' to all those who possess property and assets as well as identity cards of Gilgit-Baltistan, which includes the Pakistani citizens who have been residing in Gilgit-Baltistan since 1947. This is a matter of concern for the locals as it will alter the ethnic and religious demography permanently and reduce opportunities for natives in jobs, service, quotas and social benefits. Further, the ordinance places certain conditions on the elected representatives and legislature of Gilgit-Baltistan. Islamabad, through the prime minister, governor and the council, will reserve the right to veto the bills. For instance, local laws and resolutions passed by assembly will have to comply with Pakistani laws. Further, the representatives must ensure the security, integrity, solidarity and strategic interests of Pakistan.[18] The oath format prescribed for political and judicial officers requires them to swear loyalty to Pakistan in writing, otherwise the privilege to hold such an office will be denied. This is a direct attack on the autonomy of the Assembly and a clear violation of UNCIP resolutions. Such restrictions are against the true spirit of delegating authority to local institutions and promoting democracy and freedom of speech and expression in Gilgit-Baltistan. It is also written in the order that the laws passed by the Assembly will be vetoed if they are in violation of the *Sunnah* and Quran. Since the Shias and Sunnis cannot agree on a clear single definition of *Sunnah*, such restrictions will become dividing factor and a cause of sectarian clashes. Further, because of disagreement over definitions of religious terms, Shia and Nurbakhshi texts will not find place in government educational syllabi and institutions.

Articles pertaining to mineral development, industries, electricity and water storage, school curricula, tourism, sanctioning of cinematography, forests and many others have been put under the Council list rather than the legislative assembly list. The right of veto over such issues provided to federal government through the Council will curb the authority of the local administration and developmental departments to perform and function. Further, as per the order, the ratio of gazetted officers from Pakistan who will serve in Gilgit-Baltistan is very high which will ensure the permanent hegemony of Pakistani officials over the local administration.[19]

Fearing the expansionist motives hidden in the fine print of the ordinance, India expressed its concerns regarding the design to annex these regions by appointing a Pakistani Governor. Further, India has demanded that genuine autonomy should be granted to the people of Gilgit-Baltistan. Jammu & Kashmir has its own constitution and no Indian law pertaining to J&K can be implemented unless approved by the J&K legislature. Local judicial matters are dealt under the Ranbir Singh Penal Code of J&K. India has allocated 24 seats in the Jammu and Kashmir Legislative Assembly for the representatives of AJK and Gilgit-Baltistan.[20] Further, according to the State Subject Rule, no citizen of India living outside J&K can purchase assets in J&K, which protects the local demography and ensures social security. This is a strong commitment by India to promote genuine autonomy for the people of J&K. On the other hand, similar laws that existed in Gilgit-Baltistan until 1974 have been abrogated which shows the lack of sincerity on the part of Pakistani rulers. Pakistan's behaviour towards the people of Gilgit-Baltistan is reflective of its strategy to occupy and oppress rather than be a benign benefactor.

Although the majority of the people of Gilgit-Baltistan are not happy with the self-governance package,[21] they hope that the newly created legislative assembly will amend the package to suit their needs. The new legislative assembly, has enabled the locals to pass laws favouring common people. However, if the Gilgit-Baltistan Council packed with Pakistani federal ministers restricts the powers of the Assembly, then the same Assembly may also become a source of tension and conflict. Shias and Sunnis will have to reconcile to the fact that the legislative assembly can work to benefit both communities. The ordinance is the first baby step taken by Pakistan in 63 years and all stakeholders should give the political process a chance to evolve and mature.

For most people in Pakistan, the Empowerment and Self-governance Presidential Order 2009 of Gilgit-Baltistan is a political gimmick that falls far short of granting the AJK-style self rule, which has been the longstanding demand of the people of Gilgit-Baltistan. Political leaders from Indian Kashmir and Muzaffarabad—the capital of Pakistan-controlled Kashmir—have also expressed their opposition to the ordinance. For instance, members of the 'Azad' Jammu & Kashmir (AJK) Legislative Assembly convened an urgent All Parties Conference (APC) on September 1, 2009 and demanded that Pakistan reunite Gilgit-Baltistan with AJK, which is currently under Pakistani control. Similarly, the retired Chief Justice of the AJK Supreme Court termed the ordinance a ploy to harm the Kashmir cause. The Chairman of the United Jehad Council, Syed Salahuddin has said that the ordinance is one more evidence of a weakened

Pakistani stand on the Kashmir issue. He feels that Pakistan is deliberately providing an excuse for India to convert the LoC into an international border and annex Kashmir, Jammu and Ladakh. Pro-Indian Kashmiri groups have termed the ordinance, as yet another violation of the UNCIP resolutions by Pakistan. Kashmiri politicians from AJK are dismayed since they were not consulted during the process; only inputs from the federal ministers of Pakistan were taken. Even the local people of Gilgit-Baltistan were kept in dark till the last moment. Representatives of the Pakistan Muslim League (Nawaz), an ally of the governing Peoples Party, are also offended at being ignored during the consultative sessions. The Pakistan Muslim League (Q) and National Front of Pakistan have opposed the ordinance and have termed it an executive order. The Human Rights Advocacy Network has opposed the ordinance since it fails to fulfil the genuine aspirations and demands of the people of Gilgit-Baltistan. The spokesperson of the Balawaristan National Front (BNF) said that if Pakistan claims to follow the AJK model, then the people of Gilgit-Baltistan should be allowed to elect their own president and prime minister. He is concerned that the Pakistan's prime minister would be the Chairman of Gilgit-Baltistan Council. He says that the constitution of Pakistan does not permit any Pakistani to hold such a post. Even the UNCIP resolutions bar Pakistanis from interfering in the administrative affairs of Gilgit-Baltistan.

The only good thing that came out of the ordinance was the renaming of 'Northern Areas' as Gilgit-Baltistan. The renaming has hyphenated Gilgit and Baltistan, which can be deciphered from the following paragraph:

> In fact, the [Jammu & Kashmir] State contains *at least* five distinct regions. First, there is Kashmir proper…Second, there is the State of Jammu...Third, there is the district Poonch: and *fourth, the very extensive tract of Ladakh and Baltistan*. Finally, in the northwest is the Gilgit region, comprising Gilgit, Gilgit Wazarat, Gilgit Agency, Yasin, Ishkuman, Hunza, Nagir and tribal territories.

The above quote from *Crisis of Kashmir* by Alistair Lamb affirms that Gilgit and Baltistan are parts of Jammu & Kashmir. Further, as the *fourth distinct region*, Baltistan was part of the Ladakh Wazarat (Governorate). These two regions were integrated into the Maharaja's domain a decade before the Dogras got control over Kashmir valley. The Baltis and Ladakhis have a shared ethnicity, language and traditions. The neighbouring Gilgit region, similar to Kashmir, is home to the Dardic people. Shina, a sister language of Kashmiri, is the lingua franca of the region and natives share their Shia religion with the inhabitants of Baltistan and Ladakh.

In short, the order establishes the Gilgit-Baltistan Legislative Assembly (GBLA) and Gilgit-Baltistan Council (GBC). It also creates the post of a chief minister; and a governor, who will represent the president of Pakistan, and function as the de facto ruler of Gilgit-Baltistan. Despite local demands, Pakistan has refused to give a parliamentary system, and a president and prime minister to the people of Gilgit-Baltistan. It refused Gilgit-Baltistan the representation in the Pakistani Parliament, the Council of Common Interests, the National Hydro-electric Board, the Indus River System Authority, the National Judicial Council and the National Finance Commission. The natives are denied access to Pakistani apex courts, and also continue to be denied their own high and supreme courts, a penal code and reinstatement of State Subject Rule (SSR).[22] Instead of the chief minister, the order vests all administrative, political and judicial authority with the governor, which makes him the supreme authority and makes the Assembly a toothless tiger. At best, the order legitimises Pakistan's occupation, and claims to grant political rights to the locals without changing the power equation.

The governor will appoint, transfer and fire heads of apex departments including the public service commission, election commission, boundary commission, judiciary, auditor general, commissioner of excise, taxation and revenue, chief judges of appellate and chief courts, regional cabinet members and advisors, the Inspector General of Police, chief secretary, departmental secretaries and directors, regional commissioner and deputy commissioners. Further, he is also authorised to approve the budget, dissolve the cabinet and assembly, and impose emergency. The governor resides in Islamabad instead of staying in Gilgit-Baltistan, which deprives the locals of access to his office.[23] He is also the Vice Chairman and voting member of the Council, and has veto right over the laws passed by both Assembly and the Council. The Council, with an in-built majority status for Pakistani federal ministers, can veto laws passed by the locally elected legislature.[24] More significantly, it is not the Assembly but the Council, which takes decisions relating to natural resources including minerals, forests, electricity, water reserves, industries, tourism, school curricula, religious affairs, cinematography etc.

A similar in-built majority is provided to the federal bureaucrats serving in Gilgit-Baltistan, which ensures their hegemony over the local administration.[25] The order makes no mention of a leader of the opposition, which means a disarrayed and friendly opposition with no checks and balances on government.[26] Called an eyewash by the locals, international rights organisations have rejected Governor's rule as a sinister design of Pakistan to complicate the constitutional impasse[27] and eventually annex this region.[28] In a reaction filled with angst, prominent pro-Pakistani politicians, including Miss Malika Baltistani, demand absolute independence for Gilgit-Baltistan.[29] Prominent constitutional experts of Pakistan, including Abid Hassan Minto, who supports a provisional parliamentary set up for Gilgit-Baltistan on the lines of AJK,[30] terms Pakistan's rule illegal. He objects to Pakistan's mega projects in Gilgit-Baltistan, which continue without the consent of locals and without payment of royalty and water usage compensation.

This is not the first time that Pakistani legal experts have admitted that Gilgit and Baltistan are not a constitutional part of Pakistan. For instance, in 1963, the Supreme Court of Pakistan declared Gilgit and Baltistan as part of Jammu & Kashmir, and lying outside the territories that are defined as parts of Pakistan. Similarly, in 1978, in response to a petition filed in the Lahore High Court, Justice Javed Iqbal described Gilgit-Baltistan as part of Jammu & Kashmir. In 1990, a petition was filed in the Lahore High Court which demanded merger of Gilgit-Baltistan with Pakistan, thereby extending all political and judicial rights to the locals of these regions, that other Pakistanis enjoy. The High Court summoned the Deputy Secretary of the Kashmir Affairs and Northern Areas (KANA) Division to represent the government of Pakistan. The secretary stated that as per Article 1 (2) of the constitution of the Islamic Republic of Pakistan, the Northern Areas (Gilgit-Baltistan) and 'Azad' Jammu Kashmir (AJK), are not a part of Pakistan. Both these regions are linked with the Kashmir dispute, and pending the final settlement of the Jammu & Kashmir dispute, Northern Areas cannot become part of Pakistan.

It was further, stated that granting of constitutional rights would become possible only if Pakistan unilaterally annexed the 'Northern Areas', which would weaken Pakistan's stand on Jammu & Kashmir issue. Such a unilateral annexation would be deemed illegal as per the UN resolutions. In the end, the deputy secretary falsely claimed that until the final settlement of the Jammu & Kashmir dispute, Pakistan is authorised by the United Nations Commission on India and Pakistan (UNCIP) to administer the 'Northern Areas'. The UN resolutions on Jammu & Kashmir clearly state that until the J&K dispute is resolved, the civil administration of Gilgit-Baltistan will lie with its native people and the defence matters will be the responsibility of the UNCIP.

Again, in September 1994, the Supreme Court of Pakistan held that while the Gilgit-Baltistan regions are 'not part of 'Azad' Kashmir as defined in the 'Azad' Kashmir Interim Constitution Act', these regions are indeed 'part of Jammu & Kashmir State' as it existed until 1948. Further, it also made clear that since the Gilgit-Baltistan regions are not part of Pakistan, the apex court does not have the legal authority to take up cases concerning these regions. As per the UN resolutions on Jammu & Kashmir, the judicial matters pertaining to the 'Northern Areas' are considered to be outside the purview of the Pakistani courts. This ironic situation is a judicial impasse since the people of Gilgit-Baltistan do not have their own courts to seek legal justice, nor do they have any access to the Pakistani courts, to question their disputed status.

Another petition regarding the status of 'Northern Areas', was filed in the Lahore High Court in 1998, and when the court summoned the representative of the government of Pakistan for clarification, he admitted that Gilgit and Baltistan were part of Jammu & Kashmir state and not Pakistan. He also admitted that Pakistan had not annexed the regions as generally perceived. Later the Attorney General of Pakistan clarified, that historically, the 'Northern Areas' remained part of J&K until 1947. The Chairperson of the Federal Ombudsman of Pakistan, Justice Usman Ali Shah also described these regions as part of Jammu & Kashmir and lying outside the Pakistani territorial boundary. In his statement, he made it clear that since Gilgit-Baltistan was not part of Pakistan, the government does not have the right to impose and collect tax from the people of the region.

In 1972, a landmark resolution passed by the Legislative Assembly of POK described the 'occupation' of Gilgit-Baltistan by Pakistan as unconstitutional and stressed that the government of POK should extend its political, administrative and judicial authority to these regions. Similarly, in 1995, representatives of the political parties from the Diamer district of the Northern Areas, desiring reunification of Gilgit-Baltistan and AJK, filed a petition in the Supreme Court of AJK stating that since Gilgit-Baltistan are part of Jammu and Kashmir, the government of AJK should resume control of the regions. The apex court of POK agreeing to the matter of the petition ordered the then government to 'resume' the administration of Gilgit-Baltistan. Further, the apex court ordered that the political, judicial and administrative services available to the people of AJK should be extended to Gilgit-Baltistan.

Under pressure from Islamabad, Prime Minister Sardar Qayyum Khan, refused to comply with the orders of his own Supreme Court. He, however, declared that Gilgit and Baltistan are an integral part of Jammu & Kashmir state and that with the approval of Pakistani government, POK will resume the civil administration. On the other hand, Pakistan refused to comply with the AJK Supreme Court ruling, claiming, that as per the Karachi Agreement of 1949, the leaders of J&K Muslim Conference had accepted Pakistan's administration of Gilgit-Baltistan.

In response to the decision of the AJK Supreme Court, Fauzia Saleem Abbass, a Balti leader from Islamabad, filed a petition in the Supreme Court of Pakistan in 1995. She demanded that the Pakistani government extend political and judicial rights to the people of Gilgit-Baltistan. The case remained pending until 1999, when finally the apex court agreed to discuss it. The apex court in its judgment endorsed the Pakistani government's stand that Gilgit and Baltistan are part of Jammu & Kashmir state; therefore, political and judicial systems of Pakistan cannot be extended to these regions. Further, before the settlement of the dispute of Jammu and Kashmir, these regions cannot be made part of Pakistan either. The Supreme Court admitted that Pakistani regimes have committed human rights violations in Gilgit-Baltistan by denying basic rights to the people. Further, the apex court stated that the locals are deprived of a representative government and Pakistan should make arrangements to grant self rule to Gilgit-Baltistan. The Supreme Court, before closing the case, clarified that since Gilgit-Baltistan is not part of Pakistan, a Pakistani court cannot proceed with the case.

The timing of current ordinance is significant particularly when the country has been grappling with rising separatism and simmering Talibanisation. While minorities clamour for political autonomy in other parts of the country,[31] the strategically-located Gilgit-Baltistan topped the priority list of Islamabad for granting the so-called empowerment and self-governance. The order allows Pakistan to reap the benefits of Gilgit-Baltistan's strategic location, at a time when China, its all weather ally, is investing more than $20 billion in the region. With no legal right to administer Gilgit-Baltistan, the order conveniently enables Pakistan to exploit its natural resources and fill the coffers of Islamabad, as both countries want to maximise revenues in shortest possible time, even at the cost of environmental, demographic and cultural degradation. The Karakoram Highway (KKH), which passes through Gilgit-Baltistan into Xinjiang, is the direct and shortest transport route connecting Pakistan with China. Further, the Karakoram Highway allows arms to flow between both countries.[32] In view of its significance, China is converting KKH into a four-lane highway with three times more capacity to accommodate heavy-laden vehicles in extreme weather conditions. As per plans, a railroad will run parallel to the KKH connecting Kazakhstan via Kyrgyzstan, China and Gilgit-Baltistan to the port cities of Karachi and Gawadar in Pakistan. This will enhance China's connectivity with the energy-laden countries on the Persian Gulf. [33] Further, Pakistan's ports are far nearer to some of China's industrial zones than the eastern Chinese ports and shorten the distance between China and the Suez Canal like never before. Gilgit-Baltistan's importance as a trade, water, gas and oil corridor[34] increased after Pakistan signed a Free Trade Agreement with China in 2007, and established dry ports at Sost (Gilgit) and Tashkorgan (Xinjiang). Pakistan expects China to invest approximately $10 billion in power generation, infrastructure, telecommunications and mineral extraction. Bunji and Diamer dams are expected to cost around $19.6 billion and generate 12,000 megawatts of electricity. With 125 ongoing projects and 12,000 Chinese working in Pakistan, both countries have identified another 55 initiatives and signed 42 MoUs in less than a year. The Sino-Pak friendship, flourishing through the corridor of Gilgit-Baltistan, allows China to emerge as Asian economic and military power, and enables Pakistan to explore ways and means for its survival in the next century.

While the order is claimed as enabling the winning of hearts and minds, it instead extends the long arm of Islamabad into Gilgit-Baltistan. Further, it fails to stem the rising separatism among the aggrieved people and provides fewer or no benefits to the poverty stricken and largely illiterate masses.[35] The definition of the 'citizen of Gilgit-Baltistan' in the order itself poses grave threats to the locals, and allows foreigners to acquire local citizenship if they possess assets and local identity cards. This may benefit the hundreds of thousands of Pakistanis living in the region since 1947, and allow them to further their stakes in local jobs, resources, social services and revenues, and thereby deny opportunities to the marginalised locals. The order restricts local laws which do not comply with the Pakistani laws. Further, it requires the locals to ensure the security, integrity, solidarity and strategic interests of Pakistan. In the same manner, the order prescribes an oath-format for local officials, which requires them to swear loyalty to Pakistan. Since the order as well as the constitution of Pakistan do not consider Gilgit-Baltistan as part of the country, the locals challenge such restrictions as an attack on local autonomy; defying the true spirit of delegation of authority to local institutions and hindering democracy, and freedom of speech and expression. In the current context of political engagement, above-mentioned conditions are designed to bar involvement of the nationalists and separatists in the political decision-making process, and safeguard the interests of foreigners involved in resource exploitation in the region. The absolute authority and veto power vested in the governor is bound to create disharmony among ethnic and religious factions and lead to a political impasse.[36]

Yet another example of how this order will exacerbate the social divide and enable Pakistan to further weaken the locals is embedded in the right of the Council to veto laws which contradict the Quran and *Sunnah*.[37] This will prevent the Shias from studying their religion in government schools.

On the other hand, the Sunni immigrant minority also fears for its long term survival and socio-economic interests in the region, which became their home only three decades ago. As social friction and polarisation over *who controls what* intensifies, it will lead to further sectarian killings, long-term religious and ethnic feuds, and the destruction of the regional socio-economic fabric. This can be assessed from the results of recently held assembly election on November 12, 2009, in which the majority of voters of Gilgit-Baltistan voted along sectarian lines.[38] The fear of losing their political leverage has forced the conservative Sunnis to seek the support of their allies, the Taliban and the Al-Qaida[39] who use sectarian rift to enhance their influence in Gilgit-Baltistan. As a result of heightened religious feuds, urban centers like Gilgit and Skardo have become militarised ghettos. Owing to the Taliban influence, women were barred from voting during the recent election.[40]

One way of tackling the rising extremism is to promote the indigenous secular cultural assets of Gilgit-Baltistan as a potential bulwark. However, Pakistan believes that the promotion of indigenous cultures will advance ethnic nationalism. In fact, successive regimes have dealt with the nationalists with a heavy hand to curb pan-ethnic sentiments. During the recent assembly election, the authorities intimidated, abducted and tortured hundreds of nationalists.[41] They were banned from electioneering in Gilgit-Baltistan and in one incident [42] a bomb was hurled at the residence of a nationalist election candidate.[43] Security forces tortured and killed Zubair, a nationalist worker, on November 23, 2009, when he was protesting against rigging of elections. The ranks of nationalists will swell further if the Governor authorises the foreigners to compete with the locals in resource exploitation.[44]

During the election, the ruling party in Islamabad, the Pakistan People's Party (PPP) managed to win a two-third majority amidst accusations of rigging and ballot stuffing.[45] However, a legislature with no freedom to use the two-third majority will only serve to promote Pakistan's interests like a rubber stamp and allow the gradual annexation of Gilgit-Baltistan.[46] At the inauguration of international investment conference for Gilgit-Baltistan, Governor Kaira affirmed that the, "PPP-led government was taking solid steps to strengthen the federation and reform the system of the country".[47] The recent remarks of the newly appointed chief minister of Gilgit-Baltistan, Syed Mehdi Shah that Gilgit-Baltistan is the fifth province of Pakistan and is not connected with J&K,[48] echo a similar message. Recently, he toured Punjab and Sindh to encourage Pakistanis to invest in Gilgit-Baltistan. Such short-term and quick fix solutions for economic development of Gilgit-Baltistan might help in developing the region but will not benefit the locals, who are the real owners of the resources.[49] Rumours abound in Gilgit government circles, that an engineered two-third majority has been made possible to allow the powerless Assembly to pass a resolution declaring the region an integral part of Pakistan. This would be approved by the Council and Governor, and culminate with the President of Pakistan signing it into a binding document.[50]

The creation of two separate assemblies and councils within PoK is part of the grand scheme of divide and rule which will engulf both regions of PoK complicating the political tussle over the nature of the Kashmir dispute. As Pakistan claims Gilgit-Baltistan as its own; the policy shift on Kashmir will force India to convert the LOC into a permanent border. While the regime in Islamabad may fail to sell the idea of the permanent division of J&K to its public; the presidential order does take the nation in that direction but without much fanfare.

The Kashmiri leaders have begun to realise that Pakistan is encroaching on their territory and nibbling parts of it, the way it annexed Shinaki-Kohistan in 1955 and Chitral in 1971.[51] Now, they demand Pakistani withdrawal from PoK and the reunification of the entire state.[52] The order has internationalised the Gilgit-Baltistan[53] issue and placed the region back on the political map of J&K. The presidential order is the first baby step taken by Pakistan in 63 years and it will be some time before Shias and Sunnis will reconcile to the idea of co-existence and use the legislative assembly for the benefit of both communities. In addition, the unity among the natives of Gilgit-Baltistan will help them seek genuine political freedom and control over their resources. On the other hand, Pakistan's excessive dependence on China for economic growth complicates the Kashmir issue and makes India wary of China's intentions in the region. This may prolong the impasse on Kashmir and also the resource exploitation and political oppression in Gilgit-Baltistan. Pakistan's exploitative and oppressive attitude towards the people of Gilgit-Baltistan needs to change to that of a benign benefactor. Presidential orders and legislative assemblies can become meaningful only if the trust deficit between the Pakistanis and the locals is removed to unite them in their endeavours to halt the advancing Taliban.

NOTES

1. In 1949, the political leadership of PoK signed "Karachi Agreement" with their counterpart in Islamabad which allowed Pakistan to occupy Gilgit-Baltistan and maintain its armed forces and civil administration there.
2. Shia-Sufi strand of Islam is prevalent in Gilgit, Baltistan, Ladakh and Kashmir. In Gilgit-Baltistan, more than 75% of the population claim to follow Shia-Nurbakhshi

Islam, whereas the rest are Sunnis and *Ahl-hadith*. Further, Ladakhis and Baltis have Tibetan ethnicity and speak the same language. Shias are a small minority in the rest of Pakistan (12 per cent) and remain target of religious persecution, which affects local perception about Pakistan's attitude towards the Shia minority.

3. Term used by Pakistan for Mirpur-Muzaffarabad region of J&K, which is currently under Pakistani occupation.
4. http://www.jammu-kashmir.com/shabir/shabir_1949_03_1.html
5. The technical name for Baltistan in the UN resolutions as well Pakistani and Indian documents is Ladakh, since it was part of Ladakh before partition.
6. http://www.newasiabooks.org/publication/last-colony-muzaffarabad-gilgit-baltistan
7. http://www.globalsecurity.org/intell/world/pakistan/law.htm
8. http://www.kashmirnewz.com/a0012.html
9. http://ips-pk.org/content/view/234/259/
10. http://www.dawn.com/wps/wcm/connect/dawn-content-library/dawn/the-newspaper/national/gilgitbaltistan-package-termed-an-eyewash-089
11. International Crisis Group, Human Rights Watch and the European Union have pressed upon Pakistan to deliver political rights to the people of Gilgit-Baltistan on many occasions and these are well documented.
12. http://www.thehindu.com/2009/09/15/stories/2009091553521100.htm
13. http://www.kashmirnewz.com/a0012.html
14. http://www.kashmirwatch.com/showheadlines.php?subaction=showfull&id=1251678701&archive=& start_from=&ucat=1&var0news=value0news
15. Secretary General of Jamaat-i-Islami, Liaqat Baloch stated that through the new ordinance, Pakistan desires to impose Governor's rule in Gilgit-Baltistan since all the powers will rest with the Governor. He proposed a joint council functioning like a senate for both Gilgit-Baltistan and AJK. See *Weekly Waadi Gilgit-Baltistan*, Volume 11, Issue 4, 1-11, November 2009.
16. http://skardu.blogspot.com/2009/09/gilgit-baltistan-self-governance.html
17. *Weekly Qayadat Gilgit-Baltistan*, Vol. 32, Issue No. 1, , November 4-10, 2009.
18. The following passage contradicts the true spirit of the legislative right of the Assembly as well as the Council....[When the Governor has returned a Bill to the Assembly, it shall be reconsidered by the Assembly and, if it is again passed, with or without amendment, by the Assembly, by the votes of the majority of the members of the Assembly present and voting, and in accordance with the provision of this Order and in not in any manner prejudicial to the security, integrity, solidarity and strategic interest of Pakistan, it shall be again presented to the Governor and Governor shall not withhold assent there from].. Gilgit-Baltistan is not part of Pakistan as per Pakistani constitution and, therefore, the citizens of Gilgit-Baltistan are not bound to defend integrity and strategic interests of the country.
19. For grade 20 and 21, quota for Pakistani officers is more than 60%, which means that local officers will fail to manage their own institutions. Such fabricated rules are in violation of UN Resolutions, which give authority of civil rule to locals.
20. *Balawaristan National Front* has demanded that India should allow people of Gilgit-Baltistan to fill their share of the seats in J&K legislature. http://www.hvk.org/articles/1101/199.html
21. The prominent religious scholar of Baltistan and a close associate of Zulfikar Ali Bhutto, Allama Shiekh Mirza Yusuf Hussain, termed the whole process eyewash. He said that federal parties are not sincere as they make false promises and exploit sentiments

of people. He believes that a local political party can address needs of local people. See *Weekly Qayadat Gilgit-Baltistan*, Vol. 32, No. 1, , November 4-10, 2009.

22. SSR protects demographic characteristics of J&K. In 1974, Pakistan abrogated SSR in Gilgit-Baltistan, which paved way for Pakistanis to claim stake in local immovable assets and natural resources. Today major businesses in Gilgit and Skardo are owned by Pathans and Punjabis, which has affected the local demographic character. This not only impacts resource sharing and competition over jobs and services, it also alters local linguistic and cultural heritage and damages religious harmony. Shia-Sunni feuds have been simmering since then and have consumed thousands of lives and damage to property worth billions of rupees.
23. *Weekly Qayadat Gilgit-Baltistan*, Vol. 32, Issue 1, November 4-10, 2009.
24. http://www.hindustantimes.com/News-Feed/newdelhi/Gilgit-Baltistan-is-part-of-Kashmir-asserts-India/Article1-492780.aspx
25. For the executive positions like secretaries and directors, quota for Pakistani bureaucrats is more than 60 per cent, which means that local officers of these grades remain in a minority when it comes to heading institutions of their own region.
26. http://dailyk2.com/large.php?id=9002
27. http://skardu.blogspot.com/2009/09/gilgit-baltistan-self-governance.html
28. http://www.unpo.org/content/view/10307/83/
29. Chairperson of the *Gilgit-Baltistan National Alliance*, Malika Baltistani, who also led *Ladakh Baltistan United Front* in 1963, demands complete independence from Pakistan and rejects the order. She says, "We demand that this Constitutional package may immediately be abolished and Gilgit Baltistan may be granted independent status under the fourth-option proposed by GBNA to the United Nations in 1996". Once known as the proponent of 'fifth province for Gilgit-Baltistan', successive ordinances have forced many like her to change the political ideology and demand separation of Gilgit-Baltistan from Pakistan; http://balawaristantimes.blogspot.com/; http://www.balawaristan.net/index.php?option=com_content&view =article&id=1748%3Agilgit-baltistan-conference-in-new-york&Itemid=64
30. The term used for Muzaffarabad–Mirpur in Pakistan.
31. In Pakistan, Urdu-speaking Karachiites, Pashtuns of Baluchistan, Seraikis of Punjab and NWFP, Hindkos of NWFP, and Pothohars of Punjab demand separate provinces to offset their socio-economic marginalisation. Further, Baluchistan demands the independent status it enjoyed on August, 11, 1947. Other provinces like NWFP and Sindh demand provincial autonomy and creation of a confederation of loose states, which will weaken the federation and take away authority from Islamabad; http://www.thesouthasian.org/archives/2009/empowering_gilgitbaltistan_or.html
32. M.Z. Isapahani, *Roads and Rivals: The Politics of Access in the Borderlands of Asia*, I.B. Tauris, London, 1989, p. 199 & ff.
33. In December 2009, China secured oil contracts in Iraq, which makes KKH even more significant for its needs.
34. http://www.thesouthasian.org/archives/2009/empowering_gilgitbaltistan_or.html
35. Per capita per annum income of Gilgit-Baltistan, which is less than US$268 is one fourth of Pakistan's national average PCI (AKRSP socio-economic surveys SESNAC 2005).
36. http://dailyk2.com/large.php?id=9064
37. *Sunnah* is the Arabic term for Prophet Mohammad's practices and customs, that he expects all Muslims to follow in word and deed.

38. In order to win over Sunni immigrant-votes in Gilgit (GBLA-2), Pakistan's ruling party (PPP) fielded a Sunni candidate. However, Sunni vote divide between PPP and Muslim League-N allowed independent Shia candidate to win a seat previously held by a Sunni. Success of Shia candidates in Gilgit-Baltistan (People of Gilgit, Skardo, Ghizer, Hunza-Nagar and Ganche districts returned Shia-Nurbakhshi-Ismaili candidates) may also lead to further sectarian clashes and casualties; *Daily K2*, Issue 179, November 2, 2009, p. 1.
39. In 1988, a Shia genocide in Gilgit-Baltistan, killed thousands. Local Sunnis received support from the tribal conservative Sunnis of Swat, Dir, Kohistan, Bajour, Waziristan and Khyber.
40. http://www.dawn.com/wps/wcm/connect/dawn-content-library/dawn/news/pakistan/07-polling-underway-in-gilgit-baltistan-polls-ha-05
41. http://mygilgit.wordpress.com/2009/11/page/2/
42. *Daily Baad-e-Shimal Gilgit-Baltistan*, November 3, 2009.
43. http://gecanews.wordpress.com/2009/11/07/news-in-brief/; *Weekly Baang-e-Sahar Gilgit-Baltistan*, November 7-13, 2009, p. 1.
44. http://www.thaindian.com/newsportal/india-news/gilgit-leaders-ask-china-not-to-invest-in-disputed-region_10043318.html
45. http://www.theresearchers.org/Post&Update/Gilgit-Baltistan%20Elections.pdf
46. http://www.expressbuzz.com/edition/story.aspx?Title=India,+Pak+blow+hot+and+cold&artid=fc0TNJ2A4eQ=&SectionID=b7ziAYMenjw=&MainSectionID=b7ziAYMenjw=& SectionName=pWehHe7IsSU=&SEO=
47. http://www.app.com.pk/en_/index.php?option=com_content&task=view&id=93177&Itemid=2
48. http://www.thaindian.com/newsportal/south-asia/gilgit-baltistan-is-part-of-kashmir-asserts-india_100297603.html
49 http://dailyk2.com/large.php?id=9066
50. Based on conversations with resource persons from Gilgit-Baltistan.
51. Both were part of J&K until November 4, 1947.
52. http://www.iakf.org/main/index.php?module=article&view=309&lay_ quiet=1
53. The members of the European Union Parliament have recently formed a 'Friends of Gilgit-Baltistan' at Brussels.

11

Role of Political Parties in Pak Administered Kashmir and Gilgit-Baltistan

Shaukat Kashmiri

'Azad' Kashmir is the southern-most political entity within the Pakistan controlled part of Jammu and Kashmir. It borders the Indian state of Jammu and Kashmir in the east, the North Western Frontier Province (Pakhtoonkhwa) of Pakistan in the west, Gilgit-Baltistan in the north as also Pakistan's Punjab province. These areas were separated following the Pakistani tribal invasion in 1947 which was soon followed by an attack by Pak military regulars on the former princely state of Jammu and Kashmir.

The total area of this region is 13,297 sq kms. It consists of 8 districts, 19 towns and 182 union councils. Gilgit-Baltistan, which is to the north of the former princely state, was cut off by Pakistan in 1949 and placed under the direct control of Islamabad. Both regions have been marginalised in every respect and remain backward in all the social, economic, democratic and political aspects that benefit people in democratic societies. This paper focuses on the role played in the region by political parties and political leaders of various hues. The 18th century was the century of revolutions and freedoms; the 19th century was the century of reason; while the 21st century is the era of technology and information. Several political parties in the so called 'Azad' Kashmir and also in Gilgit-Baltistan, have been demanding the unification of this area with the rest of Jammu and Kashmir. Some political parties in Gilgit-Baltistan are also demanding sovereignty as they have been politically and democratically marginalised by the state of Pakistan. No political party or leader from 'Azad' Kashmir entered Gilgit-Baltistan, until the United Kashmir People's National Party broke through the invisible circles of Pakistani authorities in early 1990s. The civil society and political leaders of that area have strengthened their ties with the nationalist political parties of 'Azad' Kashmir, simultaneously demanding independence and sovereignty. The first political partnership was established between the Balawaristan National Front and the United Kashmir People's National Party to wage a collective struggle for securing a constitutional status for this region, and to counter radical forces.

The two undemocratic and unrepresentative institutions that have been imposed by Pakistan on the people of this region are:

1. Ministry of Kashmir Affairs and Northern Areas (KANA).
2. Kashmir Council.

The Ministry of Kashmir Affairs and Northern Areas (KANA), located in Islamabad, is headed by a federal minister, who plays a role akin to that of a Viceroy and has absolute powers, including the power to change the local authority besides manipulating the politics of the region.

The Kashmir Council is described as Senate, but its members are not democratically elected by the people of 'Azad' Kashmir. Six members are nominated by the pro-Pakistan Legislative Assembly of 'Azad' Kashmir and seven are nominated by the federal government. The Kashmir Council is headed by the prime minister of Pakistan who is also its chairman. In fact, the Legislative Assembly has no powers, which is why the local authority can always be changed, with every change of regime in Islamabad.

The Muslim Conference has enjoyed power whenever there has been a right wing or military government in Pakistan. Islamabad ensures that the same political party is in power and in opposition both in Islamabad and Muzaffarabad. The first political party in this region was the Muslim Conference which was founded in 1932, i.e. before the partition of the sub-continent. Its name was changed to the National Conference by Sheikh Mohammad Abdullah, its founding father who was a nationalist, and the pro-democracy leaders in that political era, who had a deep knowledge and understanding of Kashmir's history and culture. He sought to involve all ethnic groups in Jammu and Kashmir in the struggle for social and poltiical rights and freedom. The National Conference has been representing all regions and religions of former princely state of Jammu and Kashmir. However, after 1947 the National Conference was completely wiped out in the areas that fell under Pakistan. Some leaders revived the

Muslim Conference in the early 1940s, and raised slogans of Muslim brotherhood and Muslim nationalism and claimed to work for the rights of Kashmiri Muslims. In the meantime, the Muslim Conference also established a realtionship with the Pakistan Muslim League. Thus the Muslim Conference and the National Conference were the only political parties in the State of Jammu and Kashmir that entered into alliances with the non-Kashmiri political parties. The Muslim Conference was inclined towards the Muslim League, while the National Conference was close to the Indian National Congress.

The National Conference wielded power in the Indian state of Jammu and Kashmir, while in Pakistani Administered Kashmir, the Muslim Conference has been in power, with the blessings of Islamabad and its security establishment. The National Conference has always adhered to its manifesto while implementing its socio-economic and political agenda. Its leadership has been struggling and has even faced many ups and downs in the endeavour to secure maximum political rights for the people of Jammu and Kashmir.

But the Muslim Conference did not stand firm on its principles and it practically, became a tool and proxy for undemocratic forces and Pakistan's Ministry of Kashmir Affairs and Northern Areas. Due to this compromising attitude, the young and local leadership of 'Azad' Kashmir like Sardar Muhammad Ibrahim Khan revolted and founded the 'Azad' (Free) Muslim Conference, free from the influence of Ministry of Kashmir Affairs and Northern Areas and other Pakistani institutions. In this regard the Azad Muslim Conference was the sole voice in that period which vigorously raised its voice against the unnecesary intervention of Pakistani institutions in the political matters of the region.

The All Jammu and Kashmir Muslim Conference (AJKMC), was the single majority party in the region after the division of Jammu and Kashmir. From day one, its leadership has compromised on the fundamental rights of the people of this region that was separated from the rest of Jammu and Kashmir, following the tribal invasion in Kashmir. The Muslim Conference is the only political party of that era the members of whose working committee have been on the pay roll of the Ministry of Kashmir Affairs and Northern Areas (KANA). When the government of Sardar Muhammad Ibrahim Khan was dismissed in the 1950s, a popular uprising erupted in the Poonch and Bagh districts, adjacent to the border of Pakistan. The government of Pakistan sent its para-military troops (Pakistan Constabulary) and army to crush this movement against the interference of Pakistan in the political affairs of the region.

The leadership of the Muslim Conference can be divided into local and refugee leaders such as Chaudhary Ghulam Abbas and Sardar Abdul Qayyum Khan. While Chaudhary Ghulam Abbas was the President of Muslim Conference, it remained subservient to Pakistan. But after his death, the Muslim Conference along with K.H. Khursheed and the Azad Muslim Conference of Sardar Ibrahim Khan entered into a tripartite alliance for securing the democratic rights of the people. As a result of their struggle, adult franchise came to be recognised and an interim constitution was adopted for the region in 1970. From time to time, regional political parties and leaders like Chaudhary Noor Hussain, Sardar Muhammad Ibrahim Khan, Sardar Abdul Qayyum and Abdul Khaliq Ansari of the Jammu and Kashmir Plebiscite Front have given vent to their grievances and resentment towards Pakistan for rigging the elections as also their policy of picking and choosing. It may however be pointed out, that their role and attitude has always been in accordance with the instructions of Pakistan. They did not play an independent role in Jammu and Kashmir. The local tribal clans and people believed that they have got this area without any external help, but their perception of freedom or self-rule in these areas was influenced by the state institutions of Pakistan. The Muslim Conference helped these institutions to take control over this region, that covers a territory of approximately 33,000 sq miles.

Gilgit-Baltistan is the cockpit of Asia, as its boundaries are co-terminous with Afghanistan in the north, China to the northeast, Pakistani Administered Kashmir ('Azad' Kashmir) to the south, and Jammu and Kashmir to the southeast. Its estimated population is about two million. Pakistan further gifted the Shaksgam tract to China in 1963. The government of Pakistan had no mandate to take administrative control of this region as per the United Nations resolution of 1948, according to which Pakistan was asked to vacate the territory and to help local people establish a local government to run the state—temporarily—under the supervision of the United Nations. But the pledges made by Pakistan, both to the people of this region and to the world community, were not implemented. Pakistan did not fulfil the UN stipulations of complete withdrawal, but instead started a campaign, that the people of this region wanted to remain as part of Pakistan.

The Muslim Conference has been raising the bogey of the two nations theory and Muslim brotherhood in the region, but it has never created any awareness or campaigned for the democratic, political and socio-economic rights of the people of 'Azad' Kashmir and Gilgit-Baltistan. There was no local representation in the so called Karachi Agreement signed between Sardar Muhamamd Ibrahim Khan, the President of Azad Kashmir,

Chaudhary Ghulam Abbas, President of the Muslim Conference and Mushtaq Ahmed Gormani, a federal minister without portfolio, who was the former prime minister of the state of Bahawalpur. It may be recalled that Sardar Muhamamd Ibrahim publicly denounced the Karachi Agreement of 1949. At that time, both Sardar Muhammad Ibrahim Khan, President of Azad Kashmir and Chaudhary Ghulam Abbas were the members of the ruling Muslim Conference in the area. In all the 20 points of the Karachi Agreement signed between the government of Pakistan, the government of so called 'Azad' Kashmir and the Muslim Conference, there is no mention of the social, political, economic, cultural, constitutional and democratic empowerment of the local people of Gilgit-Baltistan. The constitutional rights of the people of the entire region have been at the mercy of a judicial commissioner and a section officer in the Ministry of Kashmir Affairs and Northern Areas based in Islamabad.

The leadership of the Muslim Conference never supported the democratic aspirations of the people of this region. In fact, this was the only organisation which helped the Pakistani state and security establishment to strengthen their hold over the region. They kept the local people engaged by raising various issues such as: implementation of UN resolutions, while Pakistan itself violated those resolutions; the demand for a plebiscite while Pakistan did not comply with the UN stipulations with regard to the same; and self-determination, while Pakistan itself advocates that the Kashmiri people have only two choices—acceding either to India or to Pakistan without having any right of self-rule or sovereignty over the territory of the former princely state of Jammu and Kashmir. Pakistan and its government institutions have perpetrated human and political rights violations in the entire region. Other political parties in the territory have also advanced the theo-fascist agenda and the expansionist designs of the Pakistani establishment under various slogans and platforms. It is unfortunate that the Muslim Conference, even though it is an indigenous political party, did not play the role that was expected and required of it, as it has been collaborating with Pakistan since the 1950s. It was the Muslim Conference President who was the first to use the term 'military democracy'—just to please the Pakistani military junta, to enhance his power—which he lost as soon as the military dictatorship in Pakistan lost power.

The United Kashmir People's National Party (UKPNP) which was founded by the young progressive youth of the region in 1985, was in its earlier avatar known as the Jammu and Kashmir People's National Party. The party aimed to secure the constitutional, political, democratic, socio-economic and cultural rights of the people under Pakistani administration and was recognised by regional and international progressive forces. The party was renamed as the United Kashmir People's National Party in 1993. The young and dynamic leadership of the party has disseminated its message to every corner of the state and challenged the undemocratic rule of Pakistan. It advocates that Pakistan should guarantee the human rights of people living under Pak administration. The Pakistani state security apparatus has been used against the party leadership and its cadre, to muzzle their voice.

The party leadership is of the view that the former princely state needs to be oriented in accordance with the socio-economic and political realities of 21st century. The party recognises the rights of all nationalities in the former princely state of Jammu and Kashmir. The idea of a United States of Kashmir was supported by many in political and academic circles of the region. The United Kashmir People's National Party has identified eight political and cultural entities that constituted the former princely State of Jammu and Kashmir as: (1) Kashmir (2) Jammu (3) Ladakh (4) Kishtwar (5) Poonch (6) Gilgit (7) Hunza and (8) Baltistan. The party believes in the equality of all and all these states will be completely independent in the legal and internal spheres, with the exception of defence, currency and foreign affairs, which shall remain with the union of states.

The United Kashmir People's National Party is the only organisation which opposes the use of religion to achieve political objectives. It is the first organisation to have stood up against expansionist designs of Pakistan in the region and has started a vigorous campaign against its proxy war and proxy politics in Jammu and Kashmir. The party has condemned and opposed Pakistan's policy to use this area as a launching pad and training camp. The party has also condemned the killing and displacement of the Kashmiri Pandit community from the valley of Kashmir.

In view of these endeavours, the party cadres became the targets of Pakistani security agencies, and its leader was kidnapped and held in solitary confinement. The United Kashmir People's National Party stands by the United Nations Commission for India Pakistan (UNCIP) resolution as per which the world community called upon Pakistan to withdraw its troops and tribals from the entire region of 'Azad' Kashmir and Gilgit-Baltistan, so that the local authorities are able to rule and administer the area politically, democratically and constitutionally. But Pakistan has violated all those resolutions and has waged a proxy war to suppress voice of the people of the former princely state of Jammu and Kashmir. The party also seeks to protect the natural resources of the state and has called upon the government of India not to trade the resources of Kashmir with Pakistan. Under the Treaty of Accession of Kashmir with India, it is the primary responsibility of the Union of India to protect the socio-economic and political rights of the people of the entire state.

The party has always raised its voice, at both national and international forums for the restoration of civil and political rights, the independence of judiciary, freedom for student union activities, local bodies elections, employment, and merit based recruitment to state institutions. The party has also established its units in Gilgit-Baltistan to revive its historical ties with the people of this region and to wage a struggle to safeguard the rights of this region. The party has raised its voice against religious extremism and sectarianism. The party believes that Pak security institutions are promoting, patronising and exporting terrorism to advance their agenda and to garner financial and economic benefits from the world community in the name of terrorism and fundamentalism.

The All Parties National Alliance (APNA) is an amalgam of nationalist political parties of so called 'Azad' Kashmir which wants the independence and unification of former princely state of Jammu and Kashmir. The nationalist political parties of both regions, civil society organisations and academicians are all part of this alliance.

Simultaneously the nationalist parties of Gilgit-Baltistan have also established the Gilgit-Baltistan Democratic Alliance (GBDA), and both alliances are working together for the social, economic, democratic and political emancipation of these regions, that are under the illegal administration of Pakistan. Together the APNA and GBDA hold press briefings, seminars, rallies and conferences to raise awareness about the fundamental rights of the people. In this endeavor, the nationalist leadership has been facing many obstacles created by the Pakistani security agencies particularly the Inter Services Intelligence (ISI). The nationalist political parties of Gilgit-Baltistan like Balawaristan National Front, Karakoram National Movement, Karakoram Students Organisation, Thinkers Forum, are all united under the umbrella of GBDA, which is striving for the constitutional and democratic rights of this region.

Religious groups and religious armed groups like Lashker-e-Tayyeba, Jaish-e-Muhammad, Harkat ul Mujhadeen, Hizbul Mujhadeen, the armed wing of Jamaat-e-Islami, Harkat ul Ansar, Jamaat-ud Dawah, Al Rasheed Trust and United Jihad Council (UJC) have established training camps in the area. They have been abducting local people and forcing them to labour for them and to feed them. In many border areas and in the Neelam valley women and local village people have demonstrated against these groups and the Pakistani military because they enter their houses and commit human rights violations. Such incidents have been reported by the BBC local correspondent at Muzaffarabad. As there is no local media, many such incidents and crimes committed by these armed groups under the protection of the Pakistani military go unnoticed and undocumented. These religious groups are threatening nationalist workers and no action is taken against them.

Some popular slogans that are often raised by the political parties in Pakistani administered Kashmir have had an impact on the daily life of people. These include: the right to self-determination; accession to Pakistan; plebiscite; Kashmir will be *Dar-ul-Islam*; Kashmir will be an independent state. Interestingly all these slogans have their origin in Pakistani administered Kashmir, where people are marginalised and voiceless, where no political party is ready to address their problems and grievances. Ironically, most of the political parties do not even know the demographic composition and topography of the former state of Jammu and Kashmir.

All the literature published in 'Azad' Kashmir is biased and communal and fosters hatred. Both K.H. Khursheed and Sardar Ibrahim Khan being practicing attorneys at law, were competent in their profession. Unfortunately, both succumbed to the patronage of Pakistan and they did not play any effective role as true Kashmiri leaders. Both of them later regretted this and revealed the true story in public meetings and writings, exposing Pakistani ambitions to enslave the people of this region.

Pakistan has also used the Kashmiri refugees of 1947, who had settled mainly in Punjab province. Until the 1970s there was no political system in 'Azad' Kashmir. In 1970, a constitutional act was imposed on the area that was later amended as the Act of 1974. This imposed tough restrictions on the political parties of the area. By virtue of that Act, freedom of assembly and political activities are banned and fundamental rights of the people and political activism is constitutionally suppressed. The political party that supports the unification and independence of the former princely state of Jammu and Kashmir is not allowed to take part in the democratic process. Section 7 (2), of the Act stipulates that, "No person or political party in Azad Kashmir shall be allowed to take part in activities prejudicial or detrimental to the ideology of State's accession to Pakistan." This is clearly contrary to the UNCIP resolution and the Pakistani mandate regarding temporary administration of these areas. Another controversial clause of the Act of 1974, is Article 56, which maximises Pakistani authoritarian control over the territory. This Act allows any government in the area to be either dismissed or changed. Pakistan has used this power many times in the history of this region. Pakistan has also created large constituencies consisting of Kashmiri refugees of 1947 in all the four provinces. There are 12 seats within Pakistan for such refugees. With the result, the members who win elections with the blessings of provincial assemblies and state security agencies, have been playing a vital role in the formation of so the called 'Azad' Kashmir government. They are the trump cards in the hands of Pakistani security establishment for influencing any government in Muzaffarabad, or even replace it.

In our view, the Republic of India has a constitutional responsibility: (a) to unify the whole state; (b) to push back all infiltrators; (c) to ask the government of Pakistan to vacate the occupied areas, so that until the final settlement, these areas are administered in accordance with the international law on disputed territories and entities; and (d) to ensure that the democratic, progressive and secular forces of 'Azad' Kashmir and Gilgit-Baltistan are supported by the civil society and democratic forces of India and Jammu and Kashmir.

The fight against terrorism, extremism and fanaticism can be won only by strengthening pro-people democratic forces in other part of the divide.

One could say that all political parties operating in Pakistani administered Kashmir are deluded and are ignorant of the legal aspects of the Jammu and Kashmir issue. We have been challenging the political role played by the Ministry of Kashmir Affairs and Northern Area and Kashmir Council, and have been criticising and opposing the interference of Pakistani state secret agencies in the political and social affairs of both regions.

The United Kashmir People's National Party has for long been warning the world community, that the ISI has strong links with extremist forces and that it is patronising the Taliban in the name of the good Taliban. The huge amount of aid that has been given to the government of Pakistan for relief and rehabilitation has always gone to the Taliban factions through different means. Jihadis in Pakistan have been declared the strategic assets of Pakistani military. In fact the Pakistan military and its secret agencies are running a parallel government and a parallel foreign policy contrary to the official stand of government of Pakistan today.

Various political parties in Pakistani administered Kashmir have been struggling for the unification of the state. These parties have been working to secure the people's rights. Whatever political development we are seeing in the region today, is the result of many sacrifices made by these political parties.

One needs to remember that Zulfiqar Ali Bhutto was hanged and Benazir Bhutto who was twice prime minister of Pakistan, was assassinated in broad day light. The late Khan Abdul Wali Khan, Atta Ullah Mangel and G.M Syed faced imprisonment and torture at the hands of Pakistani state institutions. It is not easy to struggle for the rule of law in the prevailing social and political order in Pakistan. Pakistani state instituions are more brutal and insulting towards those officers of Gilgit-Baltistan who were trained at the Dehradun Military Academy. They were demoted and were not commissioned as officers. It is against this background that Pakistan has tactically used the passion of the people for freedom and sovereignty and channelised it against the democratic forces of Indian state of Jammu and Kashmir, to deflect attention from its own wrongdoings.

12

Demography and Discontent

Crisis of Modernity and Displacement in Undivided Jammu and Kashmir

Praveen Swami

In October 1947, Abdul Rashid Butt took the last bus from Baramulla to Muzaffarabad: the very last commercial transport which would traverse that route for almost six decades. Butt was just 16 when he took the last bus to Muzaffarabad: he, with two cousins and two servants, left never having considered the possibility that he would not be able to return home. His family had dispatched him to enquire about the fate of a cargo of fruits and spices they had sent to Kohala, the small town that marked Jammu and Kashmir's border with a new country that had come into being two months earlier, Pakistan. Normal public transport had come to a standstill since Pakistan had blocked fuel supplies to Jammu and Kashmir, claiming it had none to spare. Butt and his cousins succeeded in using their contacts to board a bus chartered by a Lahore-based leader of the Muslim League to evacuate his British wife and three children who were on vacation in Srinagar. By Butt's account, he spent the night at a hotel in Muzaffarabad, and then took a horse-drawn cart to Kohala the next morning. There, he learned that the goods that his family had sent had disappeared—and that Pakistani irregulars had entered Jammu and Kashmir.

Without cash or hope of returning home, Butt stayed on in Muzaffarabad, and eventually made a life for himself in the city. He obtained a degree, set up a business and married. Across the Line of Control in Srinagar, his parents and four siblings went about their own lives, and eventually passed away. In 2005, when Butt's son, Saqib Butt, told him that India and Pakistan bus service was about to be started linking with Muzaffarabad, a journalist, Tariq Naqash, recorded that he "started crying like a child". [1]

Emotional stories like these have deeply influenced the contours of the peace process in Jammu and Kashmir, in many unacknowledged ways. Policy-makers on both sides have been working towards that end. Ever since 2005, bus services have been operating across both sides of Jammu and Kashmir: a small, symbolic gesture, but none the less significant; trade has also been initiated. In recent years, there have been repeated calls for the creation of political institutions and mechanisms that cut across the Line of Control.

There has been little debate, though, on whether erasing the Line of Control will in fact address the multiple crises of demography and dislocation that exist in undivided Jammu and Kashmir. We are accustomed to thinking of the conflict in Jammu and Kashmir as a single entity, framed by the competing national interests of India and Pakistan and with ethnic-Kashmiri nationalism as its core, and it has led policy-makers into profound fallacies. There is, in some key senses, no one thing called the Kashmir Problem, either: it is, rather, an agglomeration of multiple crisis of identity, born of the diverse experiences of its peoples with that great historical force, modernity.

This paper argues that the political contours of each part of Jammu and Kashmir are being driven by very distinct demographic contestations: each driven by an experience of profound demographic dislocation, but each unique in its specific characteristics. It examines the experiences of the Pakistan-occupied province of 'Azad' Kashmir, then the 'Northern Areas' (Gilgit-Baltistan), a part of the pre-1947 state of Jammu and Kashmir, which has been directly administered by Pakistan, and, finally, the Indian state of Jammu and Kashmir.

The Indian state of Jammu and Kashmir consists of the two major provinces from which it takes its name, and a third province, Ladakh. It has had varying degrees of democratic rule since 1947, but has in place a functional system of elections, constitutional safeguards and autonomy from the central government in New Delhi. 'Azad' Kashmir, for its part, consists of those parts of the pre-1947 state of Jammu and Kashmir which were occupied by Pakistani troops in 1947-1948. The use of the term "Kashmir" is misleading, since the bulk of 'Azad' Kashmir's population comprises Mirpuri, ethnic Punjabis closely linked by language and culture to the peoples of the province of Jammu. Much of the population of the

'Northern Areas' (Gilgit-Baltistan), for their part, is ethnically and culturally allied with the residents of the Ladakh province. Pakistan directly administers the 'Northern Areas', which have no meaningful form of elected government, on the grounds that leaders of these areas rebelled against the monarchy in 1947.

Dislocation and Diasporic Nationalisms in 'Azad' Kashmir

'Azad' Kashmir's landscape, wrote the British scholar Roger Ballard of the proliferation of diaspora-owned mansions across Mirpur, "is now peppered with symbolic monuments proclaiming the clearest possible message: the route to real prosperity lies overseas".[2]

Understanding the curious play between demographic-economic change and support for the jihad in Jammu and Kashmir requires an engagement with the complex experience 'Azad' Kashmir has had of modernity. Mirpur was made over to the Maharaja of Kashmir, after the British took control of Punjab, and the region to the east of the Jhelum thus saw few investments in economic infrastructure or education. Located some 10 miles north of the Grand Trunk Road, and sundered from it by mountains, the Mirpur belt was moreover peripheral to the enormous processes of modernisation that swept through Punjab's Doaba region, just a few miles away, under colonial rule. Backwardness, thus, is a central part of 'Azad' Kashmir's historical legacy—and also an important determinant of its political present.

Much debate in India has focussed on the large-scale influx of ethnic Punjabi migrants into Mirpur, the heart of 'Azad' Kashmir. The scale of such migration is however not clear. Moreover, unlike the Indian state of Jammu and Kashmir, 'Azad' Kashmir does not have legislation prohibiting outsiders from buying land. Pakistan's Military is known to have made grants of agricultural and residential land to former soldiers, but no ethnic conflict provoked by migration has been seen there. Regional anger does exist, notably against the use of 'Azad' Kashmir's hydroelectric resources to feed industry in Punjab, to its south. However, there has been no internal demographic conflict, perhaps because Mirpuris are closely bound to Punjabis by language, ethnicity and, often, kinship.

Developments in the mid-nineteenth century played a major role in shaping the character of what is now 'Azad' Kashmir. A major source of employment in Mirpur was the recruitment of crews for merchant boats which sailed along the Indus and its tributaries, carrying cargo to the major trading centres of Punjab. As railway connections were built between Lahore and Karachi, however, this river-based economy collapsed almost overnight. At around the same time, however, new opportunities opened up for the Mirpuri boatmen who had been redundant—as coal stokers on Britain's merchant fleet, which was in the process of shifting from sail to steam. Mirpuris occupied this niche in the global economy rapidly: by the early 1880s, the great majority of stoker-foremen in British ships sailing out of Karachi and Mumbai are believed to have been from the region.

Mirpuri seamen were to play a central role in shaping the region's identity. An ethnic colony of some size had begun to evolve in the port of Sydney by the end of the first quarter of the last century, and substantial enclaves of Mirpuris also emerged in the United Kingdom during the Second World War. Using these toeholds, Mirpuri immigrants began to feed the United Kingdom's growing post-war industrial labour needs, and succeeded in defying official efforts to restrict new immigration. With strong ethnic networks binding them to Mirpur—reinforced through the institution of cousin-marriage—Mirpuris in the United Kingdom made large scale remittances back to their home province. Immigration grew sharply after the large-scale inundation of agricultural land after the construction of the Mangla Dam in 1966, and a massive flow of remittances began into Mirpur from the beginning of the next decade.

To students of the conflict in Jammu and Kashmir, this period is of obvious significance. Although this is not the place to recount the long history of Pakistani covert warfare in Jammu and Kashmir, the period after the war of 1971 was one of crisis for the jihadi enterprise and its state sponsors.[3] Al-Fatah, the last major Pakistan-backed terrorist group to operate until 1988, had fallen apart soon after the conflict, and the attention of the Inter-Services Intelligence (ISI) had turned firmly towards countering sub-nationalist movements in Baluchistan and the North-West Frontier Province. At this precise moment, diasporic wealth made it possible for both Islamists and Kashmiri nationalists in Mirpur, who were increasingly convinced that the Pakistani State could not liberate Jammu and Kashmir, to begin their own anti-India movement: it was called the National Liberation Front (NLF), which would in later years become the Jammu and Kashmir Liberation Front (JKLF).

What meaning did the formation of the NLF have? It was, of course, intended to secure the secession of Jammu and Kashmir from India—but the fact that the NLF also represented a loss of faith in the Pakistani State is of enormous significance. Much of the NLF's work was conducted amongst Mirpuri immigrants in the United Kingdom. Its most visible pre-1988 operation, the assassination of the Indian diplomat Ravindra Mhatre in 1983, was carried out in Birmingham. To these immigrant communities, who lived in conditions of extreme hardship, deferring everyday pleasures in the hope of gratification on their return home one day, the NLF was a source of pride and meaning. It gave Mirpuris an identity distinct from that of other Pakistanis, and the prospect of homeland which the increasingly affluent community could one day dominate. As Sultan Shaheen has perceptively noted, the Kashmiri nationalism of the Mirpuris was hostile to ethnic-Kashmiris themselves: none were "prepared to accept the inevitable domination of the better educated and numerically stronger 'hatos' (coolies, manual labourers) as they contemptuously refer to the Kashmiris of the Valley in case Kashmir is united".[4]

Kashmiri nationalist tendencies, along with Islamist groups, were strengthened by a second economic boom in the 1980s: the availability of new remittance-economy opportunities in West Asia; investments in property made by early immigrants to the United Kingdom in lands and built-up properties; and the income injected by the United States-led jihadi war against the erstwhile Soviet Union's forces in Afghanistan. Transnational networks forged during this boom were critical, as is well known, to the course of the jihad in Jammu and Kashmir, notably the hawala channels used to funnel funds from West Asia and Europe to terrorist groups operating out of Srinagar.[5] A less well-understood consequence of the economic boom in Mirpur was the decline of agriculture in the region. As the relative returns on agriculture diminished in comparison with what could be made from the remittance or immigrant economies, a large pool of unskilled poor became available for recruitment by organisations engaged in the jihad in Jammu and Kashmir, ranging from Al-Badr in the early stages to Lashkar-e-Taiba today. Mirpur's poor also became increasingly vulnerable to the Islamists' network of patronage, notably schools, hospitals and seminaries.

Why is this history important for Indian policy-making? Most importantly, it makes clear that Kashmir nationalist or Kashmiri-Islamist tendencies in 'Azad' Kashmir are not part of some undifferentiated millenarian urge. While Islamist-millenarian tendencies undoubtedly feed and inform mass support for anti-India jihadi groups in 'Azad' Kashmir, this is underpinned by distinctly local concerns. Mirpuri support for the jihad in Jammu and Kashmir, in this key sense, is not *about* Kashmir: it is, rather, about a way of translating the region's affluence, and the new elites it has spawned, into concrete political power. Within the current structures of power in 'Azad' Kashmir, Mirpuri elites cannot have a say in local affairs commensurate with their affluence. As such, their political power remains considerably lower than that of their close relatives, the ethnic Punjabis who live just kilometres away. What Mirpuris hope for, therefore, is not so much the liberation of Indian Jammu and Kashmir—but a share of any devolution of powers from the principal states that would benefit their own position.

For Indian policy-making, this represents opportunity. In important ways, the interests of Mirpur elites and Pakistan's Punjab-driven military establishment do not coincide. As the memoirs of the soldier who commanded Pakistan's 1947-1948 offensive in Jammu and Kashmir make clear: the war was not just concerned with "the safety and wishes of our brethren in Kashmir", but also to "our own safety and welfare".[6] He wrote:

> One glance at the map was enough to show that Pakistan's military security would be seriously jeopardised if Indian troops came to be stationed along Pakistan's western border. Once India got the chance, she could establish such stations anywhere within a few miles of the 180 miles long vital road and rail route between Lahore and Pindi. In the event of war, these stations would be a dangerous threat to our most important civil and military lines of communication.... From an economic point of view the position was equally perilous. Our agricultural economy was dependent particularly upon the rivers coming out of Kashmir. The Mangla Headworks were actually in Kashmir and the Marala Headworks were within a mile or so of the border. What then would be our position if Kashmir was in Indian hands?[7]

Mirpur elites are asking the question: What does their future look like irrespective of whose hands the territory remains in? Indian policy-maker must defend the Mirpuri case for greater federal autonomy—and demand that Pakistan negotiate with the 'Azad' Kashmir leadership in parallel to India's own efforts to engage with Kashmiri secessionists in the six districts of the Valley.

Demography and Discontent in the 'Northern Areas'

If Mirpur's role in the jihad in Jammu and Kashmir was shaped by economic immigration, a full understanding of the processes underway on the Pakistani side of the Line of Control needs engagement with another demographic dislocation. What kinds of demographic shocks have those parts of pre-1947 Jammu and Kashmir which are under the undisguised administration of Pakistan—that is, the 'Northern Areas' of Gilgit, Hunza and Baltistan—experienced? What might their possible policy-consequences be?

Unlike much of northern and eastern India, the 'Northern Areas' did not experience large-scale demographic shocks in the immediate aftermath of Partition. General Mohammad Zia-ul Haq's regime initiated efforts to change the demographic composition of the 'Northern Areas' in the wake of the 1979 Islamist revolution in Iran. Hoping to counter the growing ethnic-religious consciousness of the 'Northern Areas' Shia population, Pakistan's military encouraged the large-scale migration of Sunni Muslims, many retired soldiers, from other provinces. Grants of agricultural land seem to have been a major instrument through which this demographic engineering was achieved.

Although verifiable data is hard to come by, most estimates suggest that Shia and Ismaili Muslims, who were about 85 per cent of the population of the 'Northern Areas' in 1948, constitute only about half of the region's inhabitants today. Analyst B. Raman has noted that this demographic shift also had a specific ethnic manifestation, other than just sectarian or religious. While in 1948, ethnic groups affiliated to those living in the Kargil and Leh districts of Jammu and Kashmir had formed the overwhelming majority of the population of the 'Northern Areas', they are today only a thin majority. According to Raman, Pashtuns from the North-West Frontier Province constitute about 24 per cent of the population, Punjabis about six per cent, Mirpuris from Pakistan-administered Kashmir about three per cent and Pashtuns from the Federally-Administered Tribal Areas, Balochis and migrants from Sindh about one per cent each. The ethnic and religious origin of some 11 per cent of the population is unknown.[8]

A key manifestation of General Zia-ul Haq's anxieties about Iranian fundamentalism penetrating the 'Northern Areas' was the decision to commit the Pakistani State to supporting an anti-Shia terrorist group, the Sipah-i-Sahaba Pakistan (SSP). Led by Maulana Haq Nawaz Jhangvi, the SSP was at the centre of massive terrorist violence that claimed the lives of 1,016 people between 1987 and 2002.[9] For much of its early existence, the SSP's strongest bases of influence were in the Pakistani province of Punjab, where it drew on tensions between the mainly-Sunni industry and business-owning bourgeoisie and industrialists and the Shia feudal elite.[10] However, in the 'Northern Areas', the SSP functioned as an instrument of Zia-ul Haq's Islamist state apparatus, setting up seminaries and military training facilities for the region's growing Sunni community.

Shia resentment against the creeping demographic shock—and the injection of Sunni-fundamentalist tendencies—took the form, in 1988, of demands for an autonomous Shia province, to be called Karakoram State. Zia-ul Haq responded to Shia mobilisation with military force. Pakistan's former President, General Pervez Musharraf in 1988 (as Brigadier) led a ruthless campaign against Shia dissent with the assistance of Islamist militia groups led by a then-obscure Saudi jihadi named Osama bin-Laden. A subsequent investigation by a Pakistani magazine, *The Herald*, reported that the army and Osama bin Laden's forces "destroyed crops and houses, lynched and burnt people to death in the villages around Gilgit town. The number of dead and injured was put in the hundreds. But numbers alone tell nothing of the savagery of the invading hordes and the chilling impact it has left on these peaceful valleys".[11]

Zia-ul Haq's subsequent death in an air crash has been attributed, amongst other things, to a suicide-assassination by his pilot, a Shia from the 'Northern Areas'. Whatever the truth, tensions created by the Pakistani State's demographic interventionism continued to simmer in the subsequent years. In the summer of 2004, Shia demonstrators took to the streets to protest against government textbooks which were perceived as hostile to their religious beliefs. Gilgit Shias were incensed by passages and images in the state-prescribed religious studies textbooks which they believed promoted a Sunni-chauvinist vision of Islam. Around the same time, Sunni chauvinists attacked staff working for the Aga Khan Foundation in the Gilgit area. In the wake of the violence, schools and educational institutions in the region had to be closed for six months. Pakistan's Islamist parties had been claiming that the Aga Khan Foundation, which runs a wide network of educational and health-related charities in Pakistan, was engaged in spreading Shia apostasy.

In January 2005, sectarian tensions again exploded after Sunni fundamentalists attempted to assassinate Aga Zia-ud-din, a Shia community leader and the imam of the main mosque in Gilgit. Two of Zia-ud-din's bodyguards were killed in the assassination attempt, while the cleric was seriously injured. At least 14 people were killed, six of them by being burnt alive, in retaliatory Shia mob attacks. Curfew had to be imposed in Gilgit to restore order. Interestingly, the violence seemed, once again, to have been linked to the Pakistani State's efforts to use Islamist groups to secure national objectives. Following the assassination attempt, the head of the Lashkar-e-Taiba's parent political organisation, the Markaz Dawa wal'Irshad, claimed that the Pakistan Government's failure to crack down harder in the 'Northern Areas' meant it was "supporting the so-called 'heresy' of Ismaili and Shia Islam".[12] Saeed's remarks were evidently intended to provide ideological legitimacy to the assassination attempt, and protect its perpetrators against legal action. Ever since its cadre were used in low-level logistical support roles in the 1999 Kargil war, the Lashkar-e-Tayyeba had set up bases in the Northern Areas, exacerbating Shia-Sunni tensions in and around Gilgit.

What lessons can Indian policy-makers draw from the 'Northern Areas' experience of the relationship between demographic change and political discontent? First, Indian diplomats need to place the 'Northern Areas' at the foreground of dialogue on the conflict in Jammu and Kashmir. Migration into this part of the pre-1947 state of Jammu and Kashmir is, in itself, a powerful argument against those who argue for the de-facto partition of the territories to be reversed, whether through a referendum or other means. Second, democratic movements within the 'Northern Areas' need the unequivocal support of the Indian Government. Leaders from the 'Northern Areas', like the All-Parties National Alliance's (APNA) Shazia Ghulam Din, have long demanded inclusion in any dialogue between India and secessionist groups in Jammu and Kashmir like the All Parties Hurriyat Conference.[13] Both in India's tactical interests, and on principle, the inclusion of 'Northern Areas' political groups in dialogue makes not a little sense. Most important, though, it is clear that the Pakistani State's efforts to counter political challenges, in this case Shia fundamentalism, through demographic intervention, has served to perpetuate a problem—not solve it. Providing state incentives for Sunni migration has created new ethnic and religious fault lines, which will more likely deepen in the future. If nothing else, this should provide food for thought for those in India who believe that opening up Jammu and Kashmir to large-scale migration from elsewhere will help strengthen its relationship with the Union of India.

Tectonic Shifts in Indian Jammu and Kashmir

Islamist political flags fluttered from atop the clock tower in Srinagar's historic Lal Chowk tower on August 15, 2008, the anniversary of India's independence. Even during the worst days of the long jihad in Jammu and Kashmir, Indian forces in Srinagar had ensured the national flag flew from the Lal Chowk tower. As usual, security force personnel had hoisted India's flag at Lal Chowk that morning. But late that afternoon, Islamist protestors marched on Lal Chowk. With strict orders not to use force on the unarmed protestors, police stationed at Lal Chowk brought down the flag and withdrew.[14] Elsewhere in Srinagar, mobs destroyed police and CRPF posts, attacked police stations and burned down the offices of pro-India politicians.[15]

What the two-decade jihad in Jammu and Kashmir had not achieved, six weeks of protests had succeeded in bringing about. The Indian State appeared to be on retreat—and this, just weeks before elections were scheduled to be held. Few believed an election in Jammu and Kashmir was even possible. Mirwaiz Umer Farooq, Chairman of the secessionist All Parties Hurriyat Conference, had insisted that "we are sure there will be 100 per cent poll boycott".[16] In an article on October 31, 2008, commentator Hassan Zainagiri reported in *Greater Kashmir* that Kashmir's "people are quite jubilantly supporting the boycott schedule of the Coordination Committee".[17] Eminent scholar, journalist and author Prem Shankar Jha even prophesied that "the Government will be lucky if they get more than 10 percent [*sic*] of people to come out and vote".[18] Most major political parties were less than enthused at the prospect of facing the electorate; India's Election Commission was also concerned.[19]

Then, the apparently-inexplicable happened: Jammu and Kashmir saw record numbers of voters participating in a peaceful election. How did this come about? And how did what appeared to be a mass uprising against the Indian rule yield so quickly to competitive democratic politics? The local agitation over a grant of few hundred acres of barren forest land for constructing pre-fabricated huts was driven by ethnic-religious anxieties which remain unresolved. All parties attempted to profit from these anxieties; none, however, was able to leverage them in order to become the sole spokesperson of the state's conflicting ethnic-religious communities.

Back in the summer of 2004, Jammu and Kashmir's then Chief Minister, Mufti Mohammad Saeed, and the state's then Governor, S.K. Sinha, had locked horns over the management of the Amarnath Yatra—an annual pilgrimage to a cave-temple in the mountains above Pahalgam. Saeed shot down Sinha's decision to extend the pilgrimage to eight weeks from four. Five cabinet ministers from the Jammu region—all members of Saeed's coalition partner, the Congress, and all Hindus—submitted their resignations in protest.[20] It was an early round in a series of skirmishes that would lead to the eventual collapse of the Congress-People's Democratic Party (PDP) alliance.

Amidst this feud, the Jammu and Kashmir High Court ordered the government to give the Shri Amarnath Shrine Board (SASB), which manages the pilgrimage, the right to use forest land to provide shelter and sanitation for pilgrims. It took another two years of legal wrangling, though, before the SASB was given permission to raise "pre-fabricated structures only for camping purposes of pilgrims without going in for construction of permanent structures". The government order granting permission made clear that the "proprietary status of [the] forest land shall remain unchanged".[21]

Kashmir's Islamist patriarch, Syed Ali Shah Geelani, saw political opportunity in the decision. He claimed that the order was part of a conspiracy to settle Hindus in the region. At one press conference, he warned that Sinha had been working "on an agenda of changing the demography of the state".[22] "I caution my nation", he warned "that if don't wake up in time, India and its stooges will succeed and we will be displaced". Later, he asserted that the land-use rights granted to the SASB were part of a covert enterprise code-named Operation Yatra, which was "devised on the lines of Israel's strategy of settlement in Palestine".[23] The SASB, he went on, was "pursuing the similar method to settle Hindus here". He was later to hold out dark hints that a genocide of Kashmiri Muslims, modelled on the Partition of India pogroms, was being planned.[24]

Geelani's position stemmed from his long-standing belief that Islam and Hinduism were locked in an irreducible civilisational opposition. At an October 26 rally in Srinagar, Geelani had explained this position, saying that "the people of state should, *as their religious duty*, raise voice against India's aggression" [my emphasis].[25] This duty, he argued, stemmed from the fact that to "practice [*sic*] Islam completely under the subjugation of India is impossible because human beings in practice worship those whose rules they abide by".[26] Geelani had long located the legitimacy of the secessionist movement in Jammu and Kashmir in the supposed oppositional dualities of Hindus and Muslims. In matters of faith, belief and customs, he argued in his prison diaries, Hindus and Muslims are set irrevocably apart, as they are divided by such matters as food, clothing and lifestyle. He described it as being as difficult for Muslims to live in a Hindu milieu as "for a fish to stay alive in a desert". Muslims, he argued, "cannot live harmoniously with a Hindu majority without their own religion and traditions coming under a grave threat, one major factor being Hinduism's capacity to assimilate other religions. For Islam to be preserved and promoted in Kashmir, it is necessary for it to be separated from India."[27]

Matters came to a head when Saeed's PDP, whose ministers had supported the land-use orders in the state cabinet, threw its weight behind Islamist calls for them to be revoked. PDP leaders were driven by the fact that a significant part of their constituency was affiliated with Kashmir's religious right. However, PDP's coalition partner Congress was unable to meet its demand, afraid it would undermine its position amongst its core constituency of Jammu Hindus. Sinha's successor as Governor, N.N. Vohra, in his capacity as Head of the Shrine Board, attempted to resolve the stalemate. He offered to surrender the land-use rights if the state government itself would provide all facilities to pilgrims, as it had been doing since 1979. Hoping to avert a showdown with the PDP, the then Chief Minister Ghulam Nabi Azad, a Congress leader, agreed. Later, under pressure from the Congress central leadership in New Delhi to save the Congress' alliance with the PDP, Azad revoked the land-use order altogether. However, the PDP pulled out of government days before a deadline it had set to resolve the crisis.[28]

Then, a second phase of the crisis began. Hindu groups in Jammu began an agitation demanding the land back. Elements among them threatened to blockade traffic to Kashmir. It is unclear whether there was, in fact, a significant blockade.[29] But the threat itself provided leverage to Geelani and Mirwaiz Umar Farooq, a Srinagar-based cleric who chairs a rival secessionist formation, All Parties Hurriyat Conference (APHC).

Acting on a call from the Pakistan-based United Jihad Council, both groups organised a march across the Line of Control, which divides Indian-administered and Pakistan-administered Kashmir, saying the economic blockade necessitated the opening of traffic from Srinagar to Muzaffarabad.[30] India had, in fact, been calling for free trade along the route, a demand Pakistan had rejected. However, the defiance of the Line of Control was an act the state simply could not countenance. To no-one's surprise, force was used to stop the marchers: three people were killed, including a mid-ranking APHC leader. Over 20 other people died in subsequent clashes between the police or army and the protestors, often a consequence of attacks on the bunkers of police and army personnel by enraged mobs.[31]

Ever since 2002, when levels of jihadi violence in Jammu and Kashmir began to decline, Indian policy-makers assumed that the anti-India movement in the region would also slowly disappear. It was a seismic error of judgment. Faith and xenophobia became the twin poles of a long-running and powerfully effective Islamist campaign that began in 2005, after it became evident to Islamists that the jihad on which their political position had been predicated was in terminal decline. Economic change and the social dislocation it had brought about provided the firmament for their revival. Islamists began to make the wider case that the secularisation of culture in Kashmir—in turn the consequence of economic growth—constituted a civilisational threat. In an article published in May 2006, Islamist leader Asiya Andrabi wondered what would happen if "Muhammad (S.A.W.) will come to know that the Muslim youth of Kashmir are busy in vulgarity, obscenity, waywardness?" She attacked "young Muslim girls who have lost their identity of Islam and are presenting the look of a Bollywood actress, but not Fatima and Aisha (R.A.) (respectively, Muhammad's sister and wife)".

Later, Islamists leveraged the uncovering of a prostitution racket in Srinagar to argue that secularism and modernity were responsible for this, and that it was an Indian conspiracy to undermine Jammu and Kashmir's

Islamic character. Pro-Islamist scholar Hameeda Nayeem even claimed that the scandal pointed "unequivocally towards a policy-based state patronage (of prostitution)".[32] Significantly, the prostitution protests saw the first large-scale Islamist mob violence that went unchecked by the state. Geelani's supporters were allowed to gather at the home of alleged Srinagar prostitution-ring madam Sabina Bulla and raze it to the ground. Mobs also attacked the homes of politicians charged with having used her services.[33]

In the summer of 2007, the rape-murder of north Kashmir teenager Tabinda Gani was used to initiate a xenophobic campaign against the presence of migrant workers in the state. Addressing a June 24, 2007 rally at the town of Langate, Geelani said that "hundreds of thousands of non-state subjects had been pushed into Kashmir under a long-term plan to crush the Kashmiris".[34] He claimed that "the majority of these non-state subjects are professional criminals and should be driven out of Kashmir in a civilised way". Geelani's political ally, Hilal War, claimed that migrant workers' slums were "centres of all kinds of illegal business".[35] The use of such language incited a series of terrorist attacks on migrants, the last of which was the bombing of a bus carrying workers from Srinagar just as the Shrine Board protests began.[36]

From these events, Islamists learned that the objective conditions existed for xenophobic politics to succeed. Even on the eve of the Shrine Board protests, Islamists mobilised against a career counsellor who, they claimed, had been despatched to Srinagar schools to seduce students into careers of vice. An Anantnag school-teacher also came under attack, after a video surfaced showing that a group of his students had danced to pop film music on a holiday in Anantnag.[37]

Part of the reason for Geelani's success was the absence of secular voices—both in political life and amongst public intellectuals—challenging his contentions. No political grouping condemned his actions. Indeed, elements in Congress made opportunistic use of his mobilisation. PDP politicians sought to appropriate Geelani's rhetoric, in an effort to draw the electoral endorsement of his supporters. So, too, did the National Conference.

Across the Pir Panjal Mountains in Jammu, a near-identical chauvinistic mobilisation was underway—one that was even more invisible to analysts and the government than its Islamist counterpart. In the build-up to the 2002 elections, the Bharatiya Janata Party (BJP) found itself discredited by its failure to contain terrorism. Much of the Hindutva movement's cadre turned to a new grouping, the Jammu State Morcha (JSM). JSM leaders wanted a new, Hindu-majority state carved out of Jammu and Kashmir.

In the event, both the JSM and the BJP were wiped out in the elections, winning just one seat each.

A new generation of Hindutva leaders then took control of Hindu neoconservative politics in Jammu. Soon after the Congress-PDP Government came to power, this new Hindutva leadership unleashed its first mass mobilisation. Reacting to PDP leader and former Chief Minister Mufti Mohammad Saeed's calls for demilitarisation and self-rule, pointing to the expulsion of Pandits from Kashmir at the outset of the jihad, Hindutva leaders claimed that Saeed was now preparing the ground for the expulsion of Hindus—and Hinduism—from Jammu.

From 2003, Hindutva groups sought to forge these anxieties into a concrete political mobilisation around the issue of cattle-slaughter. Hindutva cadre would interdict trucks carrying cattle, and then use their capture to stage protests. It was not as if the anti-cow-slaughter movement had stumbled on a great secret. For decades, cow-owning farmers had sold old livestock, which no longer earned them an income, to traders from Punjab and Rajasthan. In turn, the traders sold their herds to cattle traffickers on India's eastern border, who fed the demand for meat in Bangladesh. But Hindutva groups understood that the cow was a potent—and politically profitable—metaphor. In December 2007, for example, VHP and Bajrang Dal cadre organised large-scale protests against the reported sacrificial slaughter of cows at the villages of Bali Charna, in the Satwari area of Jammu, and Chilog, near Kathua District's Bani town.[38] Riots had also taken place in the villages around Jammu's Pargwal area in March 2005, after Hindutva activists claimed that a cow had been raped.[39]

It should be noted, however, that these mobilisations, though built around religious themes, were led by politicians and not clerics. For example, south Kashmir-based Jamiat Ahl-e-Hadis neo-fundamentalist activist Maqbool Akhrani, while mobilising against migrant workers in 2006, stated that they were part of a campaign by India's intelligence services to "divert attention from real issues and that is why new things like country made liquor are pushed into the valley".[40] Similar xenophobic claims informed the shrine war. However, though Akhrani and the Jamiat Ahl-e-Hadis participated in the anti-shrine land mobilisation, they were at best marginal to the course of subsequent events. Indeed, senior Ahl-e-Hadith leaders continued to engage with the Jammu and Kashmir Government to build an Islamic university, and refused to condemn Governor S.K Sinha.[41] Kashmir's quasi-official Grand Mufti, Maulvi Mohammad Bashir-ud-Din, also made interventions in the course of the shrine issue.[42] However, it bears note that like the Jamiat Ahl-e-Hadis leadership, Bashir-ud Din did not address a single rally of consequence.

That task was left to leaders of the Tehreek-i-Hurriyat and APHC, none of whom barring Mirwaiz Farooq was a religious leader—and even in this one case, a religious leader with influence only in a small part of Srinagar.

Hindu religious leaders like Swami Dinesh Bharati, who played roles in the Hindu agitation there, were also leaders of obscure denominations and temples, with no real clerical authority.[43] No figure associated with major temples, like the priests of the Mata Vaishno Devi or Raghunath Mandir, appear to have participated in the protests.

Underpinning the shrine war lie broader demographic contestations. On September 7, 2000, the Hizb ul-Mujahideen commander Masood Tantrey warned of an Indian conspiracy to alter the state's demographic profile, and demanded that the census process be terminated.[44] "If the government does not adhere to the warning", he said, "we will not desist from opening our guns at them". "If any one of the 22,000 government employees is seen participating in the census operation", Abu Ubaid, a Lashkar-e-Taiba commander, affirmed in turn, "he or she will be killed without warning".

It is rare for a census operation to provoke such passion—and it points, as nothing else does, to the existence of a tectonic demographic shift that is underway in Jammu and Kashmir. In the first two parts of this paper, I have addressed demographic shocks witnessed in the two major Pakistan-occupied parts of Jammu and Kashmir, and looked at the role they have played in the India-Pakistan conflict over the territory. The third demographic crisis is the slow but certain shift in power relations between the province of Kashmir and the province of Jammu, and its possible long-term consequences.

Voices on the Islamist right were not the only ones to oppose the census process in Jammu and Kashmir: mainstream figures in the politics of the Kashmir valley also did so. At a September 6, 2000 press conference, Saifuddin Soz charged that census figures had been manipulated to show that the Muslim population of Jammu and Kashmir had been declining as a percentage of the total population, and that its growth in the Jammu region had been dramatically lower than that of Hindus. In a written statement issued at a subsequent press conference on September 13, Saifuddin Soz fleshed out his position: "The lone Muslim majority State had been characterised as one of the strongest elements of India's secular edifice", he noted, "and any manoeuvring and dishonest effort to tamper with this character of the population ratio must be ruthlessly discouraged and condemned".

Leaving aside the perhaps unfortunate polemic about ruthlessness, Soz's assertions were ill founded. He insisted, for example, that census figures showed a fall in the Muslim population in the state, whereas in fact they only recorded a decline in its percentage share of the total population. The 1961 census recorded that Muslims constituted 68.30 per cent of the state's population of 35,60,976. In 1971, that figure fell to 65.85 per cent, and then to 64.19 per cent in 1981. By contrast, the percentage of all non-Muslims, overwhelmingly Hindus, grew from 31.70 per cent in 1961 to 34.15 per cent in 1971, and then 32.24 per cent in 1981. No census could be conducted in 1991, because of the emergence of large-scale terrorist violence in the state. Soz's statement focussed further on events within Jammu. In the district of Doda, he noted, census figures showed that the Hindu population had grown by 47.23 per cent between 1971 and 1981, but that of Muslims by only 11.97 per cent. In Udhampur, the figures for the same period were 45 per cent against 6.35 per cent and in Rajouri, 47.72 per cent against 33.01 per cent. Muslim populations in two districts showed a decline. The Hindu population of Kathua grew by 39.31 per cent, while that of Muslims actually fell by 14.57 per cent. The fall was most precipitate in Jammu, where the Hindu population grew by 36.14 per cent, and that of Muslims fell by 29.98 per cent. Soz did not even take into account the forced exodus of over 400,000 Kashmiri Pandits from the Valley, most of whom have been camping in Jammu and Udhampur since 1990.

What do these figures actually show us? Part of the problem with Soz's reading of the data is that he was misled by the failure to examine the sampling procedures used in the census; in 1961, census operations were conducted in February, and in 1971, in mid-March. Census operations in 1981 were, however, conducted in April. Large populations of Jammu and Kashmir Government employees move between Jammu and Srinagar for six months a year. During the 1961 and 1971 census operations, over 15,000 employees and their families would have been present in Jammu, but, in 1981, they would have begun the process of moving back to Srinagar and would have been enumerated there. What Soz did not tell the media also bears recording. For example, the population growth of Muslims massively outstripped that of Hindus in five of six districts in Kashmir valley between 1971 and 1981. In Badgam, the one district where Hindu population growth was higher than that of Muslims, it was because the Kashmiri-Pandit dominated areas of Barzulla, Rawalpora and Hyderpora, on the outskirts of Srinagar city, had been transferred to the revenue district of Badgam. Another important factor is that the Total Fertility Rates for rural Hindus in Jammu and Kashmir has been established, in successive studies, to be higher than that of Muslims—education, healthcare and economic well-being define fertility rates, not religion.

Census data in fact elucidates two stark facts. First, the emergence of Jammu as a major industrial hub over the last two decades has brought in large numbers of economic migrants from other parts of the country, feeding the growing need for labour in the state's economy. Without doubt, this appears to be the most plausible explanation for the overall decline in the Muslim population as a percentage of total population. With the ongoing construction of a railway line from Jammu to Baramulla, such migration is likely to accelerate. Similarly, the welter of large-dam projects now under construction in Jammu and Kashmir will have a similar impact.

To understand where events might go here, it is useful to turn to history. From an early stage, urban Kashmiri support for the jihad marked a crisis of modernity: a rebellion by classes who had acquired economic power but were denied political representation by parties like the National Conference which drew their legitimacy from the countryside. Consider, for example, the social composition of the Master Cell, a terrorist group which operated in the mid-1960s. One member, Abdul Hamid Khan, was a junior technician at the Government Medical College in Srinagar, another, Mohammad Yusuf Butt, an Assistant Engineer in the Electrical Department, while Ali Mohammad Malik and Mehboob Husain were both students of the Regional Engineering College in Srinagar. Broadly, this pattern is mirrored through the overall composition of the cells. Of a total of 44 residents of the Indian state of Jammu and Kashmir identified as cell members, the largest single category, 20, were government employees or contractors, in a variety of fields. The second largest category were students, of whom there were 19. Only five cell members had independent businesses or professions. All but three were from Srinagar or its immediate vicinity; none was a peasant.

One thoughtful analysis of political contestation in Jammu and Kashmir has suggested that National Conference's successful efforts to widen education may have created a class whose aspirations it could not meet. Eminent scholar Sumit Ganguly has pointed to a dramatic growth in education in Jammu and Kashmir from the 1960s onwards, a process that took place in a growing economy and which at once found expression in a dramatic escalation in newspaper circulation.[45] In Ganguly's view:

> Young Kashmiris acquired a modicum of education and became aware of improved economic prospects. They were no longer content to seek employment in the traditional sectors of the economy, namely, the handicraft industry or the tourist trade. The National Conference did

> little to expand employment growth in new sectors of the economy. Inevitably a reservoir of discontent among the quasi-educated and largely prospect-less youth of the Kashmir valley.[46]

In demographic terms, we can understand the Islamist uprising of 1988 as a final effort by ethnic Kashmiri elites to retain their primacy in state politics: within a democratic structure, urban and affluent Kashmiri elites could simply no longer hang on to a monopoly of power. Two decades of war later, however, it has become clear that sub-conventional war will not lead to the Indian State being pushed aside. It is in this context one must understand the growing ethnic-Kashmiri consensus behind securing greater federal autonomy for the state—a demand which, in reality, means the perpetuation of the hegemony of the new elites which have emerged after Jammu and Kashmir's accession to India. Indian policy-makers engaged in dialogue with secessionists must understand that negotiating postures in Kashmir are the consequence of desperation: desperation to secure a deal with India before the processes of modernisation transfigure political and economic realities in Jammu and Kashmir beyond recognition and sweeps away the class they represent once and for all.

In the cases of 'Azad' Kashmir and the 'Northern Areas', crisis of modernity have provoked destabilising outcomes. Could another crisis of modernity in Jammu and Kashmir itself, this one mediated through the instrument of democracy, lend itself to a stable outcome? Indian policy-makers need to consider the possibility—and see just kinds of interventions might be appropriate to the situation.

Conclusion

Multiple crises of modernity, linked to demography and displacement, are at work in undivided Jammu and Kashmir's several regions. Indeed, within these regions, complex internal processes and divisions are also at play. If in the 'Northern Areas', state-engineered immigration has led to the creation of a murderous ethnic-religious conflict, a history of skewed development has led to crisis of identity which was adroitly utilised by Islamists and nationalists in Mirpur. In the Indian state of Jammu and Kashmir, there has been almost no serious thinking on the consequences demographic processes that are underway might be. Careful introspection is clearly necessary to shape adequate policy responses.

Some lessons are, however, immediately apparent. To seek to engage with a single Kashmiri voice that claims to speak for all ethnic categories and groups, convenient as it might be for policy-makers and states, is an exercise in futility. What is needed instead, and what India must press for, is for a dialogue that engages states and regional politicians on both sides of the Line of Control—not just one. Some progress has been made in this direction, with informal discussions between regional leaders taking place in New Delhi, Srinagar and Jammu, but its scale and character is inadequate. Notably, Pakistan has not been pushed to start a dialogue with politicians from Pakistan-administered Jammu and Kashmir; nor have Indian politicians outside of the All Parties Hurriyat Conference been allowed to reach out across the Line of Control. Just as Pakistan asserts it has equities in the Indian state of Jammu and Kashmir, so does India on the Pakistani side—equities that must be asserted not just for tactical ends, but because they are critical to an abiding peace.

NOTES

1. Tariq Naqash, 'Bus Service Thrills Divided Families', *The Dawn*, Karachi, April 5, 2005.
2. Roger Ballard, *Growth and Poverty Reduction: Reflections on the Basis of South Asian Experience*, DFID, London, 2002, p. 28.
3. For a full discussion of these groups, see: Praveen Swami, *Covert War in Kashmir, 1947-2004*. Routledge, London, 2006.
4. Sultan Shaheen, 'How "Azad" is "Azad" Kashmir', undated, at http://www.jammu-kashmir.com/insights/insight990902.html.
5. For a thorough discussion of these networks and their origins, see Roger Ballard, *A Background Report on the Operation of Informal Value*, CASS, London, 2003.
6. Akbar Khan, *Raiders in Kashmir*, National Book Foundation, Islamabad, 1970, p. 9.
7. Ibid., pp. 9-10.
8. B. Raman, 'Unrest in Gilgit-Baltistan', Paper 1241, South Asia Analysis Group, February 3, 2005, at http://www.saag.org/papers13/paper1241.html.
9. Muhammad Amir Rana, *A to Z of Jehadi Organizations in Pakistan*, Translated by Saba Ansari, Mashal Books, Lahore, 2004, p. 140.
10. Ibid., pp. 193-194.
11. Cited in B. Raman, 'Pakistan: The Shia Anger', Paper 810, South Asia Analysis Group, October 7, 2003, at http://www.saag.org/papers9/paper810.html.
12. Editorial: 'Story of Gilgit Deaths Foretold', *The Daily Times*, Karachi, January 10, 2005.
13. Praveen Swami, 'PoK Leader Calls for a Wider Dialogue', *The Hindu*, Chennai, September 2, 2004.
14. Avijit Ghosh, 'Tricolour at 8 a.m., Flags of Separatists at 4.00 p.m.', *The Times of India*, Mumbai, August 16, 2008, at http://timesofindia.indiatimes.com/JK_Tricolour_at_8am_separatist_flags_at_4pm/articleshow/3369371.cms.
15. Hakeem Irfan, 'Angry Mobs Storm CRPF Bunkers, Police Stations', *Rising Kashmir*, Srinagar, August 14, 2008, at http://www.risingkashmir.com/index.php?option=com_content&task=view&id=5879&Itemid=1.
16. 'We'll Carry on Anti-Poll Campaign: Mirwaiz Umar', *Greater Kashmir*, Srinagar, November 22, 2008, at http://www.greaterkashmir.com/full_story.asp?Date=2211_2008&ItemID=72&cat=1
17. Hassan Zainagiri, 'Engineering Elections', *Greater Kashmir*, Srinagar, October 31, 2008, at http://www.greaterkashmir.com/full_story.asp?Date=31102008&ItemID

=27&cat=11.

18. 'Voting Begins in Indian Kashmir', *Alwahy News*, November 17, 2008, at http://alwahy.com/news/article/asiapacific/5661/1/print/.
19. Muzamil Jaleel, 'Kashmir', *The Indian Express*, New Delhi, November 16, 2009, at http://www.indianexpress.com/story-print/386152/.
20. Luv Puri, 'Amarnath Yatra: Court Vests Authority with Shrine Board', *The Hindu*, Chennai, April 17, 2005, at http://www.hindu.com/2005/04/17/ stories/2005041706750700.htm.
21. Praveen Swami, 'Anatomy of the Shrine Board Crisis', *The Hindu*, Chennai, June 30, 2008, at http://www.hindu.com/2008/06/30/stories/2008063059891300.htm.
22. Zulfikar Majid, 'I Caution My Nation: Wake Up: Geelani', *Greater Kashmir*, Srinagar, June 24, 2008, at http://www.greaterkashmir.com/full_story.asp?Date=24_6_2008&ItemID=61&cat=1.
23. Hakeem Irfan, 'Operation Yatra Devised on Israeli Lines: Geelani', *Rising Kashmir*, Srinagar, June 13, 2008, at http://www.risingkashmir.com/?option=com_content&task=view&id=4330.
24. Ahmad Ali Fayyaz, 'Stronger Geelani's New Slogan: *Ham Pakistani Hain*', *Daily Excelsior*, Jammu, August 19, 2008, p. 1.
25. AM Dar, "Geelani Slams Mainstream Politicians". *Greater Kashmir*, Srinagar, October 27, 2007, at http://www.greaterkashmir.com/full_story.asp?Date=27_10_2007&ItemID=35&cat=1.
26. Ibid.
27. Yoginder Sikand, 'For Islam and Kashmir: The Prison Diaries of Sayyed Ali Gilani of the Jama'at-i-Islami of Jammu and Kashmir', *The Journal of Muslim Minority Affairs*, Vol 18, No. 2, 1998, p. 243.
28. Chander Suta Dogra, 'Echoes in Hell', *Outlook*, August 18, 2008, at http://www.outlookindia.com/fullprint.asp?choice=1&fodname=20080818&fname=Jammu+Main+%28F%29&sid=1.
29. "Centre: No Economic Blockade of Valley, Pak Cashing In on Turmoil", *The Indian Express*, New Delhi, August 17, 2008, at http://www.indianexpress.com/printer Friendly/349694.html.
    Also see Harmeet Singh, 'Army Controls Highway, Traffic Restored', *Greater Kashmir*, Srinagar, August 4, 2008, at http://www.greaterkashmir.com/full_story.asp?Date=4_8_2008&ItemID=45&cat=1.
30. 'March towards Muzaffarabad: UJC', *Rising Kashmir*, Srinagar, August 7, 2008.
31. Ahmad Ali Fayyaz, 'Toll Reaches 21 as One More Killed in CRPF Firing', *The Daily Excelsior*, Jammu, August 15, 2008, p. 1.
32. Hameeda Nayeem, 'Unite, in Humanity', *The Indian Express*, New Delhi, May 11, 2006, p. 6.
33. For a full account, see Praveen Swami, 'Righteousness, Religion and Right-wing Politics', *The Hindu*, Chennai, May 15, 2008 at http://www.hindu.com/2006/05/15/stories/2006051504021000.htm.
34. 'Non-Kashmiris Should be Seen Off: Geelani', *Greater Kashmir*, Srinagar, July 25, 2007, p. 3.
35. 'Construction Works to be Hit by Labourers Exodus', *Daily Excelsior*, Jammu, August 4, 2007, p. 1.
36. Praveen Swami, 'Bombing in Srinagar a Response to Islamist Calls', *The Hindu*, Chennai, July 25, 2008, at http://www.hindu.com/2008/07/25/stories/

2008072556861500.htm.

37. Praveen Swami, 'Kashmir: the War for Hearts and Minds', *The Hindu*, Chennai, June 4, 2008, at http://www.hindu.com/2008/06/04/stories/2008060455311000.htm.
38. 'Tension over Cow Sacrifice', *The Daily Telegraph*, Kolkata, December 23, 2008, at http://www.telegraphindia.com/1071223/jsp/nation/story_8700385.jsp.
39. '"Unnatural Act"' with Cow Leads to Protests in Akhnoor', Expressindia.com, March 28, 2005, at http://www.expressindia.com/news/fullstory.php?newsid=44002.
40. Hilal Bhat, 'Bihari Labourers Producing Desi Liquor in South Kashmir', *Greater Kashmir*, Srinagar, June 29, 2006, p. 3.
41. Praveen Swami, 'Islamic University Falls Victim to Kashmir's Shrine War', *The Hindu*, Chennai, August 21, 2008, at http://www.hindu.com/2008/08/21/stories/2008082155121100.htm.
42. 'Lift Blockade or We Lift Durbar', *Rising Kashmir*, Srinagar, August 3, 2008, at http://www.risingkashmir.com/?option=com_content&task=view&id=5616.
43. 'Dinesh Bharti's Detention under PSA Ordered', *The Daily Excelsior*, Jammu, August 26, 2008, p. 1.
44. B.L. Kak, 'Govt Won't Permit Interference by Lashkar, Hizbul Mujahideen', *The Daily Excelsior*, Jammu, October 20, 2002.
45. Sumit Ganguly, *The Crisis in Kashmir*, Woodrow Wilson Center Press and Cambridge University Press, Washington DC, 1997, pp. 31-37.
46. Ibid., p. 74.

13

Hydropower Exploitation in Gilgit-Baltistan and Pakistani Administered Kashmir

Shabir Choudhry

> *If the wars of this century were fought over oil, the wars of the next century will be fought over water.*
>
> **Ismael Serageldin,** Vice President of the World Bank

Today, several countries have serious shortage of water and energy, and the demand is increasing. Lack of sufficient clean and useable freshwater has adverse impact on the economy and prosperity of countries. Due to this scarcity, water has assumed strategic importance, and could be the cause of armed conflicts in future. As freshwater resources transcend national boundaries, its management poses a major challenge. Water is crucial to life—it is a necessity. Yet, more than a billion people in the world do not have access to safe drinking water. According to the United Nations' World Water Development Report, the total actual renewable water resources in Pakistan decreased from 2,961 cubic metres per capita in year 2000 to 1,420 cubic metres in 2005. A more recent study indicates an available supply of water of little more than 1,000 cubic metres per person, which puts Pakistan in the category of a high stress country.

Due to inefficient water management, lack of proper investment and poor planning water and energy shortage has assumed serious proportion in Pakistan. And because of rapid growth in population, urbanisation and increased industrialisation, the situation is likely to get worse. According to a 2006 World Bank report, Pakistan is fast moving from being a "water stressed country to a water scarce country". Water is also essential for power generation in Pakistan. The country has the potential to generate as much as 50,000 MW of hydroelectric power. The current need of Pakistan is around 17,000 MW, and it does not produce enough to meet that demand. This is partly because the "transmission system has continued to languish, and up to one-third of all electricity that passes through its lines is 'unaccounted for' (either stolen or wasted though the poorly maintained system)".[1]

Despite these serious problems, Pakistan has failed to reach a consensus on constructing Kala Bagh Dam, initial planning for which was made in the 1950s, and several million pounds have already been spent on various designs and feasibility studies. Jamil Yousaf, editor of *Nazriyas*, stated at a seminar on "Quaid: A Role Model" held in Islamabad Club that it was Mohammed Ali Jinnah who had first decided in a Cabinet meeting held on March 15, 1948 to construct Kala Bagh Dam in order to meet the energy requirements of the country.[2] In the 1950s, apart from the Kala Bagh Dam, the Government of Pakistan also planned to construct Mangla Dam in Mirpur—a city in the Pakistani Administered Kashmir. After some opposition from the local people and some politicians, the authorities, however, postponed the proposed construction of the Kala Bagh Dam. All the reports suggest that the project is economically viable and highly beneficial to Pakistan, yet the politicians and provinces have not reached an agreement regarding its construction.

In contrast, Pakistani leaders are very keen to build mega dams within the territory of Jammu and Kashmir under its control, and which is not legally part of Pakistan. As a result of Pakistani-backed tribal invasion in October 1947, and subsequent accession by the Maharaja of Kashmir to India, the princely State of Jammu and Kashmir was divided between India and Pakistan. Areas under Pakistani control are known as 'Azad' Kashmir (AJK) and Gilgit-Baltistan. Pakistan separated the areas of Gilgit and Baltistan from AJK and ruled them as a colony. Vast areas of Gilgit and Baltistan, around 28,000 sq. miles were further divided and an area of approximately 2,200 sq. miles was ceded to China in 1963, what was termed as border adjustment.

The area of AJK is approximately 5,000 square miles, and as per the census of 1998, it has a population of 2,973,000. The area enjoys semi-autonomous status. The interim constitution of AJK, commonly known as Act 1974 is the biggest hindrance towards genuine democracy as it prohibits all those parties and individuals from participating in the political process that do not support the idea of Kashmir's accession to Pakistan. The relevant clause reads as follows:

> No person or political party in Azad Jammu and Kashmir shall be permitted to propagate against or take part in activities prejudicial or detrimental to the ideology of the State's accession to Pakistan.[3]

The AJK electoral law further elaborates this point by stipulating that, a person shall stand disqualified for running for an elective office: "If he is *propagating any opinion or acting in any manner prejudicial to the ideology of Pakistan, the ideology of the State's accession to Pakistan or the sovereignty, integrity of Pakistan or security of Azad Jammu and Kashmir or Pakistan, or morality, or the maintenance of public order, or the integrity or independence of the Judiciary of Azad Jammu and Kashmir or Pakistan, or who defames or brings into ridicule the Judiciary of Azad Jammu and Kashmir or Pakistan, or the Armed Forces of Pakistan.*"[4] Apart from that, all Assembly members of Pakistani Administered Kashmir, President, Prime Minister and Speaker, take the following oath: "*I will remain loyal to the country and the cause of accession of the state of Jammu and Kashmir to Pakistan.*"

This area is known as AJK, but nationalist Kashmiris like to call it Pakistani occupied Kashmir (PoK). However, the area is hardly *azad* (free). Thinking and nationalist Kashmiris view Pakistani Government and its officials as occupiers. Pakistan's relationship with these areas is of unequal relationship—that of an occupier and exploiter—and is designed to help Pakistan to plunder and exploit the natural resources of the Kashmiri territory.

Pakistan exploits the resources of Pakistani Administered Kashmir and Gilgit-Baltistan in different ways. Most significantly, the Government of Pakistan established Water and Power Development Authority (WAPDA) in 1958 as a semi-autonomous body to coordinate and plan schemes in water and power sectors. This white elephant of Pakistan was established to look after the national interests of Pakistan, and has mastered the art of exploiting Kashmiri resources. Its approach is that of an imperial organisation like the East India Company, determined to wrench every resource from its colony. Pakistan has its own water and energy requirements, but to meet these challenges it needs to use its resources and build dams within the Pakistani territory.

Construction of Mangla Dam

The state of Jammu and Kashmir is endowed with natural resources, including vast reservoirs of water. Notwithstanding the Indus Waters Treaty, water could be a likely source of future conflict between India and

Pakistan. Foreign Minister of Pakistan, Shah Mahmood Qureshi in his recent statement said that "the water dispute may create tensions between India and Pakistan in future and that was why he had asked Indian PM Man Mohan Singh during a meeting in the past to include the issue in composite dialogue".[5] Keeping this issue as a background, this section discusses the construction of Mangla Dam.

Mangla Dam was built from 1961 to 1967 with funding from the World Bank, after India and Pakistan agreed on a water sharing mechanism in the Indus Waters Treaty, which was signed in Karachi on September 19, 1960.[6] It must be noted here that the people of Mirpur and Kashmiri politicians protested against the construction of the Mangla Dam in Mirpur; however, their opposition was put down with brutal force, and Pakistan went ahead with the construction of the Mangla Dam, which was duly completed in 1967.

The Mangla Dam project was designed and supervised by Binnie & Partners of London, and it was built by Mangla Dam Contractors, a consortium of eight U.S. construction firms, sponsored by Guy F. Atkinson Company of South San Francisco. Mangla Dam Contractors employed Pakistani, American, British, Canadian, German and Irish personnel.

Mangla Dam is the 12th largest dam in the world. The main structures of the dam include four embankment dams, two spillways, five power-cum-irrigation tunnels and a 1,000 MW power station. The main dam is 10,300 feet (3,140 m) long and 454 feet (138 m) high (above core trench) with a reservoir of 97.7 square miles (253 km^2). The power station of Mangla Dam consists of 10 units each having capacity of 100 MW.

Though under the State Subject Regulations, non-Kashmiris cannot purchase any land inside the state, WAPDA constructed the dam on disputed territory and against the wishes of the local people. Due to this illegal construction, over 280 villages and the towns of Mirpur and Dadyal were submerged and over 110,000 people were displaced from the area as a result. Some of those affected by the dam were given work permits for Britain by the Government of Pakistan. Thousands of the affected people were not even appropriately compensated. Most of the promises made to the people of Mirpur were not honoured, and people were left helpless and without alternative subsistence arrangements.

No royalty for the dam was paid to the Government of Pakistani Administered Kashmir until few years ago. This is in contrast to Pakistan's treatment of North West Frontier Province, which has been receiving royalty for Tarbela Dam ever since its completion in 1976. After repeated requests from the Government of Pakistani Administered Kashmir, the

Pakistan Government set up a Committee in 1987 under the Chairmanship of Mehboob ul Haq to look into the royalty issue. The Committee had recommended that the Government of NWFP should get royalty of Rs. 2 billion per annum for the Tarbela Dam; and the Government of Pakistani Administered Kashmir should get Rs. 2 billion for the Mangla Dam. Yet no royalty was paid to Pakistani Administered Kashmir until few years ago, and it was at a much reduced rate—less than Rs. one billion; whereas the Government of NWFP now gets Rs. 8 billion for the Tarbela Dam.

When the construction of the Mangla Dam was at its planning stage, the Government of India raised objections at the United Nations Security Council, arguing that this construction was inside the "Indian territory". In a letter to the President of UN Security Council, India's Permanent Representative to the United Nations, Arthur S Lall stated:[7]

> The execution of this Dam project is a further instance of consolidation by the Government of Pakistan of its authority over the Indian territory of Jammu and Kashmir, which it continues to occupy by force, and of the exploitation of the natural resources of the territory to the disadvantage of the people of Jammu and Kashmir and for the benefit of the people of Pakistan. The members of the Security Council are aware of the categorical assurances given to the Prime Minister of India by the Chairman of the United Nations Commission for India and Pakistan that the Government of Pakistan will not be allowed to consolidate its position in the territory it had unlawfully occupied. Part 2, section A, Paragraph 1 of the Commission's resolution of 13 August 1948 (S/1100, para 75), under which Pakistan troops are required to vacate the territory unlawfully occupied by them and of the recognition of the Government of the State of Jammu and Kashmir as the only lawful Government of the State underlying the Commission's resolutions of 13 August 1948 and 5 January 1949 (S/1196, paragraph 15). The commencement of the execution of the Mangla Dam Project by the Government of Pakistan violates not only the provision of the 17 January 1948 but also the assurances given to the Prime Minister of India by the Chairman of the Commission for India and Pakistan and the provisions of the two resolutions adopted by the Commission.

In reply, Pakistan's Representative, Agha Shahi wrote to the President of the Security Council:

> We fully realise that the people of Azad Kashmir will also benefit from the Mangla Dam. Completion of this project will lead to economic, agricultural and industrial progress in the area. The people of Azad Kashmir will find new avenues of employment through this project

and it will help raise their standards of living.[8]

However, after both governments agreed on the water sharing formula and signed the Indus Waters Treaty in 1960, India chose to remain quiet.

Pakistan made a fortune from the construction of Mangla Dam. The dam provided water and energy to landlords and industrialists of Pakistan, but the people of Jammu and Kashmir were the losers, as they were uprooted by the dam. The agitation by affected people was brutally crushed, and historical, cultural sites of the area and graves submerged under the water of the Mangla Lake. People of Mirpur pay more per unit of electricity than the people of Pakistan are paying 15-20 miles away from Mirpur in Dina and Jhelum. Thousands of people who were uprooted from Mirpur were shifted to remote areas of Pakistan with a piece of paper in their hands, and they were denied access or control over their allotted lands. The local landlords and criminal groups treated them disgracefully. Many people were looted and harassed, and women were raped, which forced thousands of people to come back to AJK and make a new beginning.

Whereas there is water around the city of Mirpur to irrigate lands in Pakistan, there is not enough drinking water for the suffering people of the area. In summer, people have to buy water to survive. Despite serious economic crises and widespread unemployment and poverty, people of the area are forced to pay Rs. 1,000 for a tanker of water.[9]

The prosperity or development which is visible in Mirpur or some other parts of Pakistani Administered Kashmir is not due to economic policies of the government or the Mangla Dam. It is the result of the remittances by more than 1.5 million strong Kashmiri diaspora settled in various parts of the UK, Europe, America and the Middle East.

Upraising of the Mangla Dam

Since its construction in 1967, sedimentation has occurred to the extent of 1.13 million acre feet, and the present gross storage capacity has declined to 4.75 million acre feet from the actual design of 5.88 million acre feet. The live capacity has declined to 4.58 million acre feet from 5.34 million acre feet. It means that the dam's water storage capacity has been reduced by 19.22 per cent. Yet despite the serious water and energy shortage, authorities in Pakistan did not construct the Kala Bagh Dam, but once again decided to uproot the people of Mirpur by upraising the existing Mangla dam. Pakistan decided to raise the dam by 40 feet (12 m), to 494 feet (151 m) high. This will increase the reservoir capacity by 18 per cent and provide an additional 644 MW of power. But it will uproot more than 100,000 people currently living near the reservoir.[10]

For implementation of any development plan, it is necessary to look into the viability, technology, methodology, human resources/technical expertise and capital investment. All these elements do exist for construction of the Kala Bagh Dam, but there is no political will and vision to do so. The Kala Bagh Dam project is still gathering dust on files, despite millions having been spent on various feasibility reports and changes in the plans. This is in spite of the fact that Pakistani military dictators have held absolute power in their hands, and if they wished they could have brushed aside opposition and constructed the Kala Bagh Dam. But their preference was, still is, not to uproot Pakistani people, but to exploit Kashmiri resources and construct dams in Pakistani Administered Kashmir and Gilgit-Baltistan. Thus, the plans for construction of Kala Bagh Dam were abandoned. Instead the plan to upraise the Mangla Dam to increase its water storage capacity was implemented. It will provide more water and electricity to Pakistan, at the cost of suffering and miseries of the people of Mirpur.

The decision to upraise the Mangla Dam was taken by WAPDA, and the government of so called 'Azad' Kashmir was not part of it. Even the agreement was signed by three Pakistanis representing and protecting interests of Pakistan but stationed at different places. The agreement was signed on June 27, 2003 by Chairman WAPDA Lt. General Zulfiqar Ali Khan, Secretary Water and Power Saeed Ullah Jan and Chief Secretary of Pakistani Administered Kashmir Shahid Rafiq. It must be noted that the Chief Secretary of Pakistani Administered Kashmir is always a Pakistani, who controls and runs the show protecting the interests of Pakistan. The Prime Minister and President of Pakistani Administered Kashmir have no power to overrule him. He is practically a Viceroy or a Governor General. In this agreement, WAPDA acknowledges that thousands of people uprooted in 1967 were not compensated:

> The Ministry shall help in ensuring that governments of the Punjab and Sindh will grant proprietary rights to the 562 families who have not yet been given proprietary rights to their land and allotment of residential plot to 2799 families subject to verification by the Government of the authenticity of power of attorney of the affectees.[11]

It took the Pakistani authorities 40 long years to realise that the people who were uprooted in 1967 to benefit Pakistan were not compensated. Tens of thousands of people were forcibly evicted and not appropriately compensated; and according to WAPDA's own admission, 2,799 families have not been given proprietary rights.

The Upraising Agreement promised the people of Mirpur that:

- The WAPDA shall build one city near Mirpur and four towns as close as possible to the affected area. The WAPDA will provide the required facilities/infrastructure.
- The Ministry shall establish a major vocational training institute at Mirpur. In addition, four new male vocational training centres will be established in the proposed townships, and existing four centres for females will be strengthened. In addition, the WAPDA will take steps for imparting skills in other fields.
- Following works shall be undertaken as part of the Project:
  (a) Construction of land links for Kharak and Pinyam(Chohan) disconnected by the Project;
  (b) Provision of water supply and sewerage to Mirpur city and four hamlets from PSDP.[12]

This author visited Mirpur in May 2009, and spoke to many people and personally witnessed the progress of the work. The construction work related to upraising of the Mangla Dam was almost complete, but the work related to public welfare or new city and new hamlets, in most cases had not even started. However, in some areas, they had completed about 5 per cent of the work.

Najib Afsar, Spokesman of anti-Mangla Dam Extension Action Committee said: "Call it WAPDA or call it government of Pakistan—they have done it again, they have uprooted the people of Mirpur for the second time to promote interest of Pakistan and deserted us again. All work related to the public welfare has been abandoned, although they have levelled some hilly areas to show that they were doing some work. It is like fooling people with some window dressing. In places like Chakswari and Dayal they have not even made a start".[13] I can substantiate my claim by recent visual footage of the area. Moreover, a documentary has been compiled to be shown by an international TV channel in the near future.[14]

The work related to the public welfare was also part of the Upraising Project. Since it didn't benefit the WAPDA or its officials, they completed the upraising work benefitting Pakistan, and as in 1967, dumped tens of thousands of people of Mirpur on the streets with nowhere else to go. Moreover, due to climate changes and other factors, there is severe shortage of water, and this is also the case in Mirpur. Nevertheless, the WAPDA goes on to store enough water in the Mangla Dam Lake so that it touches new level, ignoring the suffering of the local people. The agony and suffering of the affected people will touch new heights after their houses will be submerged in water, and they will have no alternative place to go to.

Neelum-Jhelum Hydropower Project

At a time when different provinces and politicians of Pakistan were arguing with each other whether to construct the Kala Bagh Dam or not, the puppet leaders of Pakistani Administered Kashmir said: "For the sake of Pakistan we will build 100 dams in Azad Kashmir", blithely ignoring the harsh reality faced by the local people.

Neelum-Jhelum Hydroelectric Project is located near Muzaffarabad, the capital of Pakistani Administered Kashmir. It aims to dig a tunnel and divert the water of Neelam river from Nauseri, about 41 km east of Muzaffarabad. A powerhouse will be constructed at Chatter Kalas, 22 km south of Muzaffarabad; and after passing through the turbines, the water will be released in Jhelum river, about 4 km south of Chatter Kalas. Once completed, the Neelum Jhelum Hydroelectric Project will produce 969 MW of electricity annually at the cost of US$ 2.16 billion.[15]

This hydroelectric project was formally announced by former Minister Omar Ayub on June 10, 2007. WAPDA selected MWH, a global provider of environmental engineering, strategic consultancy and construction services, to provide engineering and construction management services for the Neelum-Jhelum Hydroelectric Project. It is a joint venture led by MWH and consisting of MWH, Pakistani firms NESPAK, ACE and NDC, and Norwegian firm NORPLAN. The MWH will provide design, prepare construction drawings and manage construction services. The project is proposed to be completed in eight years.

The construction contract was awarded on July 7, 2007 to M/s CGGC-CMEC Consortium China for implementation of the project at a cost of Rs. 90.90 billion. Construction Agreement was signed on December 19, 2007 and letter of commencement was issued on January 30, 2008. Neelum Jhelum Consultants (NJC), which is a joint venture comprising of MWH International Inc. USA, NORPLAN A.S., Norway, National Engineer Services Pakistan (Pvt) Limited, Associated Consulting Engineers ACE (Pvt) Limited, National Development Consultants of Pakistan, have been selected for engineering design and supervision (EDS) as Project Consultants. Consultancy Agreement was signed on May 15, 2008; and letter of commencement was issued on May 16, 2008. Services have been started since June 03, 2008. The Project is slated to be completed in 93 months.

Financing

The Government of Pakistan has approved financial arrangements for the project as follows:

- Established Neelum Jhelum Hydropower Company for the project implementation.
- Imposition of surcharge at 10 paisa per unit on power tariff for NJHEP fund providing for 50 per cent fund requirement.
- Balance equity to be arranged through loans and bonds, etc.
- Revised PSDP (2007-2008) allocation of Rs. 5,700 million.

Land Acquisition

- Project envisages acquisition of about 2,400 kanals of private and state land in the project area in Muzaffarabad District.
- So far WAPDA has transferred Rs. 705 million to Government of Pakistani Administered Kashmir, as provisional cost of the notified private and state land.
- WAPDA has taken possession of 80 per cent land; and arrangements are being made to acquire the remaining land.[16]

A concrete gravity dam, 135 m long and 47 m high will be constructed on Neelum river at Nauseri. The dam is designed for over-topping. The dam will create a head pond of 8 million cubic metres which will allow a peaking reservoir of 2.08 million cubic metres to meet daily peaking of power for more than 4 hours. A six gate tunnel intake structure of 280 cusec capacity will be connected with three conventional flushing surface basins installed at their end for taking sediment back into the river.[17]

The total length of head race tunnel is 28.5 km. A 15.1 km stretch of the tunnel from Nauseri will be constructed as a twin tunnel system each with cross section of 42 sq. m. The remaining head race tunnel down to the surge chamber will be a single tunnel having cross section of 82 sq. m. The tunnels are shotcrete lined with a concrete invert. The tunnel crosses Jhelum river approximately 380 metres below its bed. The tunnel will be accessed by seven adits for removal of excavated spoil.

The Surge Chamber consists of 340 m high riser shaft and 820 m long surge tunnel, four steel lined Penstock tunnels 150 m long and having 3.8 m internal diameter will also be constructed. The underground power station will have four units with a total capacity of 969 MW. The power station will be connected with Rawat Grid station (in Pakistan) through 500 KV double circuit transmission line.[18]

Salient Features of the Project

Overall Project Cost	Rs. 130 Billion (US$ 2.16 billion)
Installed Capacity	969 MW Four Units @ 242 MW each
Dam Type	Concrete Gravity
Height/Length	47 / 135 m
Annual Energy	5.150 Billion electricity Units
Average Head	420 m
Design Discharge	280 Cumecs
Tunnelling	Two; each dia; 7.3 m - 15 km, One; dia; 9.6 m-17 km (Total 47 km)
EIRR	26 per cent
Implementation Period	8 Years

Project Benefits as Explained by WAPDA

- Reduction of dependence on thermal power
- Savings in foreign exchange
- Employment opportunity during construction and operation
- Improved standard of living infrastructure
- Social-economic uplift of the area

Critique of the Project

1. Like other projects conceived and completed by the WAPDA in Pakistani Administered Kashmir, this project is also designed to benefit Pakistan at the expense of the local people of Pakistani Administered Kashmir.
2. Although the work has already started on the project, no written agreement has been signed between WAPDA and the Government of Pakistani Administered Kashmir. This shows that the Government of Pakistani Administered Kashmir has no role or influence over this matter; or any matter related to development and welfare of the people and local environment.
3. Contrary to WAPDA claims, the project will not help the local people in any form or shape. The employment opportunities are for the people of Pakistan or foreign workers. So far only five jobs of chefs, cleaners and watchmen have been given to the local people.[19]
4. Majority of population live in rural areas and their existence and life largely depends upon forestry, livestock and agriculture. River water and natural springs are the main source for drinking and irrigation of land; and this diversion of river will cause serious water shortage, which will make life miserable for the local people.

5. The project will have very serious impact on environment of the area, as it plays a key role in the configuration of Himalayan ecosystem. Environmental groups have expressed their concerns about prospective environmental hazards on the local economy and biodiversity.
6. According to ecologists, the project area has significant conservational importance due to abundance of forests, aquatic life and presence of many species of wildlife, which have been declared endangered globally.
7. The project will also have serious impact on the habitat of various rare species considered on the verge of extinction. Developmental activities in the area and other changes will surely have negative impact on the natural habitat of wildlife.
8. The river and the beauty of the area attract tourists and provide clean water to the local people and citizens of Muzaffarabad; and this diversion of water will deprive the area of clean water and reduce the Neelam River to "Nalah Lahi" in Rawalpindi which has dirty water and creates enormous problems for the citizens.[20]

Other Hydropower Projects in Pakistani Administered Kashmir

The following small projects have been completed: Kundal Shahee, Kathai and Leepa. Another project at Jagran with a maximum capacity of 30.4 MW is also completed, and has been connected with National Grid system. Besides, some micro-level plants are in operation at Kail. The Government of Pakistan in its *Water Vision 2025 Programme* announced plans for construction of several dams in Pakistani Administered Kashmir. These are as follows:

- **New Bong** with capacity of 74 MW
- **Gulpur** with capacity of 60 MW
- **Rajdhani** with capacity of 86 MW
- **Chakhoti** with capacity of 123 MW
- **Abbasian** with capacity of 244 MW
- **Harrihgel** with capacity of 53 MW
- **Kotli** with capacity of 97 MW

Besides, there are some micro and small-sized projects under consideration, and these are as follows:

- **Batar** with capacity of 4.8 MW
- **Kathai** with capacity of 2.4 MW
- **Batdhara** with capacity of 10.2 MW
- **Riali** with capacity of 24.9 MW and
- **Dhakari** with capacity of 3.2 MW.

Kohalla Hydropower Project

This is run-of-river project and the project site is located at Dhal Chattian 22 km from Muzaffarabad, upstream on river Jhelum. Powerhouse is at Barsala 7 km from Kohalla. Pre-feasibility studies have been completed. Interim report on feasibility has also been prepared. The completion period is about nine years at a total cost of US$ 1,381 million.

Diamer Bhasha Dam

Pakistan has declared its plans to construct dams in the Gilgit-Baltistan region of the state of Jammu and Kashmir. General Pervez Musharraf in his address on January 17, 2006 announced Pakistan's plans to construct five multi-purpose storages in the country during next 10 to 12 years. Diamer Bhasha Dam Project is being undertaken in the first phase. Diamer Bhasha Dam Project is being built on the river Indus, about 300 km upstream of Tarbela Dam, and about 40 km downstream of Chilas Town, which is the headquarters of Diamer District of Gilgit and Baltistan. Initial Feasibility report of Diamer Bhasha Dam Project was prepared by Canadian Consultants Montreal Engineering Company (MONENCO) during 1981-1984. WAPDA appointed local consultants in December 1989 for upgradation of the Initial Feasibility Report.

In 2002, WAPDA appointed M/S NEAC Consultants, a joint venture of local and foreign firms, NESPAK (Lead Firm) for the upgrade of the Initial Feasibility Study. The Upgraded Feasibility Report of the Project was submitted by M/s NEAC on 31 August, 2004. International panel of experts declared that the Project was technically feasible. The contract for review of feasibility studies, detailed engineering design and preparation of tender documents was awarded to Diamer Bhasha Consultants (DBC) (Joint Venture of local and foreign firms, with M/s Lahmeyer a leading firm).[21] Work on the project started after the ground-breaking ceremony by the President of Pakistan.

Diamer Bhasha Dam Project will be the highest Roller Compacted Concrete Dam in the world having a height of 272 metres. Salient features of the project are as follows:

Location	40 km down steam of Chilas
Main Dam	
Maximum Height	272 m
Type	Roller Compacted Concrete (RCC)
Diversion System	2 No. Diversion tunnels
	1 No. Diversion channel
	Upstream and Downstream Cofferdams

Main Spillway	
No. of gates	14
Size of gate	11.5 × 16.24 m
Reservoir Level	1160 m
Gross capacity	8.1 MAF (10.0 BCM)
Live capacity	6.4 MAF (7.9 BCM)
Min. operation level	El. 1060 m
Outlets	
Low level	2
Sluicing	5
Powerhouse(s)	2
Total installed capacity	4500 MW
Location and type	Two, one each under the right and left abutment
No. of units	12 each of 375 MW
Average generation	18,000 GWh/year

Financing of Project

- The cost of the Diamer-Bhahsa Dam is $12 billion (2008 estimates).
- Rs. 27.824 billion are required for the acquisition of land and resettlement of the people to be affected in the wake of the construction of the dam.
- Under the proposed project, Rs. 10.76 billion will be spent for the acquisition of agriculture-barren land, tree and nurseries.
- Rs. 1.638 billion to be utilised for properties and infrastructure.
- Rs. 8.8 billion for establishment of nine model villages.
- Rs. 62.119 million for pay and allowances for administrative arrangements.
- Rs. 17.7 million for contingent administrative expenses.
- The project also includes an escalation cost of Rs. 2.234 billion at the rate of 6 per cent per year for five years and interest of Rs. 4.309 billion during the implementation at the rate of 9 per cent.

Project Benefits as Claimed by WAPDA

- Availability of about 6,400,000 acre feet (7.89×109 m^3) annual surface water storage for supplementing irrigation supplies during low flow periods;
- Harnessing of renewable source of clean and cheap energy through installed capacity of 4,500 MW;
- Reduction of dependence on thermal power, thus saving foreign exchange;
- Employment opportunity, particularly to the locals, during the construction and operation; and
- Creation of massive infrastructure leading to overall socio-economic uplift of the area and standard of living of people.

Pre-Requisite Activities

Following are the pre-requisite activities:

- Construction of a new bridge on Indus river at Thakot. The existing bridge is unable to sustain anticipated transportation load during construction of Diamer Bhasha Dam Project.
- 323 km of Karakoram Highway (KKH) from Havalian to Dam site is to be upgraded by NHA for transportation of heavy machinery and equipment.
- 100 km of KKH will be submerged due to impounding of reservoir; this portion is to be relocated to a higher elevation.
- Land acquisition.

The work to develop infrastructure for communication link of Diamer Bhasha Dam, and on Karakoram Highway to link the dam has already started. The Karakoram Highway would be upgraded at the cost of Rs. 11.578 billion.

Diamer Bhasha Dam: A Critique

- The project is located in a mountainous, earthquake-prone area. World Bank report suggests that the Bhasha site being located in the highly unstable seismic zone in a narrow valley of the upper Indus could be vulnerable to some extraordinary safety hazards. Apart from that there are signs of seismic activity at its actual site within the 40 km radius of the project site.[22]
- It is partly because of this and partly because the dam is being built in a disputed territory that the World Bank refused to provide funds for this project. However, China has not only agreed to provide funds on very low rates, but also agreed to provide its expertise in the working on big dams and machinery. China has offered to provide skilled labour for the construction of the Bhasha dam as it has 17,000 skilled labourers who have worked on three dams in China, which are generating 30,000 MW electricity.[23]
- Furthermore there are many engineering challenges due to the local topography, including widening and relocating 100 km of the Karakoram Highway; and construction of a new bridge over river Indus so that all materials and heavy equipment could be transported. These factors contribute to the project's hefty price tag.
- Contrary to WAPDA claims, German company Lehmar which issued the final draft of Diamer Bhasha Dam indicated that as many as 37,000 people would be affected following the construction of the dam.[24]
- Just like Mangla Dam, whose construction and upraising uprooted

tens of thousands of people, (and thousands are still in search of permanent settlements), Diamer Bhasha Dam will also uproot more than 37,000, people, and destroy local flora and fauna and forests.

- 200 sq. km reservoir of the Diamer-Bhasha Dam would flood 100 km of the Karakoram Highway, and the villages and farms of over 35,000 people would disappear. Tens of thousands of thousand-year old rock carvings would vanish.[25]
- Experience of the construction of Tarbela and Mangla dams indicates that the construction of Diamer Bhasha Dam will result in loss of habitat, changes in downstream water quality, adverse effects on river temperature, nutrient load, turbidity, dissolved gases, concentration of heavy metals and minerals, changes in downstream morphology of river bed, delta coastline due to altered sediment load and reduction of biodiversity due to blocking of movement of organisms.[26]
- People of the area have raised strong objections to the Project, as there is widespread fear among the local people that the project would eat away all fertile land in the area, and that only those paying bribes would be compensated for their losses. They fear that "they will be having no land to settle down and become *mohajareen* (refugees)".[27]
- There is also the issue of royalty for the Dam. Most of the area submerged by the lake belongs to Gilgit and Baltistan, with only a tiny bit of area being taken up from NWFP. But the dam has been designed in such a way that the powerhouse is located in NWFP territory, so that the royalty will be granted to the government of NWFP.
- As noted elsewhere, the Government of NWFP receives Rs. 8 billion per annum for the Tarbela Dam, which is more than the total budget of the areas of Gilgit and Baltistan. The Diamer Bhasha Dam is economically very attractive, as it is expected to pay off its cost within seven years of commissioning. It would generate electricity worth $1.5 billion and supply irrigation water worth $ 600 million per year.[28]

Threat to Buddhist Artefacts

It was reported in several South Asian papers on April 4, 2008 that thousands of Buddhist artefacts were recovered at the site of the Diamer-Bhasha Dam. It was reported that more than thousand rare stone carvings, sculptures and statues of Buddha were found at the construction site of the dam. As the Pakistan Government is a signatory to international covenants for protection of culture, history and archaeology, it is imperative that steps should be taken for the protection of this unique heritage and culture. Prof. Harald Hauptmann, a leading archaeologist of the region, fears that the construction of Dam will destroy the greatest part of the rock art galleries. He said, "Forget everything. More than 80 per cent will be submerged and the remaining rock carvings on the slopes will be destroyed because of the construction of the new 100-km stretch of Karakorum Highway."[29] According to him, these rock carvings testify about great cultures that have inhabited and travelled the Indus Valley. Some examples of the rock carvings near Chilas date back to pre-historic times. Some of these also testify to the Islamic heritage in the region since 14th century. Many of these carvings were done by merchants and pilgrims who travelled the paths along the Indus Valley that constituted branches of the Silk Road.[30]

Apart from the Diamer Bhasha Dam, WAPDA plans to construct more dams in Gilgit and Baltistan. Brief details of some of these dams are as follows:

Bunji Hydropower Project

The project is located on Indus River near Gilit. Power House and Dam sites are 560 km and 610 km, respectively, from Islamabad.

Salient Features

Installed Capacity (MW)	7100
Annual Energy (GWh)	24000
Design Discharge (m^3/sec)	1900
Design Head (m)	428
Tunnel Length (km)	8.5
Height of Dam (m)	200

Basho Hydropower Project

The proposed scheme is identified along 1 km lower stretch of Basho Lungma, a left tributary of Indus River. The confluence of Basho Lungma with Indus River is located about 40 km north-west of Skardu town and 704 km north-east of Islamabad.

Salient Features

Design Capacity (MW)	28
Design Discharge (m3/sec)	3.5
Gross Head (m)	949
No. of Units Horizontal Type (Pelton)	3
Energy Generated (GWh)	135

Phandar Hydropower Project

The project area is located between Phandar Lake and Chhashi Gol, near the Chhashi village on the right side of Ghizar River in Ghizar District of Northern Areas. Phandar Lake is located about 160 km north-west of Gilgit town and 775 km north of Islamabad.

Salient Features

Design Discharge (m^3/s)	40
Gross head (m)	237
Installed Capacity (MW)	80
Mean annual flow (m^3/s)	29.275
Net head (m)	233
Mean Annual Energy (GWh)	348

Conclusion

As Pakistan is facing water and energy problems mainly due to bad planning, lack of political will and wrong priorities, WAPDA is going ahead with all the proposed dams in Gilgit-Baltisan and Pakistani Administered Kashmir. And if one goes by the experience of WAPDA, one can surmise that after completion of these dams they will abandon the uprooted people of these areas. Majority of the affected people will suffer and will eventually have to sort out their problems on their own, with the help of family and friends. They will have to learn the art of survival from those who were uprooted in 1967 due to construction of Mangla Dam, and get dispersed in various parts of Pakistan without any care or help.

A scholar from Pakistani Administered Kashmir, who doesn't want to be named fearing reprisals, while discussing the issue of compensation and completion of water dams, said that "WAPDA officials have two sets of policies, one for those uprooted from Pakistan; and one for those who are uprooted from Pakistani Administered Kashmir and Gilgit-Baltistan". He informed that he visited a village near Kamra in Pakistan where those are settled who were uprooted as a result of the construction of Tarbela Dam in Pakistan, and that he was impressed to see the facilities they enjoyed. All the affected people he spoke to, informed him that they were very happy with the compensation and facilities provided by WAPDA. These people were grateful to the WAPDA for providing them with all the facilities which they could not even dream while living in their villages of origin.

Importance of the state of Jammu and Kashmir is becoming more perceptible with growing demand and appreciation of water resources. India, which claims the state of Jammu and Kashmir as its integral part, complained to the United Nations when Pakistan was planning to construct the Mangla Dam in Mirpur, on the basis of the accession of the State by the Maharaja of Kashmir in 1947. After the Indus Waters Treaty was signed in 1960, India remained quiet on the issue of the Mangla Dam and its adverse impact on the population of Mirpur. This area was also part of the Jammu and Kashmir state at the time of signing of accession, which imparts the legal authority to India over the entire state of Jammu and Kashmir and not for the areas currently under India. From a legal point of view, Pakistan's case on the Kashmir dispute is much weaker. It is time for India to assert its position over the state of Jammu and Kashmir, and to take lead in ensuring social, economic and political rights of the people of Jammu and Kashmir, both under Indian control and under Pakistani occupation.

NOTES

1. http://www.internationalrivers.org/en/node/3293.
2. Statement in Seminar organised by Nazriya Pakistan Council in Islamabad Club in connection with the birth anniversary of Mohammed Ali Jinnah.
3. Part 7(2) of the Azad Jammu and Kashmir Interim Constitution Act, 1974.
4. *Azad Jammu and Kashmir Legislative Assembly Ordinance 1970*, Muzaffarabad, Azad Jammu and Kashmir Election Commission, 2002. Chapter 3, 2(vii).
5. *The Nation*, Pakistan, June 7, 2009.
6. Article III of the Treaty reads: "Pakistan shall receive for unrestricted use all those waters of the Western Rivers which India is under obligation to let flow under the provisions of Paragraph (2). India shall be under an obligation to let flow all the waters of the Western Rivers, and shall not permit any interference with these waters, except for the following uses, restricted in the case of each of the rivers, The Indus, The Jhelum and The Chenab, to the drainage basin thereof: (a) Domestic Use; (b) Non-Consumptive Use; (c) Agricultural Use, as set out in Annexure C; and (d) Generation of hydro-electric power, as set out in Annexure D".
7. Letter dated August 23, 1957 from India's Permanent Representative to the United Nations Arthur S. Lall, to President of the Security Council, UN Document No 3869.
8. Letter dated January 24, 1958 from Pakistan's Representative to the United Nations, Agha Shahi to the President of Security Council, UN document no S/3943.
9. *Daily Ausaf*, London, June 6, 2009, p. 5.
10. http://www.wapda.gov.pk/htmls/ongoing-index.html.
11. Agreement for Raising of the Mangla Dam was signed on June 27, 2003. For text, see Appendix.
12. Ibid.
13. Interview with Najib Afsar, Spokesman of Anti-Mangla Dam Extension Action Committee on June 7, 2009. Najib Afsar is from Mirpur and lives in England. He vigorously campaigned against the upraising of the Dam.
14. Ibid.
15. http://www.wapda.gov.pk/htmls/ongoing-index.html.
16. Ibid.
17. Ibid.
18. Ibid.

19. Author's interview with local people during his visit to the area in April 2009.
20. Author's interview with political activists, environmental experts and educationists during his visit to the area in April 2009.
21. http://www.wapda.gov.pk/htmls/future-index.html.
22. Zulfiqar Halepoto, 'Diamer-Bhasha Dam: Risks and Controversies', *Daily Dawn*, November 17, 2008.
23. 'China to Fully Finance Diamer Bhasha Dam in Pakistan', *Pakistan Daily*, August 15, 2008, at http://www.daily.pk/business/55-businessnews/6415-china-to-fully-finance-diamer-bhasha-dam-in-pakistan.html.
24. http://www.internationalrivers.org/en/south-asia/pakistan/diamer-bhasha-dam.
25. Ibid.
26. Zulfiqar Halepoto, No. 22.
27. http://www.internationalrivers.org/en/south-asia/pakistan/diamer-bhasha-dam/south-asia's-most-costly-dam-gets-infusion.
28. Zulfiqar Halepoto, no. 22.
29. http://www.internationalrivers.org/en/node/3293.
30. Ibid.

APPENDIX

Agreement for Raising of the Mangla Dam

Chairman WAPDA Lt.General (Retd) Zulfiqar Ali Khan, Secretary Water and Power, Saeed Ullah Jan, and Chief Secretary AJK Shahid Rafiq signing the agreement for raising of Mangala Dam during a signing ceremony in Islamabad on June 27, 2003. Prime Minister of 'Azad' Kashmir, Sardar Sikandar Hayyat Khan and Aftab Ahmed Khan Sherpao, Federal Minister for Water and Power witness on the occasion.

This Agreement is made at Islamabad on the 27th day of June, 2003 among the Ministry of Water & Power, Government of the Islamic Republic of Pakistan (here in after referred to as "the Ministry", which expression shall include legal representatives and assignees) of the First Part,

The Azad Government of the State of Jammu and Kashmir (hereinafter referred to as "the Government", which expression shall include the legal representatives and assignees) of the Second Part,

AND

The Water and Power Development Authority, a body corporate established under the Pakistan Water and Power Development Authority Act,1958 (W.P. Act XXXI of 1958) (hereinafter referred to as "the WAPDA", which expression shall include successors-in-interest and legal representatives) of the Third Part.

WHEREAS, the Government of Pakistan felt the necessity of raising the height of Mangla Dam to save and utilise the available water and to further utilise the hydro power potential which would result in displacement of people living in Mirpur District of the Azad Government of the State of Jammu and Kashmir and submergence of their properties;

WHEREAS, the Azad Government of the State of Jammu and Kashmir, having the support and consensus of the people of the state in general and those to be displaced in particular, agreed that the Mangla Dam raising project hereinafter referred to as "the Project") may be executed for the well being and prosperity of the people of Pakistan and the AJK.

AND WHEREAS, negotiations were held between the Government of Pakistan and the Azad Government of the State of Jammu and Kashmir in which both the parties agreed on terms and conditions which were drawn before the inauguration of the Project and are being made part of this Agreement;

NOW, THEREFORE, this Agreement has been signed among the Parties mentioned here in before.

Clause 1: Scope

1.1) The height of the Mangla Dam under the Project shall be raised by 30 feet.

Clause 2: Old Affectees

2.1) The old affectees of Mangla Dam comprising 7707 families and having land holding of half an acre or more per family, shall be compensated at the rate of Rs. 2,00,000/- (two hundred thousand) per family after verification of their exact number. The claim of WAPDA that 4481 families had given an undertaking that they did not require land will be verified by a joint committee of the Government and WAPDA already set up. The 6126 families who owned less than half an acre land shall not be further compensated as they have already been fully compensated.

2.2) The ministry shall help in ensuring that governments of the Punjab and Sindh will grant proprietary rights to the 562 families who have not yet been given proprietary rights to their land and allotment of residential plot to 2799 families subject to verification by the Government of the authenticity of power of attorney of the affectees.

Clause 3: Acquisition of land and built up property:

3.1) The Government shall make available land required for the raising of Mangla Dam for perpetual use by the Ministry for the said purpose, subject to the condition that the Government shall retain proprietary rights over such land.

3.2) The WAPDA shall pay land compensation the new affectees at the market rate plus 15 per cent compulsory acquisition charges in accordance with Land Acquisition Act, 1894(Act NO.1 of 1894) as enforced in the territory of the Azad Government of the State of Jammu and Kashmir.

3.3) The WAPDA shall pay market price (replacement cost) to the owners of the houses and additional 10 per cent shall be given above the price. The affectees shall also be allowed to carry the 'malba" of the houses. The refugees of IOK settled on the AJK and WAPDA lands shall be paid minimum Rs. three lacs per family plus five marla plot free of cost. Those refugees of IOK who are living on their own land, shall be paid compensation as paid the other affectees and shall also be entitled to plots between five marlas and one kanal on payment of cost of land and the development charges shall be borne by the WAPDA, the AJK affectees including those occupying APODA/Government lands will also be paid minimum compensation for a house @ Rs. 3 lacs and shall also be entitled to plot of five marlas to one kanal on payment of cost of land. The development charges shall, however, be borne by WAPDA.

Clause 4: Package for new affectees:

4.1) The WAPDA shall build one city near Mirpur and 4 towns as close as possible to the affected area. The WAPDA will provide the required facilities/infrastructure. The Government shall make state land available to the WAPDA on payment at site-II for new city. A part of site-II is under the use of the Army as grassland. The Government shall offer to the Army alternate land for use as grassland at site-I. The Minister for Kashmir Affairs and Northern Areas and States and Frontier Regions, Government of Pakistan will co-ordinate with the Government and the Army for relocating the Army grassland from site-II to site-I.

4.2) The Ministry shall establish a major vocational training institute at Mirpur. In addition, four new male vocational training centres will be established in the proposed townships, and existing four centres for females will be strengthened. In addition, the WAPDA will take steps for imparting skills in other fields.

4.3) The compensation package shall be implemented by a Committee under the Ministry of KANA, which shall comprise of representatives of the Government, the Ministry and the WAPDA.

Clause 5: Power Sector

5.1) The WAPDA shall drop its claim of outstanding liability of Rs. 0.9 billion against the Government. Similarly the Government shall also drop its claim with regard to any reimbursements from the WAPDA. The AJK Council shall drop its claim of re-imbursement against the Government for the amount of Rs.1.4 billion already paid to the WAPDA by the Council as ordered by the competent authority vide C.E. Secretariat U.O. No. 1313/DS(C-2/2000,dated 29-6-2000.

5.2) **a)** At present the Government of Pakistan has fixed the rate at Rs. 4.20/ KWH for the AJ&K. The WAPDA shall bear Rs. 0.71 on the basis of 17% losses. The Government shall pay Rs. 2.44 and the Ministry shall pick up Rs. 1.05 as subsidy. In case of budgetary constraints of the Government, the Ministry shall pick up the additional liability of Rs. 0.12. This rate shall be deemed to have become effective from September, 2002 and shall be frozen till September, 2003.

b) The future power tariff(beyond September 2003) for Azad Jammu & Kashmir shall be fixed by Government of Pakistan on the recommendation of a standing sub-committee already notified by the

Ministry of KANA & SAFRON vide Notification No.F.3/10/92-F&B dated June 6, 2003, copy of which is appended to this Agreement.

5.3) The Ministry shall ensure that the CBR does not levy the GST on electricity generated in and supplied to the AJ&K since the GST is applicable in Pakistan and the AJ&K already charges GST through their Tax Department. All rules prescribed by the Government of Pakistan with respect to the GST would be applicable to the Government.

5.4) The responsibility of distribution of electricity may be withdrawn from the Government and assigned to the AJ&K Council or any other relevant organisation. A study in this respect will be made by the Ministry of KANA & SAFRON/AJK Council and the Government.

5.5) The WAPDA shall construct five grid stations along with associated transmission lines, as included in the WAPDA five year plan 2002-07. It shall also construct an additional new grid station at Chittarpari.

5.6) The Government will get net hydel profit/water usage charges royalty from the Mangla Dam with effect from the entry into force of this Agreement @ Rs. 0.15 per KWH as per the policy laid down.

Clause 6: Allied matters

6.1) The WAPDA shall construct a bridge at Dhangali. The construction of another bridge(Mirpur to Islam Garrh) shall be taken up by the Ministry of KANA & SAFRON, Government of Pakistan and the Ministry of Finance and Revenue, Government of Pakistan shall provide fund under PSDP.

6.2) The WAPDA shall cater for the drawing of drinking water from the lake. The Government's requirement of water for irrigation purposes shall be taken up with IRSA. The Ministry of KANA and SAFRON, Government of Pakistan shall represent the "Government" at IRSA.

6.3) Fishing rights will be given to the Government. The tender for fishing shall be floated on all Pakistan basis.

6.4) The "Government" shall be responsible for maintaining recreation facilities in the Mangla Dam reservoir.

6.5) Following works shall be undertaken as part of the Project:

- **a)** Construction of land links for Kharak and Pinyam (Chohan) disconnected by the Project;
- **b)** Provision of water supply and sewerage to Mirpur city and four hamlets from PSDP;
- **c)** Establishment of Resettlement Organisation as approved by the Steering Committee notified vide the Ministry's letter No.3(1)2002-AG dated April 15, 2003 of the Project.

6.6) The former owners shall be permitted to cultivate the land on recession of water provided that no compensation shall be paid for damages due to fluctuation in reservoir water level.

Clause 7: Arbitration

7.1) The Parties shall, while executing the Project, in case of any difference or dispute arising out of the application and/or interpretation of the Clauses hereinbefore, at the first instance settle by negotiations. If no settlement is arrived at, the matter shall be referred to arbitration of three arbitrators namely:-

- One arbitrator to be nominated by the Ministry and the WAPDA in consultation with each other;
- One arbitrator to be nominated by the Government; and
- The Chief Justice of Pakistan or a person nominated by him, shall be the Chairman of the Arbitral Tribunal.

The award made by the Arbitral Tribunal shall be final and binding on the Parties.

Clause 8: Entry into Force

This Agreement shall enter into force on the date of signatures.

In Witness Whereof, the Parties aforementioned have signed this Agreement at the place and date above mentioned.

Ministry of Water & Power
AJK Government WAPDA

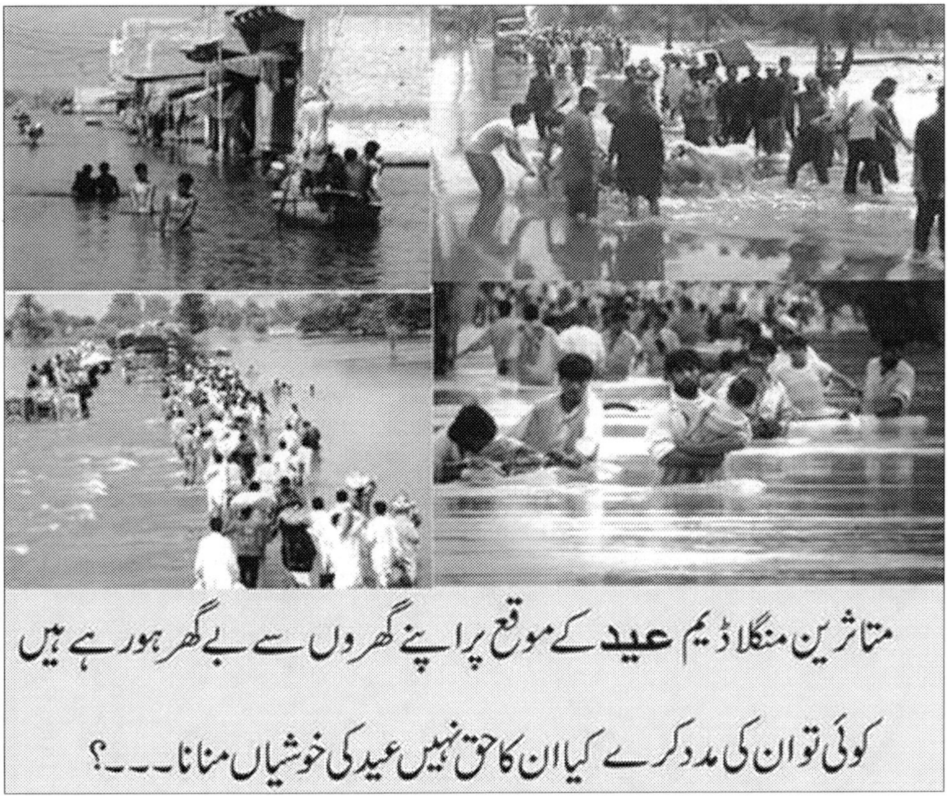

Displacement of People from their Homes in Mirpur due to the Upraising of the Mangla Dam

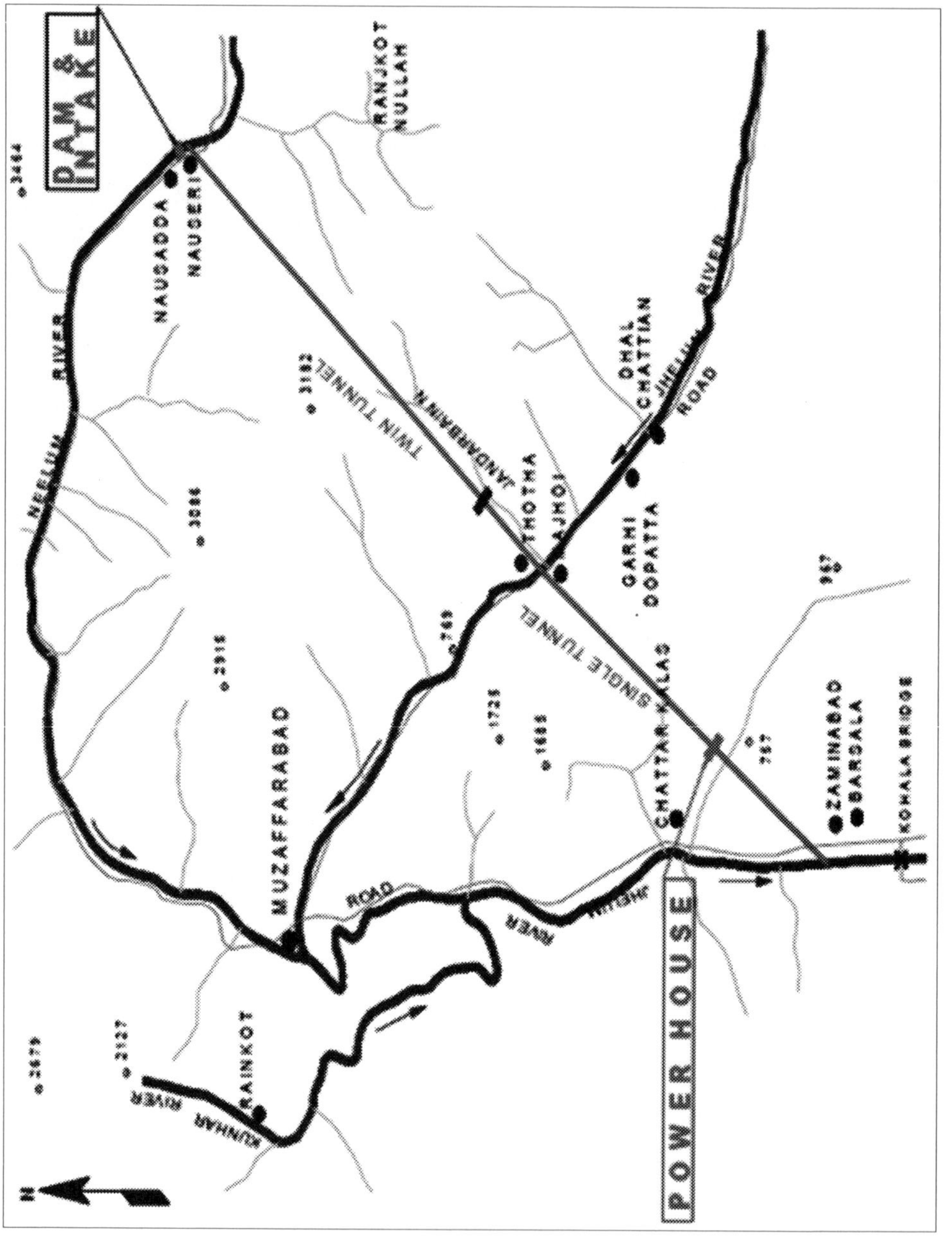

Neelum-Jhelum Project

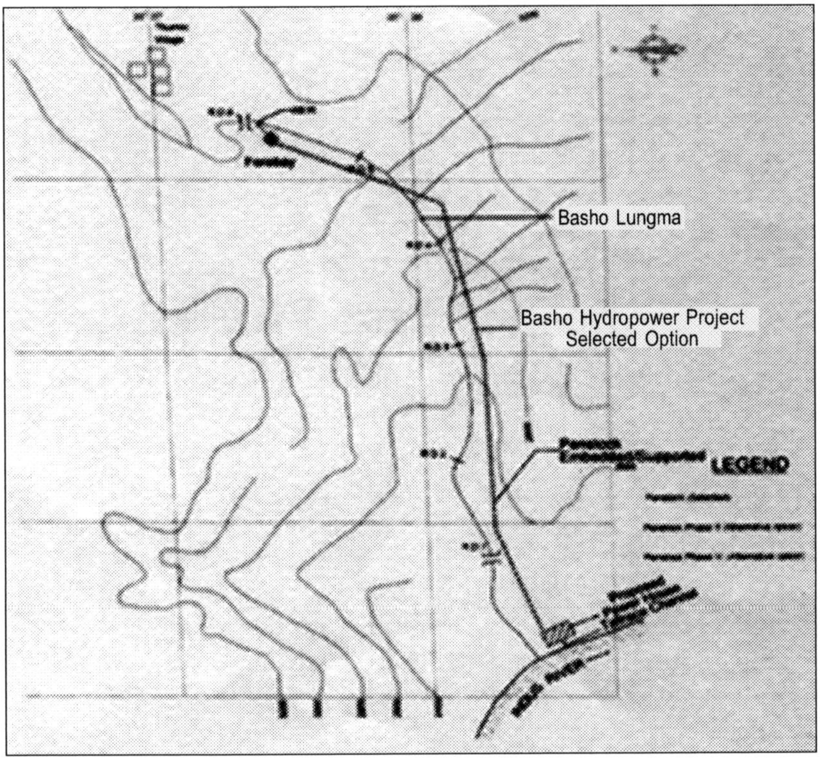

Basho Hydropower Project

14

Bhasha Dam Project

Geographical, Historical and Political Perspectives

Safdar Ali

Historical documents and recorded events provide perspectives that help to analyse a given problem and also find amicable workable solutions. This paper aims to provide recommendations regarding the Bhasha Dam project based on certain geographical, historical and political perspectives.

The Bhasha dam site of Chilas sub-division of Gilgit Agency on the river Indus was first surveyed for dam construction by English Royal Corps of Engineers, Brered Major Alexander Cunningham, Lieutenant Henry Strachey and Dr Thomas Tomson. After the conquest of Chilas by Kashmir in 1851, the Maharaja of Kashmir imposed a tribute in gold dust, and administered the territory as part of the Gilgit district. A British Agency was established in Gilgit in 1889, which included among other areas, the Chilas sub-division. It started from the junction of Ramghat, that is, the meeting place of the rivers Astor and Indus: on the right bank stand Gor, Kinergah, Hodar, Darel, Tangir, Khilli and Seo, and on the left bank, Bunar, Thak, Butogah, Giche, Thor, Harban, Sazin and Jaglot. Under the revised arrangements made in 1897, these states paid small fixed sums to the Maharaja of Kashmir, and in 1899 Thor was incorporated in Chilas. Darel rendered a tribute of gold dust to Kashmir since 1866, when the Maharaja's troops had raided the country. The tribute was later paid through the Punial Governor. Tangir also paid a small tribute to the Governor of Yasin.

The British era General Staff India maps, attached with their military reports, clearly show that along the westward flow of river Indus, Giche

Levy Post, Hodar, Morushi on Thor Nullah, Dudishal, Harban, Shatial, Sazin Ferry Site, Banda-i-Sazin, Shumar Nullah, Shekh and Diamir Lurg are very visible part and parcel of Darel. The United Nations map, especially the map attached with United Nations Commission for India and Pakistan (UNCIP) report, clearly displays Sazin within the "Jammu and Kashmir and Gilgit Agency". The Survey of Pakistan map sheets (in the scale 1:10,00,000), published under the direction of Maj. Gen. Mehboob ul Muzaffar, Surveyor General of Pakistan, First Edition, Map Sheet NI 43 (KASHMIR) Eastings/Latitude 73.4 degree and Northings/longitude 35.7 degree, very precisely indicates Banda-e-Sazin as part and parcel of Chilas district of Gilgit region.

Lt. Colonel D.W.K. Barr, Resident in Kashmir, in his letter no.1814, dated May 8, 1893, to Raja Sir Amar Singh, Vice President of the Jammu and Kashmir State Council, while referring to the fighting in Chilas on March 5, 1892, conveyed the Viceroy's deep regret at the loss of the Kashmir State Army personnel's lives. The Deputy Secretary in his letter to the Foreign Department, Government of India, No 246-F, dated April 24, 1911, to Lieutenant Colonel K.D. Erskine, Resident in Kashmir, Srinagar, conveyed the approval of the Viceroy of India for holding a Durbar at Gilgit to recognise Mehtar Pukhtun Wali (from Yasin) as ruler of Darel, Harban, Sazin and Shatial.

As regards the administration and position of the Gilgit Agency, contemporary accounts and records show that the Gilgit Agency includes the following:

1. The Gilgit Wazarat, comprising the Tehsil of Astore and Gilgit and the Niabut of Bunji
2. Punial Jagir
3. The States of Hunza and Nagir
4. The Governorships of Yasin, Kuh and Ghizar
5. The Governorship of Ishkuman
6. The republican communities of the Chilas district
7. The western portion of the Taghdumbash Pamir

The valleys which have some political connection with Gilgit are Darel, Tangir and Kandia on the right bank of the Indus, and Harban, Sazin and Jalkot on the left bank. The official correspondence between External Affairs Department, Government of India, New Delhi, the Resident in Kashmir, Deputy Commissioner of Hazara, Political Agent, Gilgit and Assistant Political Agent, Chilas on the subject "Action Against the Jalkotis by the Gilgit Scouts" clearly states that the Jalkotis were placed under the political control of the Deputy Commissioner, Hazara, till as recently as 1933. Prior to that they were under jurisdiction of Political Agent, Gilgit.

Since time immemorial, the entire Shinaki Kohistan area, that is, up to Jalkot including Koli-Palas on the left bank and Seo (ferry site) on the right bank along the river Indus remained culturally, racially, linguistically, geographically and politically part and parcel of Chilas sub-region of Gilgit-Baltistan. In 1933, due to difficulties in Jalkot area, the Indus Kohistan area was temporarily transferred to Deputy Commissioner of Hazara, North-West Frontier Province (NWFP), in the same way as Chitral was temporarily transferred to Deputy Commissioner, Malakand, NWFP. However, Yaghistan portion, including Sumar Nullah Junction with river Indus, very clearly remained and continues to be the part of Chilas sub-division of Gilgit Agency, which is included in the former State of Jammu and Kashmir. NWFP of Pakistan has nibbled away very quietly entire Yaghistan, is now prying on Chilas, Jaglot, Gilgit and is also cunningly laying claims on the Bhasha Dam royalty. The entire proposed Bhasha Dam site, including many miles downstream of the river Indus, is actually part and parcel of the territory of Gilgit-Baltistan of the Jammu and Kashmir state.

In view of the above histotical, political and geographical pacts, the proposed Bhasha dam should be abandoned till Yaghistan and Chitral regions are not reallocated to the motherland of Bolor and the Local Authority Government in Bolor.

Recommendations

1. Area up to Babosar top and Shinaki Kohistan including Jalkot is part of Gilgit (Diamer). So, boundary demarcation of the whole Diamer including Babosar top, Jalkot and whole Shinaki Kohistan should be done under the auspices of international bodies such the United Nations or World Bank, which can stand as the guarantor.
2. Right of ownership of Diamer over the whole area including the proposed dam area should be accepted in presence of international guarantors.
3. When in future the water storage capacity in the Diamar dam decreases due to mud and sand, Pakistan would be bound to increase its level, which in turn will lead to the whole area including Gilgit town being submerged. Pakistan should, therefore, provide guarantee that it will not raise the level of the dam in future.
4. Pakistan should undertake that it shall not deploy Pakistani forces for the protection and security of the dam. The security should be the responsibility of the local Gilgit Scouts, Northern Scouts and

NLI soldiers and police from Gilgit-Baltistan only. It may be noted that Pakistan Army is planning to depute 2 Division troops, on the pretext of protecting Diamer Dam, Skardu, Bonji and other dams in Gilgit-Baltistan.

5. All the workers on the dam (both technical and non-technical) should be appointed from the Gilgit-Baltistan region.
6. Compensation should be given according to the rates prevalent in Islamabad in one instalment to the effected people.
7. Royalty of Rs. 10 billion per annum should be given to Gilgit-Baltistan and not to the NWFP. Royalty rate should be increased according to the rate of inflation.
8. Bank accounts and billing should be handled by the citizens of Gilgit-Baltistan only.
9. Sufficient power to meet the electricity requirements of Gilgit-Baltistan be provided at subsidised rates.
10. Income from this dam be used for the development of Gilgit-Baltistan.
11. Compensation should be given to Gilgit-Baltistan if any atmospheric/weather change occurs and causes any damage in the area.
12. Pakistani citizens including military forces should not be stationed/settled/deputed temporarily or permanently on the soil of Gilgit-Baltistan.
13. Experts from Gilgit-Baltistan only should be responsible for recruitment. Experts from outside of this area should be appointed with the permission of the local elected body like NALA, if local experts are not available in Gilgit-Baltistan.

15

Political Unrest in Pakistan occupied Kashmir (PoK)

A View from the Pak Press

Priyanka Singh

Pakistan occupied Kashmir (PoK), legitimately an integral part of the Indian state of Jammu and Kashmir, has been under Pakistan's control after it occupied the territory in 1947. It covers one-third of the total area of 86,023 sq. miles (222,236 sq. km) of the state of Jammu and Kashmir. The area under occupation comprises two administrative units: Mirpur-Muzaffarabad and Gilgit-Baltistan referred as 'Azad Kashmir' and the Gilgit-Baltistan (Northern Areas), respectively, by the Government of Pakistan. Pakistan ceded a portion (2,700 sq. miles) of this occupied territory lying to the north-east border of the Gilgit-Baltistan known as the Trans Karakoram Tract to China in 1963.[1]

Pakistan invaded Kashmir on the eve of independence and subsequently signed the Karachi Agreement with the 'Azad Kashmir' Government in April 1949. The agreement was signed between the Minister from Pakistan, President of the 'Azad Kashmir' and the Muslim Conference.[2] The Muslim Conference was the only political party in the occupied Kashmir and with the passage of time its voice for the Kashmir cause was lost in oblivion. The PoK comprising so-called 'Azad Kashmir' and 'Northern Areas' now known as Gilgit-Baltistan is till date an amorphous entity.

Pakistan's approach towards the PoK is bedevilled with inherent contradictions. It does not consider Gilgit-Baltistan as part of the so-called 'Azad Kashmir'. However, the Karachi Agreement, which governs the political structure of Gilgit-Baltistan, was signed between the 'Azad Kashmir' Government and the Government of Pakistan. This fact again fails to provide any rationale. The moot question is: How could the fate of people in Gilgit-Baltistan be subjected to the will of 'Azad Kashmir' which technically is not associated with Gilgit-Baltistan at all? Irrespective of the nature of government in Pakistan, this issue has been kept in a state of suspended animation.

In this backdrop, the paper argues that Pakistan over the last 65 years has made baseless allegations against India about violation of human rights in Jammu and Kashmir. The paper also argues that the voice of the people of PoK has been silenced over decades of India-Pakistan fight over Kashmir currently under India's control. Pakistan over the years has been successful in digressing the attention of the world community from serious issues of human rights violations, spurting sectarian tensions amongst its own people with evil designs. Since the paper attempts to capture the view of the Pakistan press, newspaper articles and the Internet sources account for most of the references.

Existing Political Structure

Gilgit-Baltistan

The Government of Pakistan announced the comprehensive "Gilgit-Baltistan Empowerment and Self Governance order 2009" on August 29, 2009. As a result, the 'Northern Areas' was renamed as Gilgit-Baltistan, which was a long-standing demand of the people of the region. Pakistan's then Prime Minister Gilani while announcing the package claimed that the order would guarantee full internal autonomy to Gilgit-Baltistan, giving it somewhat the status of a province just as the other four provinces of Pakistan. The change of name is significant keeping in view the sentiments of the local population; what is ironic is lack of veracity in the official claims on ensuring total autonomy to Gilgit-Baltistan.[3]

The package has allegedly deceived the genuine political and constitutional demands of people. It has failed to fulfil the constitutional lull existing for decades. The promise of autonomy is a farce, as according to the provision given in the package, the region would be put under the rule of a Governor appointed by the establishment in Islamabad.[4] The President is not authorised to pass any legal decisions on Gilgit-Baltistan, as the status of the region is not defined in the successive constitutions of

Pakistan. Moreover, the order does not establish PoK's "institutional link with the four provinces or the Pakistani constitution".[5]

The package evoked mixed reactions both from political and non-political quarters. Pakistan Muslim League-Nawaz (PML-N) agreed to it after initial hesitation as they complained that they were not consulted during the preliminary stages of the formulation of the order.[6] Pakistan Muslim League-Quaid (PML-Q) rejected it completely on the pretext that the order failed to provide Gilgit-Baltistan a provincial status.[7]

Before this, Gilgit-Baltistan was known as 'Northern Areas' which fell under the direct rule of federal government in Pakistan under the Legal Framework Order of 1994.[8] There was Northern Areas Council headed by the Minister for Kashmir Affairs and Northern Areas (KANA). The Council meetings were presided over by the Minister. Gilgit-Baltistan is situated in one of the most important regions of the world in the strategic context.[9] It was deliberately separated from the so-called 'Azad Kashmir' so that it is isolated from any foreseeable settlement on the Kashmir issue. Some political groups have even denied the existence of any such document stating that Gilgit-Baltistan never wanted to unite with Pakistan. If this was not the case, why has Pakistan denied basic political and economic rights to the people of Gilgit-Baltistan for more than 60 years?[10]

Former President Pervez Musharraf announced the "Constitutional Package for Northern Areas" in October 2007 after incorporating some amendments to redress the grievances of the people in Gilgit-Baltistan.[11] Apparently the powers of the Ministry of Kashmir Affairs and the Northern Areas were reduced in favour of the elected governing structure. It bestowed the Legislative Council with the status of a Legislative Assembly which could take important decisions.[12]

'Azad' Jammu and Kashmir (AJK)

The territory of the so-called AJK is governed in accordance with the interim AJK constitution formulated in 1974. According to the UN resolutions, the area is neither a sovereign state nor a province, and the so-called government of AJK is a localised authority. The incumbents stay in office during the pleasure of the federal government in Islamabad. The executive is divided in two branches: the AJK Government in Muzaffarabad and the AJK Council in Islamabad. The council is headed by the Prime Minister of Pakistan which leaves little room for the Legislative Assembly to exercise effective powers.[13]

Important Political Groups Making Demands

Gilgit-Baltistan United Movement (GBUM) is a prominent local political autonomist movement, supported by local politicians which demands a fully autonomous state comprising of Gilgit and Baltistan, also known as 'Northern Areas'.[14]

Balawaristan National Front (BNF) came into existence on July 30, 1992 and is based in Majini Mahla, Gilgit, Balawaristan. The group was founded by Nawaz Khan Naji and is presently led by its Chairman, Abdul Hamid Khan. The party claims to enlighten the people of Gilgit-Baltistan about their state of deprivation over the years and demands an independent republic of Balwaristan. It considers Pakistan as a "usurper" and its control over the region as "illegal" according to the international law.[15]

Balawaristan Student National Organisation (BSNO) is the student wing of the BNF and is a group of young activists who are pursuing the struggle to gain independence from the rule of Pakistan which they consider tyrannical and colonial.[16] There is BSNO cabinet which tries to enhance the level of awareness amongst the youth and inspires them to struggle for attaining their basic political rights.[17] The BSNO is known to have extended its activities to as far as Karachi in Pakistan.[18]

Unrepresented Nations Peoples Organisation (UNPO) is an important platform where issues related to the plight of the people of PoK are very often raised. The organisation emphasises the miserable lives and conditions of the local population who are forced to live as aliens in their own state in the absence of basic rights and freedom.[19]

Gilgit-Baltistan Democratic Alliance (GBDA) is the group of several political groups operating in the PoK including the GBUM. According to UNPO, it is "an umbrella organization [*sic*] which also represents groups such as the *Balawaristan National Front, Karakoram National Movement*, the *Bolor Research Forum* and the *Gilgit-Baltistan Ladakh Democratic Movement*. These groups remain committed to non-violent methods, despite the deteriorating situation."[20]

Political Unrest in Pok as Reflected in Pakistan Press

Due to long stints of military rule in the country, the media in Pakistan has not flourished too much during the last 65 years. In the PoK, the media is suppressed, and as a result, very little is known to the outside world about the situation prevalent there. The mainstream media reports on selective issues such as political developments and structural changes, giving little space for human rights violations and sustained deprivation of the local population. It is only the news sources which are run by political groups that come out with reportage on such issues. But the reach of these private news sources is not as good as those of the mainstream dailies such as *Dawn, Daily Times* and *The News*. The entire plethora of socio-economic and political problems in the PoK as stated in Pakistan and local PoK media could be broadly classified under the following categories:

1. Lack of Constitutional and Political Status
2. Appalling Socio Economic Conditions and Human Rights Violations in PoK
3. Issue of Identity
4. Demographic Changes
5. Lack of Freedom of Press and Expression
6. Chinese Inroads in PoK
7. Militant Training Camps in PoK
8. The Taliban Threat in PoK
9. Comparing PoK with Jammu and Kashmir

Lack of Constitutional and Political Status

PoK has no clearly defined constitutional or political status as the successive constitutions of Pakistan have not done so.[21] A section of people in Gilgit-Baltistan demanded an AJK like structure, if not a better one. The government was slated to take a final decision on the matter last year after a report was submitted to it by political groups on the socio-economic backwardness of the region. The absence of political structure is mainly responsible for lack of development during the last 62 years.[22] The All Parties National Alliance (APNA) leaders state that "the nationalist and progressive forces, both in Pakistan-administered Kashmir and Gilgit-Baltistan, should join hands and launch struggle for attainment of socio-political and constitutional rights usurped by the rulers of Pakistan for the last over six decades".[23]

The GBUM is one of the important groups that has long been pursuing an agenda calling for independence of the region and asking for freedom of expression. The interim constitution of AJK prohibits such freedom of "association and assembly" and any such activity which is against Pakistan's control over the region.[24] The police has brutally crushed such movements in the past; particularly in 2005, when Shia students carried out a protest march against the Pakistan Government. At least 10 people were reportedly killed in the incident.[25]

The deprivation of political and civil rights for decades has led to a discourse on what is best for the people in PoK amongst groups representing different interests of the society. These groups ruminate on these issues and develop their ideology accordingly. Therefore, whereas some groups demand an AJK like set up for Gilgit-Baltistan, others are of the opinion that there is nothing ideal in AJK for Gilgit-Baltistan to imitate. Shafqat Inquilabi, leader of GBDA, opines that even if the Government of Pakistan grants an AJK like structure, it would do no good to their wretched lives. GBDA insists that such action would further deteriorate their socio-economic and political condition.[26] Some religious groups, namely the Central Mosque, Gilgit, and Ittehad Ulema Council, Northern Areas, also demand the merger of Gilgit-Baltistan with the AJK stating that both entities belonged to single geographical entity in the past.[27]

November 16, 2008 was widely observed as a Black Day in PoK to oppose its illegal occupation by Pakistan.[28] Addressing a press conference on the occasion in Skardu, Manzoor Hussain Parwana, Chairman of the GBUM, urged Pakistan to withdraw its military and civil establishment from the region. GBUM calls Pakistan's rule as "usurped control". Parwana further noted: "We will reject any package granted by the government of Pakistan because we are a nation and the nation needs independence, not package." The group is concerned over the economic drain of its homeland, resources and natural wealth by outsiders who have no right to do so. In this regard, the GBUM demanded that "the right of using local resources should be given to local people, and illegitimate and unconditional construction of Skardu and Diamer Dam should be halted".[29]

Sometime back, the Prime Minister of AJK was removed and replaced by Sardar Yaqoob Khan as the new Prime Minister.[30] Soon after his appointment, Yaqoob Khan sacked the existing heads of the civic bodies and public institutions. This only underlines the instability and lack of continuity not only in the political system but also the institutions and offices there under.[31] Similarly, there was sharp controversy on the appointment of a former judge of Pakistan as Chief of the Supreme Appellate Court of Gilgit-Baltistan. Leaders of the GBUM noted that "the appointment of a non-local, retired and above all a PCO judge as the Chief of the SAC" was not acceptable to the people of Gilgit-Baltistan.[32] Such appointments were allegedly made to suppress the rising discontent amongst the people and to extend firm control of Islamabad over the area.

The pro-independence political groups especially GBUM believes that Kashmir does not solely belong to Muslim inhabitants. This refutes the Pakistani contention that since the majority of population was Muslim, Pakistan being a Muslim state had a legal right on Kashmir. The GBUM leader holds this contention responsible for prolonged subjugation of the region over the decades, and he believes that Kashmir belongs as much to the Hindus and Sikhs as to Muslims.[33]

The Skardu Declaration of June 2008 went a long way in drawing world attention to the multi-dimensional problems of the PoK at least in the media circles. It raised pertinent issues related to the identity of the region which was reduced to a mere geographical indicator for this culturally rich land. The declaration was made under the aegis of GBUM and sharing the same platform the members of the alliance vehemently demanded the formation of a constituent assembly which could be entrusted with the work of drafting a just and fair constitution for the people of Gilgit-Baltistan.[34] As mentioned earlier, the region does not have a constitution of its own, neither does it figure anywhere in the several constitutions of Pakistan. The forum also voiced concern on issues of gross human rights violations in the region over the years. The leaders requested the international community, the UN and EU to pave way for ensuring basic rights of life to the people of Gilgit-Baltistan.[35]

Socio-Economic Conditions and Human Rights Violations in PoK

The region accounts for immense poverty, unemployment and low level of illiteracy especially amongst women. The so-called AJK was ravaged by a massive earthquake on October 8, 2005 which further exacerbated the state of lack of development. There is complete absence of freedom of expression. There is a sort of censorship which restricts exposure of any development in the PoK to the outside world. This is why level of gross human rights violations taking place in the area is not known outside. Amir Hunza, a PoK leader once admitted in a letter published in Urdu newspaper *Jasarat,* "It is a fact that people of this region (Northern Areas) are facing more human rights violations and whenever the official media talks of repression in (Indian) Kashmir, people with strong hearts laugh at this hypocritical attitude and people with weak hearts cry."[36]

An important issue which has generated considerable unrest at all levels is the construction of the Diamer Bhasha dam in PoK.[37] The ambitious venture was announced during the Musharraf regime in January 2006.[38] The project which has attracted massive foreign investment especially from China[39] is alleged to inundate large tracts of low lying land and displace the population therein. The dam is named after a village Basha in NWFP even though its site is in Gilgit-Baltistan.[40] The decision to build the dam was arbitrary as the local leadership or people at any level were not consulted.[41] There is resentment over the state's indifference on the fact that the site of the dam is located in an extremely sensitive seismic zone. The region survived an earthquake in October 2005 and is far from recovery despite several billion dollars of foreign assistance. Ironically, the government has shown no predisposition on such environmental factors.[42]

This insensitivity has aggravated the situation and people feel further alienated. There is widespread apprehension on the eventuality where Gilgit-Baltistan does not get any share in the royalty of the said dam.[43] Local groups demand creation of an independent commission so that the boundary issues related to the dam could be adjudicated.[44]

Political unrest is also based on issues of gross irregularities in the day-to-day administrative affairs of the region. Leaders and some civil society organisations in Gilgit-Baltistan have accused the administration of favouritism and nepotism especially while making government appointments. There is widespread discrimination in public life based on region and sect.[45] One such case was related to the merger of the Azad Kashmir Rural Supports Programme (AJKRSP) with a controversial Pakistani Non-governmental Organisation (NGO) known as National Rural Supports Programme. The latter is charged with siphoning off money from the earthquake relief fund for other purposes.[46] The issue of non-completion of rehabilitation projects and rebuilding the earthquake affected areas has been a major source of discontent not only at the political level but also at the individual level.[47] One of the reports brought about the dismaying statistics, wherein out of the 15,000 houses that were damaged due to the 2005 earthquake, only 450 were partially constructed, and thousands of people are as a result compelled to live in refugee camps.[48] This is after almost four years during which foreign aid and assistance have poured in the region on a massive scale mostly from European countries including Britain.[49]

Similarly, the Benazir Income Support Programme (BISP) was also embroiled in controversy in March 2009. The scheme sought to help the people who were living below the poverty line. There was a demand made by the Northern Areas Legislative Assembly that the application forms be distributed by legislators and not through any other authority.[50] During the winter months when the temperatures are remarkably low after the snowfall, no relief was provided by the government for the poor. That there is no electricity in the far flung areas and the absence of fuel in sufficient quantity, only worsened the situation. The people were forced to live a "miserable life" as noted by one of the local leaders in Skardu in February 2008.[51]

Issue of Identity

The underlying factor in the all-pervasive political unrest in PoK is the issue of identity: cultural, social and political. Some groups have spoken about the "ideological terrorism" which could possibly ruin the "ideological boundaries" of the region.[52] They consider this possibility as a part of the larger conspiracy to usurp the political and cultural identity of PoK. Earlier, when Gilgit-Baltistan was referred as the 'Northern Areas', there was an array of protest on the name 'Northern Areas' as it is a mere "geographical connotation", and it seeks to deprive the natives of their history and culture which is known to be very different from the Pakistani side.[53] Political groups from Gilgit-Baltistan often refer it as Balawaristan, which is the ancient name of the region. This shows how strongly they feel for their cultural heritage and ancient identity.[54]

Some of the serious grievances that were emphasised during a political meeting were opening up of routes between the two parts of divided Kashmir and the strict enforcement of State Subject Rule (SSR) to recover land from outsiders. The SSR prohibits purchase and sale of lands in the PoK by people who are not the original inhabitants of the region. Ironically, the law has been utterly violated by the establishment in Islamabad in order to alter the demography of the region suiting their political objectives.[55]

Demographic Change

The population in Gilgit-Baltistan was originally predominantly Shia. However, the establishment in Pakistan, primarily a Sunni state, has adopted ulterior means to change the demography of the area by giving incentives for the settlement of outsiders, mostly Sunni Punjabis so as to outbalance the Shia majority. Today, the Shias and Ismailis fear being pushed to minority in their own homeland.[56]

The bias against Shias dates back to late 1980s when the military dictator and then President of Pakistan Zia-ul-Haq staged a conspiracy to alight sectarian violence between the Shias and the Sunnis. Notably, the Shias were in majority in the PoK at the time Pakistan annexed it. Therefore, successive rulers in Pakistan pursued a policy of demographic change where Sunnis from other parts of the country were not only shifted to the region but also encouraged to develop their financial stakes here. This reality very often finds vent in the local media which describes the apathy of the population who have lost not only their identity but also their land and resources to outsiders.[57]

Lack of Freedom of Press and Expression

The interim constitution of 'Azad Kashmir' states, "No person or political party in Azad Jammu and Kashmir shall be permitted to propagate against or take part in activities prejudicial or detrimental to the ideology of the State's accession to Pakistan."[58] This provision ensures that people neither have any choice as far as governance is concerned nor can they express resentment against the annexation of their land by Pakistan 65 years back.

A comprehensive report published by the *Human Rights Watch* dubbed 'Azad Kashmir' as "a land of strict curbs on political pluralism, freedom of expression, and freedom of association; a muzzled press; banned books; arbitrary arrest and detention and torture at the hands of the Pakistani military and the police; and discrimination against refugees from Jammu and Kashmir state". The report speaks volumes of Pakistan's policy of using the PoK as a safe haven for the militant organisations at the cost of development activities for the well-being of the common people.[59]

Most of the nationalists from PoK have been forced to flee their homeland and live in other countries. This is apparent when one comes across the press releases issued by prominent political parties from the PoK. These statements are either issued in some European country or released on websites.[60] The authoritarian system in Pakistan does not allow free interplay of ideas and expressions in public life. Not only this, there have been reports that these leaders are subjected to atrocities if they are caught by police or intelligence agencies.[61]

There were several incidents in the year 2007 which indicate the high handedness of authorities in such cases. In October 2007, the police detained protesters who were demanding the shift in the capital from Muzaffarabad, and in November of the same year, members of APNA (favours independence of the region) were held while demonstrating in connection with the cross-LoC trade.[62] In November 2007, a group of journalists in Mirpur launched a protest against the government after an emergency was imposed in Pakistan which put effective curbs on the freedom of press. The protest was organised by Pakistan Federal Union of Journalists (PFUJ).[63] Various NGOs, particularly those run by Aga Khan Foundation in PoK, have been threatened from time to time against any activities which purportedly highlight the discrepancies on the part of the state apparatus.[64]

Chinese Inroads in PoK

Another turning point in the history of the PoK region was the opening of the Karakoram Highway, which is the highest international road in the world. The highway connects China and Pakistan across the Karakoram mountain range via the Khunjerab Pass and has unfolded tremendous trading opportunities between the two countries. There are plans to further widen the highway and also build a railway track there. It connects China's Xinjiang region with 'Northern Areas', now renamed as Gilgit-Baltistan. In addition to what China had already occupied, Raskam and Taghdumbash, which formed part of the Hunza Division, Pakistan ceded Shaksgam area in 1963 primarily as a payoff for building the Karakoram

Highway. More than the trading activities, the road is widely used for the transfer of missiles and nuclear material from China to Pakistan. Notably, China has also built as many as 16 air strips on the road to facilitate the jet planes, a development which is quite alarming for peace and stability in the entire South Asian region.[65]

Developments in Pakistan augur a bleak future for the country at least for the next few years, and this turmoil may well give China a fair chance to further strengthen and diversify these inroads in PoK. There is absence of socio-economic development: poverty, illiteracy and unemployment prevalent in PoK has increased the vulnerability to Chinese influence. As Pakistan on its own could not do anything for the upliftment of people here and, therefore, depends very much on the "Joint Ventures" with China for the purpose.[66]

China's economic intervention in its neighbourhood is not new and its interest in the PoK is not an isolated issue. A piece of land (read PoK) which for several years has been wilfully neglected to fulfil unjustifiable political objectives by Pakistan would surely look up to such openings which could rid the people of misery and poverty. The level of receptivity in PoK towards the Chinese trade openings is so high that it has attracted people from other parts of Pakistan to come and settle there in search of better lives.[67] Gilgit as a backward region has been fortunate to access this trading route and witness appreciable economic betterment.

China of late has made immense financial commitments in PoK especially in the wake of the 2005 earthquake and the ongoing reconstruction efforts. China had also shown considerable interest in the Kohala Power Project.[68] In early 2009, it proffered a whopping $ 300 million for undertaking development projects in the quake affected cities of Muzzaffarabad, Rawlakot and Bagh.[69] The agreement to this effect was signed in Islamabad between Earthquake Reconstruction Rehabilitation Authority (ERRA), the body responsible for undertaking development work in the earthquake affected areas of the PoK, and the Chinese Ambassador Luo Zhaohui.[70] Notably, ERRA has been levelled with several charges of gross irregularities and failure to complete its work on time. The region has stagnated for over six decades under Pakistan's control.

Militant Training Camps in PoK

The Mumbai attacks in November 2008 turned the focus on PoK under immense media glare. The perpetrators of the attack were known to have been trained in the PoK and had travelled all the way to Mumbai from Baitul-Mujahideen in Muzaffarabad via Karachi.[71] This was not the first occasion when close ties had been established between PoK and cross-border militancy sponsored by Pakistan. In fact before the devastating earthquake of 2005, this region was kept under wraps by the rulers in Pakistan so that the people there could not give vent to their overwhelming anti-Pakistan sentiments. It was only in the aftermath of the earthquake, after foreign aid coupled with international NGO offices poured into the area that the harsh realities related to lack of development and overall situation of the people in PoK were noticed.[72] It was during the post-earthquake relief programmes that the increasing involvement of militant organisations camouflaged as social workers was also noticed in the PoK.[73] People who were neglected and unheard in the wake of the calamity, developed receptivity for these terrorist organisations that were providing them at least with food and medicine in their moment of distress.[74] This factor significantly accounts for the proliferation of militant training camps in the PoK, and which are responsible for horrific incidents of violence, such as the attacks of 26/11.

In February 2008, some of the banned terror outfits who in the past have carried out lethal cross border terrorist attacks in India held a meeting under the aegis of the Pakistan Army at Muzaffarabad. The matter which was reported by the BBC, showed the complicity of the Pakistani State in promoting and nurturing cross-border terrorism against India.[75] As many as 12 groups attended the meeting: notable amongst them were Lashkar-e-Toiba (LeT) and the Jaish-e-Mohammed (JeM).[76]

The Taliban Threat in PoK

The free play of Taliban in Pakistan's tribal areas is a cause of concern for people in the PoK territory. They are well aware of their vulnerabilities in case of Taliban emergence as they are dependent on Pakistan for their security. Keeping in view the failure of the Pakistan Army to stop Taliban in the heartland, the region has valid apprehensions on security issue against dreaded groups such as the Taliban.[77] It is apprehended that the Taliban may take control of the Karakoram Highway to achieve strategic depth not only in their apparent fight against Pakistan security forces but also against India.[78] The fear is entrenched among the local population as their memories of the Shia purge in the late 1980s are still fresh. The population which is primarily non-Pashtun (Shias and Ismailis) is, therefore, strongly opposed to any emergence of Taliban militancy in their land. Zia-ul-Haq organised the mass killing in the region with a view to alter the demographic balance of the region. Women and children were subjected to atrocities and their houses were destroyed in this conspiracy.[79] Since then, "latent sectarianism coupled with lack of constitutional avenues has aggravated the sense of alienation" in the people of Gilgit-Baltistan.[80]

It was around the same time that Arif Shahid, a leader of the Jammu and Kashmir National Liberation Front (JKNLF) predicted that Shariat Law might be implemented in the PoK following the example of the restive Swat Valley. In an interview, Shahid admitted that the military establishment of Pakistan may plant Taliban militants in the PoK to ensure that "the issue of PoK is settled in favour of Pakistan". He also alleged that the probability of Shariat Law was all the more likely as the Qazis already exercise good deal of influence in the courts in PoK.[81] Also, Pakistan reportedly allowed at least 28,000 Afghan settlers to establish themselves in the PoK to proliferate the jihad ideology and drain the resources of the region.[82]

Comparing PoK with Jammu and Kashmir

Amir Humza Qureshi, leader of the Gilgit-Baltistan Jamhoori Mahaz once noted, "India is not perpetrating even one hundredth part of the repression that people spread over an area of 28,000 miles have been facing for the past 60 years. The Indian Government has given people all their fundamental human rights and in spite of that they are in a state of confrontation against the government. But the people of this region (PoK) are far behind the rest of the world in matters of fundamental human rights, justice and economic development."[83]

In the light of the aforementioned statement, it is useful to draw comparison between the two parts of Kashmir to bring out harsh realities existing on the Pakistani side.[84] Jammu and Kashmir is an integral part of India and is run by a legitimate and democratic governing structure duly elected in free and fair elections held every six years. There is great deal of stability in the political system despite incidents of violence perpetrated by Pakistan-backed militants since late 1980s. The regional parties exercise considerable influence in the local politics which is evident from the fact that the state governments are formed by Kashmiri political parties. There is overwhelming participation in both state and general elections, and the voter turnout in 2009 was approximately 62 per cent, which is higher than any other part of the country. Despite call from pro-independence political groups such as Hurriyat Conference to boycott the polls, such evidence of participation in elections nevertheless further strengthens India's legitimate claim on Kashmir. The realisation of disparities as far as basic rights of life are concerned has also escalated the discontent amongst the unfortunate people of PoK.

Conclusion

In the wake of the new package for Gilgit-Baltistan, India registered protest by handing a demarche to the Pakistani High Commissioner in India.[85] In this document, India clearly stated that Pakistan has no right to take decisions for Gilgit-Baltistan, as it is not an integral part of Pakistan and legally belongs to the state of Jammu and Kashmir. The Indian High Commissioner in Pakistan was handed the reply on the same day, wherein the Pakistan Government stated that the PoK was beyond India's locus standi.[86]

Due to preoccupation in countering cross-border terrorism sponsored by Pakistan over the years in the state of Jammu and Kashmir (which now engulfs the heartland too), India has not been able to focus much on the miseries on the other side of the border. These reports, which have been taken primarily from the Pakistani media sources, have endless tales to narrate about the state of affairs prevailing in PoK. In July 2009, prominent leaders from PoK participated in the conference on society, culture and politics in Karakorum Himalayas held in New Delhi. These leaders urged India to undertake a greater and more substantial role in helping the people from the region attain their basic rights and freedom from Pakistan's tyrannical rule.[87]

It should be noted that these news reports have not only been filtered but also escaped the stringent controls that Pakistan has imposed on the press and media in the PoK. Hence, it is not very difficult to imagine the degree of discontent prevailing there. Things are worsening as there is inadequate international attention to take note of gross scale of human rights violation in the PoK. There is more hue and cry internationally over such violations in Jammu and Kashmir due to false rhetoric and propaganda doctored by Pakistan since over the past six decades. Since its inception in 1947, Pakistan has fed the world with false information on Jammu and Kashmir and has astutely hidden its stark transgression in the PoK. It is ironical that Pakistan has succeeded in befooling countries and has generated tremendous aid both military and non-military, which could be employed in sponsoring militancy against India.

Press has a vital role to play in troubled societies, and in the past, media is known to win wars for the oppressed people. Keeping in view the turbulent past and the current bizarre security situation in Pakistan, it may not be advisable to be too prescriptive about the desired role of media in PoK. Nevertheless, a greater role of media with adequate authenticity can bring about sea change by dismantling the terror infrastructure which has proved an existential threat to regional security especially India. This would also wreck Pakistan's sinister strategy of pushing the PoK to abyss of backwardness and misery so that its clandestine activities in the region are not known to the outside world. Pakistan realises rather well that development will bring the region under some sort of media glare which could unravel its militant network operating in the PoK. Once the region is rid of these hideouts and training camps, normalcy could be restored as was the case before Pakistan deceitfully occupied it.

The step-motherly treatment that the people of PoK have been subjected to for years has aggrieved them immensely. Pakistan invaded the territory merely for ulterior motives of territorial aggrandisement, but never really owned the people of the land. They were kept in a state of lurch with no political and economic rights. The loss of faith in the Pakistani system has yielded political dissent on a large scale evident in the selected reports that were referred while writing this paper.

It is high time that the international community and especially India take note of this boiling spot right in the heart of South Asia and act suitably. The human rights activists and organisations should help the people of PoK in acquiring the basic rights of life as their case has been neglected for years. These organisations could also help them fight against the economic exploitation of their land and their marginalisation. These people are suffering due to irrational behaviour of Pakistan, which neither wants to free the land of its occupation nor is inclined to carry out development activities for the well-being of the local population.

NOTES

1. 'A Comprehensive Note on Jammu & Kashmir', Pakistan Occupied Kashmir, at http://www.indianembassy.org/policy/kashmir/kashmir_mea/POK>html (Accessed August 1, 2008).
2. Full text of the Karachi Agreement, signed in April 1949, at http://www.kashmir.ahrchk.net/mainfile.php/after1947/43/ (Accessed January 6, 2009).
3. 'Gilgit-Baltistan Package a Big Joke with People of Gilgit-Baltistan', *Hunza Times*, September 1, 2009, at http://hunzatimes.wordpress.com/2009/09/01/gilgit-baltistan-package-a-big-joke-with-people-of-gilgit-baltistan/
4. Rekha Chowdhary, 'Northern Errors', *The Indian Express*, September 8, 2009.
5. Ismail Khan, 'Gilgit Baltistan Autonomy', *Dawn*, Karachi, September 9, 2009, at http://www.dawn.com/wps/wcm/connect/dawn-content-library/dawn/news/pakistan/04-gilgit (Accessed September 9, 2009).
6. "PML-N Welcomes Approval of Self Governance for NA: Ahsan", at http://www.onlinenews.com.pk/details.php?id=151049 (Accessed August 31, 2009).
7. "PML-Q Rejects New Package". *Daily Times*, Lahore, August 30, 2009, at http://www.dailytimes.com.pk/default.asp?page=2009%5C08%5C30%5Cstory_30-8-2009_pg1_4 (Accessed September 2, 2009).
8. Vijay K. Sazawal, "The 'Self Governance' Bogey". Kashmir Forum, August 22, 2006, at http://www.kashmirforum.org/the-self-governance-bogey.htm (Accessed August 26, 2009).
9. B. Raman, "Unrest in Gilgit Baltistan", Paper no. 1241, February 3, 2009, at http://www.southasiaanalysis.org/%5Cpapers13%5Cpaper1241.html (Accessed May 27, 2009).

10. Abbas Ali, "Political Unrest in Gilgit-Baltistan". *Dawn*, Karachi, July 26, 2009, at http: //www.dawn.com/wps/wcm/connect/dawn-contentlibrary/dawn/in-paper-magazine/encounter/politicalunrest-in-gilgitbaltistan-679 (Accessed August 10, 2009),
11. "Constitutional Package for N. Areas", *Dawn*, Karachi, October 24, 2007, at http:// www.dawn.com/2007/10/24/top1.htm (Accessed March 6, 2009).
12. "The Gilgit Baltistan Reforms Package 2007: Background, Phases and Analysis". *Gilgit Baltistan Tribune*, March 2009, at http:// gbtribune.blogspot.com/2009_03_01_ archive.html (Accessed June 3, 2009).
13. "Constitutional Structure of Azad Kashmir and Its Relationship to Pakistan", at http: //www.hrw.org/reports/2006/pakistan0906/4.htm (Accessed 3 June 2009).
14. Official Website of the Gilgit Baltistan United Movement. at http:// skardu.blogspot.com/.
15. Official Website of the Balwaristan National Front, at http://www.balawaristan.net/
16. "Rising Popularity of BNSO in Hazara Division Hailed". *Bang-e-Sahar* (Weekly), November 15-21, 2008, at http://gilgitbaltistantimes,blogspot,com/2008/11/rising-popularity-of-bnso-in-hazara.html.
17. "Youth Last Ray of Hope for GB People: BNSO Chief". *Bang-e-Sahar* (Weekly), April 14-20, 2009 http://weeklybaang.blogspot.com/2009/04/weekly-baangkarachi-volume-02-issue-08_3275.html.
18. "BNSO Karachi Extends Activities to Other Cities". *Bang-e-Sahar* (Weekly), February 27 - March 2, 2009, at http://weeklybaang.blogspot.com/2009/02/weeklybaang-issue-01-back-page.html.
19. Website of the Unrepresented Nations Peoples Organization, at http:// www.unpo.org/.
20. "Gilgit Baltistan", at http://www.unpo.org/content/view/8727/256/ (Accessed August 25, 2009).
21. Emma Nicholson, *Report on Kashmir: Present Situation and Future Prospects*. Committee of Foreign Affairs, European Union, April 25, 2007.
22. *Discord in Pakistan's Northern Areas*, Asia Report N 131, April 2, 2007, International Crisis Group.
23. "Gilgit-Baltistan's Constitutional Status". *Bang-e-Sahar* (Weekly), September 6-12, 2008.
24. "Freedom in the World 2008—Kashmir [Pakistan]", Refworld, UNHCR, at http:// www.unhcr.org/cgi-bin/texis/vtx/refworld/rwmain?page=printdoc&docid= 487c (Accessed August 28, 2009).
25. Ibid.
26. Shafqat Ali Inqilabi, "Is Azad Kashmir Independent?"*Bang-e-Sahar* (Weekly), November 22, 2008, at http://balwaristan.blogspot.com/2008/11/is-azadkashmir-independent.html.
27. "Call to Include Gilgit and Baltistan in AJK". *Bang-e-Sahar* (Weekly), June 14-20, 2008, at http://gilgitbaltistantimes.blogspot.com/2008/06/call-toinclude-gilgit-and-baltistan-in.html.
28. "Kashmiri Leadership Sees Light at the End of the Tunnel". *Pakistan Observer*, October 29, 2008, at http://pakobserver.net/200810/29/Editorial02.asp (Accessed August 31, 2009).
29. "Pakistan Asked to Withdraw Its Civil and Military Colonial Rulers from Gilgit Baltistan", Press Conference, November 16, 2008, at http://skardu.blogspot.com/ 2008/11/pakistan-asked-towithdraw-its-civil.html (Accessed November 20, 2008).
30. "Change of Government in Azad Kashmir". *Daily Times*, Lahore, January 8, 2009, at

http://www.dailytimes.com.pk/default.asp?page=2009%5C01%5C08%5Cstory_8-1-2009_pg3_1 (Accessed August 25, 2009).

31. "Political Heads of Development Authorities & Civic Institutions across AJK Removed". *Associated Press of Pakistan*, January 7, 2009, at http://www.app.com.pk/en_/index.php?option=com_content&task=view&id=64247&Itemid=2.
32. "Appointment of SAC Chief Aimed to Suppress People's Voice: GBUM", January 27, 2009, at http:/skardu.blogspot.com/2009/01/appointment-of-sacchief- aimed-to.html (Accessed January 31, 2009).
33. "Kashmir Is Not a Property of Its Muslim Inhabitants", at http://skardu.blogspot.com/2008/10/kashmir-is-notproperty-of-its-muslim_20.html.
34. "Skardu Declaration of GBUM", June 15, 2008, at http://skardu.blogspot.com/2008/06/skardu-declarationof-gbum15-june-2008.html.
35. Ibid.
36. "Revolt Brewing in the so-called Northern Areas of Pakistan Occupied Kashmir". J&K Insights, at http://www.jammu-kashmir.com/insights/insight980201.html (Accessed September 20, 2009).
37. Khurshid Anwer, "Bhasha Dam Blunder?" *The News*, Karachi, August 23, 2009, at http://www.thenews.com.pk/daily_detail.asp?id=194463 (Accessed September 20, 2009).
38. Alok Bansal and Priyanka Singh, "Bhasha Dam: A Tombstone for Gilgit Baltistan's Aspirations". IDSA Strategic Comments, January 31, 2009, at http://www.idsa.in/publications/stratcomments/AlokBansalPriyankaSingh310109.htm. (Accessed January 31, 2009).
39. "Bhasha Dam Construction Tenders Summoned". May 21, 2009, at http://www.apakistannews.com/bhasha-dam-construction-tenders-summoned-121645 (Accessed May 30, 2009).
40. Md. Sadiq, "Bhasha: The Damned Dam", J&K Insights, May 20, 2006, at http://www.jammu-kashmir.com/insights/insight20060520a.html (Accessed November 30, 2009).
41. "Conditions for Diamer Dam by the People of Gilgit-Baltistan". *Balawaristan Times*, at http://balawaristantimes.blogspot.com/2009/02/conditions-for-diamer-dam-by-people-of.html.
42. Zulfiqar Halepoto, "Bhasha Dam: Socio-Economic and Environmental Impacts". *Indus Asia Online Journal*, November 17, 2008, at http://iaoj.wordpress.com/2008/11/17/bhasha-damsocio-economic-and-environmental-impacts/.
43. Md. Sadiq, "Diamer-Bhasha Dam Controversy: The Rights of the People of Northern Areas Must be Respected...", November 12, 2008 http://letusbuildpakistan.blogspot.com/2008/11/diamerbhasha-dam-controversy-rights-of.htm.
44. "Independent Commission to Resolve the Boundaries of Diamer Bhasha Dam: BNF". *Dardistan Times*, July 7, 2009, at http://dardistannews.wordpress.com/2009/07/06/independent-commission-to-resolve-the-boundaries-ofdiamer-bhasha-dam-bnf/ (Accessed August 15, 2009)
45. "People of Hunza Feel Strongly against Job Discrimination". *Hunza Times*, September 18, 2008, at http://hunzatimes.wordpress.com/2008/09/18/people-of-hunza-feel-strongly-against-job-discrimination/ (Accessed September 24, 2008).
46. "Prime Minister of Azad Kashmir in the Line of Fire". *Kashmir Watch*, August 27, 2009, at http://www.kashmirwatch.com/showajnk.php?subaction=showfull&id=1251385725&archive=&start_from=&ucat=18&var1news=value1news (Accessed

August 30, 2009).

47. Zafar Iqbal, "Post Traumatic Earthquake Scenario of AJK". *Kashmir Watch*, July 9, 2009, at http://www.kashmirwatch.com/showajnk.php?subaction=showfull&id=1247140423&archive=&start_from=&ucat=18&var1news=value1news (Accessed August 10, 2009).
48. James Palmer, "Thousands in Tents after '05 Pakistan Quake". *Chronicle Foreign Service*, November 15, 2008, at http://www.sfgate.com/cgi-in/article.cgi?f=/c/a/2008/11/15/MNBS13RI53.DTL&type=printable (Accessed November 30, 2009).
49. "UK to Continue Reconstruction Efforts in Quake Hit Areas". *Daily Times*, Karachi, July 3, 2008, at http://www.dailytimes.com.pk/default.asp?page=2008%5C07%5C03%5Cstory_3-7-2008_pg7_25 (Accessed August 2, 2008).
50. Shabbir Ahmed Mir, "Muzaffarabad Migrants Decry Official Apathy, Distribution of BISP Forms through Legislators Sought". *The News*, Karachi, March 20, 2009, at http://www.thenews.com.pk/daily_detail.asp?id=168118.
51. "Gilgit Baltistan: Miserable Life Condition", at http://www.unpo.org/content/view/9192/254/.
52. "Gilgit Baltistan: Ideology Dissuaded". March 12, 2009, Statement issued by Manzoor Hussain Parwana, Chairman, Gilgit Baltistan United Movement, at http://www.unpo.org/content/view/9347/254/.
53. "Save Gilgit-Baltistan from Pakistani Jackboots", at http://globalpoliticsnews.com/?p=163 (Accessed March 31, 2009).
54. "Plight of the People of Balawaristan". *Balawaristan Times*, January 26, 2009, at http://balawaristantimes.blogspot.com/2009/01/plight-ofpeople-of-balawaristan.html.
55. "Call to Reinforce State Subject Rule in Gilgit Baltistan". *Balwaristan Times*, at http://balawaristantimes.blogspot.com/2009/02/call-toreinforce- state-subject-rule-in.html.
56. "Divided We Fall", Editorial, *Bang-e-Sahar* (Weekly), March 24-30, 2009.
57. "Pakistan Plundering Northern Areas Resources, UN Told". *Bang-e-Sahar* (Weekly), September 6-12, 2008, at http://gilgitbaltistantimes.blogspot.com/2008/09/pakistan-plundering-northern-areas.html (Accessed September 30, 2009).
58. See *Azad Jammu and Kashmir Interim Constitution Act, 1974*, p. 5.
59. "With Friends Like These...Human Rights Violations in Azad Kashmir". *Human Rights Watch Report*, 18 (12), (C), September 2006.
60. "Abdul Hameed Khan, "Chairman BNF's Speech at European Parliament". *Balawaristan Times*, at http://balawaristantimes.blogspot.com/2008/12/abdulhameed-khanchairman-bnfs-speech.html.
61. "Gilgit Baltistan: Deteriorating Freedom of Press", Statement released by the Gilgit Baltistan United Movement, March 23, 2009, at http://www.unpo.org/content/view/9393/254/.
62. "Freedom in the World 2008-Kashmir [Pakistan]", no. 24.
63. Mirza Sajid Bashir, "Azad Kashmir Journalists Protest against Media Curbs", November 22, 2007, at http://www.groundreport.com/World/Azad-Kashmir-Journalists-protest-against-media-Cur/2838355 (Accessed October 20, 2009).
64. B. Raman, "Gilgit-Baltistan: The AQ Khan Proliferation Highway—Part VII", Paper no. 3428, September 22, 2009, at http://www.southasiaanalysis.org/%5Cpapers35%5Cpaper3428.html.
65. Letter from Abdul Hamid, Chairman, Balwaristan National Front, to Javier Solana, Secretary General of the Council of the European Union, dated August 19, 2009, at

http://www.gwank.org/August09/Chinas_Occupation_Balwaristan20090820.htm (Accessed September 18, 2009).

66. "Chinese Public Sector Keen to Enter into Joint Ventures". *Associated Press of Pakistan*, April 19, 2009, at http://www.app.com.pk/en_/ index.php?option=com_content&task=view&id=73980&Itemid=1.
67. Ayesha Siddiqa, "Deadly Social Change". *Dawn*, Karachi, May 1, 2009, at http://www.dawn.com/wps/wcm/connect/dawn-contentlibrary/dawn/the-newspaper/columnists/16-ayeshasiddiqa-deadly-social-change-hs-05 (Accessed June 7, 2009).
68. Sher Baz Khan, "Kohala Power Project Attracts Chinese Firm". *Dawn*, Karachi, October 10, 2008, at http://www.dawn.com/2008/10/10/top17.htm (Accessed October 31, 2009).
69. "China to Provide $ 300 Million to AJK Quake Affected", February 15, 2009, at http://www.sananews.com.pk/english/2009/02/15/china-to-provide-300-millions-to-ajk-quake-affectees/ (Accessed February 20, 2009).
70. Khalid Amin, "Chinese Firms to Undertake Urban Development Project". *Daily Mail*, February 15, 2009, at http://dailymailnews.com/200902/15/news/dmcitypage01.html (Accessed February 20, 2009).
71. Praveen Swami, "Lashkar Tested Sea Route to Mumbai in 2007 Dry Run". *The Hindu*, New Delhi, November 28, 2008, at http://www.hindu.com/2008/11/28/stories/2008112861921200.htm (Accessed December 1, 2008).
72. Shabir Choudhary, "Emma Nicholson and the EU Report". *Asian Tribune*, December 14, 2006, at http://www.scribd.com/doc/983377/Emma-Nicholson-and-EU-Kashmir-report (Accessed August 25, 2009).
73. Steve Coll, "Lashkar-e-Taiba". *The New Yorker*, December 1, 2008, at http://www.newyorker.com/online/blogs/stevecoll/2008/12/lashkaretaiba.html.
74. "Rooting out the JuD". *The News*, Karachi, January 27, 2009, at http://www.thenews.com.pk/print1.asp?id=159205 (Accessed January 30, 2009).
75. "Banned Pakistan Militants Gather", British Broadcasting Corporation, at http://news.bbc.co.uk/2/hi/south_asia/7869697.stm.
76. "Pak Guards Terror Conclave in PoK". *Economic Times*, New Delhi, February 5, 2009, at http://economictimes.indiatimes.com/articleshow/ 4078240.cms?prtpage=1.
77. "Afghans to be Kicked out of Gilgit-Baltistan". *Bang-e-Sahar* (Weekly), October 18-24, 2008, at http://gilgitbaltistantimes.blogspot.com/2008/10/afghans-to-be-kicked-out-of-gilgit.html.
78. "Taliban Threat to Gilgit". *Pakistan Tribune*, April 28, 2009, at http://www.paktribune.com/news/index.php?id=214213.
79. "The State of Sectarianism in Pakistan". *Asia Report Nº95*, April 18, 2005, at http://www.crisisgroup.org/library/documents/asia/south_asia/095_the_state_of_sectarianism_in_pakistan.pdf (Accessed May 27, 2009).
80. Alok Bansal, "Gilgit Baltistan: The Roots of Alienation". *Strategic Analysis*, January/February 2008, at http://pdfserve.informaworld.com/590783_751313386_790950216.pdf (Accessed December 16, 2008).
81. "Shariat Law May Soon be Implemented in POK", April 19, 2009, at http://kashmirihindu.wordpress.com/2009/04/19/shariatlaw-may-soon-implemented-in-pok/.
82. Sultan Shaheen, "How Azad is Azad Kashmir?", at http://www.jammu-kashmir.com/insights/insight990902.html (Accessed October 20, 2009).
83. "Kashmir is Not a Property of Its Muslim Inhabitants", no. 33.

84. "Shariat Law may soon be implemented in POK", no. 81.
85. India Protests Pak Plan for Gilgit-Baltistan, August 31, 2009, at http://www.kashmirobserver.net/index.php?option=com_content&view=article&id=2860:india-protests-pak-plan-for-gilgit-baltistan&catid=4:world-news&Itemid=5 (Accessed September 20, 2009).
86. "Pakistan Rejects Indian Protest on Gilgit-Baltistan, Bunji Dam". *The News*, Karachi, September 12, 2009, at http://www.thenews.com.pk/updates.asp?id=86825 (Accessed September 14, 2009).
87. Amitabh Sinha, "PoK Leaders Seek India's Help in Fight against Pak", at http://www.defence.pk/forums/strategic-geopoliticalissues/30552-pk-leaders-seek-india-s-help-fightagainst-pak.html (Accessed August 24, 2009).

16

Religious Extremism in NWFP, Swat and Chitral

Impact on Gilgit-Baltistan

Manzoor Hussain Parwana

Extremism does not belong to any religion, school of thought or special geographical condition. Extremism is an attitude, which develops in human beings due to the surrounding conditions, injustice and unusual training. Though Islam gives the universal message of peace and harmony, some of its followers have used Islam as the religion for victory. Some scholars have even interpreted that there is no nation superior than the followers of Islam. The concept of superiority over human beings and greed to enter the paradise pushed a sizeable section of Muslims in the marsh of extremism.

The beginning of the present era of Islamist extremism starts with the Cold War, in which Pakistan become the frontline state in the war to evict Russia from Afghanistan, and as a result, Pakistan developed the jihad culture at its official level. North-West Frontier Province (NWFP), 'Northern Areas' and Tribal Areas because of their contiguous boundaries with Afghanistan were thus used for war purposes. General Zia-ul Haq provided military training in Pakistan to millions of terrorists around the world in the name of Jihad-e-Afghanistan. These Mujahideen, who were filled with the spirit of jihad, proceeded from Pakistan to conquer Afghanistan and Kashmir. After the eviction of Russian forces from Afghanistan, these Mujahideen scattered around the world and organised themselves under the name of al-Qaida and Taliban to implement their concept of religious extremism.

Gilgit-Baltistan was a peaceful land, free from religious extremism, sectarianism and prejudice. People from all schools of thought were like members of one family, even though Shia Muslims were in majority. Government of Pakistan in violation of the State Subject Rules, settled thousands of people from NWFP in Gilgit-Baltistan and converted the local majority into a minority. The language, culture, customs and social values of Gilgit-Baltistan were thus ruined, and sectarian movements emerged. Settlement of outsiders in Gilgit-Baltistan was done under proper planning. For this purpose, administrative heads from NWFP were sent to Gilgit-Baltistan and million acres of land was distributed amongst these outsiders. In this manner, a different school of thought from NWFP and Punjab was established there. Besides business, high administrative posts were awarded to outsiders. As a result, the local people of Gilgit-Baltistan have been facing external interference.

Gilgit-Baltistan became victim of religious extremists in May 1988 when at the behest of General Zia-ul Haq and official agencies, thousands of militants called *Lashkar* attacked Gilgit-Baltistan. These *Lashkar* comprised tribesmen and natives of NWFP and Afghanistan, and under the supervision of government agencies reached Gilgit after covering a distance of 600 km. The genocide of Shia Muslims was the main aim of this attack. They were fully armed, and resorted to killings and terror activities in Gilgit. Settlements were ruined, in particular, the Shia majority locality of Jalalabad was put on fire; human beings, animals and standing crops were also put on fire. They also targeted the people of Ahal-e-Sunnat. When the invaders returned to Islamabad, they were treated lavishly by the officials there. No case was registered against these militants nor were they asked to explain their attack on Gilgit-Baltistan. The invasion and killing of local people was kept secret from the world community.

Religious extremism in NWFP and Chitral and the ongoing fighting there has been directly affecting Gilgit-Baltistan. The peaceful land of Gilgit-Baltistan is the new target of these terrorists. Religious extremism or Talibanisation in NWFP, Chitral and Swat Valley has adversely affected Gilgit-Baltistan. Asian Human Rights Commission revealed in its report of June 1, 2009 that the Government of Pakistan intended to use force against the people of Gilgit and Baltistan under the pretext of eliminating the Taliban. It stated: "A recent announcement of the Pakistan Army and its intelligence agency (ISI) stated that the Taliban are taking shelter in the Gilgit and Baltistan areas." The purpose of using the pretext of the presence of the Taliban in the area is to mislead the US and North Atlantic Treaty

Organisation (NATO) forces, who are involved in the war on terror. They want to project that the Taliban is a menace in the construction of the big dams, and wish to occupy Gilgit and Baltistan themselves. The announcement has created insecurity among the two million people who have been already denied development for the last 65 years, that is, since the creation of Pakistan.

The following are the main causes of Talibanisation in the region:

Geography of Gilgit-Balistan

Gilgit-Baltistan is situated in the north and northwest of Swat, Chitral and NWFP. District Ghizar of Chitral, Tangeer Darel of Swat and Kohistan and Chilas are geographically contiguous to Gilgit-Baltistan. Nowadays, these 'Northern Areas' of Pakistan are the abode of terrorists. Though Gilgit-Baltistan is not a constitutional part of Pakistan, yet Pakistan has firm administrative control over it. The name 'Northern Areas' is itself a threat to the identity and survival of Gilgit-Baltistan because the extremists easily penetrate and seek safe haven in this region.

Area of Shia Majority

The status of Shia majority is deteriorating day by day in Gilgit-Baltistan as it is being converted into a minority. After the assumption of control by the Government of Pakistan in Gilgit-Baltistan in 1947, people belonging to Sunni school of thought from other provinces and particularly tribal areas from NWFP were settled here, which changed the demography there. Even though a lot of sectarian violence took place in Gilgit-Baltistan, the terrorists involved in these incidents enjoyed official support. As such no arrests were made, nor was any one punished.

These immigrants of the Ahal-e-Sunnat school of thought residing in Gilgit-Baltistan have a soft corner for the Taliban of Swat, Waziristan and NWFP, and many of them even received military training and even participated in jihad. Thousands of these armed *Lashkar* from tribal areas declared the Shias of Gilgit-Baltistan as infidels and attacked them, killing hundreds of Shias.

NLI Youth of Gilgit-Baltistan

In 1988, when the *Lashkar* attacked Gilgit-Baltistan, they were repulsed by the local people, and both the retired or serving soldiers of Northern Light Infantry (NLI) put up a determined fight against the invaders. Thousands of soldiers of the NLI Regiment are today fighting against terrorism in tribal areas, Swat and NWFP. The youth of Gilgit-Baltistan are directly bearing the brunt of operations by the terrorists. It remains to be seen if the Taliban get defeated at the hands of the youth of Gilgit-Baltistan. Will this situation lead to further hatred and sectarian violence against the youths of NLI and thus cause harm to Gilgit-Baltistan and its people? Keeping in view these facts, it is not advisable to post the soldiers from Gilgit-Baltistan for a longer duration. When the dead bodies of the soldiers belonging to Gilgit-Baltistan are received here from Tribal areas and NWFP, the society of Gilgit-Baltistan is adversely affected. People are all the time worried about the safety and welfare of their relatives, which causes breakdown in social and economic activities. And they are spending thousands of rupees in *Nazar-o-Niaz* for the safety of their kith and kin.

Karakoram Highway

The people of Gilgit-Baltistan call Karakoram Highway (KKH) the bloody road, or the killer road. This is the only land route which connects Gilgit-Baltistan with Pakistan. The Taliban influence over the population is merely 500 km away. In the past, there have been several incidents in which the people of one school of thought were killed after getting down from the vehicles on the KKH. Though this highway is unsafe, it being the only route for transportation of goods and movement of people, one is compelled to travel on this road. If this road gets temporarily blocked, then the communication of Gilgit-Baltistan with the outside world is cut off. The economic development of Gilgit-Baltistan depends upon the KKH. The Taliban activities in this area began after American war against the Taliban. Many terrorists have fled due to army operations in Swat against the Taliban and are hiding in the settlements adjoining KKH. China is working on the extension plan of KKH. In case fighting against the Taliban takes place at KKH, then the people of Gilgit-Baltistan will be deprived of their travel facilities and all commodities.

Unsatisfactory Security Measures

The feeling of insecurity is increasing day by day amongst the people of Gilgit-Baltistan. Government has already deployed Frontier Constabulary (FC), Rangers and paramilitary forces to maintain law and order in the region. Billions of rupees have been spent on such forces from the development budget of the area, yet terrorists have extended their activities to Gilgit-Baltistan. Inside the city of Gilgit, on every roundabout and on roads, armed forces are deployed. On entering the city and when moving from one place to other, people are routinely searched, and citizens are harassed without any cause. Yet, the terrorists continue their activities easily, notwithstanding the presence of these forces. The persons involved in the sectarian violence of 2005 have not been arrested till date nor has anyone been punished. In early 2009, Syed Asad Zaidi, the Deputy Speaker of Northern Areas Legislative Assembly (NALA), and some other persons were assassinated within a distance of a few metres from the Ranger's checkpost. This case is yet to be investigated. The people believe that the terrorist activities in Gilgit are being backed by the non-local civil administration.

In Gilgit-Baltistan, secret agencies also interfere in the daily lives of the people, and instead of improving the deteriorating law and order situation, they only destabilise Gilgit-Baltistan. There are so many incidents, in which these official agencies picked the local people and tortured them to death. In June 2009, Sadiq Ali was killed while he was in police custody. It is common belief that official agencies killed him by torture during confinement. The law enforcement agencies especially Frontier Constabulary (FC), which is from the tribal areas and NWFP, are the main security threat for the local people. Due to these factors, Talibanisation has made its presence in Gilgit-Baltistan. Though the Inspector General of Police and Chief Secretary of Gilgit-Baltistan have ruled out the possibility of the threat of Talabanisation in Gilgit-Baltistan, they revealed that "Great Game" would soon start in Gilgit-Baltistan.

Alien Civil Administration

The highest posts in the judiciary, administration and security are held by persons who belong to other provinces of Pakistan, and they are all from one school of thought. With the security and political control of Gilgit-Baltistan in their hands, they have vested interests, particularly the extension of their tenure, in maintaining an uncertain security situation in the area. Interestingly, whenever law and order is seriously disrupted in Gilgit-Baltistan, these people come from Islamabad to offer condolences.

In 2005, when there was sectarian violence on the issue of curriculum after the murder of Shia leader Syed Ziauddin Rizvi, the administrative heads, Chief Secretary, I.G.P. and Home Secretary, were in Islamabad. And in 2009, too, when the Deputy Speaker of NALA was murdered, I.G.P., Chief Secretary, Home Secretary and Deputy Commissioner, Skardu, were in Islamabad. People protested against this situation and demanded the removal of non-locals from the administration. Since the administration, which comprises non-locals, is not aware about the geographical conditions, mountain paths and caves, they are unable to provide security, which in turn promotes the Taliban activities in Gilgit-Baltistan.

Impact of Swat

The operations against terrorists in NWFP and Swat led to the exodus of over a million people, which has begun to impact Gilgit-Baltistan. These people are reaching out to their relatives, who are the inhabitants of Gilgit-Baltistan. Their arrival may lead to the entry of extremists and terrorists in Gilgit and Baltistan. The people of Gilgit-Baltistan are scared due to the unsatisfactory security situation. Moreover, Gilgit-Baltistan is suffering from economic stringency after the arrival of these immigrants. There is no indication that these people will return to their homes after the end of the operations there. The government is even in favour of settling the non-locals in the region, which will only give further impetus to extremism in Gilgit-Baltistan.

Conclusion

As Gilgit-Baltistan borders Afghanistan, China and India, in case of the rise of extremism or Talibanisation in Gilgit-Baltistan, these three countries will be directly affected. The extremists can enter the nearby areas of these three countries, which will lead to a bigger crisis and turn the peaceful land of Gilgit-Baltistan into a zone of war. International community needs to play its role to save Gilgit-Baltistan from the imminent threat of Talibanisation.

The following measures can be adopted to keep Gilgit-Baltistan safe from religious extremism or Talibanisation:

1. In 2008, NALA had recommended through a resolution that the area be called by its historical and actual name 'Gilgit-Baltistan', in place of the so-called 'Northern Areas'. The government did not approve this resolution. Gilgit-Baltistan in respect of its geography and history is not the northern area of Pakistan, but by calling this area as 'Northern Areas', Gilgit-Baltistan has been included as part of the northern and tribal areas of Pakistan. It is a matter of satisfaction that Pakistan has realised its mistake and has renamed the region by its historical and original name, Gilgit-Baltistan, vide its Ordinance of 2009.
2. Both the domestic and international media have put spotlight on the fight against terrorism in the northern areas, and common people erroneously believe that it is taking place in Gilgit-Baltistan, which is actually 800 km away from the northern areas of Pakistan. The name 'Northern Areas' is misleading; a consequence of which is that foreign tourists are not visiting Gilgit-Baltistan, causing huge losses to the local economy. Thousands of people, particularly associated with the tourism industry, have become jobless.

3. Socio-economic development and law and order in Gilgit-Baltistan depend upon the restoration of State Subject Rules (SSR). The Government of Pakistan violated the SSR to convert the local population into a minority by the settlement of non-residents in the area. After dissolving SSR the economic, political and social circumstances changed in Gilgit-Baltistan. If the non-residents are not evicted through the strict implementation of SSR, then the Taliban may take up residence here, and the houses of non-residents could provide safe haven for the Taliban. The restoration of the SSR becomes necessary for saving Gilgit-Baltistan from religious extremism and Talibanisation.
4. Public demand regarding the setting up of Local Authority Government has been increasing, because the non-residents have been holding their administrative posts for the last 62 years. The administration of the area can improve only by stationing of local persons on high administrative posts, which in turn will block external intervention.
5. The security of Gilgit-Baltistan is in the hands of non-resident forces, that is, FC and Rangers. The eviction of FC and Rangers is necessary to improve the security situation in Gilgit-Baltistan, because they have been blamed for their involvement in sectarian violence. The local people consider themselves unsafe in the presence of FC and Rangers. To create a secure feeling for the people, the security of Gilgit-Baltistan needs to be handed over to NLI and Northern Scouts, who can block the entry of extremists and Taliban at the entrance gates of Chitral, Swat and NWFP.
6. War against terrorism has been severely affecting the economy of Gilgit and Baltistan. In order to enhance its economic activities, all historical and business corridors joining Gilgit-Baltistan, should be opened. Opening the traditional Kargil-Skardu, Ishkoman-Tajikistan and Astor-Srinagar routes for trade purposes will revolutionise the economic lives of the people, who will thus not be dependent on the Karakoram Highway as they will get alternative corridors for trade. The number of tourists will increase in Gilgit-Baltistan, as the tourists from India and Tajikistan shall get an opportunity of safe tourism on transit visa, which is beneficial for the area.
7. Religious extremism has no place in Gilgit-Baltistan. If there is any attempt to target its local population, or there is Talibanisation of the area, then certainly it will lead to conflict with the two million indigenous population of Gilgit-Baltistan. Today, the beauty, culture, folklore, archaeological monuments and thousand-year-old

historical heritage and heavenly valleys of Karakoram, Himalayas and Hindu Kush, which are facing the threat of religious extremism and Talibanisation, need to be saved. Mountains, glaciers, water resources, minerals, wildlife, archaeological monuments and culture are the assets of humanity, and it is the duty and responsibility of the world community to secure these assets. It is in this context that Gilgit-Baltistan needs to be saved from religious extremism.

17

Human Rights Situation in Pakistan Administered Kashmir

Nasir Aziz Khan

'Azad' Kashmir territory comprises about 5,000 sq. km of area. In 1988, the total population was 3 million, of whom 87.5 per cent lived in rural areas and 12.5 per cent in urban areas. The population density is 246 persons per sq km. 'Azad' Kashmir is divided into eight administrative districts: Muzaffarabad, Neelam, Bagh, Poonch, Sudhnutti, Mirpur, Kotli and Bhimber. Muzaffarabad is the capital of this region. According to the constitution of Pakistan, this area is neither a part of Pakistan nor an independent entity. The Government of Pakistan maintains complete control through the 'Azad' Jammu and Kashmir (AJK) Council, which is dominated by the Prime Minister of Pakistan who controls the development funds. The local interim authority powers are also limited to utilisation of local revenue generated within the territory itself. The Council's decisions are final and not subject to judicial review, either by the judiciary of Pakistan or by that of local judiciary at Muzaffarabad.

Power, however, rests with the officials of Pakistan and the Ministry of Kashmir Affairs and Northern Areas in Islamabad with regard to all legislation and appointments, questions of general policy, budget, security and matters related to civil supplies. People in this area were completely denied of the right to adult franchise till 1960, as no elections were held until then. Indirect elections were later held between 1960 and 1975 through the system of so-called "basic democracies" propounded by the then Pakistani ruler General Ayub Khan. Those political parties who believe in the unification and independence of former princely state of Jammu and Kashmir cannot operate independently. The nationalist political activists can not seek justice against impunity and violations of right to life. The culture of personal likes and dislikes and nepotism prevails in local institutions.

Every candidate has to take an oath of loyalty to Pakistan, and has to declare that he/she is Muslim, believes in the state's accession to Pakistan and that Qadianis are non-Muslims. Such written and oral statements have been verified by the local Pakistani intelligence personnel, and it is on the recommendations of secret agencies that executive posts from grade 16 and above are filled. Rest are under the jurisdiction of Chief Secretary who enjoys absolute authority over the Government of 'Azad' Kashmir. If the Chief Secretary is against any project proposal, the same cannot be accomplished by the local authorities at any level. The bureaucracy of 'Azad' Kashmir is directly under the control of Pakistani establishment and all key portfolios such as Chief Secretary, Inspector General of Police, Director General Health and Finance Secretary are bestowed to Pakistani nationals rather than to the inhabitants of the land.

There is widespread resentment amongst the local people and nationalist political parties regarding identity issues, socio-economic and political development of this region. The development schemes are often distributed among the pro-Pakistan political workers who are unqualified and incompetent in building infrastructure. Any one speaking out on such issues faces harassment, and even torture through different means, by the local authorities and the intelligence agencies.

Gilgit-Baltistan, which comprises about 28,000 sq. miles, has a total population of over two million. Islamabad rules this area through its bureaucracy and intelligence agencies which are not accountable and enjoy unlimited powers. Thousands of people are politically victimised and socially and economically marginalised. Majority Shia population, which constitutes 55 per cent of the total population, in the region is forced to study a particular Saudi-imported Wahhabi curriculum in the schools. Demographic change is being encouraged by settling non-locals. People have no constitutional forum or institution to get their grievances redressed. These areas are very important strategically; Gilgit-Baltistan is called the cockpit of Asia. It may serve as an alternative trade route as its borders are linked with China, India and the Central Asian states.

The constitution of Pakistan and the Survey of Pakistan map do not show 'Azad' Kashmir and Gilgit-Baltistan as belonging to Pakistan. On the one hand, the constitution of Pakistan states that the future of Jammu and

Kashmir shall be decided according to the wishes of the Kashmiri people, on the other hand, it bars and denies the right of independence of the people of the former princely state of Jammu and Kashmir by imposing the Constitutional Act of 1974. According to this Act, "No person or political party shall be allowed to take part in activities prejudicial or detrimental to the ideology of state's accession to Pakistan." This clause is in clear violation of the freedom and fundamental rights, and is contrary to the claims of Pakistan itself at national and international fora. In addition, it is contrary to Pakistan's claim of supporting the right of self-determination of the people of Jammu and Kashmir.

Although 'Azad' Kashmir has its own constitution, the Interim Constitution Act of 1974 and a locally chosen parliamentary form of Government, which in theory establish the structures that comprise a self-governing state, including a legislature elected through periodic elections, a Prime Minister who commands the majority in the Assembly, an indirectly elected President, an independent judiciary and other local government institutions. But in practice, these provisions have turned out to be hollow. Under Section 56 of the Jammu and Kashmir Interim Constitutional Act (which was drafted by the Ministry of Kashmir Affairs and Northern Areas and imposed by Azad Kashmir Council, Ministry of Kashmir Affairs, in Islamabad), the Government of Pakistan can dismiss and change any elected Government or its head in 'Azad' Kashmir irrespective of the support it may enjoy in the Legislative Assembly. The Interim Constitution Act provides for two executive forums: the 'Azad' Kashmir Government in Muzaffarabad and the 'Azad' Kashmir Council in Islamabad.

'Azad' Kashmir Council, presided over by the Prime Minister of Pakistan, exercises paramount authority over the AJK Legislative Assembly, which cannot challenge the decisions taken by the Council. The Council is under the control of the federal government in Islamabad, as in addition to the Pakistan's President or Prime Minister, it comprises six other federal ministers, the Minister of Kashmir Affairs as the ex-officio member, the Prime Minister of 'Azad' Kashmir, and six 'Azad' Kashmir members elected by the members of local Legislative Assembly. The Interim Constitution Act lists 52 subjects, virtually everything of any importance, which are under the jurisdiction of the 'Azad' Kashmir Council, which has been described as the "supra power" by the 'Azad' Kashmir High Court. Its decisions are final and not subject to judicial review. Because of the mandate of the AJK Legislative Assembly and its particular division of power with Pakistan, the elected political leaders of 'Azad' Kashmir essentially remain titular heads of the territory, while the real power rests with the Ministry of Kashmir Affairs and Northern Areas in Islamabad. This requires a compliant 'Azad' Kashmir administration, which explains the repeated changes in 'Azad' Kashmir's leadership as per Pakistan's desires from time to time.

Another instrument of exercising control is through assigning virtually all major civil and police administrative posts to Pakistani civil and military officials who are "on deputation" from Islamabad. The 'Azad' Kashmir Government is also totally dependent on the federal government of Pakistan for its finances. Power in 'Azad' Kashmir is exercised primarily through Pakistan Army's General Headquarters in Rawalpindi, just outside Islamabad, and its Corps Commander based in Murree. It is widely understood in Pakistan and privately admitted by virtually all politicians from 'Azad' Kashmir that the Corps Commander in Murree is known to summon the 'Azad' Kashmir Prime Minister, President and other government officials regularly to outline the military's views on all political and administrative issues in the territory. In 'Azad' Kashmir people believe that Corps Commander (GOC Murree) is the real ruler of so-called 'Azad' Kashmir.

Whereas the Pakistani bureaucracy wields the real administrative power, the Inter-Services Intelligence (ISI) and the Pakistan Army exercise coercive power. And under the constitution, the elected representatives are subservient to the Kashmir Council controlled by Pakistan. High Court and Supreme Court Judges can only be appointed with the approval of the Ministry of Kashmir Affairs in Islamabad. That is why there is a subservient judiciary. Junior Judges are appointed as Chief Justice of Supreme Court and in High Court as well. Fundamental freedoms such as freedom of movement, expression, assembly and association are often infringed in AJK.

The Pakistani accountability law, deemed draconian by some, is also applicable in AJK. The Minister of Kashmir Affairs can dismiss the Prime Minister, as also the Chief Secretary-another Islamabad appointee. Under Article 56, the President of Pakistan can dissolve the Legislative Assembly. According to United Nations resolutions dating back to 1948, 'Azad' Kashmir is neither a sovereign state nor a province of Pakistan, but rather a "local authority" with responsibility over the area assigned to it under a 1949 ceasefire agreement with India. It has remained in this state of legal limbo since that time. In practice, the Pakistan Government in Islamabad, Pakistan Army and the Pakistan's intelligence services, the ISI, control all aspects of political life in 'Azad' Kashmir. Though 'Azad' means "free", the residents of 'Azad' Kashmir are anything but 'Azad'. There are strict curbs on political pluralism, freedom of expression and freedom of association; a muzzled press; banned books; arbitrary arrest and detention and torture at the hands of Pakistan's military and the police and discrimination against refugees from the Jammu and Kashmir state.

Kashmiri nationalists who do not support the idea of Kashmir's accession to Pakistan are singled out. Anyone who wants to take part in public life has to sign a pledge of loyalty to Pakistan, while anyone who publicly supports or works for an independent Kashmir is persecuted, tortured and harassed by the intelligence agencies through different means. Torture is routinely used in Pakistan, and acts of torture by military agencies primarily serve the purpose of "punishing" errant politicians, political activists and journalists, particularly in 'Azad' Kashmir. Ever since 1947, there has been not even a single case in which members of military and paramilitary, security and intelligence agencies have been prosecuted or even disciplined for acts of torture or mistreatment.

Tight controls on freedom of expression have been a hallmark of Pakistan Government's policy in 'Azad' Kashmir. This control is highly selective. Pakistan-backed militant organisations promoting the incorporation of Jammu and Kashmir state into Pakistan have had free rein, particularly from 1989 when militancy began in Kashmir. They have been propagating their views and disseminating literature. By contrast, groups promoting an independent Kashmir are curbed to express their views.

October 8, 2005 Earthquake and its Aftermath

In October 2005, the devastating 7.6 magnitude earthquake hit Kashmir. More than 80,000 people were estimated to have been killed, which included 17,000 children. Around 3.5 million people were rendered homeless as cities, towns and villagers throughout the region were razed to the ground. However, politicians and officials continue to pat themselves on the back, while survivors organise protests against the slow pace of reconstruction, lack of compensation and government corruption. Several demonstrations were held in the Pakistani capital of Islamabad, Muzaffarabad, Neelam Valley, Bagh, and Rawlakot. Thousands of people from the quake-affected areas of Bagh, Muzaffarabad, Neelam Valley, Battagram, Rawlakot gave vent to their anger against the government's woefully insufficient aid efforts. Wearing black and red stripes around their heads and arms, they complained about intimidation, flawed policies, lengthy procedural delays and rampant corruption.

They held up placards and banners declaring: "Who is the killer of thousands of children in earthquake?", Stop taking bribes", etc. Some displayed cheques which they said had bounced back. Hundreds of survivors from the earthquake affected area staged another demonstration in 'Azad' Kashmir over the non-receipt of any financial compensation. Placards included: "Where is the $6 billion in donations?" and "Stop discrimination against the quake-affected people."

According to official statistics from Pakistan's Earthquake Reconstruction and Rehabilitation Authority (ERRA), some 600,000 rural and 30,000 urban homes were damaged or destroyed by the October 2005 quake across a 30,000 square kilometres region of mountainous terrain, covering nine districts and 4,000 villages. The ERRA annual report admitted that rehabilitation work has been limited. Even after several years, still many more people remain in unofficial camps, in tents or other makeshift shelter. Essential services have been affected. More than a million school children were affected by the quake. Around 8,000 schools were destroyed or damaged across the region. Many children still go to school in makeshift tents.

In the first 72 hours after the earthquake, thousands of Pakistani troops stationed in 'Azad' Kashmir prioritised the evacuation of their own personnel over providing relief to desperate civilians. The international media began converging on Muzaffarabad within 24 hours of the earthquake and fanned out to other towns in 'Azad' Kashmir shortly thereafter. They filmed Pakistani troops standing by and refusing to help because they had "no orders" to do so, even as locals attempted to dig out those still alive, sending a chilling message of indifference from Islamabad. Having filmed the refusal, journalists switched off their cameras and joined the rescue effort themselves; in one instance, they shamed the soldiers into helping. But unlike death and destruction, the media were not everywhere. The death toll continued to mount. Many Kashmiris told *Human Rights Watch* that prior to the earthquake, the Pakistani Military kept a close watch on the population to ensure political compliance and control; this was facilitated by the placement of military installations frequently in close proximity to populated areas. In the context of a military presence and domineering Pakistani political control, the failure of the authorities to respond quickly and more humanely to the after-effects of the earthquake in 'Azad' Kashmir came as little surprise. That failure generated massive public resentment against the Pakistani State, and it highlighted the need for an examination of the conduct of Pakistan authorities in 'Azad' Kashmir.

The earthquake put the international spotlight on 'Azad' Kashmir for the first time. Previously, attention had been almost wholly on the Indian state of Jammu and Kashmir, which since 1989 has endured brutal militancy. Human rights abuses by the Indian security forces and separatist forces in Jammu and Kashmir have been relatively well documented and often condemned. But the world knows little about 'Azad' Kashmir, excepting that the territory has been used by Pakistan-backed militant groups as a staging ground for attacks in Jammu and Kashmir.

Aid organisations and donors keen to learn about 'Azad' Kashmir after the earthquake, so that they could respond in a useful and informed manner, soon discovered that there was virtually no published information. This is because prior to the earthquake, 'Azad' Kashmir has been one of the most closed territories in the world. While the Indian state of Jammu and Kashmir received considerable tourist traffic prior to the beginning of militancy there, the areas of Kashmir on the other side of the Line of Control (LoC) had seen little external interest or presence after the end of the British colonial era in 1947: a situation used by Pakistan to exercise absolute control over the territory. Information, particularly about the human rights situation, governance, the rule of law and the institutions that hold real power in 'Azad' Kashmir is more important than ever as the territory rebuilds and, by necessity, opens up to the international community in the aftermath of the earthquake. In the coming years, international engagement with the territory is likely to be intense. For that engagement to be effective and beneficial to the people of 'Azad' Kashmir, it is essential that international actors approach the territory with an awareness of its particular history and its often tense and unhappy relationship with the Pakistani State in general and the Pakistani military in particular.

Since 1994, when the ISI organised 13 militant groups operating in Jammu and Kashmir state into the United Jihad Council (UJC), army-backed militant organisations have shared with the Pakistani Military through the ISI, real decision-making authority and the management of the "Kashmir struggle". Even mainstream political parties allowed representation by Pakistan in the 'Azad' Kashmir Legislative Assembly are largely sidelined. As the government-backed militant groups gained strength and dominance, Kashmiri nationalist militants left the movement or were sidelined and eventually began to be persecuted by the authorities and their proxies in Pakistani administered Kashmir. Soon after Pakistan began supporting the US-led "global war on terror" in 2001, the UJC ceased to operate publicly. Several groups simply changed their names and are now operating independently or through clandestine underground networks. The Pakistani intelligence apparatus retains close association with these groups. Interestingly, these groups have been described as the strategic assets of the Pakistani Military. Virtually all independent commentators, journalists, former and serving militants and Pakistan-backed 'Azad' Kashmir politicians openly state that there has been continuing militant infiltration from 'Azad' Kashmir into the state of

Jammu and Kashmir. And there have been no indications that the Pakistani Military or militant groups have decided to abandon infiltration as policy.

It was no accident that militant groups were the first on the scene dispensing relief goods and other aid after the earthquake in 2005. Nor was it a sign of their great organisational skills. As the Pakistani military prioritised the rescue of its own personnel, it probably sought the assistance of its closest allies, the militant groups in 'Azad' Kashmir. These groups, which had undoubtedly suffered the loss of personnel and infrastructure themselves in the earthquake, won much local appreciation for their rescue and relief efforts. This public relations coup could not have been possible without the logistical support from sections of the Pakistani military apparatus. For example, one of the first groups to set up operations was the Jamaat-ud-Dawa. This was the Lashkar-e-Tayyeba (LeT) group operating under a new name, as in January 2002, the Pakistani Government had banned the LeT as a terrorist group. However, in the aftermath of the earthquake, the then President Pervez Musharraf went out of his way to praise its relief work and brushed off calls to restrict its operations. The Pakistani Military apparently used the earthquake as an opportunity to craft a new image of these militant groups rather than as an opportunity to disband them.

Successive Pakistani governments have asserted that Kashmir's political future must be determined in accordance with the wishes of the people. But the reality of 'Azad' Kashmir has been that there are governmental restrictions on fundamental rights and freedoms. As the international community supports the task of reconstruction, it must insist on a new respect by Pakistan for the human rights of the people of 'Azad' Kashmir. No viable solution to the Kashmir issue can exclude the exercise of fundamental civil and political rights for the people of 'Azad' Kashmir in an environment free of coercion and fear. The October 2005 earthquake brought into focus the dominant role of Pakistan Army in the governance of 'Azad' Kashmir and the almost complete absence of any independent civil society in the territory. It also highlighted the inability of Pakistani Military to assume the role of civil society in times of crisis.

The reality is that Pakistani security forces continue to torture persons in custody throughout the country. The methods include beating, burning with cigarettes, whipping the soles of the feet, prolonged isolation, electric shock, denial of food or sleep, hanging upside down, etc. Politically motivated torture is typically used to compel politicians, political activists and journalists critical of the government to change their views or at least to silence them. There are large numbers of Kashmiri detainees being held for long periods by the Pakistani military in secret detention facilities in

'Azad' Kashmir and in Pakistan. Their families are unaware of their existence and are suffering. The poor human rights situation in Pakistani administered areas of so-called 'Azad' Kashmir and in Gilgit-Baltistan is well documented by the European Parliament resolution of May 24, 2007 and *Human Rights Watch* report of 2006 and Human Rights Commission of Pakistan findings of 2004. The army needs to greatly reduce its political role in 'Azad' Kashmir in order to make way for genuinely civilian governmental institutions that respect basic rights.

18

Sectarian Conflict in Gilgit-Baltistan

Alok Bansal

Sectarian violence in Pakistan is a manifestation of its flawed ideology. When a state was created on the basis that Muslims cannot coexist with non-Muslims in a unified India, the next logical question was bound to be: Who is a Muslim? As early as 1950, a judicial commission set up to investigate whether Ahmediyas were Muslims came to the conclusion that no two ulemas could agree on the definition of a Muslim. After the separation of East Pakistan (now Bangladesh), when the numbers of non-Muslims, became insignificant in Pakistan, the fanatic adherents of this exclusivist ideology turned their ire towards their co-religionists, who differed from their own version of Islam. Consequently, the violence was used to settle scores not only between Shias and Sunnis, but also between different strands of same sects. This ideological schism, a natural corollary of divisive "Two Nation Theory" has permeated the high Himalayas and is most stark in Gilgit-Baltistan, than in any other part under Pakistani control.

Amongst all the territories under Pakistani control, Gilgit-Baltistan is the only political unit where the followers of different strands of Shiism are in majority. Pakistani establishment especially since the 1970s has been dominated by the Sunnis and has been extremely wary of this Shia majority region. As a result attempts have been made to change the sectarian composition of this region since 1970s, when State Subject Rule enacted by the Dogra Maharajas to preserve the unique identity of the region was abrogated by the then Prime Minister of Pakistan, Zulfiqar Ali Bhutto. The law barred outsiders from seeking permanent residence or naturalisation in the princely states. However, its abrogation opened the floodgates of immigration. Interestingly both in the Indian state of Jammu and Kashmir as well as in other areas of Pakistan occupied Kashmir the rule is still in force.[1] This is one of the clearest manifestations of the intent of the Pakistani State to change the demographic profile of the region. The attempts by the successive Pakistani administrations to bring in people from various parts of Pakistan have created fear of ethnic marginalisation in their own traditional homeland in the minds of Balti and Dardic people. This has manifested in violence, mainly against those who are perceived to be outsiders, particularly government employees. The local sects enjoyed peaceful coexistence for many years. Things turned nasty with the "outsider" Pakhtoons, Kashmiri and the jihadi elements coming into play in the area. The administration suffers from a total lack of trust from those living in the area.[2] In any case, grafting population as insurance in sensitive areas is an exercise in futility, which only serves to alienate the local population and fuels rifts, as are being witnessed now.[3]

Genesis of Sectarianism

Gilgit-Baltistan contains a high percentage of people from the Shia sect, many of them are Ismailis, the followers of Aga Khan, who are considered heretics by hard-line Islamists, whilst others are Twelver Shias, who are predominantly tribal in their ethnic origin.[4] From being a completely Ismaili (a Shia sub-sect) region in history, it has been injected with external populations with the connivance of the government from the rest of Pakistan. As a result, in the subsequent years, there has been competition of sorts between the big sects, and clerics from other parts of the country introduced the Twelver Shia (*Athna Ashari*, the official religion of Iran) and Sunni faiths too. This has resulted in creation of an area where geographic and linguistic boundaries often coincide with the sectarian identities. Different valleys speak different languages and follow different denominations. Today Gilgit is 60 per cent Shia, 40 per cent Sunni; Hunza, Punial, Yasin, Ishkoman and Gupis are 100 per cent Ismaili; Nagar 100 per cent Shia; Chilas and Darel/Tangir 100 per cent Sunni; Astor 90 per cent Sunni, 10 per cent Shia; Baltistan 96 per cent Shia, 2 per cent Nurbakhti (or Nurbakhshi—followers of Mohammed Nur Baksh) and 2 per cent Sunni.[5]

Poor economic conditions and lack of educational facilities have made Gilgit-Baltistan a hub of sectarian strife during the last two decades. The basic ingredients of sectarianism in this region under Pakistani occupation since 1947 have been similar to that of other parts of Pakistan, as they have been subjected to the similar state policies. External involvement, mostly from "brotherly" Islamic countries, a weak judicial system, proliferation of small arms, mushrooming of sectarian madrassas and the use of religious groups to meet Pakistan's internal and external policy objectives are cited as the major reasons for the current sectarian situation.[6] Ironically, the impoverished populace of the region does not have any realistic alternative to putting their children in madrassas, the ubiquitous nurseries of religious extremism. Consequently, the region is churning out more ulemmas (religious scholars) than most other parts of Pakistan. These half-baked ulemmas, often due to the lack of true understanding of Islamic teachings and aversion to the modern education of science and technology, intentionally or unintentionally instigate sectarian hatred that frequently leads to violence.[7]

Traditionally, the people of Gilgit and Baltistan have been non-violent. Different sects there lived peacefully, and even inter-married. A vast majority of Shias in the region feel that an attempt is being made to marginalise them with the connivance of Pakistani Government. However, the activities of religious militants in the wake of Pakistan's involvement in the Afghan war and the rein given to religious groups have vitiated the atmosphere. They site the incidents of 1988 as proof because the complicity of Zia's government was clearly evident when Gilgit was attacked by Sunni *Lashkar*. The civil and military law enforcement agencies had made no attempts to intervene.[8] Subsequently, the sectarian riots were engineered to divide the people whenever they demanded their legitimate political riots. There were newspaper reports that officials themselves were encouraging riots to prolong Islamabad's unconstitutional rule.[9] Thus Gilgit-Baltistan in recent decades has witnessed many sectarian clashes and strife resulting in the loss of innocent lives.

The absence of any say in the governance has exacerbated the alienation of people of this region, who have been denied their democratic rights. The region does not have any local government system, and bureaucrats from outside the region have lorded over the local populace like colonial masters. The people do not have recourse to any judicial review. The constitutional status of Gilgit-Baltistan has remained ambiguous and attempts have been made to subsume the distinct cultural and ethnic identity of the people under an all encompassing Islamic identity. Locals believe that their resources are being exploited by the government in Islamabad without any benefit accruing to the locals. The immense water resources of the region are being harnessed in such a way that the fertile valleys in Gilgit-Baltistan are being flooded to meet the electricity requirements of Pakistan. This sense of economic exploitation is making the people quite restive.

The growing alienation of the people of Gilgit-Baltistan has led to a demand from the people of the region (mainly Shias) for a separate Karakoram province with real executive and legislative powers; the hardliners amongst them are even demanding a sovereign Balawaristan. On the other hand, many amongst the Sunni minority are seeking the merger of the region with 'Azad Kashmir', the other part of Pakistan occupied Kashmir (POK) comprising Mirpur and Muzaffarabad: a demand that has been upheld by the 'Azad Kashmir' judiciary. The sectarian fissures, which are present across the entire Islamic world have aggravated since the Iranian revolution. Pakistan's political and religious collusion with Pan-Arab countries follows a latent anti-Iran and anti-Shia line. There has been subtle discrimination against the Shias of Gilgit-Baltistan, who have been denied their legitimate share of developmental funds. The Pakistan Government perceives that the creation of a separate Shia-dominated province could further disturb the existing delicate Shia-Sunni relations in the rest of Pakistan, and as a result has dithered in granting provincial status or autonomous status akin to 'Azad Kashmir' to this region. This has particularly exacerbated the alienation of the local population and has taken sectarian hue. It is estimated that over thousand lives have been lost since 1988, when the sectarian conflicts surfaced in the region.[10]

After the abrogation of State Subject Rule in 1974, it became legally feasible for outsiders, mainly Pakhtoons, to acquire property and settle down in the region. The construction of Karakoram Highway brought in a fresh wave of Pakhtoon entrepreneurs and workers initially to Gilgit city and subsequently to other parts of the region. Almost all of them were adherents of Sunni Deobandi Islam. This influx was resented by the local populace who saw the business and jobs slip from their hands and go to the Pakhtoon immigrants. Thus, an uneasy peace was maintained; further, the state patronage accorded to the Sunni-Deobandi Islam under General Zia-ul-Haq led to the introduction of Sunni Deobandi ulemmas in the region. In due course, Sunni militant groups, mainly Sipah-e-Sahaba, emerged in the region, and with state patronage succeeded in spreading their tentacles in this remote, mountainous, tribal and hitherto peaceful region. The Shias and the Ismailis were made to submit to the state-sponsored puritanical aggressive onslaught of Sunni Deobandi ideology.[11] The local population viewed the local administration dominated by the Pakistani bureaucrats to be aiding and abetting the Sunni extremists. The feeling of being discriminated against and an alien religious belief being thrust upon led the majority Shia population of Gilgit to come out and participate in the first major violent demonstration in May 1988. Zia-ul-Haq perceived it as a personal challenge to his beliefs and authority. He deputed a Special Service Group (SSG) group commanded by the then Brigadier Pervez Musharraf to suppress the revolt and restore order. Musharraf decided to penalise the local Shias by transporting a large number of Wahabi Pakhtoon tribesmen from the North-West Frontier Province (NWFP), FATA and Afghanistan to Gilgit to teach the "apostate" Shias a lesson.[12] These Pakhtoon tribesmen massacred hundreds of Shias in Gilgit and the surrounding areas.

According to *Herald*, "In May 1988, low-intensity political rivalry and sectarian tension ignited into full-scale carnage as thousands of armed tribesmen from outside Gilgit district invaded Gilgit along the Karakoram Highway. Nobody stopped them. They destroyed crops and houses, lynched and burnt people to death in the villages around Gilgit town. The number of dead and injured was put in the hundreds. But numbers alone tell nothing of the savagery of the invading hordes and the chilling impact it has left on these peaceful valleys."[13]

Musharraf also initiated a process that involved large-scale induction of Punjabis and Pakhtoons into the sparsely populated Gilgit-Baltistan to convert the Shia majority of the region into a minority. The influx continues to this date, and the proportion of Shias and Ismailis in the overall population has come down significantly. The state-sponsored influx of Punjabis and Pakhtoons from outside has created an acute sense of insecurity amongst the Shia population.[14] It is widely believed in Pakistan that a Shia airman from Gilgit, wanting to take revenge for the May 1988 carnage, was responsible for the air crash that killed General Zia.[15] After 1988, sectarian riots have become a regular feature in Gilgit-Baltistan. The pattern shows that whenever people demanded their constitutional rights, sectarian riots were engineered to divide them. There were media reports that officials themselves were encouraging riots to prolong Islamabad's unconstitutional rule.[16]

On Zia's death anniversary on August 17, 1993, there were massive riots, and over 20 persons were killed before the Pakistani Army managed to restore a modicum of order. The army then accused the Shias of amassing weapons brought in from Iran in their mosques. This was followed by large-scale persecution and arrest of Shias within the region.[17] Subsequently, Lashkar-e-Tayyeba gained influence in the 'Northern Areas' during the Kargil War in 1999. Today, the entire population is divided on the lines of belief and faith (sect). Different interpretations of the same faith (Ismailis consider themselves distinct from other Shias) have bifurcated the society into hard-line groups. Though people of differing shades of faiths normally live side by side in the region, yet petty issues tend to spark bloody clashes amongst them. Latent sectarianism coupled with lack of representation has aggravated the sense of alienation in the populace and led to the creation of ultra-nationalist political groupings like Balwaristan National Front (BNF). During 2003-04, Shias objected to certain portions of the school course curriculum, particularly the contents of *Islamiyat* and Urdu text books, and popular discontent was so high that the authorities were forced to accept the Shia viewpoint after the violent riots in June 2004. Imam Aga Syed Ziauddin Rizvi, the local Shia cleric helped the authorities in trying to resolve the issue to the satisfaction of Shias.[18] However, the issue was so emotive that all schools in Gilgit-Baltistan remained closed for one full year till April 2005 and could only be reopened after all controversial portions were removed to the satisfaction of all sects.[19]

Assassination of Aga Ziauddin

Sunni radicals who had hitherto got used to getting their way did not like the government's accommodation of the Shia viewpoint, and this sense of outrage led to the assassination of widely respected Shia cleric Aga Ziauddin. On January 8, 2005, Aga Ziauddin Rizvi was critically injured when gunmen fired at his car in Gilgit. 15 persons died in violent protests before law and order was restored. On January 13, 2005, Aga Ziauddin died of his wounds in the military hospital in Rawalpindi. The news of his death enraged Shias not only in Gilgit-Baltistan but also across Pakistan. Curfew had to be imposed in Gilgit and Skardu, the two major towns of the region. Government buildings, officials and their families were attacked, and troops had to be deployed to restore law and order. Gilgit-Baltistan continued to simmer weeks after the incident. A number of towns remained under curfew for weeks,[20] telephone lines were disconnected and night time curfew continued for over a month.

After the incidents of January 2005, a façade of normalcy was maintained for some time, but violence kept erupting from time to time. As a stark reminder, the Inspector General of Police (IGP), the highest-ranking police officer, was assassinated along with his bodyguards on March 23, 2005 while travelling between Gilgit and Hunza. He was known to have been imbued with extreme Sunni views during his earlier assignment in Afghanistan as a diplomat and was considered to be biased against the local Shia community.[21] His murder sent shock waves through the establishment and at least three senior police officers of the rank of Superintendent of Police (SP) refused to join duty in Gilgit-Baltistan and preferred being dismissed.[22] With the senior police officers preferring to be sacked rather than serving in the region, the state of other civilian government officials can easily be visualised. The situation forced the government to close all educational institutions and impose curfew. The

Pakistan Army, a contingent of the Punjab Rangers and the Northern Area Scouts were called in to restore a semblance of administration.[23] On April 23, 2005, a bus carrying passengers from Skardu to Islamabad was intercepted at Bhasha right across Gilgit-Baltistan's boundary, and two ethnic minorities from Baltistan were shot at point blank range.[24] When the bodies reached Skardu, the entire Baltistan was up in flames.

In an apparent attempt to cool down passions and restore normalcy, the government agreed to withdraw the controversial textbooks of *Islamiyat* and Urdu from the curriculum.[25] However, a fresh wave of violence engulfed Gilgit and surrounding areas, when five passengers of a bus travelling from Gilgit to Islamabad were killed and six others injured on the Karakoram Highway near Chilas on July 17, 2005.[26] Six more deaths were reported in revenge attacks, which left the region paralysed for over a week. Gilgit was still reeling from the shock of fresh spate of sectarian attacks when a union council chairman and three others were gunned down in a suburban area, triggering clashes between the residents and police. Subsequently, the house of a local journalist was bombed in Gilgit on July 25, 2005.[27] The situation turned so bad that shoot-at-sight orders had to be issued.[28] Despite such strong measures, sporadic cases of violence continued in the region.

In the immediate aftermath of the earthquake in October 2005, when entire Pakistani State's attention was focussed on 'Azad Kashmir' and NWFP, Gilgit-Baltistan erupted again. The new cycle of violence started on October 11, 2005, when a group of Sunnis opened fire on a Shia group, 58 km from Gilgit at Basen killing two and wounding others. Two of the gunmen escaped, but one of them was injured and was nabbed by the local police. The police took him to the district headquarters in Gilgit, but the Pakistan Rangers took him out of the custody of the local police. When the Shia community found out about this change of hand, they protested and were dispersed by the Rangers using tear gas. Out of the 10 protesters arrested by the Rangers was 15-year-old Maqsood Hussain, whose body was found on October 12 in a *nalla* leading to more protests and demonstration by the people.[29] On October 13, 2005, a group of Shia students clashed with the Pakistan Rangers in Gilgit, and in the fracas that followed, six people, including two Rangers personnel, were killed. This aggravated the situation and led to renewed violence, which resulted in more deaths. The Shia community thereafter blocked parts of the Karakoram Highway to protest against the deaths.[30] Curfew was imposed in the city for weeks. Several people were arrested and a cache of weapons, including rocket launchers and AK-47 rifles, were recovered. At least 15 people were in killed within only two days of sectarian violence in Gilgit town. This was the first time when heavy weapons like rocket launchers and bombs were used in the region.[31]

Since October 2005, sporadic cases of violence have been reported from the region. The buses plying on Karakoram Highway have been regularly attacked especially in the Sunni-dominated Chilas Valley, where inhabitants are known for their hostility against Shias living further north.[32] The government officials, including those of the army, Northern Light Infantry and police, have been identified and murdered while travelling in buses in areas falling under the control of rival sects. Casualties due to bomb explosions, ambushes and sniper firing have become a daily routine and so is the blockade of the Karakoram Highway. There were more than 100 fatalities in 2005, a large figure for a sparsely populated region. In March 2006, a day after Muharram Shia protesters blocked the strategically located Gilgit-Skardu and the Gilgit-Hunza roads over Islamabad's decision to incarcerate senior Shia cleric Aga Rahat Kazmi.[33] In April 2006, the government move to shift the district headquarters of newly created Astore district from Shia-dominated Idgah town to Sunni-dominated Gorikot saw nightlong gun battles being fought between police and Shia residents resulting in the death of two women.[34] Again after a brief lull, a judge, Jamshed Khan, of the anti-terrorism court, who had been conducting trials in the cases related to previous sectarian clashes in the region, was shot dead in Gilgit on June 24, 2006.[35]

The declaration by General Musharraf that Bhasha Dam will be the first mega dam to be constructed and the subsequent inauguration of the project by President Musharraf on April 26, 2006 has caused immense consternation in the region as it will inundate large tracts of land in Diamer district of Gilgit-Baltistan. In addition, a huge 35 million acre feet dam has been proposed at Skardu, which will submerge the entire Skardu bowl, the hub of Balti cultural heritage. The Baltis feel that the proposed dam is a deliberate attempt to decimate their culture and identity. It sees this dam as an attempt to marginalise Baltis in Skardu.[36] Allama Hassan Turabi, a renowned Shia cleric from Baltistan, was assassinated in Karachi on July 14, 2006.[37] Ironically, no one has ever been arrested or punished for his assassination.

Current Status

The year 2007 was fairly peaceful and despite provocations, there was hardly any significant case of sectarian violence in the region. The year 2008, though relatively peaceful, saw 18 people being killed in sectarian violence, including the Director of Agriculture Department of Gilgit. However, 2009 again saw a spurt in sectarian violence. It started on

February 19, 2009, when two Shias were killed in an attack on their van in Gilgit. Syed Asad Zaidi, a native of Kharmang Valley in Baltistan and the Deputy Speaker of 'Northern Areas' (earlier, the official name of Gilgit-Baltistan) Legislative Assembly, was shot dead along with his companion, and his driver was injured as they arrived in Kashrote, Gilgit on April 19, 2009. Although perceived as a pro-government leader, he was accused of having delivered a strong anti-Sunni speech in Gilgit in 1971.[38]

Subsequently, a Shia political activist, Sadiq Ali from Jafrabad, Nagir was arrested and tortured to death on June 26, 2009 whilst in detention.[39] Two months later, the killing of rabidly anti-Shia party Sipah-e-Sahaba Pakistan's leader Allama Ali Sher Hyderi in Sindh resulted in widespread rioting in Gilgit. There were fierce gun battles between the two sects in Gilgit and all the markets and commercial establishments were forced to close. Again in September 2009, two Sunni Pakhtoon migrants and three native Shias were killed in Gilgit; in addition, a bus with Shia passengers from Baltistan was torched.[40] On September 26, 2009, just three days ahead of the then Pakistani Prime Minister Gilani's visit to Gilgit, a bomb planted in a stationery shop blew up and engulfed the city in a fresh bout of sectarian riots.[41] Gun battles in the aftermath of the blast devoured more than 12 people including Raja Ali Ahmed Jan, a prominent leader of the Pakistan Muslim League.[42] After a brief pause, again on November 10, in the final stages of electioneering for the newly constituted assembly, three employees of Pakistan State Oil including the Area Manager Ali Mohammad were killed and two others injured when their vehicle while coming from Astore was attacked by unidentified gunmen near Pari 35 km from Gilgit, clearly indicating that the sectarian violence continues unabated in the region.[43]

Of late, there have been reports of collusion between the Taliban and Sunni extremists in the region, as with the operations in Swat valley and other parts of Malakand a large number of them have moved to Gilgit-Baltistan, which adjoins Malakand. Over 300 suspected terrorists without valid identity documents were expelled from Gilgit and its adjoining areas in October 2008, ostensibly to ensure security of Chinese engineers and workers working on Karakoram Highway. This clearly indicated the increased presence of Taliban cadres from outside in Gilgit-Baltistan.[44] The Taliban presence has resulted in the mode of sectarian violence graduating from sniper firings to bomb blasts. It is believed that local Sunni youth have acquired from Taliban expertise in making bombs and suicide jackets. The Taliban has also succeeded in indoctrinating local Sunni youths with their extremist brand of Islam. An Al Qaeda member, Abdullah Rehman, in April 2009, threatened to blow up a four-star hotel in Baltistan. In May 2009, following a bomb blast in Baltistan, two Sunnis were arrested with a large cache of explosive material and hand grenades. Subsequently in July 2009, a bomb was hurled in Gilgit at Bagrot Hostel, which killed two students and injured several others. In February 2012, 18 people from Gillgit-Baltistan were target-killed by gunmen in a bus after being identified as Shias. In August 2012, at least 22 passengers, who were going home from Rawalpindi to Gilgit, were gunned down at Mansehra area of Khyber-Pakhtoonkhwa after being identified as Shias.[45] Increasing influx of Taliban, has not only exacerbated the sectarian tensions, but is also leading to change of demographic profile and erosion of local cultural identity. The usage of Northern Light Infantry, which has predominantly Shia troops from Gilgit-Baltistan, in operations against Taliban in FATA, has further accentuated the sectarian divide in this region where Taliban now has a fair presence.[46]

Empowerment and Self-Governance Ordinance 2009 and Elections

It has widely been believed that Pakistani intelligence agencies trigger sectarian and ethnic tension whenever locals demand political and constitutional rights. Killing of Syed Asad Zaidi, a prominent Shia leader, in a Sunni locality in the neighbourhood of Gilgit town was probably intended to trigger anti-Shia riots and to create divisions between Gilgit and Baltistan. It came at a time when the demand for political rights was becoming louder in the region. The fact that a separate commissionerate for Baltistan was set up just a few months later gives credence to this "Divide and Rule" strategy.[47] However, after failing to create large-scale divisions amongst the people, government announced certain concessions to locals in the form of Gilgit-Baltistan (Empowerment and Self-Governance) Order 2009.

The Order renamed the region as Gilgit-Baltistan, which was hitherto called 'Northern Areas', fulfilling a longstanding demand of the residents of the region. It has also given the region a local administration headed by a "Chief Minister", a post that did not exist in the region. It provides for the Chief Minister, to be elected by the Gilgit-Baltistan Legislative Assembly, who would head a council of ministers, comprising six ministers and two advisors. The legislative assembly now consists of 24 directly elected members and 6 women as well as 3 technocrats to be elected by the members. The Order has provided some financial autonomy for the region, and a consolidated fund has accordingly been created. The budget for the region would here and after be presented and approved by the Gilgit-Baltistan Legislative Assembly. The Order has introduced a judicial set-up with the establishment of an Appellate Court comprising of a Chief justice and two other judges. There is also a provision in the Order to eventually increase the strength of the court to five. Besides, the order has provision for a separate Public Service Commission, a Chief Election Commissioner and an Auditor General for the region.[48]

However, what is significant is that by introducing this Order the Pakistani Government has taken the first step towards amalgamating this strategically significant part of the former state of Jammu and Kashmir into Pakistan. The Order does not provide either the Chief Minister or the Legislative Assembly with any worthwhile powers; the real powers lie with the Governor of Gilgit-Baltistan, who is an outsider appointed by the President of Pakistan on the advice of the Prime Minister. Although a Legislative Assembly has been elected, the real powers vest with the Gilgit-Baltistan Council, whose Chairman is the Prime Minister of Pakistan and most of whose members are the appointees of the Pakistani Government. Although, the number of subjects on which the assembly can make law has been increased from 49 to 61, the Council retains the exclusive power to legislate on 55 issues, which are of much greater significance. In any case, certain issues like defence, foreign affairs and security are beyond the purview of both the Assembly and the Council. Similarly, the Chief Justice of the Appellate Court is appointed by the Chairman of the Council (Prime Minister of Pakistan) on the advice of the Governor (another Pakistani appointee). Other judges will also be appointed by the Chairman on the advice of the Governor after seeking views of the Chief Justice. The order stipulates that the budget will be presented to the assembly and passed by it; however, what is significant is that it would be prepared by the Pakistani bureaucrats. Similarly, all members of Public Service Commission, the Auditor General or the Election Commissioner are to be either the direct or indirect appointees of the Pakistani government. Similarly, all the key functionaries of the administration like the Chief Secretary, the Finance Secretary and the IGP will be Pakistani bureaucrats deputed from outside. It is significant to note that the region has no representation in either the Pakistani Parliament or the Council of Ministers, which would have the final say in the future set-up of the region.[49]

Thus, the Order vests all the real executive, legislative and judicial powers with outsiders or their appointees, whereas the Assembly or the Council of ministers would be devoid of any worthwhile powers. The fact that the terminologies like the Governor and the Chief Minister have been used rather than the "President" and the "Prime Minister", which are used for the heads of 'Azad Kashmir', indicates a more sinister design to the whole exercise. The cosmetic changes that have been incorporated are intended to give an impression of autonomy, where as the real attempt is to separate this strategic region, which has been an inalienable part of the state of Jammu and Kashmir, from the other part of Pakistan occupied Kashmir (POK) and eventually to gobble it. Right from 1947, Pakistan has systematically worked towards this end. Immediately after occupation, it separated State of Chitral, a vassal of Maharaja of Kashmir from the region and incorporated it in NWFP.[50] The very fact that President and the Government of Pakistan have passed orders on the future governance of an area that is not Pakistan's part even according to its constitution indicates its sinister designs on the area. The Order also has an interesting clause, which states that any law passed by the Assembly will be null and void if it contradicts *Sunnah* and Quran. As Shias and Sunnis have a differing perception of what constitutes *Sunnah*, the order could thus provide fuel to sectarian rifts.

The elections based on the order were held on November 12, 2009; most of the Pakistani political parties and local groups participated in the elections. Leaders of most political parties campaigned in the region during elections. Almost 40 per cent of 714, 966 eligible voters participated in the elections.[51] As has always been the case in POK, the ruling party in Islamabad, namely the Pakistan People's Party (PPP), emerged as the winner in these elections as well. During electioneering there was heavy presence of security forces, and women participated freely in the elections in most parts of Gilgit-Baltistan. However, in Diamer a district which has come under heavy Taliban influence in recent times, women were not allowed to participate in the elections. Sunni hardliners also tried to prevent women from voting in the area of two polling booths in Danyor, near the city of Gilgit.[52] The elections saw the advent of secular parties like Mohajir Quami Movement (MQM) in the region, but an undercurrent of sectarianism was clearly evident in the polling. Mostly voting took place along sectarian lines. The elections saw PPP fielding a Sunni candidate for the first time in immigrant-dominated Gilgit-2 constituency, but it resulted in splitting of Sunni votes between PPP and PML (N), resulting in the victory of a Shia independent candidate.[53] This resulted in all six seats in Gilgit district being won by Shia candidates, which could lead to sectarian clashes in future. Similarly, in Ganche district of Baltistan, sectarian polarisation helped Grand Nurbakhshi Mufti M. Abdullah to win against PML (Q) candidate Amina Ansari.[54] Despite lack of media coverage and intimidation by the security forces, the nationalist groups working against continued Pakistani occupation of the region, did fairly well. All Parties National Alliance (APNA), a grouping of nationalist parties boycotted the elections, viewing them as a prelude to Pakistan's intentions of annexing this strategically significant region. Of the parties that participated, campaigning by BNF and Gilgit Baltistan Democratic Alliance (GBDA) was banned and many of their activists were arrested. House of BNF candidate in Gilgit-2 was bombed. [55] Many opposition parties and Non-Governmental Organisations (NGOs) including Human Rights Commission of Pakistan (HRCP) found flaws with the conduct of elections and accused the federal government of using the government machinery to influence voters.[56] The elections to LA19 in District Ghizer, which were held later on December 21, 2009, were allegedly rigged by the agencies to deprive Nawaz Naji, a leader of BNF, a well-deserved victory. Nawaz Naji was widely expected to win the seat with a big margin and during counting, reports till 8 p.m., from all 12 polling stations indicated that he was leading the polls, but at 9 p.m. it was declared that PPP candidate Pir Saeed Karam Ali Shah had won the elections. This led to rioting by BNF supporters and government property was damaged.[57]

Conclusion

Gilgit-Baltistan has enormous strategic significance, it connects Pakistan with China and provides Pakistan with most of its fresh water resources. The region is also rich in natural resources. Pakistan is keen to prolong its control over the region with the intention of eventually incorporating this part of Jammu and Kashmir into its own territory. Any clamour for autonomy is dissipated by creating divisions amongst the local populace and instigating sectarian disturbances. The social divide along ethnic and religious lines has been exploited by the Pakistani intelligence agencies and security forces to weaken the demand for genuine political autonomy and basic human rights by the local populace. State-sponsored Shia-Sunni and Shia-Nurbakhshi riots have aggravated the socio-political polarisation in Gilgit-Baltistan. On numerous occasions, agencies have used religious leaders of different sects to fan hatred. In one of the bizarre incidents, intelligence agencies released a Punjabi cleric, Allama Ghulam Raza Naqvi, of Sipah-e-Muhammad from prison to "be sent to Gilgit where he would head a seminary to keep the pot of sectarian violence boiling". His release was used as quid pro quo to grant freedom to Maulana Muhammad Ludhianvi, a rabidly anti-Shia leader of banned Sunni outfit Sipah-e-Sahaba, and other imprisoned leaders of Lashkar-e-Jhangvi.[58] The authorities have often used local Sunni minority in Gilgit-Baltistan to act as their accomplices in order to deprive the majority of their political rights. Even the IGP of Gilgit-Baltistan, Syed Tehseen Anwar, admitted the involvement of police personnel in sectarian causes and in sustaining the network of banned sectarian outfits in Gilgit-Baltistan.[59]

The agencies have also used the sectarian tensions to diffuse the opposition of the local population to Bhasha Dam, which will inundate large tracts of land in Gilgit-Baltistan and 120 km stretch of Karakoram Highway, which links China with Pakistan and provides the main access to Gilgit-Baltistan. The students in Gilgit-Baltistan have also started asserting that Chitral and Kohistan in NWFP are part of Gilgit-Baltistan and were separated by Pakistan as part of a conspiracy. They have emphasised that the region is a disputed territory and Pakistan should not build a mega dam without resolving its status.[60] These newer and growing demands are nothing but a manifestation of increasing alienation of the population from Pakistan. Pakistani establishment will continue to foster sectarian divisions to counter the growing alienation of the local population with Pakistan.

NOTES

1. M. Ismail Khan, "Demystifying Kashmir", *The International News*, Internet Edition, January 23, 2006.
2. Amjad Bashir Siddiqi, "Conflict in Gilgit", *The International News*, Internet Edition, November 14, 2005.
3. Ibid.
4. Stephen Philip Cohen, *The Idea of Pakistan*, Oxford University Press, New Delhi, 2005, p. 222.
5. "Story of Gilgit Deaths Foretold", Editorial, *Daily Times*, January 10, 2005.
6. Zaigham Khan, "Gilgit on Fire". *The International News*, Internet Edition, January 15, 2005.
7. Ershad Mahmud, "Challenges before the New Government in NAs". *The News*, Internet Edition, December 11, 2004.
8. *The State of Sectarianism in Pakistan*, International Crisis Group Asia Report No 95, April 18, 2005, p. 12.
9. Samuel Baid, 'Northern Areas', in Jasjit Singh (ed.), *Pakistan Occupied Kashmir: Under The Jackboot*, Siddhi Books, New Delhi, 1995, pp. 131-132.
10. Sarmad Abbas and Imtiaz Ali Taj, "Brothers with Arms",*The Herald*, April 2005, p. 63.
11. Khaled Ahmed, *Pakistan: The State in Crisis*, Vanguard Books, Lahore, 2002, p. 38.
12. B. Raman, "Biography of General Pervez Musharraf: His Past and Present", at http: //www.angelfire.com/al4/terror/musharraf.htm (Accessed June 26, 2006).
13. *The Herald*, May 1990.
14. *The Friday Times*, October 15-21, 1992.
15. B. Raman, no. 12.
16. Samuel Baid, no. 9, p. 139.
17. Ibid.
18. Ashok Behuria, "Rumblings in Northern Areas". *Journal of Peace Studies*, Vol. 11 No. 4, October-December 2004, p. 79.
19. "Gilgit Schools Re-Open Today after One-Year". *The News*, Internet Edition, April 27, 2005.
20. Alok Bansal, "Riots in PoK", *Central Chronicle*, Bhopal, February 10, 2005, p. 7.

21. Khaled Amed, "The Trouble in Gilgit", *The Friday Times*, July 8-14, 2005, p. 8.
22. Ansar Abbasi, "Three SPs Sacked for Not Joining Duty in Gilgit", *The News*, Internet Edition, May 3, 2005.
23. Amjad Bashir Siddiqi, "Police, DMG Officers Refuse to Join Duty in Gilgit", *The News*, Internet Edition, May 1, 2005.
24. M. Ismail Khan, "The Highway of Death". *The News*, Internet Edition, May 5, 2005.
25. M. Ismail Khan, "Northern Areas: Heading back to Normalcy", *The News*, Internet Edition, May 2, 2005.
26. "Violence in Gilgit", Editorial, *Dawn*, Karachi, July 25, 2005.
27. "Violence Grips Gilgit", Editorial. *The Nation*, July 27, 2005.
28. "Shoot at Sight Ordered", *Dawn*, Karachi, July 26, 2005.
29. Gulmina Bilal, "While Gilgit Burns...", *The News*, Internet Edition, November 22, 2005.
30. "Violence Grips Gilgit", no. 27.
31. Ahsan Wali Khan, "Lawless in Gilgit", *The News*, Internet Edition, October 25, 2005.
32. "Violence Grips Gilgit", no. 27.
33. "Shia Protesters Continue to Block Keys Roads in Gilgit", at http://www.newkerala.com/news2.php?action=fullnews&id=7379 (Accessed March 2, 2006).
34. Sarmad Abbas, "Sectarian Conflict Spills Over into Astore District", *The Herald*, May 2006, p. 50.
35. "Gunman Shoots Dead Pakistan Judge", at http://news.bbc.co.uk/2/hi/south_asia/5114670.stm (Accessed June 27, 2006).
36. M. Ismail Khan, "Skardu Dam; Recipe for Disaster", *The News*, Internet Edition, March 16, 2005.
37. A.H. Khanzada, "Allama Hassan Turabi Assassinated", *The News*, Internet Edition, July 15, 2006.
38. Senge H. Sering, "Talibanization of Gilgit-Baltistan and Sectarian Killings", IDSA Strategic Comment, October 19, 2009.
39. "ISI Killed Innocent Youth in Gilgit", at http://www.balawaristan.net/index.php?option=com_content&view=article&id=1770%3Aisi-killed-innocent-youth-in-gilgit&Itemid=64 (Accessed December 10, 2009).
40. Senge H. Sering, no. 38.
41. Shabbir Ahmed Mir, "Four Die as Blast Triggers Riots in Gilgit", *The News*, Internet Edition, September 27, 2009.
42. Senge H. Sering, no. 38.
43. Shabbir Ahmed Mir, "Three Killed in Gilgit-Baltistan Ambush", *The News*, Internet Edition, November 11, 2009.
44. "300 Suspected People Expelled from N Areas, Gilgit", *Dawn*, at http://www.dawn.com/wps/wcm/connect/dawn-content-library/dawn/news/pakistan/nwfp /300-suspected-people-expelled-from-n-areas-gilgit (Accessed October 21, 2009).
45. Anita Joshua, "22 Shias Shot Dead in Mansehra", *The Hindu*, 17 August 2012, p. 13.
46. Senge H. Sering, no. 38.
47. Inputs received during my discussions with Senge H. Sering, Abdul Hamid Khan, Manzoor Hussain Parwana and other political leaders from Gilgit-Baltistan during their participation in the international conference on Karakoram Himalayas at Delhi.
48. Alok Bansal, "Gilgit-Baltistan Amalgamation: India Must React", at http://headlinesindia.mapsofindia.com/international/international-affairs/gilgitbaltistan-amalgamation-india-must-react-22032.html (Accessed September 10, 2009).
49. Ibid.

50. Ibid.
51. "Muttahida Alleges Worst Rigging as PPP Leads in Gilgit-Baltistan Polls", *Khaleej Times*, Online Edition, November 13, 2009.
52. "PPP in Sight of Majority in Gilgit-Baltistan", *Dawn*, November 13, 2009.
53. *Daily K2*, November 2, 2009, Issue 179, p. 1.
54. http://dardistannews.wordpress.com/2009/11/14/unofficial-results-of-election-in-gilgit-baltistan/ (Accessed December 21, 2009).
55. *Daily Baad-e-Shimal Gilgit-Baltistan*, Vol. 93, No. 12, November 3, 2009.
56. "Muttahida Alleges Worst Rigging as PPP Leads in Gilgit-Baltistan Polls", no. 51. Also see "HRCP Sees Flaws in Gilgit-Baltistan Elections", *Dawn*, November 14, 2009.
57. Inputs received from Shafqat Inquilabi, a leader of BNF.
58. "President Musharraf and His Dangerous Ambiguities", Editorial, *Daily Times*, May 21, 2006.
59. *Weekly Qayadat Gilgit-Baltistan*, Vol. 32, No. 1, November 4-10, 2009.
60. "NA's Students Claim Chitral as Part of Gilgit-Baltistan', at http://www.chitralnews.com/LN144.htm (Accessed March 2, 2006).

19

Pakistan Occupied Kashmir

An Emerging Epicentre of Global Jihad

Wilson John

Pakistan occupied Kashmir (PoK) (or 'Azad' Kashmir) has long been a gateway of jihad with the Pakistani State setting up a vast network of terrorist training camps, religious schools and centres and weapons stores. As a result, all terrorist groups based in Pakistan, some 104 of them on the last count,[1] have maintained a training base in towns and villages in PoK like Muzaffarabad, Kotli and Balakot. So long as these terrorist groups remained focussed on carrying out violence against India, particularly in Kashmir, the world, by and large, chose to ignore this terrorist sanctuary. Till today, the War on Terror, progressing in fits and starts, has not reached this mountainous area straddling between the lawless western frontiers of Pakistan and a seething eastern-most tip of China.

This paper argues that PoK will emerge from being merely an isolated jihadi outpost to become the epicentre of Global Jihad in the days to come. With Al Qaida and its allies facing the brunt of the western military might along the Durand Line dividing Afghanistan and Pakistan, the shifting of "base" from Waziristan to PoK is not inconceivable.

There are some obvious reasons as to why such a shift can be envisaged. First, PoK has always been a "colony" of the state of Pakistan, never really becoming a part of the federation, thereby making it easy for the State, i.e., the Pakistan Army and its intelligence arm, Inter-Services Intelligence (ISI) Directorate, to carve out a sanctuary for its strategic assets—the jihadi groups. Second, the area has been a laboratory of sorts for sectarian engineering with the State carrying out oppressive policies, both militarily and politically, to subjugate Shias and other non-Sunni groups. The persistent Sunnification of the area has left the communities sharply divided, giving by default and design, considerable support among the Sunnis for the Sunni terrorist and extremist groups to operate freely from the area.

With the madrasas set up by these groups providing convenient recruitment base for terrorist activities and generous funding of these groups not only by the State agencies but also by the local residents as well as the Pakistani diaspora in the UK and West Asia, PoK has flourished as a jihadi BPO for Islamabad. It was strategically convenient and tactically useful to have a base camp of terror close to the Indian state of Jammu and Kashmir which over the past 65 years has remained the raison d'etre of Pakistan Army. Terrorist groups like Harkat-ul Mujahideen (HuM), Harkat-ul Ansar (HuA), Jaish-e-Mohammad and Lashkar-e-Tayyeba (LeT), all of them blooded in so-called Afghan jihad, became an integral part of the Pakistan Army's proxy war in Kashmir or the so-called Kashmir jihad.

These terrorist groups also had tactical utility for the army. These groups, with networks across the border, in India, became the eyes and ears of the army, bringing in valuable intelligence about the social and political happenings in Kashmir and other parts. These groups have been used to stir civilian protests in the Valley, primed to launch the much-talked about Kashmir *intifada*, used as frontline troops (to camouflage the military infiltration in Kargil) and incubators of terror beyond Kashmir.

Terror Network Before 9/11

But before Kashmir, it was the US-led proxy war against the Soviet troops in Afghanistan which saw PoK turning into a Gateway of jihad. Although the so-called Afghan mujahideen were trained in camps across Afghanistan, it was the PoK camps where many of them honed their skills in guerrilla warfare. Terrorist camps began mushrooming in Muzaffarabad, Kotli and Balakot which hosted terrorists either returning from Afghanistan for rest and recuperation or for advanced training. These camps largely operated as recruitment offices and training campus for the Afghan jihad.

In the late 1980s, when LeT was created as an armed wing of Markaz Dawat al Irshad, otherwise a centre for Islamic preaching and learning, the first set of recruits were sent to two camps—the Taiba and the Aqsa—in Afghanistan. The first LeT training camp in Pakistan was set up in Muzaffarabad and was christened Baitul Mujahideen, or the House of the

Holy Warrior. A report prepared by LeT commanders about their group's history said:[2] "During those days of 1990 *mujahideen* from Kashmir started reaching the Taiba camp in Afghanistan for military training. So a different camp, called Aqsa Camp, was established near Taiba Camp just for their training. In Muzaffarabad, Baitul Mujahideen was established. Here Pakistani and Kashmiri *mujahideen* received training together...In the beginning of 1991, the first batch of *mujahideen* trained in Aqsa Camp reached Muzaffarabad. To refine their training, Badar Post was founded and a camp named Ummul Qara was established in Muzaffarabad. In August 1992, the first batch of *Lashkar-e-Taiba mujahideen* was launched in Kashmir."

According to Arif Jamal,[3] author of *Shadow Games*, an insightful study of Pakistan's proxy war against India, three of Lashkar's military training camps or cantonments functioned in PoK: "It has trained over 100,000 *mujahideen* in the military craft in these camps while those waiting for their turn to start their military training may exceed the number of the trained *mujahideen*. Only one of its military training camps, Ummul Qara, in Muzaffarabad, churns out over 500 *mujahideen*. The other two functional training camps are smaller. The Markaz has set up a huge network around the country with over 2,000 unit offices. There are few places in Pakistan where the workers of the *Markaz Dawat al Irshad* are not present."

Similarly, HuM set up a wide network of training camps in PoK and the adjacent North West Frontier Province (NWFP) besides the tribal areas which straddle the Durand Line. Other smaller groups had their little corners in the mountains and valleys of the region, surviving on the munificence of the ISI and Pakistan Army. Most of these groups shared common logistics and communication networks that linked them with their "handlers" in ISI.

The area flourished as a jihadi campus when new recruits began pouring in for Kashmir. Large segments of these new jihadis came from universities and colleges across Pakistan, particularly from Punjab. One of the primary recruiting group for jihad was Jamaat-e-Islami (JI) and its student wing Islami Jamiat Talaba (IJT).[4] The volunteers "include young college and university students with aggressive tendencies who are responding to what they regard to be a religious call".[5] Many of these students were involved in campus violence and "bloody fights, involving kidnappings and murders", of members of hooligan student unions. They had just the right mental make up for being brainwashed by hardcore JI and IJT leaders with stories of "torture, rape, and killing of Kashmiri Muslims perpetrated by the Indian law-enforcement agencies". Most of them were first sent to the military training facilities set up by the JI called

Markaz-e-Islami in Afghanistan. The exploits of jihadis in Kashmir were published in JI's fortnightly *Jehad-e-Kashmir*, and monthlies *Ham Qadam* and *Bedar Digest*. The group ran a systematic campaign to mobilise public opinion for the Afghan jihad and took part in militant activities with full zeal, producing 72 "martyrs" between 1980 and 1990.[6]

Although JI had steered the Kashmir jihad, a significant number of IJT recruits preferred to join Al Badr, a terrorist group set up in PoK with the objective of forcibly annexing Kashmir. An important reason why Al Badr drew recruits from colleges and universities across Pakistan was that educated youth preferred to work with people from a similar background and inclination, and not madrassa students who largely went to Afghanistan. They were "at ease in the company of engineers, doctors, computer scientists, and social scientists who made up the *al Badr Mujahideen*".[7] The group also adopted a more lenient view about offering regular prayers, growing a beard, or following a dress code (they often wore shirt and trousers). All the same, rigorous military training was always preceded by an equally intense religious indoctrination in the PoK camps.[8]

With the Cold War, at least the first round, getting buried in the rugged, cruel mountains of Hindu Kush, the rapid growth of these terrorist groups went largely un-noticed except by India which bore the brunt of a wave of terror that brought the spectre of endless violence to the streets of Kashmir and other parts of India. These groups remained in the shadow of global attention as the US began its military operations in the Middle East and a global terrorist group Al Qaida began to emerge from the ashes of Afghan jihad.

However, there was one other incident which focused global attention on these training camps, even if briefly, before 9/11 happened: the 1999 Kargil War. General Pervez Musharraf launched a motley group of jihadi groups across the Line of Control to infiltrate into the heights in Kargil and other areas studded along the crucial Srinagar-Leh Highway in Kashmir. The objective was to camouflage a military offensive as an infiltration and thus avoid a closer scrutiny by the Indian security forces and the global community. Cadres from Al Badr, LeT and other groups occupied some of the key areas along the ridges and mountain tops overlooking the Indian defences before the regular Army moved in to consolidate their positions along the Line of Control.

There are, however, differing opinions on the participation of the jihadi groups in the Kargil War. One version argues that the terrorist participation was merely a ploy to cover up what was essentially a military operation.[9]

Others pointed out that "at least four such (terrorist) organisations were involved in Kargil. Initially, it was *Tehrik-e-Jihad* which openly claimed that their men had taken control of large parts of Kargil. Later, three more groups, *Al Badr, Harkatul Mujahideen* and *Lashkar-e-Tayyeba* came out with similar statements".[10] It was a crafty move on the part of General Musharraf, but it backfired when the Indian security forces responded with alacrity and determination, and the global community intervened to prevent a possible nuclear conflagration.[11]

The global scrutiny on the terrorist groups operating out of PoK and the state complicity in supporting and sustaining them against India, however, remained short-lived as the then Pakistani Prime Minister Nawaz Sharif, under the then US President Bill Clinton's emphatic advice, ordered the withdrawal of the troops and the restoration of status quo at the Line of Control.

The General and Jihad

The military coup in Pakistan shifted the attention of the international community and while concerned nations, including India, grappled with the idea of living with a Pakistan under a martial regime, the terrorist groups maintained a low profile and concentrated on regrouping and strengthening their networks, training camps and launching pads.

One of the most significant developments in this context was the hijacking of the Indian Airlines IC-814 in December 1999. The passengers were exchanged for the freedom of three hardcore terrorists, two of them from Harkat-ul Ansar—Masood Azhar and Syed Omar Sheikh—and one from Al Mujahideen, Mushtaq Ahmed Zargar. In January 2000, Azhar announced the setting up of Jaish-e-Mohammad (JeM) with the sole objective of "liberating Kashmir". It was a desperate move by the Pakistan Army, which had failed at Kargil early 1999, to unleash a wave of violence across the Indian Kashmir to focus the global attention on the issue and force India to come to the negotiating table. PoK thus saw a spurt in terrorist activity during the period with JeM taking over some of the HuM/HuA assets and setting up new camps in Balakot and Muzaffarabad, all with the active assistance of ISI.

Within months, JeM's Balakot training camp became the biggest centre of terrorist recruitment and training in PoK. Over 7,000 trained at Balakot and other training centres in 2000.[12] Azhar wrote in the JeM magazine about the camp named as "Madrasah Sayeed Ahmed Shaheed Rahimullahahu Ta'la,[13] A Masjid, large water tanks, a ground for physical training, and rooms for the *mujahideen* are being constructed on its premises. Some women have sent their jewellery for the construction of the mosque and other buildings". The campus soon became the biggest terrorist camp in the region, supervised by Azhar and his confidant and trainer, Qari Shah Mansur. Besides physical training and other guerrilla tactics, the recruits were taught to use rocket launchers, automatic guns, explosives besides shooting from various positions including from moving vehicles.[14]

JeM, with ISI and Pakistan Army's support, launched a series of suicide attacks on the Indian security forces in Kashmir besides setting up a network of supporters and recruitment centres in other parts of India, particularly in north India where it drew support from its Deobandi lineage. These attacks swelled the group's ranks and coffers with money pouring in, particularly, from the Mirpuri diaspora in the UK. Recruits were also drawn from other parts of the world with internet forums and chat rooms connecting JeM with potential candidates. Within a short period, JeM became a global jihadi group, facilitating recruits from different parts of the world to join Al Qaida's training facilities in Afghanistan. In June 2001, for instance, an Australian convert, Shane Kent, reached JeM camp in PoK where he was put through the basic course in physical training and weapons handling before being sent to Al Qaida's Al Farooq camp near Kandahar in Afghanistan. It was the same camp where seven of the 19 hijackers who carried out the 9/11 attack received basic training.[15]

9/11, Al Qaida and Pakistan Jihad

The terrorist attack on the Twin Towers in Manhattan, New York, and Pentagon near Washington on September 11, 2001 forced a sudden halt to the jihadi expansion in PoK and other areas. The US bombing of terrorist camps in Afghanistan disrupted the jihadi network to a great extent. Hundreds of recruits and trainers in these camps were killed and others were forced to flee to Pakistan's tribal areas, NWFP, PoK and the 'Northern Areas'.

It is important to understand a particular chain of events that unfolded in Pakistan immediately after the US came down heavily on Al Qaida and the Taliban strongholds in Afghanistan. Fleeing Al Qaida and the Taliban leadership found easy shelter in Pakistan with the help of the ISI and religious and sectarian outfits like JI and Lashkar-e-Jhangvi (LeJ), a rabidly Sunni organisation which has been the ISI's instrument in subjugating the Shias since the early 90s. Many of the LeJ leaders had trained at terrorist training camps in Afghanistan along with the Taliban and Al Qaida recruits. The Al Qaida and the Taliban leadership found access to safe houses in major cities like Quetta, Karachi, Peshawar and Lahore, all courtesy the above-mentioned "band of brothers".[16]

Some of them had come to PoK where they took shelter in HM's camps in Kotli.[17] There were reports that in June and July 2002 "two groups of the Taliban and one of Al Qaida cadres arrive in NAs ('Northern Areas'), after entering the Dahrkoot valley from Broghok in Chitral...which links with the Wakhan corridor in Badakhshan province, Afghanistan. Each group consisted of 30-50 persons....The first group of the Taliban cadres reportedly stayed at Giyekooshi in the Dahrkoot valley for a month and were later transported towards Gilgit to head to the Darel and Tangir valley of district Diamer. Unmarked ISI vehicles were used to transport Al Qaida terrorists from Dahrkoot valley to Gilgit city between 1 am and 5 am". The reports said about 600 Al Qaeda cadres were "believed to have been relocated around Gilgit-Baltistan, mostly in Darel and Tangir". They, however, returned to the tribal areas after the US exerted pressure on the army to oust them. Today, large parts of the tribal areas are part of the Al Qaida sanctuary which acts as the recruitment and training ground as well as a wellspring for Global Jihad.

The Pakistani jihadi groups like JeM and LeT remained quiet but active in supporting the Al Qaida regrouping in Pakistan even as General Pervez Musharraf joined the US-led Global War on Terror as a "strategic ally" and promised to come down heavily on the terrorist entities sheltered in his country. ISI hastily put together a team of JeM and LeT cadre to launch an audacious attack on the Indian Parliament on December 13, 2001, barely two months after the 9/11 attack. Although the attack failed in its objectives, it provoked an unprecedented anger among the Indians and triggered a massive deployment of troops along the Line of Control, raising the possibility of a military conflict in the region. After a concerned international community leaned heavily on Pakistan, and India, to avoid such a confrontation, Musharraf was persuaded to ditch the jihadis, reform the madrasas and roll back his military dictatorship for a democratic frame-up of governance.

Although Musharraf changed his tune and made all the right noises, the actions against the jihadi groups remained cosmetic. An indicative instance was what happened on January 12, 2002, when Musharraf made his "path-breaking" speech about turning his country towards "enlightened moderation" and to plug the jihadi pipeline. Even as the world was coming to terms with this "changed" Musharraf, Jamaat-e-Islami Amir Qazi Hussain Ahmed and Hizbul Mujahideen supreme commander Syed Salahuddin were visiting a terrorist camp, Maskar-e-Rahil in Kotli, PoK. They addressed the militants undergoing training at the camp and talked to HM commanders in Poonch and Rajouri sectors through wireless.

Two months later, Salahuddin addressed a two-day meeting of Pakistan Islamic Medical Association (a facility for treating militants) at Multan. Salahuddin told the gathering that the Musharraf regime was only taking action against fake jihadi organisations. He said he had seen the list of such organisations and many of them did not even exist. Although many refused to believe the ground reality, especially those in the West, about the jihadi re-grouping in Pakistan, it became apparent subsequently that groups like JeM and LeT were allowed to retain significant portions of their infrastructure and presence although they were asked to lie low and carry out their recruitment and funding activities more covertly.

In the 'Northern Areas', General Musharraf's regime played another diabolical game. His regime systematically began driving the sectarian divide deeper by inserting objectionable chapters and sentences in school textbooks to Shias and by encouraging Sunnis to settle down in otherwise Shia-dominated areas. In fact, it was General Musharraf as Brigadier, on the orders of the then President Zia-ul Haq, who led a mixed contingent of soldiers and tribal fighters to put down a Shia rebellion in the region. The operation witnessed large scale slaying of women and children.

A closer scrutiny of the jihadi networks in PoK would prove to be instructive in understanding how the dynamics of terrorism has changed in the region after 9/11, and is likely to change further in the future. In the post 9/11 crackdown, a large number of the 2,200 centres run by LeT across Pakistan were forcibly shut down and even though some of them were revived clandestinely on a smaller scale subsequently.

Although HuM and JeM retained some of their training facilities in PoK, it was LeT which managed to expand its network considerably in the region. HuM's fate was the worst after the US bombing in Afghanistan as it lost considerable men and material in Afghanistan. Since it had a direct association with Al Qaida and the Taliban, it bore the brunt of the Global War on Terror. In 2002, HuM had 24 recruitment and other offices in Pakistan but almost all of them closed down as HuM's leader, Maulana Fazlullah Khaleel lost his hold over the jihadi network. Khaleel is today confined to a small madrasa outside Rawalpindi, working more as a fire-fighter for the ISI. Khaleel, for instance, was one of the mediators in the Lal Masjid standoff in July 2007.

JeM, on the other hand, had fared better, but the involvement of some of the JeM cadres from PoK in the twin assassination attempts on the then President Musharraf in December 2003 and the earlier arrest and conviction of JeM mastermind Syed Omar Sheikh in the Daniel Pearl murder case rendered it vulnerable to intense global scrutiny. When Musharraf asked the jihadi groups to go slow on Kashmir, Masood Azhar and others took it to the heart and accused the General of working against their Islamic cause under pressure from the US.

It was LeT which remained loyal to the ISI and Pakistan Army and managed to retain substantial part of its recruitment and training infrastructure in Pakistan, including PoK despite its clear involvement in the December 13, 2001 attack on the Indian Parliament. LeT supremo Hafiz Saeed was even arrested and kept under house arrest in December 2001. Undeterred, Saeed, who developed the Markaz-ud Dawa headquarters in Muridke, a town off Lahore, with generous help from Osama bin Laden and other Saudi benefactors, changed the name of Markaz to Jamaat-ud Dawa, separated LeT from its parent body and appointed Abdul Wahid Kashmiri as the head of LeT the headquarters of which was shifted to Indian Kashmir. Saeed has since been projecting his organisation, JuD, as a religious charitable organisation engaged in running hospitals, dispensaries and schools at several places in Pakistan.

In reality, these changes were reflected only on paper to avoid further sanctions from the US. LeT has been, and is, an integral part of JuD besides being a surrogate of Al Qaida. An article from *Ghazwah* (an Urdu weekly published by JuD) posted on its website, dated September 23, 2005, declared that "support must be resumed for *jihad* in Kashmir". At a time when America, so goes the editorial penned by Saeed, "has entangled herself into the wars of Iraq and Afghanistan and has been suffering from severe afflictions like Katrina and Rita, it's the right time for Pakistan to support the *jihad* in Kashmir".

Given the support the group enjoyed from the military establishment, it was not surprising that LeT managed to retain its four training centres in PoK even after the global sanctions of all manner:[18] Ma'askar Taiba located in Muzaffarabad with a capacity to train 500 recruits; Ma'askar Aqsa near Muzaffarabad which can accommodate and train 150; Ma'askar Ummul Qura near Muzaffarabad with a capacity for 500 trainees per month and Ma'askar Abdullah bin Masood camp which can accommodate 300 recruits.

The October 2005 earthquake in PoK saw an exponential growth and power of LeT. Among all the terrorist and religious extremist groups that carried out relief operations, Jamaat-ud Dawa (JuD) stood out for the swift manner in which it took over the responsibility of providing immediate succour to the quake victims. Even Musharraf admitted that the work done by religious groups was commendable. Groups like JuD, smaller and more dynamic, were able to reach the site of devastation more quickly, raising doubts about the intention and efficiency of the armed forces and civilian organisations. With the troops unable to reach far-flung areas in the region, JuD activists, most of them carrying Kalashnikovs along with relief materials, managed to reach even remote villages to provide food, tents and medical aid. Through its widely appreciated relief and rehabilitation measures in the region, LeT gained enormous amount of popular support as a result, attracting both donations and volunteers not only from Pakistan but also from other parts of the world. A substantial part of the funds collected for earthquake relief were diverted to bolster the terrorist infrastructure and activities. The foiled London plot, in which several planes were to be hijacked and blown up in air was partly funded from the money collected for earthquake victims in London and other areas.[19]

Along with an extensive social network in the area, LeT was able to restore and strengthen its terrorist infrastructure. LeT had lost a few hundred of its cadres and facilities in the earthquake and had moved a large contingent of jihadis to safety to new camps in NWFP's Upper Dir area. According to Pakistani media sources, at least 3,000 terrorists were moved to these camps which were set up with the help of ISI. Subsequently, these camps became the new centre of jihadi activity for both Afghanistan and Kashmir. Although JeM moved its activities to these camps and its headquarters in Bahawalpur (Punjab), LeT managed to strengthen its network in PoK. Along with mobile dispensaries, health centres and refugee camps, LeT revived its original campus, Baitul Mujahideen, or the House of Holy Warrior, at Shawai Nala, barely five km from Muzaffarabad, to train new recruits for terrorist missions into India and Afghanistan.

Campus of Jihad

Though other training centres were also restored in at Mansera, Balakot, Sialkot, Shahdodpur in Sindh, Baitul Mujahideen (BM) became LeT's operational HQs with Zaki-ur Rahman Lakhvi as its "commandant". Lakhvi was one of the first commanders who trained terrorists in LeT's Kunar and Pakhtia provinces during the Afghan jihad. Today, the complex, squatting in the midst of rolling foothills, houses a three-storied building, a mosque, hostels and an arms and ammunition warehouse. There are supplementary training camps in and around BM; for instance, Maskar-e-Ummalkura camp is located above BM, in the thick coniferous forests. The Al Aqsa camp where trainees are put through physical regimes and basic knowledge of weapons is not far from BM. These camps have few permanent structures and the trainees stay in tents, 15-20 in each tent.

All new recruits are frisked at the gate for cigarettes, opium and tobacco products before allowed in. Once inside the BM, each recruit is photographed, fingerprinted and given identity cards before being dispatched to the Maskar-e-Ummalkura training camp in the thickly wooded mountains slopes above the campus. More than 100 trainees report for each session at these camps which is the first step towards becoming a fully trained terrorist or *mujahid*.[20]

Zaki ur-Rahman Lakhvi oversaw the entire training from the beginner's course to the advance course, which spreads over a period of 12 to 18 months, until he was arrested for the Mumbai attacks. He oversaw BM and other training camps with the help of a team of loyal, hard-core trainers. The training modules at LeT camps were modelled on the training programme evolved by Al Qaida which had, in turn, picked up lessons from the US Marines. In fact, a close similarity between LeT training modules and Al Qaida manuals on Special Operations could be detected. Most often, expert trainers visited these camps from ISI and Pakistan Army and Navy for special classes. LeT also developed its maritime training facility at Mangla reservoir and its Muridke campus. Initially the maritime skills were developed in PoK where LeT used boats and rubber dinghies to ferry people and material during the rescue and relief operations after the earthquake.

Post-Mumbai Attack Developments

Despite the international hue and cry over terrorist groups like LeT after the Mumbai attack in November 2008, the terrorist group retained most of its extensive infrastructure and capability to pursue its terrorist activities without much difficulty, betraying the ISI's collusion. A telling instance of the ISI desperate bid to reorganise the jihadi structure in PoK was the joint meeting of leaders from HuM, JeM and LeT it organised in Muzaffarabad on February 3, 2009 where, among other issues, they all agreed that jihad was the only way to bring about a solution to the Kashmir conflict.[21]

No less revealing was the opinion of the policy-makers in Pakistan. On January 24, 2009, for instance, Pakistan's High Commissioner to the UK, Wajid Shams-ul-Hasan, said[22] that "*Lashkar-e-Taiba* was fighting for freedom in the Occupied Kashmir". The High Commissioner was only stating the obvious, a stand which has been consistent with Pak Army's Kashmir obsession. Two days before the Mumbai attack, the Army's Vice Chief of Staff, Mohammad Yusuf Khan, (on November 24, 2008) stated that "the international pressures notwithstanding, Kashmir shall remain an inseparable component of our national policy and consequently a vital strand of our strategy".[23]

Today, LeT, despite the crackdown, continues to run a vast network of schools, colleges, hospitals, ambulance services, seminaries, publications and charity organisations throughout Pakistan as freely as before the Mumbai attacks. Its headquarters at Muridke, Lahore, remained open, guarded by armed LeT men, as late as mid-January 2009[24] until the Punjab government decided to appoint an administrator for the complex. In any case, the Muridke complex, once the hub of trans-national terrorism, has long ceased to be of any critical importance to LeT and the restrictions imposed on its functioning remain at best symbolic.

The true intentions of the Pakistan Government were betrayed by its lack of action against LeT's new operational headquarters on Lake Road, Lahore, a double-storied mosque complex called Masjid Jamia Qadisiya, a name which evokes the historic location where the Arabs had defeated the Iranian King in 637 AD. Another major LeT establishment, which has remained untouched, is Markaz Mohammad bin Qasim at Maldasi in Shahdadpur, near Hydrabad (Sindh). It is built like a fort with high walls and has been one of the three LeT training camps in interior Sindh.

Lahore's Masjid Qadisiya is open, and Saeed's son, Mohammad Talha Saeed and LeT leader's close associate, Maulana Saifullah Khalid, leads the Friday prayers, by turn. There has been no let up in the venom of jihad despite Saeed's absence. On January 23, 2009, Maulana Khalid told the gathering at the mosque that "muslims under the leadership of *Lashkar-e-Taiba* and *Jamaat ud Dawa* will conquer South Asia. Nobody can stop us fighting India. The forces trying to suppress the *Jamaat ud Dawa* and *Lashkar-e-Taiba* themselves will be crushed".

Of the 100 and more leaders and members of LeT arrested in Punjab, as claimed by Rahman Malik, Pakistan's de facto Interior Minister, only 12 remained under house arrest for a period of one month. Hafiz Saeed was among them. Three days after his detention, he was allowed to leave his Johar Town home in Lahore and travel to a nearby mosque for offering prayers.[25] His son, Talha Saeed, remains free and leads the Friday prayers in his father's absence. There is no restriction on Saeed's family members either from visiting him frequently.

Another telling indication of the complicity was the publication of JuD's venomous weekly, *Ghazva*. The December 2008 edition of the weekly termed the Mumbai attack as "historic" victory for the Muslim warriors. On the back page, the magazine carried an appeal from the group to donate hides. The message read:[26] "Donate the hides for the war against infidels in Kashmir and to teach a lesson to the mean Hindus who have blocked Pakistan's waters...if you give Rs 25 as charity to a roadside beggar, it is not as rewarding as the charity which is used to buy the bullet that will hit the chest and forehead of a Hindu soldier who raped a Kashmiri Muslim woman." The magazine also carried an article about 4,500 women who "donated" a son each, and 83 mothers who gave two sons each, to the terrorist group for "the noble cause of promoting, preaching and defending Islam against infidels".

Seven months after the Mumbai attack, the Multi-Agency Centre (MAC), a nodal agency for collating intelligence on terrorist groups and their activities set up by the Indian Government, found 34 active and eight holding camps across the border. The 'Northern Areas' and PoK housed 17 of the active and four of the holding camps. The agency said there were over 2,200 recruits in these camps—300 of them affiliated to LeT, 240 to JeM and 130 to HuJI. The report said these camps were located in Tattapani, Garhi Dupatta, Barnala, Sensa, Forward Kahuta, Peer Chinasi, Shawai Nalla, Bhimber, Kotli, Skardu, Abdullah bin Masud, Nikial, Gulpur, Samani and Jhandi Chauntra.

Further evidence of the terrorist regrouping in PoK after the Mumbai attacks came in a BBC Report of June 30, 2009.[27] The report, quoting a confidential report sent by the police to the government in Muzaffarabad on March 25, 2009, said HuM, JeM and LeT were active in Muzaffarabad. The report said LeT had bought 65 *kanals* (a *kanal* is equal to 0.125 acres) of land in Dulai, Muzaffarabad to construct a mosque, a school and a dispensary. The report also pointed out that HuM and JeM were also setting up similar mosque-madrasa complexes in and around the city. "No officials are allowed to enter these premises to gather any information…we fear these *madrassas* may be a cover for furthering militant activities", the media quoted the confidential report. The report said the terrorist groups were visible in Neelum district where they were indulging in logging to raise funds.[28] The Indian intelligence agencies have information about terrorist groups gathering for training in Tauheed Hills, an isolated forest 40-50 km off Muzaffarabad. The Tauheed camps are training new recruits in handling of sophisticated weapons and explosives.[29]

Future Implications

In the light of above discussion, it is apparent that (a) terrorist groups, despite global pressures and proscriptions, remain a "strategic asset" for Pakistan Army; (b) These groups have considerable presence and clout in several pars of Pakistan, including PoK and 'Northern Areas'; and (c) These groups have become closer to Al Qaida and the Taliban and hence should be seen as part of the global jihadi movement.

These developments must be read with the ongoing military offensive launched against the Taliban in NWFP and the tribal areas by Pakistan Army. After months of heavy-handed military offensive (May 2009 onwards), the operations in Swat and other areas in the Frontier till now have had only a limited impact. Although the security forces were able to regain large parts of the areas controlled by the Taliban, the top leadership of the group remain intact and ready to move in and strike back at the first given opportunity. In short, the problem of the Taliban and its allies remains as grave as it was before the military operations. In fact, there are growing fears that the Taliban might emerge much more stronger if the state failed to, first, protect the citizens who are moving back to the "freed areas", and second, if the development packages are not implemented sincerely and with urgency.

This quite clearly raises the possibility of a prolonged round of military offensives in area in the months ahead, particularly in view of the fact that the real core of the Taliban in Waziristan is yet to be tackled. Likewise, Al Qaida and its allies in Afghanistan and Pakistan are likely to face increasing pressure from the Pakistan Military as well as the US in the coming days, raising the possibility of these groups looking for an alternate sanctuary. PoK fits the bill.

Here it would be relevant to underline the linkages that exist between Swat and PoK, and 'Northern Areas'. Swat, for instance, where the security forces were pitted against the Taliban and its allies, borders Chitral which is adjacent to the 'Northern Areas' and the corridors that lead to Xinjiang province in China. There are reports that the Taliban were trying to establish a presence[30] in Kohistan and Battagram districts of Hazara division and the Kala Dakha area of Mansera divisons. Since the Taliban are already aligned at the operational level with groups like LeT and JeM with bases in PoK and 'Northern Areas', it would be easier for them to find ready-made launching pad to establish their presence along the strategically important Karakoram Highway that links Pakistan with China. Likewise, the "eastern" movement of the Taliban towards Buner and then Mansera in early 2009 had raised fears about PoK turning into another sanctuary for the Al Qaida-Taliban conglomeration.

Though the Taliban have been driven out of Buner and Swat, and prevented from moving east any more, the possibility of the terrorists taking over PoK in near future cannot be discounted. It is quite obvious, considering the Taliban takeover of Swat and other areas in Malakand division, the move towards Buner and Mansera, that when pressure mounts on these groups including Al Qaida (these are in fact a conglomerate of terror, or networks of terror, working often autonomously, but under the overarching umbrella of Global Jihad), they are likely to search for a safe sanctuary in the region. PoK with its ready-made terrorist infrastructure, state support and the protective cover of mountains and valleys offer such a possibility. The Taliban militants stormed a mountaineering camp at Buner Valley in Gilgit-Baltistan, which serves as a base for maintainers headed for Nanga Parbat—the world's ninth highest peak, in June 2013 killing nine foreigners including five Ukrainians, three Chinese and one Russian tourist.[31] Tahrik-e-Taliban Pakistan claimed responsibility for this attack.

There is a growing fear that Al Qaida, and its surrogate groups could foment sectarian conflict in the 'Northern Areas' as well as in Chitral, with considerable Shia population, to gain a foothold in the region, and open a new front in Gilgit.[32] Al Qaida has flourished in conflict-ridden areas and can possibly to do so in Gilgit-Baltistan, drawing support from the considerable presence of Sunni groups in the region. A Shia resident of Lahore wrote to *Daily Times* in April 2009 that "Shias and Ismailis are the majority in Gilgit, and they depend solely on the state of Pakistan for their security. But there is a real fear among the people of Gilgit that they will be left to the mercy of the Taliban much like the people of Swat."[33]

Such a possibility gains further strength from reports that immediately after the US bombing of Afghanistan in 2001, several Al Qaida and Taliban leaders had found shelter with HuM camps in Kotli. The oft-reported presence of Osama bin Laden (at the time) in the nearby Chitral area,[34] where, in any case, ISI has been running safe-houses of Al Qaida leaders for quite some time, only added to the calculation that PoK is a prime target for Global Jihad.

Although the world has focussed on the Al Qaida-Taliban sanctuary in Afghanistan and Pakistan since 9/11, there has hardly been any concern for the mounting evidence of PoK-based terrorist groups' alliance with global terrorist network. LeT and JeM, for instance, has been running training camps for the Taliban and Al Qaida in Dir and Upper Dir since 2006. These camps have also hosted recruits from different parts of the world, including United Kingdom. It is quite apparent that the George W Bush's War on Terror and Barack Obama's Af-Pak strategy have missed these signs for short-term gains in Afghanistan and in the region.

The long-term implication of allowing terrorist networks to retain their training and recruitment bases in PoK is not hard to see: With the military offensive likely to continue along the Durand Line against the terror networks, the area has all the potential to transform from a warehouse of terror[35] to the new epicentre of Global Jihad, part of the overall Al Qaida strategy.

NOTES

1. Amir Rana, *The Seeds of Extremism*, New Millennium Publications, London, 2005, p. 99.
2. Taiba Bulletin (nadqpk@yahoo.com), "Subject: Eleven Years of Lashker-e-Taiba", April 22, 2001, at http://groups.yahoo.com/group/muslimworldnews. Quoted from Evan Kohlmann, *Synopsis of Testimony*, Regina vs Mohammad Ajmal Khan et al., Snaresbrook Crown Court, UK, 2006.
3. *The News*, February 20, 2000.
4. Wilson John, *Coming Blowback: How Pakistan is Endangering the World*, Rupa, New Delhi, 2010.
5. "Kashmiris and Jehad in Kashmir", *Frontier Post*, February 4, 1994 (Accessed from ORF Database).
6. Seyyed Vali Reza Nasr, *The Vanguard of the Islamic Revolution: The Jama'at-i-Islami of Pakistan*, University of California Press, Berkeley, 1994.
7. *The News*, August 29, 1999 (Accessed from ORF Database).
8. Wilson John, no. 4.
9. For a detailed discussions on these versions, refer to: Chris Fair, "Militants in the Kargil Conflict: Myths, Realities and Impacts", in Peter Lavoy (ed.), *Asymmetric Warfare in South Asia: The Causes and Consequences of the Kargil Conflict*, Cambridge University Press, 2009.
10. Zaffar Abbas, "Back from the Brink". *Herald*, June 1999.
11. Succinctly described in Bruce Riedel, *American Diplomacy and the 1999 Kargil Summit at Blair House*, Center for the Advanced Study of India, University of Pennsylvania, 2002.
12. Muhammad Amir Rana, *A to Z of Jehadi Organisations in Pakistan*. Mashal Publications, Lahore, 2005.
13. Masood Azhar, "Organising central office of Jaish-e-Mohammad", *Dharb-i-Momin*, Vol. 2, No. 26, January 26, February 2, 2001.
14. Amir Mir, "Manufacturing Martyrs", *Newsline*, Pakistan, September 2005.
15. Amir Rana, no. 1; *The 9/11 Commission Report: The Final Report of the National Commission on Terrorist Attacks Upon the United States*, July 22, 2004.
16. Abdul Hamid Khan, "Pakistan's Heart of Darkness", *Asia Times Online*, August 22, 2002.
17. Sushant Sareen, *The Jihad Factory*, Har Anand Publications, New Delhi, 2005.
18. Amir Rana, no. 1.
19. "Charity Funds Sent to PoK Banks for Aircraft Plot: UK Report", *The Indian Express*, August 13, 2006.
20. For detailed reference to the training and other activities at Baitul Mujahideen, refer to Wilson John and Vishwas Kumar, *Investigating the Mumbai Conspiracy*, Pentagon Press, New Delhi, 2009.
21. "Banned Pakistan Militants Gather", British Broadcasting Corporation, February 4, 2009.
22. '"Those Blaming Pakistan are Unaware of Facts': Wajid". *The News*, January 25, 2009, at http://www.thenews.com.pk/updates.asp?id=66295.

23. "Kashmir Inseparable Part of Policy: Pak Army", *The Indian Express,* November 25, 2008, at http://www.expressindia.com/fullstory.php?newsid=21883.
24. "Half-hearted Measures to Rein in JuD", *The News International,* January 10, 2009.
25. Richard Oppel and Salman Masood, "With House Arrest Pakistan Curbs, Lightly, a Leader Tied to Mumbai Attacks", *The New York Times,* December 13, 2008.
26. Shahzada Irfan Ahmed, "Popular Belief", *The News on Sunday,* December 21, 2008, at http://jang.com.pk/thenews/dec2008-weekly/nos-21-12-2008/spr.htm.
27. Syed Shoaib Hasan, "Banned Pakistani Groups 'Expand'", BBC, June 30, 2009.
28. Kanchan Lakshman, "Complicity Uninterrupted", *Outlook,* July 21, 2009.
29. Sanjeev Pargal, "PoK's Tauheed Hills New Base for LeT: HM", *Daily Excelsior,* July 17, 2009.
30. Sadia Sulaiman, "Syed Adnan Ali Shah Bukhari, Fears of a Taliban Spread", *Asia Times Online,* May 21, 2009.
31. "Taliban Kills Foreign Tourists in PoK", *The Hindu,* June 24, 2013, p. 1.
32. "Taliban Threat to Gilgit". *Daily Times,* April 28, 2009.
33. Ibid.
34. "Osama Flits between Pak, PoK: Biographer". *Press Trust of India,* July 22, 2002. The report mentioned Yossef Bodansky, the author of *Bin Laden: The Man Who Declared War on America,* claiming that Bodanski said Bin Laden "is shuttling between the Afghanistan panhandle, Pakistan-occupied-Kashmir (PoK) and certain segments of the north-western part of Pakistan and sometimes crossing into Afghanistan".
35. For a detailed exposition of Al Qaida's strategy in Pakistan, refer to Don Rassler, "Al-Qaida's Pakistan Strategy", *CTC Sentinel,* July 2009.

Bibliography

Adair, F.E.S., *A Summer in High Asia: Being a Record of Sport and Travel in Baltistan and Ladakh*. London, Thacker, 1899.

Afridi, Banat Gul, *Baltistan in History*. Peshawar, Emjay Book International, 1988.

Aitchison, J.E.T., *Handbook of the Trade Products of Leh*. Calcutta, Wynne, 1874.

Alder, Garry J., *British India's Northern Frontier 1865-95: A Study in Imperial Policy*. London, Longmans, 1963.

Anon, *Geology of the Karakoram and Hindu Kush*. Kyoto, Kyoto University, 1965.

Bailey, Grahame. *The Grammar of the Shina Language*. London, The Royal Asiatic Society, 1924.

Bajpai, Shiva Chandra, *The Northern Frontier of India: Central and Western Sector*. Bombay, Allied, 1970.

Barrow, E.G., *Dardistan and Kafiristan*. Calcutta, Aylton, 1885.

Barth, Fredrik. *Indus and Swat Kohistan: An Ethnographic Survey*. Oslo, Forende Trykkerier, 1956.

Biddulph, J., *Tribes of the Hindu Kush*. 1880. (Reprint) New Delhi, Bhavana Books, 2001.

Chohan, Amar Singh, *Historical Study of Society and Culture in Dardistan and Ladakh*. New Delhi, Atlantic Publishers, 1983.

Chohan, Amar Singh, *The Gilgit Agency 1877-1935*. New Delhi, Atlantic, 1997.

Clark, John, *Hunza: Lost Kingdom in the Himalayas*. (Reprint) Karachi, Indus, 1980.

Clarke, Graham, E., "Who Were the Dards? A Review of the Ethno-graphic Literature of the North-Western Himalayas". *Kailash*, Vol. 5, 1977, pp. 323-356.

Conway, William Martin, *Climbing and Exploration in the Karakoram-Himalayas*. 3 vols. New York, Appleton, 1894.

Cunningham, Alexander, *Ladakh: Physical, Statistical and Historical with Notices of the Surrounding Countries*. (Reprint) New Delhi, Sagar, 1970.

Dani, Ahmad H., *Human Records on Karakorum Highway*. Islamabad, Lok Virsa, 1983.

Dani, Ahmad Hasan, *Guide to Karakorum Highway*. Islamabad, Lok Virsa, 1983.

Dani, Ahmad Hasan, *History of the Northern Areas of Pakistan*. Islamabad, Lok Virsa, 1989.

Datta, Chaman Lal, *Ladakh and Western Himalayan Politics 1819-1848*. New Delhi, Munshi Ram Manoharlal, 1975.

de Filippi, F., *The Italian Expedition to the Himalaya, Karakoram and Eastern Turkestan (1913-14)*. London, Edward Arnold, 1932.

Drew, Frederic. *The Jummoo and Kashmir Territories: A Geographical Account*. 1875. (Reprint) New Delhi, Cosmo, 1977.

Dunmore, Earl of., *The Pamirs*. London, John Murray, 1893. 2 vols.

Durand, Algernon, *The Making of a Frontier: Five Years of Experiences and Adventures in Gilgit, Hunza, Nagar, Chitral and the Eastern Hindu Kush*. London, Thomas Nelson & Sons, 1899.

Dutt, N.N. and Sharma, S., *Gilgit Manuscripts*. 2 vols., New Delhi, Motilal Banarsidass, 1984.

Eckenstein, Oscar, *The Karakorams and Kashmir: An Account of a Journey*. London, T.F. Unwin, 1896.

Etherton, P.T., *Across the Roof of the World: A Record of Sport and Travel Through Kashmir, Gilgit, Hunza, The Pamirs, Chinese Turkestan, Mongolia and Siberia*. London, Constable, 1911.

Featherstone, B.K., *Unexplored Pass: A Narrative of a Thousand Mile Journey to the Karakorum Himalaya*. London, Hutchinson, 1926.

Fisher, Margaret W., Leo E. Rose and Robert A. Huttenback, *Himalayan Battleground: Sino-Indian Rivalry in Ladakh*. New York, Praeger, 1963.

Francke, August Herman, *Baltistan and Ladakh*. 1907. (Reprint) Islamabad, Lok Virsa, 1987.

Francke, August Herman. *Antiquities of Indian Tibet*. 2 vols, 1926. (Reprint) New Delhi, S. Chand, 1972.

Gazetteer of Kashmir and Ladakh: Together with Routes in the Territories of the Maharaja of Jamu and Kashmir. 1890. (Reprint) Calcutta, Gang-e-Meel Publications, 1991.

Girdlestone, Charles. *Memorandum on Chashmere and Some Adjacent Countries*. Calcutta, Foreign Department Press, 1874.

Gupta, Virendra and Bansal, Alok (Editors), *Pakistan occupied Kashmir: The Untold Story*. New Delhi, Manas, 2007.

Hamid, S. Shahid. *Karakorum Hunza: The Land of Just Enough*. Karachi, 1979.

Hamza, S. S., *Gilgit-Baltistan Lawa Ke Dhana Par* (In Urdu) [Gilgit-Baltistan at the threshold of volcanic lava]. Islamabad, Orient Printers, 1995.

Hashmatullah Khan, *History of Baltistan*. 1939. (Reprint) Islamabad, Lok Virsa, 1987.

Hashmatullah Khan, *Tareekh Jammu* (In Urdu) (History of Jammu). (Reprint) Lahore, 1968.

Hasnain, M. Sengge Thsering, *Balti Language and Script*. Skardo, Society of Asian Civilization Pakistan, 20 August 2000.

Hasnain, M. Sengge Thsering, 'The Linguistic Heritage of Balti Tibetan Muslims'. *The Tibetan Review Volume*. Volume 36, No. 2, 2001, pp. 18-20.

Hasnain, M. Sengge Thsering, Baltistan: Fifty Two Years of Agony. In *ACHA Peace Bulletin*, http://www. asiapeace.org (5 June 2002)

Hasrat, H., *Baltistan Tehzib-o-Saqafat* (In Urdu) [Baltistan's Culture]. Skardo, Baltistan Publications, 2007.

Hasrat, M. H., *Shimla se Baltistan tak* (In Urdu) [From Simla to Baltistan]. Rawalpindi, Gilgit-Baltistan Printing Services, 1997.

Hopkirk, Peter, *The Great Game*. Oxford, Oxford University Press, 1990.

Hussain, F.M., *Gilgit: The Northern Gate of India*. New Delhi, Sterling Publishers, 1978.

Hussainabadi, Y., [*Tarikh-e-Baltistan*] (In Urdu) *History of Baltistan*. Skardo, Baltistan Printers and Publishers, 2003.

Jaschke, H. A., *A Tibetan-English Dictionary*. Delhi, Motilal Barnasibass Publishers, 1887.

Jasjit Singh (Editor), *Pakistan occupied Kashmir: Under the Jackboot*. New Delhi, Siddhi Books, 1995.

Jettmar, K., 'Ethnological Research in Dardistan'. *Proceedings of the American Philosophical Society*, Vol. 105, No. 1, 1958.

Jettmar, Karl, *Antiquities of Northern Pakistan, Reports and Studies*. Mainz, Philip von Zabern, 1989.

Jettmar, Karl, *Between Gandhara and the Silk Roads: Rock Carvings Along the Karakorum Highway: Discoveries by German-Pakistani Expeditions 1979-1984*. Mainz, Philipp von Zabern, 1987.

Jettmar, Karl, *Bolor: A Contribution to the Political and Ethnic Geography of Northern Pakistan*. Islamabad, Lok Virsa, 1980.

Jettmar, Karl, ed. *The Religions of the Hindukush: The Religion of the Kafirs*. Vol.1. Warminster, Aris and Phillips, 1986.

Kaiser, M. A., *Shohda-e-Gilgit Baltistan* (In Urdu) [Martyrs of Gilgit-Baltistan]. Islamabad, R. S. Publications, 2005.

Kashmir Human Rights Forum, *High Court of Judicature Azad Jammu and Kashmir: Verdict on Gilgit and Baltistan*. Mirpur, n.d.

Kazmi, M. A., *Balti Lok Geet* (In Urdu) (Balti Folk Songs). Islamabad, National Institute of Folk Heritage, 1985.

Keay, John, *The Gilgit Game: The Explorers of the Western Himalayas, 1865-1895*. New York, Oxford, 1990.

Keay, John, *When Men and Mountains Meet: The Explorers of the Western Himalayas, 1820-75*. Hamden, Connecticut, Archon Books. 1982.

Khan, Colonel Mirza Hassan Jarral, '*Shamsheer se Zanjeer tak* (In Urdu) (from sword to chains)', Rawalpindi, K2 Group of Publishers, 2002.

Khan, F.M., *The Story of Gilgit-Baltistan and Chitral*. Gilgit, Eajaz Publishers, 2002.

Khan, Tarik A., Little Tibet—Renaissance and Resistance in Baltistan. *Himal Magazine*, Nepal, May 1998.

Klimburg-Salter, D.E., *The Silk Route and the Diamond Path: Esoteric Buddhist Art on the Trans-Himalayan Trade Routes*. Los Angeles, 1982.

Knight, E.F., *Where Three Empires Meet: A Narrative of Recent Travel in Kashmire, Western Tibet, Gilgit and the Adjoining Countries*. 1893. (Reprint) Lahore, Ferozesons, 1980.

Lamb, A., *Kashmir—A Disputed Legacy 1846 – 1990*. Karachi, Oxford University Press, 1992.

Lamb, Alastair. *The Sino-Indian Border in Ladakh*. Canberra, Australian National University, 1973.

Lawrence, Walter R., *Kashmir and Jammu: Imperial Gazetteer of India: Pronvincial Series*. 1901. (Reprint) Lahore, Sang-e-Meel. 1973.

Leitner, Gotlieb W. *Dardistan in 1866-1886 and 1893: The Hunza and Nagyr Handbook*. Woking, England, Oriental University Institute, 1889.

Leitner, Gotlieb W., *Results of a Tour in Dardistan, Kashmir, Little, Tibet, Ladakh, Zanskar, etc. in 1861*. Lahore and London, Truebner/Indian Public Opinion Press, 1868-1873.

Leitner, Gotlieb W., *The Languages and Races of Dardistan*. 3 Parts. Lahore, Government Central Depot, 1877.

Leyden, J., 'On the Language and Literature of Indo-Chinese Nations', *Asiatic Researches*, Volume X, 1808.

Lobsang, G. Hussain, 'Sang' in *Wakhsi Namkhor*. Skardo, Lobsang Publishers, 1990.

Lobsang, G. Hussain, *Balti Grammar*. Berne, Institute of Linguistics, University of Berne, 1995.

Lobsang, G. Hussain, *History of Bon Philosophy: History of Baltistan, Ladakh and Tibetan Belief System*. Gilgit, Hunza Printing Press, 1997.

Lorimer, David L.R., "An Oral Version of the Kesar Saga from Hunza". *Folklore*, Vol. 42, 1931, pp.105-140.

Lorimer, Emily O., *Language Hunting in the Karakoram*. London, Allen and Unwin.

Mahajan S. Kumar, *Debacle in Baltistan*. New Delhi, 1966.

Maraini, Fosco, *Karakorum*. Paris, Presses de la Cite, 1963.

Miller, Keith J., ed., *International Karakoram Project*. 2 vols. Cambridge, Cambridge University Press, 1984.

Mueller-Stellrecht, Irmtraud. *Hunza and China (1761-1891)*. Wiesbaden, Franz Steiner, 1978.

Parwana, M. H., *Sach Likhna Jurm Hai* (In Urdu) [Telling Truth is a Crime]. Skardo, GBUM Publishers, 2005.

Read, A.F.C., *Balti Grammar*. London, Royal Asiatic Society, 1934.

Schlagintweit, H.A. von and R. von Schlagintweit, *Results of a Scientific Mission to India and High Asia*. 4 vols. London, Atlas, Truebner, 1860-1866.

Schomberg, Reginald C.F., *Between the Oxus and the Indus*. London, Martin Hopkinson. 1935.

Schomberg, Reginald C.F., *Unknown Karakoram*. London, Martin Hopkinson. 1936.

Schuler, S., "The 'Story of the Creation of the Shigar' of Wazir Ahmad". *Central Asiatic Journal*, Vol. 22, No. 1, 1978, pp. 102-120.

Siiger, Halfdan, "Shamanism among the Kalash Kafirs of Chitral". *Folk*, Vol.5, 1956, pp.205-303.

Sikandar, K.S.K., *Qadeem Ladakh: Tarikh-o-Tamaddun* (In Urdu) [Ancient Ladakh: History and Civilization]'. Leh, Kacho Publishers, 1987.

Singh, Ghansara, *Gilgit Before 1947*. Translated by Sher Baz Ali Khan Boroha. Rawalpindi, 1986.

Snellgrove, D.L. and T. Skorupski, *The Cultural Heritage of Ladakh*. 2 vols., Warminster, Aris and Phillips, 1977.

Sprigg, R.K., *Balti-English, English-Balti Dictionary*. London, Routledge, Curzon, 2002.

Stein, Marc Aurel, *On Alexander's Track to the Indus: Personal Narrative of Explorations Carried Out on the North-West Frontier of India*. London, Macmillan, 1929.

Vigne, G.T., *Travels in Kashmir, Ladakh, Iskardo: The Countries Adjoining the Mountain-Course of the Indus, and the Himalaya North of the Punjab*. London, Colburn, 1842.

Warikoo, K., *Central Asia and Kashmir: A Study in the Context of Anglo-Russian Rivalry*. New Delhi, Gian. 1989.

Warikoo, K., Editor, *Himalayan Frontiers of India: Historical, Geopolitical and Strategic Perspectives*. UK, USA and Canada, Routledge, 2009.

Warikoo, K., Editor, *Jammu, Kashmir and Ladakh: A Classified and Comprehensive Bibliography*. New Delhi, Sterling. 1976.

Warikoo, K., Editor, *Jammu, Kashmir and Ladakh: Linguistic Predicament*. New Delhi, Har Anand, 1996.

Warikoo, K., Editor, *Religion and Security in South and Central Asia*. UK, USA and Canada, Routledge, 2011.

Warikoo, K., *Society and Culture in the Himalayas*. New Delhi, Har Anand, 1995.

Workman, Fanny B. and William H. Workman, *Ice-Bound Heights of the Mustagh: An Account of two Seasons of Pioneer Exploration and High Climbing in the Baltistan Himalaya*. London, Archibald Constable, 1908.

Workman, Fanny B., *In the Ice World of Himalaya, Among the Peaks and Passes of Ladakh, Nubra, Suru, and Baltistan*. New York, Cassell, 1900.

Younghunsband, Francis E., *Report of a Mission to the Northern Frontier of Kashmir in 1899*. Calcutta, Government of India, 1890.

Younghusband, Francis E., *The Heart of a Continent: A Narrative of Travels in Manchuria, Across the Gobi Desert, Through the Himalayas, and Chitral, 1884-1894*. London, John Murray, 1904.

Index